THE POSTCOLONIAL INTELLECTUAL

The Postcolonial Intellectual
Ngũgĩ wa Thiong'o in Context

OLIVER LOVESEY
University of British Columbia-Okanagan, Canada

LONDON AND NEW YORK

First published 2015 by Ashgate Publishing

2 Park Square, Milton Park, Abingdon, Oxfordshire OX14 4RN
52 Vanderbilt Avenue, New York, NY 10017

Routledge is an imprint of the Taylor & Francis Group, an informa business

First issued in paperback 2019

Copyright © 2015 Oliver Lovesey

Oliver Lovesey has asserted his right under the Copyright, Designs and Patents Act, 1988, to be identified as the author of this work.

All rights reserved. No part of this book may be reprinted or reproduced or utilised in any form or by any electronic, mechanical, or other means, now known or hereafter invented, including photocopying and recording, or in any information storage or retrieval system, without permission in writing from the publishers.

Notice:
Product or corporate names may be trademarks or registered trademarks, and are used only for identification and explanation without intent to infringe.

British Library Cataloguing in Publication Data
A catalogue record for this book is available from the British Library

The Library of Congress has cataloged the printed edition as follows:
Lovesey, Oliver, author.
  The postcolonial intellectual: Ngũgĩ wa Thiong'o in context / by Oliver Lovesey.
    pages cm
  Includes bibliographical references and index.
  ISBN 978-1-4094-0900-7 (hardcover: alk. paper)
  1. Ngũgĩ wa Thiong'o, 1938– —Criticism and interpretation. 2. Intellectuals—Kenya.
3. Postcolonialism in literature. 4. Pan-Africanism. 5. Decolonization. I. Title.
  PR9381.9.N45Z765 2015
  823.914—dc23
                                                                                          2014036143
ISBN 978-1-4094-0900-7 (hbk)
ISBN 978-0-367-87894-8 (pbk)

Contents

Acknowledgments   *vii*

1   The Postcolonial Intellectual   1
2   The Decolonization of James Ngũgĩ: Early Journalism   43
3   Diasporic Pan-Africanism: The Caribbean Connection   75
4   Ngũgĩ's "Aesthetics of Decolonization": Return to the Source   115
5   Postcolonial Intellectual Self-Fashioning   139
6   The Global Intellectual: Conclusion   173

Works Cited   *195*
Index   *221*

Acknowledgments

A section of Chapter 5 was first published in *Research in African Literatures* 26.4 (Winter 1995), 31–45, and is reprinted with permission by Indiana University Press. A section of Chapter 6 was first published in *Modern Fiction Studies* 48.1 (2002), 139–168, and it is reprinted with permission by Johns Hopkins University Press; Copyright © 2002 for the Purdue Research Foundation. The cover image is a photograph of Ngũgĩ wa Thiong'o by Nikki Kahn used with permission by the *Washington Post* via Getty Images.

Lavish acknowledgment is extended to Marie Loughlin for keeping everything in context.

Chapter 1
The Postcolonial Intellectual

Rumors of the death of the intellectual, as Susan Sontag asserts, are greatly exaggerated (110), though the announcement of the intellectual's demise is itself a "recurrent genre" (Collini 40).[1] The somewhat "moldy," "elitist," or "obsolete" air of the traditional, universal intellectual (and perhaps especially the professional, institutional, academic intellectual) remains, and there is a perennial discomfort with the term that carries the odor of the candle or the aura of the screen. Much has been written on the role and representation of intellectuals and clearly intellectuals like writing about themselves, though a species of anxiety or self-conscious hand-wringing often informs these reflections. There is a commonly expressed impatience with intellectual work's apparent or perceived divorce from the material realities of poverty and injustice, if not an outright death wish, as in some of the work of intellectuals as different as Jean-Paul Sartre and Amílcar Cabral. One might be forgiven for thinking that times are nearly always dark for intellectuals.[2] For many people, and even some intellectuals, like Edward W. Said, appalled by intellectual hubris,[3] the intellectual may be a useless passion.

A *PMLA* Roundtable on Intellectuals was convened in 1997 at a time when the humanities and academia in general were variously described as besieged or beleaguered (Perloff 1129; Miller 1137). Judith Butler, six years later in 2003, would also voice concerns about the role of the traditional intellectual, concerns that in her view are exacerbated for "politically minded intellectuals" in the academy due to anxiety about the effectiveness of their public communications amid "an

---

[1] This genre is accompanied with "ancient rights to a certain hyperbole" and also with the announcement of a new candidacy for a presumptive heir to fill the vacancy of the "absent intellectual" (Collini 40).

[2] See Hannah Arendt's *Men in Dark Times*. In *Representations of the Intellectual*, Edward Said writes that "[i]n dark times an intellectual is very often looked to by members of his or her nationality to represent, speak out for, and testify to the sufferings of that nationality" (43). See, too, Julia Kristeva's "Thinking in Dark Times" in *Profession*'s "The Role of Intellectuals in the Twenty-First Century" forum. In a memorial reflection on Said's intellectual mode, Gayatri Chakravorty Spivak writes of the "need for his presence in the current post-9/11 destruction of free society in the United States [which] is teaching us afresh how important he was" (Spivak, "Edward Said" 59). Adrienne Rich in 2006 asserted the need for poetry in the present "dark times" when "I live with manipulated fear, ignorance, cultural confusion and social antagonism huddling together on the faultline of an empire" ("Legislators").

[3] Said refers to "the appalling danger of thinking of oneself, one's views, one's rectitude, one's stated positions as all-important," a species of self-deluded narcissism resembling that often targeted in Swift's writings (Said, *Representations* 113).

upsurge of anti-intellectualism" (45)[4] when "anti-intellectualism has become practically institutionalized" (Feal 1).[5] The new information economy and infotainment media culture have challenged older concepts of individual intellectual expertise and of any lingering notions of a "common culture" (Miller 1138). At the same time, intellectual, knowledge capital is more marketable than ever (Graff, "Today, Tomorrow" 1133), and media exposure, particularly of African-American intellectuals (such as perhaps America's most prominent intellectual, Cornel West), has reinvigorated the role of the public intellectual (LaCapra 1134), despite Pierre Bourdieu's cautions about media intellectuals' "cultural 'fast food'" (29) and Said's warnings about media intellectuals' compromising commodification of their own expertise (Ali, *Conversations* 110). In this climate, as Dominick LaCapra maintains, the postcolonial intellectual (Walter Mignolo prefers "the postoccidental intellectual" [1141]) is well-positioned to mediate the contested terrain between "specialized research" and public address (1134), though Marjorie Perloff suggests that innovative intellectual renewal may be best effected by "poet-intellectuals" (1130).

One of the often overlooked preoccupations of the postcolonial critical project, itself one of the major academic growth industries over the past two decades, is the role of the intellectual. Simultaneously, there have been persistent questions about who speaks and for whom, and from what location and to what purpose, with a recurring anxiety that such speech, however well-intentioned, performs an authoritarian act of silencing the other and particularly the subaltern. This book aims to reengage with the figure of the postcolonial intellectual as manifested in the words and practice of a number of postcolonial intellectuals and in their relationship to the work of Ngũgĩ wa Thiong'o, and it also aims to reexamine some of the critical, historical, and cultural sources and contexts of his thought. It calls for a reconsideration of his location as a major postcolonial theorist when he is sometimes regarded as merely a novelist or dramatist who just happens to do theory. His eight critical and theoretical works, from *Homecoming: Essays on African and Caribbean Literature, Culture and Politics* (1972) to *Globalectics: Theory and the Politics of Knowing* (2012),[6] are, moreover, sometimes perceived as being mere diagrams, keys, or tool kits (or worse, guidebooks with answers, the desire for which Chinua Achebe deplores amusingly in his famous early statement

---

[4] R. Radhakrishnan finds Butler's effective voicing of the position of the "public intellectual" in her recent *Precarious Life* and *Giving an Account of Oneself* ("Theory" 791–2). Radhakrishnan's earlier account of intellectual agency, focused on Foucault and Gramsci, appeared in "Toward an Effective Intellectual" (57–99).

[5] Placing this type of critique in a strictly national context, New York punk poet Richard Hell, one-time leader of the Voidoids, refers in a different context to America as "idiotically anti-intellectual" (212).

[6] Ngũgĩ's *In the Name of the Mother: Reflections on Writers & Empire* (2013) appeared too late for consideration in the present study.

on the role of the creative intellectual in Africa, "The Novelist as Teacher")[7] for deciphering Ngũgĩ's own artistic creations. This myopic interpretation is a particular danger for a theorist who, unlike Said, Gayatri Chakravorty Spivak, or Homi Bhabha, is also an accomplished artist. Moreover, Ngũgĩ's subaltern background, his upbringing in an extended family of landless, illiterate peasants, and his lived experience of colonial violence, anticolonial resistance, and neocolonial imprisonment, make him an unusual postcolonial intellectual. Ngũgĩ's role in canon reform and educational decolonization helped to establish the discipline of postcolonial studies, even if it didn't finally "abolish" English departments. "On the Abolition of the English Department" by Ngũgĩ, Henry Owuor-Anyumba, and Taban Lo Liyong, a memo that launched a revolution, was issued at the University of Nairobi in October 1968, and included in Ngũgĩ's first volume of essays *Homecoming* (145–50). As he recalls in his most recent collection *Globalectics*, "[t]he debate and the consequences went beyond Nairobi to other universities in Africa and beyond, generating disputes, some of the earliest shots in what later became postcolonial theories" (9). Ngũgĩ is routinely named as a contender for the Nobel Prize in Literature, and odds takers estimate his chances highly.[8]

This book also calls for a reconsideration of the role of the intellectual in global leadership in speaking truth to power in the struggle for truth, justice, and reconciliation, at a time when a Kenyan-American intellectual who carries the aura of a rock star and whose father was born 40 miles from Kisumu in Kogelo, Western Kenya, is president of the United States of America for a second term of office, after two election campaigns in which issues of race, gender, religion, nationality, and culture entered public political discourse. Moreover, Barack Hussein Obama's grandfather, Hussein Onyango Obama, may well have been a survivor of torture in Britain's colonial camps for Mau Mau suspects.[9] Ngũgĩ's acclaimed novel *Mũrogi wa Kagogo* (*Wizard of the Crow*), the longest of his career, appeared in 2006; it

---

[7] Achebe refers to a letter from a student reader in Ghana lamenting the omission of questions and answers at the end of *Things Fall Apart* (42), and this leads Achebe to address his purpose in writing which he maintains is not distinct from "the deepest aspirations of my society" (44): "I would be quite satisfied if my novels (especially the ones I set in the past) did no more than teach my readers that their past—with all its imperfections—was not one long night of savagery from which the first Europeans acting on God's behalf delivered them" (45).

[8] Zoe Norridge, lecturer in Modern and Contemporary Literature at the University of York, wrote in *The Guardian*'s Book Blog on October 8, 2010:
Yesterday Ngugi wa Thiong'o didn't win the Nobel prize. A few days earlier he'd become the bookies' favourite when the odds on his being awarded literature's highest accolade fell from 75-1 to 3-1. But at midday on 7 October, Mario Vargas Llosa was announced as this year's laureate. (http://www.guardian.co.uk/books/booksblog/2010/oct)

[9] Obama outlines some of the details of his Kenyan family in *Dreams from My Father*.

uses the technique of postmodern African folk tales (a uniquely African version of magic realism) as well as Ngũgĩ's distinctive "Mau Mau aesthetics" (following the Mau Mau rebel fighters in transforming biblical stories, for example, into tools of liberation)[10] to dream a truly independent future into being. All of Ngũgĩ's novels present history "from below" and demonstrate that history is a contested terrain, open to challenge and transformation, and his novels from the 1960s have served witness to the brutality of colonial repression, especially during the Mau Mau period (Elkins 374–5). *Wizard of the Crow* appears at a time when revisionist imperial historians, particularly in Britain, are promoting portraits of benevolent empire, though other historians, like Caroline Elkins, David Anderson, and Ian Cobain are detailing the true horrors of colonialism in Kenya, and former Mau Mau detainees have been granted a voice in British courts, an action that appears set to unleash a myriad of claims from former colonies (Cobain and Hatcher 15). "[W]hat is astonishing about Kenya's dirty war [the vicious suppression of anticolonial forces in the 1950s] is not that it remained secret at the time," remarks Anderson, "but that it was so well known and so thoroughly documented" in Britain and Kenya (309). *Wizard of the Crow* tackles dictatorship in a fictional African state resembling Kenya, and its subject is particularly poignant in a period when the world lies in a state of heightened security after the bombings in Nairobi, New York, and elsewhere, followed by the "war on terror," and the "global village," to misapply Marshall McLuhan's evocative phrase,[11] seems smaller and more fragile than before. Dictators and exporters of civil war, like Liberia's Charles Taylor, are being brought to justice, and the first and second generation of African strong men, like Kenya's Daniel arap Moi, are being humbled at the ballot box and in some cases, like that of Kenya's new president Uhuru Kenyatta, potentially at the International Criminal Court in The Hague. While the forces of globalization, which Ngũgĩ faces directly in *Penpoints, Gunpoints, and Dreams* (1998), are as pervasive and destabilizing as ever, a more hopeful future, as he has recently argued, may be dawning with "the decolonization of modernity" (*Something* xi). These recent essays expand Ngũgĩ's range of intellectual engagement, which now extends from Walter Benjamin, Michel Foucault, and Plato to popular culture. There has been renewed critical interest in Ngũgĩ's works with at least six monographs, as well as a number of essay collections and comparative studies, in recent years.

The figure of the public intellectual has been most powerfully asserted in the cultural and political stance of the postcolonial intellectual who has become a kind

---

[10] See Lovesey's *Ngũgĩ wa Thiong'o* (64–5).

[11] McLuhan was concerned, in works like *The Gutenberg Galaxy* and *Understanding Media*, with the evaporation of distance within the free circuit of information, and he anticipated the extension of consciousness with a device resembling the Internet though he did not anticipate a more peaceful globe.

of global conscience as well as an engaged social critic.[12] Critics like Said, Spivak, and Bhabha have led the Western academy to reconsider its own ideological location, but Ngũgĩ has worked in this area for five decades, and he has also directly participated in grassroots cultural renewal as playwright and novelist, and engaged in political action. Ngũgĩ's contribution to a recent forum on "The Role of Intellectuals in the Twenty-First Century," in conversation with Julia Kristeva, one of the leading French intellectuals today,[13] indicates Ngũgĩ's importance in advancing the dialogue of the Black Atlantic and shows his oppositional stance to the role of universal intellectuals. As in her call in 1977 for a new type of "dissident" intellectual, in touch with the politics of gender, power, and the unconscious,[14] Kristeva, in the "dark times" of 2006, sought a "reconstructive role" for the intellectual (18; 13–21), and like Ngũgĩ, advanced the intellectual's continuing engagement with "freedom, liberation, [and] social justice" ("For Peace" 39). In 2009's *The Incredible Need to Believe*, Kristeva would call once more for a new, reformed humanism, a radical actualization of thought to confront the postmodern "empire of calculation and show business" (29) and by extension its promotion of anonymous, passive spectatorship.

Kristeva's and Ngũgĩ's positions are indebted to the radical intellectual politics of Sartre, who had a sustained if sometimes adversarial influence on the work of postcolonial theorist Frantz Fanon. In "A Plea for Intellectuals" (1965) and "A Friend of the People" (1970), the latter produced two years after May 1968, Sartre launched a harsh critique of the role of the "classical," universal intellectual that he had earlier exemplified as shown in *What Is Literature* (1948), despite his wartime adoption of the stance of the engaged Resistance writer who voices

---

[12] Focusing on J.M. Coetzee's ambivalent position regarding the postcolonial in terms of politics and intellectual orientation, Jane Poyner, using Said's conception of the intellectual in *Representations*, argues that Coetzee's work embodies "the paradox of postcolonial authorship," the notion "that writing on others' behalf threatens the ethico-politics that go to the very heart of the postcolonial text" (Poyner, *J.M. Coetzee* 3). Coetzee himself, as shown in his testy responses in an interview conducted by Poyner, appears disinterested in postcolonial critical discourse and regards revived interest in the public intellectual as a feature of the academic industry's self-promotion (Poyner, "J.M. Coetzee in Conversation" 22, 23).

[13] Kristeva describes herself as a "cosmopolitan intellectual" with her Bulgarian origins, French nationality, European citizenry, and American association with Columbia University, but she also clearly sees herself as part of the French tradition of critical debate in which the examination of the "role of intellectuals" was central (*Hatred and Forgiveness* 3–4).

[14] See Richard Wolin's discussion of this phase in Kristeva's thinking (282–3). He notes that while her arrival in Paris from Bulgaria "in French intellectual lore … has acquired an aura akin to the Second Coming" (247), her legacy is problematic. Remarking on the trend to deplore the "decline of French intellectuals" after 1980, he situates the problem in the legacy of their alliances with various forms of state, institutional, and disciplinary power, including poststructuralism and Maoism (286–7).

subaltern positions as in *Anti-Semite and Jew* (1946). Sartre's autobiography, *The Words* (1964), is partly a rigorous debunking of the illusions and delusions to which intellectuals appear surprisingly vulnerable. Sartre's was an education in disillusionment. As a gifted child who was regarded as a prodigy and who saw himself as one of the "elect" (252), Sartre entertained a view of the writer's role as a heroic, romantic, priestly, quasi-mystical vocation. He writes that "[f]or a long time, I took my pen for a sword; I now know we're powerless" (253–4). In his later works, however, Sartre advances the radical model of the "combat[ant]" intellectual, one of whose roles is to accept that he is "the monstrous product of a monstrous society" ("Plea" 249, 247), living amid instability and contradiction. He must engage in perpetual self-criticism and even "suppress himself as an intellectual" ("Friend" 293).

"[I]ntellectuals have chosen unhappiness by wanting to be intellectuals," remarked Jean Baudrillard in 1985, noting that this unhappiness results from vocational critical detachment as well as internal division (72), qualities of Sartre's "classical" intellectual. In the aftermath of the heady late 1960s when French intellectuals, like Sartre, Foucault, and Baudrillard himself stood at the epicenter of volcanic social and political battles, intellectuals often appear uneasily poised between grandiosity and despair. Their self-perception is a species of grandiose delusion about being in the vanguard of meaningful social change and a simultaneous, despairing recognition of impotence, intellectuals' having "never changed anything much" (Baudrillard 76). While admiring intellectuals' utopian imaginings, Baudrillard insists, "I wouldn't be against envisaging a world without intellectuals" (79). The year following Baudrillard's statements, one of the most prominent of America's radical, oppositional intellectuals, Noam Chomsky, speaking in Managua, Nicaragua, would echo a similar fatigue and also a certain contempt for "classical" intellectuals' apparent vocational inclination to delusional arrogance in a characteristic diatribe:

> What we often find is that the intellectuals, the educated classes, are the most indoctrinated, most ignorant, most stupid part of the population, and there are very good reasons for that. Basically two reasons. First of all, as the literate part of the population, they are subjected to the mass of propaganda. There is a second, more important and more subtle reason. Namely, they are the ideological managers. Therefore, they must internalize the propaganda and believe it. And part of the propaganda they have developed is that they are the natural leaders of the masses. (quoted in Ross, "Defenders of the Faith" 101)

In the context of this despair at intellectuals' self-delusion and anxiety of impotence, there was also a certain naïve envy of postcolonial intellectuals' importance, and an apparent disregard for the very real personal danger they faced. Baudrillard, for example, juxtaposes the vacillation of post-1968 French intellectuals with the position of "[i]ntellectuals of the Third World [who] have the privilege of holding a clear critical position and of having the possibility of struggle, which is also totally clear. Confusion, in their case, is not possible" (73).

Paris provided an important nexus for Pan-African colonial intellectuals, such as Fanon, Aimé Césaire, and Léopold Sédar Senghor, in the period leading to independence, as would London, explored in Chapter 3. The intellectuals' location informs both their role and their function. The postwar elite in France—what Claude Lanzmann, Resistance fighter, *Shoah* director, and *Le Temps Modernes* editor, called the *mandarins*, a term Simone de Beauvoir, France's foremost feminist intellectual, used as the title of her roman á clef *Les Mandarins* (1954; *The Mandarins*) (Lanzmann 235)—was preoccupied with the aftermath of the outbreak of peace in Europe and its consequences for the role of intellectuals, while rumors circulated about Soviet labor camps and the ongoing "enslavement of colonial peoples" particularly in Algeria (Beauvoir, *Mandarins* 430). As Beauvoir makes clear, French left-wing intellectuals had to decide whether to continue the struggle of the Resistance elsewhere in Europe, in countries such as Portugal, with its own African empire, and even more generally how to accommodate their personal and collective, historical and political pasts.[15] More specifically, they wondered if an art of individual solace, reflection, and entertainment—Beauvoir, Sartre, Albert Camus, and Arthur Koestler were all novelists as well as philosophers—was desirable or even morally permissible at what might be a moment of great crisis and opportunity. This is a question that would also trouble Ngũgĩ in the late 1960s. Should intellectuals be activists, and if so should they act up within political parties and political periodicals or maintain an independent detachment? Such questions had vital significance, and their discussion was of widespread interest because in France, as Nobel laureate Doris Lessing notes: "intellectuals generally, were glamorous in a way they never have been" in Britain ("Introduction" 7); Richard Wolin maintains that within France, they "have enjoyed the status of a lay aristocracy" (19). Baudrillard would concur in the mid-1980s, reflecting on the heady days of 1968 when intellectuals were in the thick of a struggle that appeared to have profound social significance: "[p]eople like technicians, who use their brain but do so through technical means, are not, for us, intellectuals. Even scholars and scientists are not, in France, intellectuals. We have more restricted and more élitist positions" (80).[16] Intellectuals' political battles, compromises, betrayals, and disagreements in the 1960s had prescience because they were not merely interpersonal power struggles or academic debates: indeed, "the future of

---

[15] If intellectuals in France belonged to a glamorous elite, their position elsewhere was very different. In America, as Anne thinks with regard to her lover Lewis Brogan, "intellectuals could live in security because they knew they were completely powerless" (394) as no one listens to their pronouncements. Later in the novel, an American writer, whom Anne had earlier considered a potential lover, says to her that political action is the "psychosis" of French intellectuals, and Anne condemns the manner in which all "American intellectuals plead impotence" (680).

[16] For Baudrillard, the status and role of French intellectuals shifted radically after this period when they appeared able "to translate an intellectual position into a political act, or into political behaviour," to the point at which he reflected "I don't think an intellectual can speak for anything or anyone" (73, 79).

the world was at stake" (Lessing, "Introduction" 9). In retrospect, Lessing refers to her own dramatic decision to join the Communist Party after arriving in London from Rhodesia as "probably the most neurotic act of my life," a manifestation of her intellectual generation's participation in "some kind of social psychosis or mass self-hypnosis" (*Walking* 52, 53).[17]

A new merging of the political and the intimate lies at the heart of Beauvoir's *The Mandarins* within the open marriage of Robert Dubreuilh and Anne, though it is tested severely. Looking at *The Mandarins* in a little more detail may give a sense of the complex of conflicting politics, including sexual politics and the politics of labor camps, within the intellectual center of France in the 1950s, with its direct and indirect implications for the postcolonial project. The original of the romantic object of desire in the novel—Jewish American novelist Nelson Algren, to whom *The Mandarins* is dedicated—was never sanguine with his position in the Sartre-Beauvoir constellation as a participant in what Beauvoir celebrated as "contingent love" (Drew 323). When the affair ended, Algren and Beauvoir would disparage each other with the most toxic words in their lexicons: he said reading some of her work was "like eating cardboard"; she said "[h]e was not an intellectual" (quoted in Drew 205). The exemplar of the model intellectual in the novel is Dubreuilh (Sartre), to whom Anne is committed. He is "able to reconcile high aesthetic standards with revolutionary inspiration"; he is "a great writer and a man who was part of the vigilance committees, the anti-fascist meetings; an intellectual dedicated to the revolution without repudiating himself as an intellectual" (45, 266). Anne's unqualified devotion to him in the novel, like Beauvoir's to Sartre, is one of the factors that makes Lawrence D. Kritzman refer to Beauvoir as a "paradoxical intellectual" who celebrated women's emerging freedom (206–13), while holding that Sartre's work was more important than her own. She was also highly ambivalent about intellectual engagement, though she publicly supported Algerian resistance worker Djamila Boupacha in the early 1960s at the beginning of the Algerian war, and later actively fought for abortion rights and the rights of the elderly. Similarly engaged with Beauvoir's apparent subservience to Sartre, Toril Moi, who calls Beauvoir "the emblematic intellectual woman of the twentieth century," intimates that it was the struggle with patriarchy that forced Beauvoir to compromise her personal freedom so radically (23). Central to Beauvoir's life work is an engagement with the public and the private and with autobiography, as attested by her many volumes of memoir and her autobiographical fiction, a concern of increasing centrality to intellectuals' work, as discussed in Chapter 5. A perpetual self-questioning defines the intellectuals

---

[17] She focuses on the "contradictions" in the membership's unwillingness to confront the realities of Stalinism: "Here we were, committed to every kind of murder and mayhem by definition: you can't make an omelette without breaking eggs. Yet at any suggestion that dirty work was going on, most communists reacted with indignation" (*Walking* 45). André Gide was a French intellectual attracted to the Soviet Union, partly because of its early endorsement of the sexual revolution. Gide planned to argue with Stalin against a recent trend toward antigay restriction during his official visit in 1936, little realizing that a reign of terror was already underway (Sheridan 473-510).

in *The Mandarins*, and particularly Dubreuilh, who wonders about the origin of the intellectual's desire for a public voice and the source of the presumption of authority. He asks, "[W]hat makes certain men decide they can speak in the name of others? In other words, what is an intellectual? Doesn't that decision make him a species apart?" (291) In a provocatively hostile expression of the presumption of intellectual difference, Anne and Robert's daughter Nadine complains to Henri (Camus): "How can anyone love an intellectual! ... you're all just a bunch of fascists" (205). The engaged Henri resents this outburst as much as the expressions of those for whom "intellectual" is an "insult" (173). The confrontation circulates around support for the Soviet Union and left politics in general despite growing, documentary evidence of the labor camps. In response to Dubreuilh's agonized refusal to relinquish his doubt about the camps in the face of this evidence so as not to empower the right and harm the utopian promise of Soviet Russia, Scriassine (Koestler) says, "You have accepted—with the natural masochism of intellectuals—the idea of a dictatorship of the mind" (384).

Unlike Sartre and Beauvoir, as well as Chinua Achebe, Léopold Sédar Senghor, and Wole Soyinka, three of the most famous African writers and postcolonial intellectuals of the independence and post-independence periods in Africa, Ngũgĩ has resisted the African public intellectual's role as leader or exemplar in favor of a model of the intellectual as a grassroots member of the masses. His position, however, has become more nuanced in his most recent writings, in which he issues a challenge to postcolonial African and diasporic African intellectuals to work for Pan-African renewal. Moreover, there has been much ambivalence in his view of intellectuals from his early novels' portrayals of deluded, messianic individuals promoting universal education as a social panacea to some of his first Gĩkũyũ fiction's celebration of militant political heroism, and his own weathering of direct and indirect attacks against Western-based, "Third World" intellectuals' inadvertent complicity in the Western academy's appropriation of postcolonial studies. His own stance as a hybridized, cosmopolitan African living in exile as a member of the African diaspora, an uncomfortable subject position that is increasingly the subject of his essays and indirectly his recent memoirs, moreover, has inevitably distanced him from the home ground of his own inquiry though he has evolved his own artistic and linguistic practice, even using Nairobi street patois, Sheng, in *Wizard of the Crow*.

While the role and representation of the postcolonial intellectual has largely been ignored in studies of Ngũgĩ, there are some notable exceptions. Patrick Williams's lucid examination of Ngũgĩ, often perceived as "*the* paradigmatic postcolonial intellectual," in his "'Like wounded birds'? Ngugi and the Intellectuals" (1997) (201)[18] is an important early study. Williams focuses on Ngũgĩ's pre-*Matigari* novels, taking an oppositional stance to Said's position in *Representations of the Intellectual* although he uses Said's thematic categories as his organizing principle. Neil Lazarus, in "(Re)turn to the People: Ngũgĩ wa Thiong'o and the Crisis of

---

[18] Williams's critique is extended somewhat in "Nothing in the Post?—Said and the Problem of Post-Colonial Intellectuals," though it is primarily focused on Said.

Postcolonial African Intellectualism" (1995), considering the pre–*Devil on the Cross* novels, commends Ngũgĩ's "contribut[ion] to the reanimation of radical African intellectualism" (12), arguing for the value of Ngũgĩ's insistent reinsertion of class and anti-imperialism into the debate. Considering Ngũgĩ's and Achebe's different views of the intellectual, Anthony Arnove's "Pierre Bourdieu, the Sociology of Intellectuals, and the Language of African Literature" (1993) presents a critical view of Ngũgĩ's framing of the African elite's alienation through attachment to colonial languages, primarily in *Decolonising the Mind*. Apollo Obonyo Amoko's *Postcolonialism in the Wake of the Nairobi Revolution: Ngugi wa Thiong'o and the Idea of African Literature* (2010) considers the problematic construction of the African postcolonial intellectual in Ngũgĩ's practice in his pre-*Matigari* novels in the context of an insightful and wide-ranging critique of the role of literature, educational institutions, and the nation-state in colonial and postcolonial Africa.

Whether Ngũgĩ's work may be considered "postcolonial" is a question raised provocatively by Pius Adesanmi (53) and Lazarus (*Postcolonial* 34),[19] and Ngũgĩ has recently added his own voice to the chorus questioning the postcolonial itself (*Globalectics* 49–50). Rumors of the demise of the postcolonial have circulated in a recent *PMLA* roundtable on "The End of Postcolonial Theory" (Yaeger 633–51) and works like Hamid Dabashi's *The Arab Spring: The End of Postcolonialism*. The announcement of the demise of postcolonial studies, however, like notices of the death of the intellectual, has almost become a recognized genre. The problematic term "postcolonial" began as periodic shorthand.[20] It has come to represent a discipline and perhaps a discursive political practice with far-reaching influence beyond the academy. A self-interrogating quality has been part of its genesis,[21] as has a perpetual questioning of the place and role of representation. The

---

[19] In a sweeping critique of the selective and repetitive nature of much postcolonial criticism, which leaves out the "world" in favour of texts and authors and is myopic about much postcolonial literature with the concentration on a select number of "consecrated writers" (*Postcolonial* 26), Lazarus targets Bhabha's narrow delimitation of the "postcolonial perspective" (32) that would not "remotely" characterize a writer like Ngũgĩ (22–36, 82). In some of his remarks about the selective designation of the postcolonial, while acknowledging the danger of universalizing the postcolonial as a category, it appears that Lazarus is advocating a type of post-postcolonial critical discourse that appears to approximate Ngũgĩ's advocacy of world literature in *Globalectics*.

[20] See Lazarus's genealogy of the term (*Postcolonial* 9–12) and also Ato Quayson's account of its prehistory (5–16) and his designation of "colonial/postcolonial space" (20) as a useful conceptual frame (16–20). Simon Gikandi adds to this consideration that "postcolonial theory emerged as a reaction against the institutionalization of English as the discipline of empire" (Gikandi, "Editor's Column: The End of Postcolonial Theory?" 635), which has particular relevance for an understanding of Ngũgĩ's position in postcolonial studies.

[21] An early manifestation of this self-interrogation took place in the pages of *Social Text* in the early 1990s. See Ella Shohat's "Notes on the 'Post-Colonial'" and Anne McClintock's "The Angel of Progress: Pitfalls of the Term 'Post-Colonialism.'"

postcolonial has been questioned, however, for its transnational, transhistorical, even transcendental, and transgenre (despite a recurring focus on the postmodern novel), homogenizing tendencies, and for its reliance on the effortless, notional hyphen in the compound of the "colonial" and the "post." It has also been unambiguously linked with a succession of "posts" that go well beyond even the moment of independence: post-structuralism, postmodernism, and post-Marxism. Moreover, it has been associated with the Western academy and seen as something white people have done to brown people to save them from other brown people, to misuse Spivak's famous "sentence" from "Can the Subaltern Speak?" in a different context,[22] or the self-proclaimed interpretive position of Sartre in 1948 explaining "to white men ... what black men already know" (Sartre, "Black Orpheus" 16).[23] One of the foremost twenty-first-century public intellectuals, the controversial, philosophical provocateur Slavoj Žižek, is particularly contemptuous.[24] The postcolonial and the postcolonial intellectual in the Western academy[25] have also been associated with various hegemonic bogey men such as the culture wars, political correctness, an open season on dead white males, and the accommodation of a displaced elite from the former colonies.[26] Yet another interpretation perceives

---

[22] See Spivak's recent reflections on this sentence's distorted readings (Bhattacharya, "Interview" 231–2).

[23] Sartre writes that in the poetry of Négritude, "[t]hese black men are addressing themselves to black men about black men." "I am talking now to white men, and I should like to explain to them what black men already know" ("Black Orpheus" 16). A few years later, Fanon would explore the gendered anxieties in racist attitudes further in *Black Skin, White Masks*: "Our women are at the mercy of the Negroes" (157).

[24] He states in an interview with Katie Engelhart from December 2012: "I really hate all of this politically correct, cultural studies bullshit. If you mention the phrase 'postcolonialism,' I say, 'Fuck It!'" Postcolonialism is the invention of some rich guys from India who saw that they could make a good career in top Western universities by playing on the guilt of white liberals" http://www.salon.com/2012/12/29/slavoj_zizek_i_am_not_the_worlds_hippest_philosopher .

[25] Bruce Robbins in *Secular Vocations: Intellectuals, Professionalism, Culture* offers a sustained, persuasive examination of changing perceptions of intellectuals as professionals in a politically fraught climate in which intellectuals' disappearance became a major source of anxiety. See, too, John Michael's *Anxious Intellects: Academic Professionals, Public Intellectuals, and Enlightenment Values*. Stanley Aronowitz, in Robbins's edited collection *Intellectuals: Aesthetics, Politics, Academics*, which contains Robbins's lucid introductory analysis of intellectuals' location or "grounding" (ix–xxvii), sets out a powerful, comprehensive exploration of intellectual autonomy and agency, amid growing concerns about the exclusive valuing of technical expertise (3–56).

[26] Arif Dirlik, however, while stressing the importance of the figure of the postcolonial intellectual and its foundational role in the postcolonial project, questions the misleading, homogenizing nature of the category. For Dirlik, the "postcolonial, rather than a description of anything, is a discourse that seeks to constitute the world in the self-image of intellectuals who view themselves (or have come to view themselves) as postcolonial intellectuals" (339). The postcolonial, he argues provocatively and perhaps somewhat facetiously, was

the postcolonial as post- or neo-orientalist in orientation and practices. However, despite persistent rumors of its demise and its expansion into postcolonialisms, even encompassing Europe's metropolitan centers (Quayson 12) and possibly the globe itself, as Ngũgĩ maintains (*Globalectics* 55), the term may still be useful (Spivak, "Subaltern Talk" 295), and, while debate continues, as Robert J. C. Young notes, "the postcolonial remains" ("Postcolonial" 19).[27]

The postcolonial intellectual is a variety of the late twentieth- and early twenty-first-century diasporic intellectual, often an exile, refugee, or escapee from political, economic, ideological, or cultural oppression.[28] The postcolonial intellectual emerged from the global geopolitical shifts of nineteenth-century imperial adventures, the rise of nationalism in its wake, the legacy of slavery and its embedding in modernity (Gilroy, *Black Atlantic* 190), and the domination of settler and resource colonization. One of the first voices of the colonized to emerge was that of Fanon, who targeted the contingent physical, psychic, and epistemic violence of colonialism, and articulated means of redress. Interpretations of Fanon's work, the crucible of the Algerian anticolonial conflict, and particularly Fanon's stance on the role of the intellectual, in both reactionary and progressive functions, in all stages of colonial violence, have been enormously influential. Sartre advanced Fanon's work. Sartre from the 1950s wrote from a philosophically and politically engaged position, but also as someone who had interrogated the implications of European anti-Semitism, as noted by Achebe (45). Some of the earliest pejorative references to self-styled intellectuals emerged in the atmosphere of virulent anti-Semitism at the time of the Dreyfus affair, a trial conducted when W.E.B. Du Bois—the founder, with Edward Wilmot Blyden, of Pan-Africanism—

---

created by postmodernism in the climate of emergent globalization and global capitalism, with the arrival of "Third World intellectuals" in "First World academe" (329, 352). Though postcoloniality's concerns predated the creation of the postcolonial in the 1980s, postcolonial intellectuals in Western universities inevitably found themselves in a position that was privileged, powerful, and compromised (343–4). The institutional ascendency of postcolonial studies as a discipline coincided with shifts of intellectual labor in the broader, global context of migration and emigration, transnational capital flows, and transnational production characteristic of late capitalism (330–1). This overlooked convergence explains for Dirlik why the potentially radical nature of postcolonial critique has become conservative and even complicit in replicating an essentialist history foregrounding colonialism, mimicking Orientalism and colonial epistemology and modes of analysis, and inadvertently reproducing power structures.

[27] A strong case for the continuing urgency of postcolonial studies and its "radical reflexivity" is made in Bill Ashcroft's introduction to *Literature for Our Times: Postcolonial Studies in the Twenty-First Century* (xv–xxxv).

[28] See Gilroy's examination of diaspora and the linkages, productive and problematic, between the Jewish and African diasporic communities in black intellectual history (*Black Atlantic* 205–12).

was in Europe (Gilroy, *Black Atlantic* 211–12).[29] Sartre's articulation of the perverse double consciousness or doubled identity of anti-Semitism, resembling Du Bois's "double-consciousness" in *The Souls of Black Folk* (5), finds a corresponding reflection in the articulation of alienated identity contingent on colonialism, as Bhabha recognizes:

> The ambivalent identification of the racist world—moving on two planes without being in the least embarrassed by it, as Sartre says of the anti-Semitic consciousness—turns on the idea of man as his alienated image; not self and Other but the otherness of the Self inscribed in the perverse palimpsest of colonial identity. (*Location* 44)

The need to defeat colonialism with violence, to address the debilitating legacy of inferiority in the colonized as raised in Fanon's work would profoundly influence later postcolonial critics, as will be explored in Chapter 3.

The major figures whose names are synonymous with the development of postcolonial studies, the famous troika of Said, Spivak, and Bhabha, have all written on the role and representation of the intellectual, partly addressing their own subject position, the location of articulation, and the question of representation. Their articulation of the postcolonial intellectual usually but not uncritically jibes with their own textual and worldly practice. Said, who has written most extensively on the subject, offers himself, though not without a studied self-irony, as a model. Said calls for the intellectual to be the face or image of his or her ideals so as to embody the representation of discursive positions, as he has done himself. While the figure of the intellectual is itself not a Foucauldian discourse, discursive position, or even counterdiscourse[30] for Said and he is equally dismissive of performing celebrity media intellectuals—despite being a highly effective media communicator who always wanted to score the winning blow—Said's emphasis in his many references to intellectuals hinges on the question of representation. Moreover, as H. Aram Veeser contends in his recent biography, *Edward Said: The Charisma of Criticism*, Said was a charismatic celebrity intellectual, who fortuitously benefited from the rise of theory's fortunes and their fall just as his own more worldly studies emerged. His work has gained even greater prestige and profundity when viewed retrospectively in a post-9/11 world. Veeser sees Said as a performative "academic intellectual"—a phrase Spivak used for Said in her remembrance of her colleague ("Edward Said Remembered" 55)—devoted to his work as a teacher at Columbia University just as Ngũgĩ has been throughout his career. Veeser frames his intellectual biography with his memories of being Said's student (and fan) and of facing Said's obstructions to his biographical research

---

[29] See Stefan Collini's astute discussion of the use of the term in light of Benda's analysis (285–90).

[30] In an essay striving to locate Said's notion of the public intellectual in a postcolonial frame, Ashcroft maintains that for Said, however, the intellectual's power is counterdiscursive, operating via "acts of counter-representation" ("Exile" 92).

and Said's encouraging exasperation with the length of time Veeser was taking to complete the task.

Said was something of a willfully intransigent, self-consciously contrapuntal, professional contrarian. He is often credited with establishing postcolonial studies despite his denials,[31] as well as being a major influence on Cultural Studies and also New Historicism (Spivak, "Edward Said" 54), but he was also a controversial advocate of a Palestinian homeland, a formalist literary critic enmeshed in Victorian and high Modernist domains, an accomplished pianist and expert on Western classical music, as well as a respected voice on the role of the dissident, oppositional intellectual. Due to the eclecticism of his multidimensional cultural, critical, and historical locations, in his autobiography *Out of Place* Said refers to himself as "Edward Said" in inverted commas. Born in an Arab Jerusalem that ceased to exist not long after his birth, the son of wealthy Protestant Christians who attempted to raise their children in a quasi-Western, colonial bubble, and exiled first in Egypt (from which he was later exiled in turn for 15 years) and then America, Said was named after the Prince of Wales and an obscure family relation. Even in childhood he developed the habit of referring to himself in the third person; as a boy he longed to be a book so as to have his identity self-evident and not requiring constant explanation and interpretation (76). His multiple dislocations would continue even later when he was denounced as a "professor of terror" in America at the same time as Yasser Arafat was suspicious of him as the quintessential representative of all-American attitudes and interests (Ali 85, 81). His was a lifelong search "for the self beneath or obscured by 'Edward'" in an existence characterized by "displacements from countries, cities, abodes, languages, environments" (Said, *Out* 294, 217). Moreover, Said was almost as hostile to postcolonial studies as he was to the intellectual orthodoxy of deconstruction that held sway in English departments in the 1960s and 1970s and particularly what he perceived as its detachment from society, history, culture, and politics. To found an academic discipline of enormous influence and then deny one's role in its establishment are perhaps emblematic of Said's willing embrace of the position of contrarian and his discomfort with anything other than the outsider status of the actual, metaphorical, and metaphysical exile.

---

[31] Veeser puts the matter succinctly: "Despite protests to the contrary, he fits into the set of themes and methods that today bear the name of postcolonial theory" (196). R. Radhakrishnan begins his entry on postcolonialism in his *A Said Dictionary*, the title itself a monument to Said's creation of a new critical language: "Every student of world literature now knows: no Edward Said, no postcoloniality" ("Postcoloniality" 86). However, as Young elaborates in "Edward Said: Opponent of Postcolonial Theory," Said was indifferent or openly hostile to the concept, and perhaps particularly because pointed hostility to Said and his *Orientalism* was often the gesture of initiation of any postcolonial critique which itself often mirrors orientalist critique; Young also points to Said's own movement away from poststructuralism and his alignment of it with the postcolonial, but mainly because postcolonialism's dominant narrative excludes the Palestinians (23–43).

Out of Place is one of a number of significant postcolonial autobiographical texts that indicate an emerging, distinct subgenre of autobiography,[32] in which Ngũgĩ's recent memoirs have an important place. Said's text appears to acknowledge that he found a home in his intellectual pursuits as he lived in exile in the global city of New York that he loved for its multicultural diversity, its rich cultural life, its proximity to ready departures, and its anonymity. His memoir is the account of "an essentially lost or forgotten world" (ix), the Palestinian Jerusalem of his youth, a record of Arabic memories translated in his own mind into English (ix–xii), and inevitably "a reenactment of the experience of departure and separation" (222). His memoir is also indirectly a biography of his parents, who colored his childhood with some of the isolationist, puritanical zeal evident in Edward Gosse's *Father and Son* and the obsessive pressures placed on John Stuart Mill's early education as outlined in his *Autobiography*, but also the eccentric postcolonial privilege of Sara Suleri's *Meatless Days*. His parents' disciplinary rigor involved the policing and perpetual criticism of every aspect of his life and extended to virtually every part and product of his body, including his seminal emissions. The disciplinary regime eventually creates a debilitating sense of inadequacy and insufficiency, and finally, internalized surveillance. In this sense as well as in its frequent references to the diagnosis of leukemia near the end of his life that provides the impetus for telling the story of his lost past, *Out of Place* is an illness or disability narrative, the story of a deep-seated psychological anxiety about unworthiness, as well as an account of life in the interzone of personal and collective dispossession and disorientation. His story of a damaged, "distorted" life (142; he refers to his own psychoanalysis 261), despite its spectacular achievements, is also inevitably a type of confession of pained, ambivalent love for his parents.

Said's encounters with British colonial schools were motivated by his father's attempt to keep Arab society outside the home and to make the home itself a parody of European or American family life. The Cairo of his youth was mainly lived within a bubble of Western high culture and privilege, just as in British colonial schools he was being trained to become a member of a colonial elite for a dead and dying empire (185–6). He experienced a sustained intellectual flowering and homecoming, paradoxically, at Princeton University, his intellectual occupations an escape from what he remembers as the dominant, resolutely anti-intellectual ethos of the campus. He finds independent intellectual sanctuary in his studies in order to distance himself from the "weekend social life of house parties, raccoon-skin coats, and endless drinking" and the "casual, pipe-smoking, tweedy anti-intellectualism of many teachers and students alike" (278).

The examinations of the intellectual that arise in Said's best-known early work on orientalism and orientalists sometimes have an autobiographical cast, partly due to his own distinctly cosmopolitan, humanist educational upbringing, his engrained tendency to self-criticism, and an anticipation of his later perception

---

[32] See Bart Moore-Gilbert's *Postcolonial Life-Writing: Culture, Politics and Self-Representation* and David Huddart's *Postcolonial Theory and Autobiography*.

of himself as a model of the dissident intellectual. Said's second major critical intervention, *Beginnings: Intention and Method* (1975), a text composed between 1967 and 1973, witnessed its own origins in a meditation on the role or dilemma of the critic, a term virtually synonymous with the intellectual in his early work as in Bhabha's. The "critic's enterprise" must unfold outside "a dynastic tradition" under the guidance of a "nomadic authority" (24, 13, 23), he says in the introduction to that work, and Said would become determined later to reclaim and reinvigorate the concept of the intellectual at a time when many theorists had "retired the category … as outmoded and even repressive" (Radhakrishnan, "The Intellectual" 48). However, Said's interest in the intellectual consciousness had been part of his very first book, which began as his doctoral dissertation at Harvard University. *Joseph Conrad and the Fiction of Autobiography* (1966), an unapologetically biographical reading of a corpus of literary work by a figure who would preoccupy Said for the rest of his life, is focused upon "the drama of the intellectual" (McCarthy 17).[33] Reading Conrad's short fiction in the light of his collected letters, Said stresses Conrad's self-fashioning and especially his construction of a public image. Said interprets the letters as "an almost embarrassingly rich testimonial" to Conrad's ideas and his persona (quoted in McCarthy 15). Said's fascination with Conrad's articulation of his own inner conflicts and extreme skepticism may reveal much about his own similarly troubled, exiled, alienated, historically haunted consciousness as revealed in *Out of Place*.

The intellectual, he maintains, has a responsibility "to remind this basically a-historical, forgetting world" about history and its human consequences, but also the intellectual must be radically free and relentlessly self-critical—"I agitate against myself!"—(Ali, *Conversations* 84, 105) and almost to be defiant by vocation, as if defiance, agitation, and dissent were part of the job description. While *The World, the Text, and the Critic*, written just after *Orientalism*, is an extended critique of post-structuralism's retreat from real world concerns, it is also a denunciation of the "cloistral world" of the university and especially the humanities' passivity and "surprisingly insistent quasi-religious quietism" (21, 25). Even *Orientalism*, however, may be read as being at least in part an attack, a "J'Accuse … !" directed at the "worldly" naïveté and state complicity of American intellectuals (McCarthy 96–7). Said asks what it means for the intellectual to have a "worldly" social identity and uses his own critical practice to exemplify his conclusions (*The World* 24). While acknowledging that the notion of the intellectual is largely a nineteenth-

---

[33] McCarthy writes in his lucid, concise, and perceptive introduction to Said's thinking that this early text is more generally

> about the drama of the intellectual coming to that definition in contexts of psychic, physical, ideological, and cultural extremity and difficulty—imperial struggle, war, exile, cultural dislocation, and assimilation. Over and over again, throughout his career, we shall see Said grappling with versions of these problems, either elucidating the struggles of writers and intellectuals who interest him … or undergoing such struggles himself, primarily in the context of his Palestinian activism. (17–18)

century invention, of which he insists a social role was an accepted component, he suggests that Jonathan Swift (1667–1745) be regarded as something of the quintessential intellectual who, despite or perhaps because of his compromised position and his meta-ironic complexity, assumes a steadfastly oppositional stance. Moreover, for Said, Swift exemplifies the intellectual who performs in his work a type of class suicide anticipating Cabral, as will be explored in Chapter 4, opposing the rank, station, and profession from which he emerged and in which he sustains his living. Swift must be understood via "his self-consciousness as an intellectual" (87) and his contrarian stance. "I'm the last Jewish intellectual," Said famously would declare late in his life, acknowledging his debt to Adorno, his provocatively contrarian and beleaguered ideological stance, and his elegiac embrace of the rhetoric of lateness (Said, "My Right" 458).[34]

Like Swift and Antonio Gramsci, Said's consideration of the role of the intellectual and his own intellectual self-consciousness lie at the center of his critique of "the modern postindustrial state" (*The World* 82). The intellectual operating within a state apparatus, like Said at Columbia University, even while advocating on a global scale for the Palestinian cause, is ever subject to ironic critique. The intellectual desires to be neither the state's propagandist nor part of its police force, but the web of state power is inevitably enclosing. Ironically, for Said, the intellectual may be regarded as dangerously subversive by the state even while being engaged in a self-reflexive critical discourse ostensibly divorced from history, society, or politics (173). Thus, perhaps, for Said, Swift's "Voyage to the Country of the Houyhnhnms" becomes an allegory of the intellectual, forced to confront an embedded Yahoo nature and the potential catastrophe of the triumph of reason, and Said's intellectual is ultimately tragic or at least ironic (89). Said's willing embrace of contradictory, even paradoxical positions may be the model for his notion of the intellectual as one who is both outsider and insider, in exile even while in the glare of publicity in a global city, passionate yet detached, theoretically dense yet accessible to a broad public (Ashcroft, "Exile" 76).

Said's best-known statement on intellectuals, *Representations of the Intellectual, The 1993 Reith Lectures*, is largely a repetition of the positions advanced in *The World, the Text, and the Critic*. However, *Representations* somewhat self-consciously performs the public role of the intellectual in voicing its opinions to a potentially mass audience in more concise, lucid terms, with Said's characteristic lists of intellectuals. *Representations* also voices contradictory positions, a feature not universally celebrated.[35] Inevitably, in this work, Said becomes, partly at

---

[34] Said ends the interview in which this statement appears with another equally controversial assertion: "I'm a Jewish-Palestinian" (458). For a detailed account of the meaning, impact, and legacy of this remark, see Bryan Cheyette's "A Glorious Achievement: Edward Said and the Last Jewish Intellectual" (74–94).

[35] Collini refers to *Representations* as "a compendium of seductive delusions," a text that shifts between definitions and prescriptions, roles and psychologies (432, 427–32). His critique is based primarily on what he regards as a confusion in Said's self-positioning as

least, the type of public media intellectual he abhorred though his sound bites were always more like gourmet mini-meals. He rehearses his framing references to Julien Benda and Gramsci,[36] supplying a more nuanced reading of Benda's formation of the intellectual "cleric," who speaks from a universal, transcendental position, aloof from "racial passion, class passions and national passions" in *La Trahison des Clercs* (Benda 3). Said's own critique of intellectuals of the present resembles Benda's but the thrust of Said's argument is nearly, but not quite, opposite. As in *The World*'s reading of nineteenth-century English intellectuals like Matthew Arnold, who celebrated a perspective of detachment and disinterestedness, in *Representations* Said acknowledges Benda's worldly concerns, if only in his examples of model intellectuals such as Jesus. Said insists on intellectual judgments made "on the basis of universal principles" of truth and justice (11). *Representations* departs farthest from *The World* in its addition of American examples of intellectuals, no doubt to address more directly his primarily American audience. His model of the oppositional, dissident intellectual is himself, one who feels compelled to represent and embody all opinions, ideas, and concerns articulated. The type of engagement Said calls for is sincere personal belief in words and deeds. His demand results from both his annoyance at the detachment of some critics and a certain exasperation at the volume of studies of intellectuals, as if talking about the roles and representations of the intellectual is itself a way of sidestepping genuine intellectual work.

While engaged in an extended definition of the intellectual in terms of "the image, the signature, the actual intervention and performance," Said is impatient with the "entire library" of works devoted to the subject:

> There are thousands of different histories and sociologies of intellectuals available, as well as endless accounts of intellectuals and nationalism, and power, and tradition, and revolution, and on and on. Each region of the world has produced its intellectuals and each of those formations is debated and argued over with fiery passion. There has been no major revolution in modern history without intellectuals; conversely there has been no major counterrevolutionary movement without intellectuals. Intellectuals have been the fathers and mothers of movements, and of course sons and daughters, even nephews and nieces. (*Representations* 10–11)

Said goes on to imply strongly that intellectual self-fashioning is itself a symptom of the proliferation of intellectuals. He points to Foucault's position

---

an intellectual: "there is a very strong personal anxiety or fantasy at work here, an anxiety which is at least in part about being corrupted by success" (429). Collini specifically attacks the delusions of grandeur hiding behind much noisy consumption of humble pie: "Throughout, Said implicitly represents himself as resisting the glamour and seductiveness of official patronage, but he succumbs to a more insidious kind of glamour, that of being the champion of the wretched of the earth" (428).

[36] Saree Makdisi calls Said's position a "synthesis" of the two (22), calling into question whether Said's resulting high modernist view of the intellectual is a useful model in the present with increasing surveillance even within universities (32–4).

on "specific" intellectuals' having taken over from universal intellectuals and Gramsci's declaration that "all men are intellectuals" (Gramsci quoted in Said, *Representations* 3) as creating a climate for ubiquitous intellectualism. What he does not consider is that intellectuals like writing about intellectuals and that such relentless self-analysis is a recognized feature of most definitions. However, Said is clearly articulating a somewhat more exclusive definition, departing from Foucault and Gramsci, and moving closer to Benda. Said's true public intellectual is not "an anonymous functionary or careful bureaucrat" (13), but one with a calling or vocation for public performance of oppositional positions and for embodying, branding, and bearing the image of such commitments and beliefs. Said's true intellectual is a living witness and exemplar.

Said's stance is ostensibly antagonistic to Benda's, but in the course of his lectures, though less stridently than in *The World*, Said, in Benda-like mode, attacks postmodern academics, sequestered in academic and specialist silos, who acquiesce to their divorce from real life and the public sphere. His work joins other texts he examines (from *The Last Intellectual* to *The God That Failed*) in deploring intellectual gullibility, narcissism, and hubris. Moreover, while Said acknowledges the limitations of Benda's quasi-religious universal, transcendental values, he readily endorses universal values of truth, freedom, justice, and equal rights, and castigates moral relativism. He cites Tocqueville's moral relativism in attacking America but not Algeria, and J.S. Mill's endorsement of democratic rights in England but not India.

Moreover, while compiling lists of good and bad intellectuals, the list being a characteristic of his writing, Said returns to his protest against the already overworked task of defining the intellectual, though he goes a step further in illuminating the features of what he calls the "true intellectual" (120). He moves beyond endorsements of other intellectuals to elucidate features, though not, so he claims, a "sealed gearbox" or manual of how to be this true intellectual (120). This elucidation endorses the intellectual's vocation, calling, and role, and outlines a code of intellectual conduct. While deploring intellectual narcissism, hubris, and widespread hand-wringing over the intellectual's predicament, Said accepts an "erosion" in the notion and status of the intellectual, partly as a result of a fracturing of the role of the traditional intellectual by national and religious obligations, but also due to the very proliferation of professional careers for intellectuals in the postmodern world and because of specialization and the dominance of expertise as well as accommodation to the dictates of power. He wonders finally if "an independent, autonomously functioning intellectual" is possible any longer (67), and advocates some radical reforms. Said strongly suggests that his true intellectual must murder the psychic inheritance of the internalized traditional intellectual in order to speak in the public sphere from an engaged position. However, as Lazarus points out, "there is … a certain romanticism of the intellectual in Said" ("Mind the Gap" 11),[37] and Said's true intellectual is nearly always a writer or academic, and not a "social movement intellectual" or a collective agent (Scalmer 46).

---

[37] Lazarus explores this further in "Representations of the Intellectual in *Representations of the Intellectual*" (118–19) and *The Postcolonial Unconscious* (196–203).

Said comes closest to considering in detail the role and the status of the postcolonial intellectual in his remarks on exile, the black intellectual tradition, and "Third World exile intellectuals" (*Representations* 51). However, as Young suggests, Said himself was uncomfortable with the postcolonial partly because its "triumphalist narrative" of homecoming or return to independence was a "post" denied Palestinians, and as a result he identified more with the long line of displaced twentieth-century European intellectual exiles in England and America than with the diasporic postcolonial exile intellectual ("Edward Said" 36–7). He also appears to have recognized how readily postcolonial studies would become a new orthodoxy.[38] Exile for Said is the actual, metaphorical, and metaphysical condition of intellectuals—his examples are Swift, V.S. Naipaul, and Theodor Adorno—but there is of course a great difference between holding that the intellectual is or should be an exile by vocation, a type of Byronic stranger alone even in a crowd, and acknowledging the number of unwilling intellectual exiles, like Ngũgĩ, forced into displaced locations due to political terror. Said and Ngũgĩ are different examples of what Abdul R. JanMohamed refers to as "border intellectuals," whose location is necessarily both ambiguous and precarious (97, 102).[39] Said controversially refers to the rewards, privileges, and "pleasures of exile" (the phrase is George Lamming's, a writer of great importance for Ngũgĩ) in heightened awareness and "eccentric angles of vision" (*Representations* 59) that enforce a style of detachment: "The intellectual in exile is necessarily ironic, skeptical, even playful—but not cynical" (61). Without fully acknowledging his privileged position in the global high-cultural mecca of New York, at a respected Ivy League university, with an enviable and deserved international celebrity status, Said does refer to American academia as potentially providing "the intellectual a quasi-utopian space in which reflection and research can go on, albeit under new constraints and pressures" (82).[40] For Said, such an exiled location allows the intellectual to resist isolation in specialized silos and to work in inter- and multidisciplinary and comparative contexts as well as voicing concerns in the

---

[38] In a 1989 interview published in 1992's *Edward Said: A Critical Reader*, Said articulates his suspicion of orthodox positions when he says, "I've been very conscious ... of not wanting to impose myself on students ... to become part of a school, to formalize what it is that I do in teachable ways" ("Interview" 248).

[39] While he does not set out to provide a typology, JanMohamed's distinction of syncretic and specular intellectuals appears to omit a figure like Ngũgĩ unless he would allow that Ngũgĩ's use of the novel genre, even of a distinctly oppositional, oral, non-English type, situates him with Soyinka, Salman Rushdie, or Achebe as a syncretic intellectual who "is able to combine elements of the two cultures in order to articulate new syncretic forms and experiences" (97).

[40] Radhakrishnan refers to "the Saidian intellectual" as a "critical-utopian individual consciousness that seeks to find a home in critical homelessness, that is, to realize the critique as a form of solidarity and historicize solidarity as a form of critical belonging" ("The Intellectual" 52).

public sphere. Moreover, such a seemingly enviable position perhaps starkly illuminated his own reflections on home.

Said examines the state of colonial and postcolonial studies as well as the location of the postcolonial intellectual in an earlier work, "Intellectuals in the Post-Colonial World" of 1986, concluding with a statement on the importance of the intellectual's vocation and offering some advice for postcolonial intellectuals. In light of an account of mid-1980s colonial nostalgia and the Raj revival, Said reflects on the colonial legacy in the heterogeneous postcolonial world and the work of intellectuals in addressing it. He name-checks Ngũgĩ in words repeated almost verbatim in *Culture and Imperialism*, though Ngũgĩ's full name is misspelled differently in each (Said, "Intellectuals" 45; Said, *Culture* 18). Said's essay refers to Ngũgĩ briefly amid a lengthy analysis of Orwell and Conrad, and an early celebration of the benefits of exilic, outsider status. Conrad for Said is a writer embedded in an imperialist ideology whose clarity of vision results from his "exilic marginality": "[Y]our self-consciousness as an outsider can provoke in you an active comprehension of how the machine works, given that you are usually out of synch with and at a distance from it" (49). Said assigns a contingent role to postcolonial novels, that, in his estimation, endlessly unfold parodic reinterpretations and reinscriptions of the colonial quest narrative. Ngũgĩ, for Said, is one of those postcolonial "intellectuals who have carried on their thought and practise publicly and courageously" (45), despite persecution, imprisonment, and exile. However, he also suggests that Ngũgĩ is one of those postcolonial intellectuals trapped in a reiteration of a "politics of blame" (45) against colonialism, and while he makes no specific reference to Ngũgĩ's novels,[41] he offers two suggestions. The postcolonial intellectual should be an outsider within the whale of Orwell's public and private imaginary, and should examine the "experience of colonialism that continues into the present" (46, 54). Said also advises an "intellectual vocation" (55) for "oppositional intellectuals," an "intellectual imperative" that, over and above the lived experience of the native informant or some species of identity politics, can authorize more "useful" accounts of the "symbiotic," "congruent," "intertwined" relationship between the colonial and postcolonial, rather than a relationship characterized by a polarized antagonism (59–64). In a panel discussion on the paper at Skidmore College, Said goes a step further in typically contrarian mode, given his endorsement of public engagement: "At some point, part of the post-colonial intellectual's agenda should be to leave aside the immediate politics in which we're all engaged. ... The most interesting aspect of the post-colonial intellectual's job is not in the arena of combat" (Said, "The Intellectual" 70).

---

[41] Similarly, in a 1989 interview in *Edward Said: A Critical Reader* in response to a reference to "N'gugi" [sic]'s remarks on his "new novel" (presumably *Matigari*)'s incorporation of innovative narrative strategies, Said notes his impatience with "prescriptive and programmatic imperatives of a particular methodological vision" and his irritation with "nativist sentiments" (Said, "Interview" 255), though in these last remarks Said does not directly refer to Ngũgĩ.

Said is writing a manifesto on the role of the true intellectual, of which he is a model. His works on this subject, taken together, may form an intellectual autobiography or what Jacques Derrida calls in a different context an "intellectual bildungsroman" (70). As Benita Parry has noted in a discussion of Said's "Third World Intellectuals/Metropolitan Culture,"

> when Said describes the revisionist projects of postcolonial intellectuals who "address the metropolis using the techniques, the discourses, the very weapons of scholarship and criticism once reserved exclusively for the European" as "original and creative work" which has transformed the very terrain of the disciplines ..., this can be read as self-referential. ("Overlapping" 20)

Said may never really exact a final distinction between being an embedded intellectual (hired to report from within and be an adjunct to state and other institutional power) on the one hand, and being a free radical intellectual boasting an independent, amateur status, while still working within institutions like the university, on the other. He displays his refusenik credentials in declining to be a paid media or government consultant, but he does separate his commitments into different intellectual spheres. For example, he places a symbolic firewall around his work in the classroom, rejecting participation in the so-called activist classroom. Said was far too astute not to recognize what might be his own self-justification in this account of intellectual roles, representations, and distinctions. He rationalized his skeptical, outsider, exile status with "the essentially impossible and generally losing results of being Palestinian," and hence "the virtues of outsiderhood" (*Representations* 108, 107). He insists upon his role of resisting stagnation or co-optation, and of speaking for "the poor, the disadvantaged, the voiceless, the unrepresented, the powerless" (*Representations* 113).

In *The Post-Colonial Critic: Interviews, Strategies, Dialogues*, a text compiled when she was nearing the height of her "grand celebrity" as a "post-colonial intellectual," Spivak presents a detailed, highly self-critical portrait of her multiple subject positions (117, 8).[42] While she is one of the founders of postcolonial studies, as well as a confirmed comparativist, Marxist, feminist scholar of Subaltern Studies, theorist of translation, and celebrated translator of Derrida, and a doyen of theory, Spivak began her intellectual career as a literary critic of Irish

---

[42] Spivak's multiple self-representations and perceptions by her critics are characterized by David Huddart within his study of autobiography's interface with theory:
> First, she is extremely critical of what she sees as metropolitan diasporic intellectuals flaunting their difference as part of some dubiously careerist manoeuvrings. Second, according to her critics she's not above flaunting her difference as part of some dubiously careerist manoeuvring. Third, her work displays an admirable honesty about how these two things co-exist, and a stern theoretical grasp of the necessity of this co-existence (122),

and finally "her work ... is not only self-obsessed but also impenetrably suffused with jargon" (123).

and nineteenth-century English texts. Her groundbreaking study of the canonical Victorian novel and prototypical female bildungsroman *Jane Eyre* (1847) is now often read as a companion piece to that novel, a contrapuntal relationship it shares with Achebe's analysis of *Heart of Darkness* (1899) as a classic racist text.[43] It also shares this type of contrapuntal relationship to some extent with C.L.R. James's more extensive analysis, first published in 1953, of *Moby Dick* (1851) as a modernist allegory, a groundbreaking analysis in postcolonial and Black Trans-Atlantic studies, as well as a critique of the reactionary American literary and critical studies establishment, written while James was imprisoned on Ellis Island as an "alien," which is explored in Chapter 3.[44] Spivak's analysis of *Jane Eyre* reexamined the figure of Bertha Mason, who had been dismissed as an incidental piece of Gothic claptrap, a convenience of three-volume plot mechanics, making the first Mrs. Rochester into a central figure conjuring the counterbalance of her wifely suicide and Jane's rise to matrimony, a pair of marriages made comfortable by the profits of slavery. Spivak's "Three Women's Texts and a Critique of Imperialism" also considered the implications of the prominence of Brontë's novel in the 1970s feminist reclamation project regarding women's literary history. In an interview in 1993, Spivak recalls reading *Jane Eyre* as a child in India, and she refers to her awareness of the role of that novel in forming "young colonial subjects" when much later she came to reread and teach it: "this book that I read with such pleasure as a child in Calcutta had things in it that I had not noticed. It taught me a lesson of what the making of young colonial subjects was like. For I was looking at myself" (Spivak, "Subaltern Talk" 288). A more detailed consideration of the role of English novels like Brontë's in colonial or postcolonial India is called for by Gauri Viswanathan, who advocates that the reception of such canonical works in an imperial context must be regarded as a constitutive part of the texts.[45] Achebe's moment of revelation about *Heart of Darkness* was similarly heightened by his memory of being hoodwinked by his childhood reading. Spivak reflects on Ngũgĩ's work on orature as part of decolonizing imaginative reading in one of the opening gestures of her influential "How to Read a 'Culturally Different' Book" (73).

Spivak's credentials as theorist and her formidable linguistic expertise were established in one of her first major works, a translation of Derrida's *De la Grammatologie* (*Of Grammatology*), but also in its lengthy preface, which raises

---

[43] As Ngũgĩ has recently noted, "[i]n the world today, some of the most penetrating readings of the same [canonical] texts have come from theorists from the colony" (*Globalectics* 12).

[44] See the restored edition of *Mariners, Renegades and Castaways: The Story of Herman Melville and the World We Live In*. For an account of the ongoing interpretive debate about this text's and especially its suppressed final chapter's political stance, see Donald E. Pease's introductory essay (vii–xxxiii).

[45] She writes that "we can no longer afford to regard the uses to which literary works were put in the service of British imperialism as extraneous to the way these texts are to be read" (169).

the question of Spivak's notion of the critic or deconstructivist intellectual's positioning. Spivak's work is a translation of a text by a philosopher whose first book was a translation, and her introductory preface, in deconstructivist mode, begins with a critique of the notion of the preface, finally asserting both that *Of Grammatology* "is infinitely translatable" and that it "denies the possibility of translation" ("Translator's Preface" lxxxvi).[46] The preface traces Derrida's work's relationships to various philosopher father figures, but it also investigates the construction of the subject partly in light of what it elsewhere refers to as "self-differentiation and self-postponement" (li), a condition partly resulting from the critic's inability to "present his own vulnerability" (lxxv). Speaking of the deconstructivist's desire, Spivak writes that "the critic provisionally forgets that her own text is necessarily self-deconstructed, always already a palimpsest" (lxxvii). The pleasure of deconstruction for the critic lies partly in the intoxication of deconstruction's limitlessness and its endless qualifications and supplementations. However, for the critic, the preface suggests, deconstruction also offers a tantalizing image of the otherness of the self:

> Thus a further deconstruction deconstructs deconstruction, both as the search for a foundation (the critic behaving as if she means what she says in her text), and as the pleasure of the bottomless. The tool for this, as indeed for any deconstruction, is our desire, itself a deconstructive and grammatological structure that forever differs from (we only desire what is not ourselves) and defers (desire is never fulfilled) the text of our selves. (lxxvii–lxxviii)

Deconstruction thus appears to enable the critic's own self-exposure or opening to her own unexamined, bottomless vulnerability. At least in part, this mode of analysis gestures in the direction of the confessional writing self. In this context, it is significant when Spivak points out that "the East is never seriously studied or deconstructed in the Derridean text" (lxxxii), and hence within this absence she may locate the origins of her own later postcolonial project.[47] However, like Chuang Tzu dreaming he is a butterfly, or "Rousseau ... dreaming of Derrida" (lxxxv), a dream with which the preface concludes, by 1986 Spivak could assert, "I'm not a deconstructivist" (*Post-Colonial Critic* 45).[48] She was rejecting what had become the hegemony of essentialist theoretical authority, a particularly ironic development given that it had begun as an anti-hegemonic practice.

Spivak has an intensified awareness of her own positionality, role, inscription, trace, construction, identity, and definition as well as the uses made of these guises

---

[46] Spivak's preface sets "a new standard for self-reflexivity in prefaces" as Donna Landry and Gerald MacLean note ("Introduction" 1).

[47] Spivak's movement toward postcolonial studies is traced indirectly in the essays within *In Other Worlds*.

[48] Importantly, Spivak's statement is qualified: "[A]lthough I make a specific use of deconstruction, I'm not a deconstructivist" (45).

and their distortions.[49] She recently reflected on the development of her ideas and their relationship to her lived experience as forming "my own intellectual autobiography, my stereotype of myself" (Bhattacharya, "Interview" 224). This problematic multiplicity, moreover, is to an extent "the predicament of the postcolonial intellectual" (*Post-Colonial Critic* 70). Spivak claims the migratory status of one who "is never at home" linguistically or geographically partly due to her birth as a Bengali Brahmin woman[50] in a Kali-worshipping sect in the "artificial construct" that is contemporary India (38, 39). In a different context, somewhat like Said, she celebrates a certain critical and historical rootlessness, maintaining that "a nostalgia for lost origins can be detrimental to the exploration of social realities within the critique of imperialism" ("Can the Subaltern" 291), and she traces a symmetry between this rejection of nostalgia and a deconstructivist examination of complicity.[51] She has been regarded by many in the Western academy as "bicultural," a diasporic Western-trained native informant, a "Third World woman," an "anomaly," "a piece of exotica" (*Post-Colonial Critic* 83, 60, 155, 94),[52] though she has recently written that she is beginning to find the endless rearticulation of her positionality and "diasporicity" to be quite "tedious" ("Preface" xiv). As a graduate of the University of Calcutta, "then the cultural centre of the British Empire as it were," she came to America, where she was regarded as resembling "women in *National Geographic*" (*Post-Colonial Critic* 84–5). At Cornell University she was denied a fellowship because her first language was not English. She has become a highly respected distinguished professor in an American Ivy League university, an "international star" (*Post-Colonial Critic* 116)—the jacket promotion for 2012's *An Aesthetic Education in the Era of Globalization* refers to Spivak unequivocally as "the world's most renowned critical theorist"—while at the same time as a divorced woman in certain communities in India she bore "the mark of bad luck" (*Post-Colonial*

---

[49] Colin MacCabe no doubt unwittingly suggests something self-serving or at least conveniently politically ambidextrous in referring to Spivak's "all purpose radical identity" (xii), though he later clarifies his regard for her astute self-consciousness: "The force of Spivak's work lies in her absolute refusal to discount any of the multiplicity of subject-positions which she has been assigned, or to fully accept any of them" ("Foreword" xxiii).

[50] Spivak defines her class position as being "from the bottom layer of the upper middle class or the top layer of the lower middle class, depending on which side of the family you are choosing" ("Bonding" 17).

[51] Spivak's articulation of deconstructivist practice clearly informs her hyper-awareness of compromised multi-positionality. She writes in her "Translator's Foreword" to her translation of Mahasweta Devi's "Draupadi" of "the recognition, within deconstructive practice, of provisional and intractable starting points in any investigative effort; its disclosure of complicities where a will to knowledge would create oppositions; its insistence that in disclosing complicities the critic-as-subject is herself complicit with the object of her critique" (246–7).

[52] See Spivak's revealing account of her academic "marginality" in the Western academic milieu in "Explanation and Culture: Marginalia" (139–60).

Critic 116). Her journey to this conflicted stature has made her recognize the vanity of institutions and intellectuals: "There is an impulse among literary critics and other kinds of intellectuals to save the masses, speak for the masses, describe the masses. On the other hand, how about attempting to learn to speak in such a way that the masses will not regard as bullshit" (*Post-Colonial Critic* 56). Her own hypercritical awareness of positionality has also made her remarkably inclusive, even toward her white male students, who feel silenced.[53] However, while she recognizes the uses and misuses others make of their construction of her, she also appreciates this construction's moral implications: "one of my projects is not to allow myself to occupy the place of the marginal that you would like to see me in, because then that allows you to feel that you have an other to speak to" (*Post-Colonial Critic* 122). She refuses to be what Sara Suleri calls in a different context an "otherness machine," a target for psychic projections.[54]

"Can the Subaltern Speak?" is perhaps Spivak's most famous essay and, despite its myriad misinterpretations,[55] it has made Spivak an expert on and voice for the question of representation in postcolonial studies. "Can the Subaltern Speak?" also directly tackles another, related question: can the postcolonial intellectual speak? Spivak's carefully articulated positions have sometimes been reduced to formulas, such as that "[t]he regulative psychobiography for Indian women, according to you, is sanctioned suicide" (*Post-Colonial Critic* 71). However, as she makes plain, she does not represent or ally herself with the subaltern; she merely acknowledges herself "as a namer of the subaltern" (*Post-Colonial Critic* 166). "Can the Subaltern Speak?" appears to have followed in the wake of her awareness of "how the [colonial] reading subject is produced" in her rereading of *Jane Eyre* ("Subaltern Talk" 288). More particularly, this essay seems to have grown from her insightful critique of Kristeva's *About Chinese Women*, and its representation of the subaltern woman, and that text's construction of Kristeva's own positionality as "the speaking, reading, listening 'I,'" though Spivak also questions Kristeva's "wishful use of history," the lack of "primary research," and a certain essentialism (Spivak, "French Feminism" 189, 190). She sees French feminism and its naïve parody in Anglo-American criticism as a continuation of the privileged perceptions of the avant-garde, and she concludes that "the First World feminist must learn to stop feeling privileged *as a woman*" (Spivak, "French Feminism" 187), as if operating on the notion that gender always trumps race, class, culture, history, and politics. She calls instead for a "metaphysics of identity": "[W]ho is the other woman? How am I naming her?" Who is the "'colonized' woman?" (Spivak, "French Feminism" 206, 207).

---

[53] "I compare myself ... sometimes to my white male students, who complain that they can no longer speak. I say to them that they should develop a degree of rage against a history that has allowed that, that has taken away from them the possibility of speaking" (*Post-Colonial Critic* 43).

[54] See Lovesey's "Postcolonial Self-Fashioning in Sara Suleri's *Meatless Days*" (35–50).

[55] Spivak explains the somewhat fraught origins of the essay, saying the first version of the article "reflects something of the struggle I went through trying to write that piece," and its radically divergent readings and misreadings (Spivak, "Subaltern Talk" 288, 287–92).

"Can the Subaltern Speak?" addresses the question of the location of articulation of the postcolonial intellectual, or as Spivak puts it "the positionality of the postcolonial intellectual as investigating subject" (296). She juxtaposes the somewhat cool disavowal of Foucault and Gilles Deleuze in "Intellectuals and Power" regarding the European ethnocentric construction of the Other and the European intellectual's denial or effacement of responsibility in answering Spivak's essay's titular question, on the one hand, with a careful promotion of Derrida's less widely acknowledged Marxist politics/theoretical praxis, on the other. She suggests that while "calling the place of the investigator into question" (271) and being "uncritical about the historical role of the intellectual" (275), Foucault and Deleuze inadvertently construct the sovereign subject of the West and the Western intellectual. In particular, Spivak famously points to their failure to distinguish the uses of representation, a distinction made in Marx's *The Eighteenth Brumaire of Louis Bonaparte* between *vertreten* or a legalistic speaking for, or on behalf of, or in the place of, or as a substitute for, another; and *darstellen* or a more aesthetic/ artistic speaking about or portraying (276–9). Foucault and Deleuze, in effect, refuse responsibility and ignore the reality of Europe's creation of empire and the place of the subaltern within it. In effect, "the intellectual is complicit in the persistent constitution of Other as the Self's shadow" (280). However, Foucault and Deleuze were primarily reacting to the hostility directed at intellectuals during the May 1968 protests in Paris, and were acknowledging the bankruptcy of the older notion of the traditional intellectual as the "conscience, consciousness, and eloquence" of any group or collective (Foucault, "Intellectuals" 207),[56] and stressing instead the intellectual's own entrapment within the mechanisms of state power. Deleuze does state categorically that "[a] theorizing intellectual, for us, is no longer a subject, a representing or representative consciousness" (Foucault, "Intellectuals" 206). They thus elaborate the figure of Foucault's "specific intellectual" who engages only in particular struggles and stands in clear opposition to the figure of the "prophetic intellectual" and "the Dreyfusard ideal of the universal intellectual" (Wolin 20–21). They sidestep the question of empire and the intellectual's responsibility, asserting that "only those directly concerned can speak in a practical way on their own behalf" (Foucault, "Intellectuals" 209); their examples are taken from the prison, the factory, and the kindergarten.

In one of the next major moves in this densely argued essay, in the direction of her final inquiry into the freight of tradition, individual free will, and law in the colonial banning of widow suicide, Spivak refers to Thomas Macaulay's famous "Minute [on Indian Education]" and its project of constructing an elite corps of native intellectuals. The essay raises the possibility by implication of a

---

[56] Foucault questions the intellectual's role as expert and distributor of knowledge or representative voice. He says that "[i]n the most recent upheaval, the intellectual discovered that the masses no longer need him to gain knowledge: they *know* perfectly well, without illusion; they know far better than he and they are certainly capable of expressing themselves" (207).

connection between the concrete effects of Foucault and Deleuze's denial of the European subject of history—"the self-diagnosed transparency of the first-world radical intellectual" and "the first-world intellectual masquerading as the absent nonrepresenter who lets the oppressed speak for themselves" (285, 292)—and the ostensible benevolence of Macaulay's program of disciplinary language learning. Macaulay called for the creation of "a class who may be interpreters between us and the millions whom we govern; a class of persons, Indian in blood and colour, but English in taste, in opinions, in morals, and in intellect" (quoted in Spivak, "Can the Subaltern" 282). In particular, this new native intellectual class would absorb the English language as a means of colonization and a method to transform an orientalist Sanskrit into a working vehicle for disseminating disciplinary knowledge. Macaulay's project, however, was partly based on an appreciation of the intellectual capacity and linguistic facility of "the learned natives," and also a conviction, confirmed in his opinion by orientalists, that Sanskrit and Arabic are "barren of useful knowledge" (Macaulay). Partly due to its growing presence in the empire, English in Macaulay's view is the best vehicle for conveying the fact- and science-based learning required. His "Minute" was driven ostensibly by concerns for thrift and pragmatism, rather than by a desire for an acceleration of the hegemonic cultural destruction and assimilation that were already underway in English India. While he is disparaging of the culture of Sanskrit and Arabic, and contemptuous about Indian spirituality in all its forms, he does not promote English study to displace Hindu "superstition" or to inculcate English values. His aim is utilitarian and seemingly more banal. He seeks to achieve an efficient filtering down of practical knowledge needed for running a colony, from an educated elite to the masses, through education and translation (Viswanathan 144–69). While perhaps inadvertently reinforcing the caste system by creating caste-segregated colleges, the English Education Act of 1835, which followed from Macaulay's "Minute," introduced class stratification in its creation of an intellectual elite.

The postcolonial intellectual's predicament is a form of abjection, a recognition of irretrievability when attempting to narrate the colonial subject's struggle, while aware that "in the context of colonial production, the subaltern has no history and cannot speak" (Spivak, "Can the Subaltern" 287). In recognizing their position regarding the text of the subaltern, "[t]he postcolonial intellectuals learn that their privilege is their loss. In this they are a paradigm of the intellectuals" (287). Spivak advocates a rigorous unlearning—or perhaps a variety of self-effacement ("Translator's Foreword" 246)—for the postcolonial intellectual but one that is not a version of what she calls "sanctioned ignorance" resting on a convenient alterity (291).[57] The postcolonial intellectual is placed at best in an absurd position,

---

[57] She explains:
That inaccessible blankness circumscribed by the interpretable text is what a postcolonial critic of imperialism would like to see developed within the European enclosure as *the* place of the production of theory. The postcolonial critics and intellectuals can attempt to displace their own production only by presupposing that *text-inscribed* blankness. ("Can the Subaltern" 294)

given that "the subject of exploitation cannot know and speak the text of female exploitation, even if the absurdity of the nonrepresenting intellectual making space for her to speak is achieved" (288). She continues:

> In seeking to learn to speak (rather than listen to or speak for) the historically muted subject of the subaltern woman, the postcolonial intellectual *systematically* "unlearns" female privilege. This systematic unlearning involves learning to critique postcolonial discourse with the best tools it can provide and not simply substituting the lost figure of the colonized. (295)

This program veers from an embrace of detachment in the face of catachresis to the elaboration of a tool box. The rigorous discipline (a version of imaginative negative dialectics) Spivak demands of herself and of the postcolonial intellectual generally begins in the space between her two sentences following from the colonial banning of widow sacrifice, which operated under the banner of the protection of Indian women and the establishment of civil society over and above a stated desire to retain traditional, custom-based jurisprudence. In this space, "the postcolonial woman intellectual ... begins to plot a history" which is "to give the subaltern a voice in history" (297, 296) over and above a transcendental, transhistorical misogyny. More recently, Spivak refers to the task as empowering the creation of the subaltern intellectual or "the hard work of learning from below the production of the subaltern intellectual" (Bhattacharya, "Interview" 232).

In this space of articulation, however impossible, "the non-self-abdicating intellectual" can and must speak. In the wake of the colonial project and against the uncommitted stance of the "first-world radical intellectual" like Foucault and Deleuze and even the postcolonial intellectual's separation from the colonial subject, intellectuals in the Subaltern Studies group accept the project of "rewrit[ing] the development of the consciousness of the Indian nation" ("Can the Subaltern" 285) and "bringing hegemonic historiography to crisis," and perhaps enabling an "emergent collective consciousness" (Spivak, "Subaltern Studies" 272, 283). Spivak ends "Can the Subaltern Speak?" with the historical and personal account of a young woman's suicide and its reinterpreted and misinterpreted motives.[58] A more recent case has provoked international attention and shown the relevance of Spivak's position. The repercussions of a 23-year-old woman's gang rape in New Delhi at the end of 2012 filled the news. Just prior to her death after the failure of medical treatment, she is reported to have said: "Mummy, I am sorry." This statement has been interpreted as a confession of guilt provoked by violation. Her case inaugurated mass protests in India against a climate of judicial silence and governmental myopia in the face of sexual violence. Objecting to the way that some international media have attempted to present this case as an example of an international epidemic of violence against women, Doug Saunders in Canada's *The Globe and Mail* newspaper wrote, "It's not a 'universal

---

[58] Spivak reflects on the personal connections of this story in a recent interview (Bhattacharya, "Interview" 224–5, 231–2).

rape culture'—it's India" to refocus attention on the specifics and contexts of the case, but in so doing he reinforced the perception that unexamined, transhistorical colonialist attitudes and injunctions, and perhaps also the subaltern's silence, did not end with independence. It is worth recalling in this tragic context that Spivak has declared that to an extent the postcolonial is itself "the child of rape" (Spivak, "Bonding" 19).

A number of Spivak's remarks on the postcolonial critic confront Foucault's universal/specific intellectual binary, but she is also impatient with Western academic insularity. She maintains that while many academic intellectuals are localized within specific institutions, many of these institutions, particularly in America, consider themselves universal prototypes (*Post-Colonial Critic* 3–6, 37). In the *Post-Colonial Critic* interviews, she refers to Ngũgĩ's injunction in *Writers in Politics* about the need for "cultural worker[s]" to break not with the universal/ specific designation, but with class allegiance and in particular their "alliance with the native bourgeoisie" (156). Elsewhere, Spivak notes Ngũgĩ's acknowledgment that this class rupture is a type of internal exile, made into a "double exile" when the intellectual is forced from the national homeland (Spivak, "More" 161). She acknowledges the risk encountered by these intellectuals, "the Third World elite who then begin to masquerade as the representatives of the third world" (*Post-Colonial Critic* 163). Echoing Ngũgĩ, Spivak cautions "vigilance" for "new immigrant intellectuals" in Western universities ("Subaltern Talk" 297). She points out that Western intellectuals are too insular and that for female academics in America, for example, political activity often fails to extend beyond the struggle for tenure (*Post-Colonial Critic* 118). While the intellectual in postcolonial countries has a stronger political voice "in the construction of national identity" (*Post-Colonial Critic* 134), this does not sanction the radical retreat from political engagement in Western academia. It also does not sanction the banal assertions that intradisciplinary battles, such as between deconstructivist and New Historicist literary critics, are somehow allegories of a wider, ideological struggle and related to global politics. Spivak does acknowledge, however, the predicament of the radical Western intellectual.[59] She remarks on the "hope" entertained, for example, by "male critics in search of a cause" when they discover "feminist criticism": "for the bourgeois intellectual to look to join other politico-economic struggles is to toe the line between hubris and bathos" (Spivak, "Politics of Interpretations" 182).

In his challenging, highly speculative, allusive work on the postcolonial condition and its hybridization, which he appears to celebrate, Bhabha only indirectly addresses the role of the postcolonial intellectual. However, he is everywhere concerned with voice, translation, enunciation, and the location of utterance. He does address the postcolonial critic in terms of what he calls the "committed intellectual"—referring to Sartre and Fanon—who seeks to unite

---

[59] Spivak remarks: "The radical intellectual in the West is either caught in a deliberate choice of subalternity, granting to the oppressed either that very expressive subjectivity which s/he criticizes or, instead, a total unrepresentability" ("Subaltern Studies" 287).

theory and practice ("The Commitment" 30). He asks who can speak and for whom and from what geographical imaginary their utterance issues. As he writes in "The Commitment to Theory":

> I want to take my stand on the shifting margins of cultural displacement—that confounds any profound or "authentic" sense of a "national" culture or an "organic" intellectual—and ask what the function of a committed theoretical perspective might be, once the cultural and historical hybridity of the postcolonial world is taken as the paradigmatic place of departure. (21)

The postcolonial critic's work is to "take responsibility for the unspoken, unrepresented pasts that haunt the historical present" (12), to "witness" to new global realities, and to intervene against "uneven development" and repetition of imperial national narratives ("The Postcolonial" 171). Speaking from the inevitable indeterminacy of migratory identity, as well as "the transnational as the translational," "the postcolonial intellectual attempts to elaborate a historical and literary project" ("The Postcolonial" 173). In some of his most recent work, Bhabha has moved into the domain of art history, but his concern with the location of and sanctions upon utterance continues. As he writes of Iran in his Foreword to *Iranian Photography Now*,

> It is one of the great tragedies of history that there are times when a whole country disappears behind a heavy curtain. Sometimes this is the result of an authoritarian regime that wants to darken the lives of its own people; at other times, those outside the country choose to see it, for their own purposes, through a veil of ignorance. Iran has suffered both fates. ("Draw the Curtain" 6)

His remarks have relevance for Ngũgĩ's experienced, represented, and remembered Kenya that has recently reemerged from its 1950s colonial image as the Happy Valley to a perception as Britain's Gulag.

Bhabha has been as much criticized as celebrated. His attack on binaries and his infusion of poststructuralist theory with the insights of psychoanalysis, Marxism, and semiotics have greatly expanded the scope of postcolonial critique, but he has been attacked for distancing his analysis from political and economic realities, for gazing at the postcolonial through a Western theoretical lens, for repackaging of old ideas, for obscurantism,[60] and for willful, if creative, misreading, particularly of the

---

[60] Bhabha's writing style is a perennial concern, and in an interview in *Critical Intellectuals on Writing* he notes that he prepares for writing sessions by reading poetry and particularly the poems of Auden and Lowell ("Homi Bhabha" 36). Moore-Gilbert refers to "the often extremely dense (or clotted) texture of his style. At times, indeed, his characteristically teasing, evasive, even quasi-mystical (or mystificatory) mode of expression seems designed to appeal primarily to the reader's intuition" (*Postcolonial Theory* 115). Mustapha Marrouchi is yet more totalizing in his assessment: "Bhabha's verbosity scarcely conceals the underpinnings of his position and his extraordinary capacity for getting nearly everything wrong" (198).

work of Fanon. Bhabha's poststructuralist interpretation of Fanon, and particularly Fanon's writings before *The Wretched of the Earth*, almost renders Fanon an embryonic poststructuralist. As an unnamed audience member complained to Bhabha at the Institute of Contemporary Arts in London in the summer of 1995: "You have managed to move Fanon from politically committed to some sort of trendy postmodern bullshitter" (quoted in Read 41). The precision of his reading of historical incidents from the colonial archive has also been questioned, as in Young's and also Bill Bell's critique of Bhabha's account of the incident, which inspires his influential "Signs Taken for Wonders" (Young, *White* 149; Bell 309–29). However, the very absence of such examinations of historical acts of anticolonial resistance over and above the new historicist anecdotes from his own or others' experience[61] that preface or document the moment of inspiration behind his papers is also not unproblematic (Young, *White* 145). Rasheed Araeen at least suggests that Bhabha's promotion of the privileged hybridity of the postcolonial intellectual makes this figure and by extension Bhabha himself a "native collaborator," and that Bhabha's acknowledgment of the necessary transformation of the colonized as a result of the colonial encounter renders him a virtual if highly nuanced colonial apologist (17). Parry concludes an influential critique of Bhabha's *The Location of Culture* with a consideration of Bhabha's self-fashioned location of articulation. She suggests that his participation in "the euphoria of celebrating the arrival of the postcolonial" and especially the hybridity of the postcolonial condition relies on an exclusive position of privilege experienced by the postcolonial elite: "the cosmopolitan artist, writer, intellectual, professional, financier, and entrepreneur in the metropolis" that is very different from the lived experience of "low-waged workers in Western capitals, and contract laborers in the Gulf states or other centers of capitalist growth within the Third World" (Parry, "Signs" 139). These marginalized groups "do not share in the freewheeling pleasures of commuting between cultures available to the privileged postcolonial" ("Signs" 140). Young in *Colonial Desire* defends Bhabha (as well as Said and Spivak) against this critique by suggesting that though these critics may appear to underplay the realities of colonial violence and anti-colonial resistance, their textual, theoretical "colonial-discourse analysis" does not impede, but rather enhances, the creation of an essential framework for materialist historical critique (163). This general suspicion of Bhabha, in particular, as being somehow hypertheoretical and divorced from material realities, however, introduces a salient criticism leveled more broadly at postcolonial intellectuals who may have been part of the colonial elite before becoming, as a result of political exile, migration, or professional performance, members of a privileged postcolonial elite. The ideological or class position of the postcolonial intellectual becomes suspect or at least presents a soft target when it issues from a handsomely endowed chair at an elite research university in a global metropolis. Moreover, there is much discomfort when this figure appears to

---

[61] See, for example, Bhabha's anecdote about Roland Barthes in a gay bar in Tangiers that begins "Postcolonial Authority and Postmodern Guilt" (56–7).

speak for the subaltern. As Simon Gikandi points out in a discussion of conflicted cosmopolitan identities, "there is an inherent tension between the self-identity of postcolonial elites and the people they claim to represent" ("Between Roots" 29).

For some critics, the apparent aloofness or arrogance of the postcolonial intellectual as exemplified by Bhabha is deeply offensive. Aijaz Ahmad most famously has taken a strident stance against those who appear to have benefited from the articulation of the postcolonial condition. In a critique of Bhabha, Ahmad asserts: "this figure of the post-colonial intellectual has a taken-for-grantedness of a male, bourgeois onlooker, not only the lord of all he surveys but also enraptured by his own lordliness" ("The Politics" 13). For Ahmad, certain postcolonial intellectuals are neocolonial mimic men who, he implies, reflect the arrogance of their colonial forebears with the decidedly patriarchal imperial gaze of those with inherited power. Ahmad concludes that Bhabha's celebration of the disinterested embrace of philosophical and cultural hybridity by the "migrant intellectual" exemplifies irresponsibility and bad faith, and ignores the reality of the majority of migrants who "experience displacement not as cultural plenitude but as torment" ("The Politics" 14, 16). Ahmad objects as stridently, however, to the notion of a "postcolonial intellectual" or a "colonial intellectual" in Said's formulation as he does to the postcolonial or postcolonial theory itself as a discourse or discipline. For Ahmad, the "analytic value, or theoretical status" of categories such as the postcolonial intellectual is questionable and their deployment tends to "homogenize very complex structures of intellectual productions or the trajectories and subjectivities of individual writers and critics or broad intellectual strata" (*In Theory* 205). His discomfort with the idea of the postcolonial intellectual or the postcolonial itself in Bhabha's work builds on his antipathy to what he considers to be Said's Western focus and Said's valorization of the postcolonial intellectual's address to the Western metropolis (*In Theory* 207). Ahmad also fiercely attacks all intellectuals who migrate to the Western academy, despite his own somewhat compromised personal position (Moore-Gilbert, *Postcolonial Theory* 155; Young, "Edward Said" 26). In Ahmad's uncompromising view, even exiled African writers and intellectuals like Ngũgĩ and Achebe who accept academic positions in the Western metropolis are complicit in maintaining the new globalized world order and its system of domination (*In Theory* 207–9).

Bhabha, however, recognizes the complex, paradoxical, hybrid, and textually inscribed position of the postcolonial intellectual, but he also sees this figure engaged in and committed to political action. In the context of a discussion of hostility toward "minority intellectuals" in general and "the black public intellectual" in particular in his October 1995 *ArtForum* essay "Black and White and Read All Over," Bhabha notes that the emergence of "new" intellectuals always raises questions about whether these individuals are sufficiently representative, authentic, autonomous, worthy, and even adequately universal. Bhabha seems to anticipate Ahmad's disquiet. In a somewhat perverse parody of colonial discovery of European books in Bhabha's "Signs Taken for Wonders," Ahmad narrates his discovery of recent texts of postcolonial analysis ("Politics" 1–3). Both accounts, the colonial encounter with the "texts of the civilizing mission" (Bhabha, "Signs" 105) and the postcolonial encounter in London with "what gets called 'postcolonial criticism'" (Ahmad, "Politics" 1), conjure the disembodied encounter with texts and their ideological legacies narrated in Tayeb Salih's *Season of Migration to the North*.

Bhabha is a major reinterpreter of Fanon and particularly Fanon's account of the effect of colonial trauma on identity. In "Remembering Fanon," the foreword to the 1986 edition of *Black Skin, White Masks*, Bhabha reads Fanon as an exemplar of the postcolonial subject's predicament. As Bhabha writes in "Interrogating Identity: Frantz Fanon and the Postcolonial Prerogative," "[t]he time has come to return to Fanon; as always, I believe, with a question: how can the human world live its difference; how can a human being live Other-wise?" (64). Bhabha suggests here the tortured, symbiotic relationship between colonizer and colonized, and the imprinting of both on the new postcolonial identity. In Bhabha's estimate, Fanon recognizes that "the liberatory people who imitate the productive instability of revolutionary cultural change are themselves the bearers of a hybrid identity. They are caught in the discontinuous time of translation and negotiation" (Bhabha, "The Commitment" 38). The outcome of colonial alienation lies in the creation of a turbulent, hybrid postcolonial identity.

Bhabha's work on *Black Skin, White Masks* has led the regard for that work to rival and even supersede the reputation of *The Wretched of the Earth*. At the time when he wrote his foreword to *Black Skin, White Masks*, Bhabha would maintain that Fanon was largely overlooked and his ideas "effectively 'out of print'" (xxii). While he is an admirer of Bhabha's critique of Fanon, Stuart Hall assesses the current vogue for *Black Skin, White Masks* as the result of its more theoretically charged discourse and a consequence of the "*jouissance* of theory," an instance of what he sees as "[t]he struggle to colonise Fanon's work [that] has been an on-going process from the moment of his death" (Hall, "The After-life" 17, 15). *Black Skin, White Masks*, in particular, has been read as exemplifying what Lyle Ashton Harris calls "Fanon's engagement with political autobiography" (182). In Fanon's work, the colonized subject's complex, conflicted relationship with the colonial homeland is part of the cause of ambivalence. As Hall points out, Fanon's postcolonial self-fashioning was always highly conflicted:

> Fanon, like many other bright young colonial intellectuals, went to study in France; became locked in a deep internal argument with the various currents of thought which he found there; and went to North Africa as a salaried member of the French colonial psychiatric service. ... [I]n Martinique, for many intellectuals, to be anti-colonial and opposed to the old white indigenous plantocracy was to be *for* French Republican ideology, with its rallying cry of liberty, equality and fraternity. Fanon may have travelled far from all that, but it is not clear that he ever left it all behind. The career of someone like his compatriot Aimé Césaire is incomprehensible without understanding the complexity of the relations which constituted French colonialism for black intellectuals in the Antilles. (Hall, "The After-life" 31)

In an examination of Fanon's conflicted identity and the rise in his critical fortunes, Henry Louis Gates points out that the newly minted postmodern Fanon tells us as much about his interpreters such as Bhabha as it does about Fanon. Gates demands that Fanon be read within his own historical contexts and not elevated into an iconic "transcultural, transhistorical Global Theorist" (470), a salient caution that also applies to Ngũgĩ. Gates reminds us "to recognize him as a battleground in himself" (470), unwittingly recalling T.E. Lawrence's self-description as "a standing civil war"[62]:

> Fanon, whose mother was of Alsatian descent, grew up in Martinique thinking of himself as white and French: ... his painful reconstitution as a black West Indian occurred only when he arrived at the French capital. ... [H]is attempts to identify himself as an Algerian proved equally doomed. ... [M]ost Algerian revolutionaries scant his role and remain irritated by the attention paid to him in the West as a figure in Algerian decolonization: to them—and how ironic this is to his Western admirers—he remained a European interloper. (468)

In the work of Said, Spivak, and Bhabha, references to Ngũgĩ—where they do arise—primarily point to his role as a voice of conscience, a writer placed in prison by the neocolonial state. The other focus, particularly in Spivak's work, is on Ngũgĩ's interventions regarding the decolonization of the imagination, his articulation of the importance of orature, and his elucidation of the African intellectual's role in directly influencing meaningful political transformation and by extension the writer's engagement in direct political action. Much less is made of Ngũgĩ's position as a political exile, though Spivak does refer to his "double exile" both in the neocolonial state and as a political refugee forced out of that state. Ngũgĩ's having lived the consequences of being an irritant to the neocolonial state gives him the postcolonial "aura" noted by Spivak ("Ngũgĩ" 6). This notion of exile is somewhat fraught, and while Said embraces a somewhat romantic, idealized exilic alienation as central to the intellectual's vocational and geographic role, and Bhabha appears to celebrate hybrid and hybridized locations, Spivak loudly rejects the notion of herself as exiled intellectual and the resulting misperception. "I'm tired of dining out on being an exile," she declares bluntly (*Post-Colonial Critic* 40). Ngũgĩ's Kenyan origins in a landless peasant family are nearly the opposite of the somewhat privileged, if differently marginalized, origins of Said, Spivak, Bhabha, and Fanon. In addition, Ngũgĩ's writing is almost transparently lucid in comparison with that of particularly Spivak and Bhabha, and unlike the members of the postcolonial troika, Ngũgĩ's work has in the main not garnered widely varying interpretations, though some have stridently contested his positions.[63] "Can the Subaltern Speak?" has been interpreted, reinterpreted, and misinterpreted as well as revised as much as a koan-like utterance and

---

[62] See Said's "A Standing Civil War: On T.E. Lawrence" (31–40).

[63] See, for example, respected Kenyan historian W.O. Maloba's position on the treatment of Mau Mau history in Ngũgĩ's works (60–75).

Orientalism, the text which may have generated postcolonial studies, has been so differently interpreted that it appears to be more than a single text or discourse, as even Said recognized (Hussein 12). While the poetic nature of Bhabha's use of language fosters creative misreading, "Can the Subaltern Speak?" and *Orientalism* are almost Rorschach "texts" that somehow reflect their readers' consciousness. Like postcolonial studies itself beginning with Fanon, the work of all three writers is heavily inflected with French poststructuralist theory, an influence that is not marked in Ngũgĩ's work, save for its early deployment of Fanon. In all five writers, however, there is a central concern with the question of representation, as in Bhabha's spatial metaphors elucidating the location of articulation, Said's return to the critical, exilic moment of *Mimesis*, Spivak's ongoing elucidation of her own positionality and that of her representation of the subaltern, Fanon's shift from West Indian French to black Algerian identification, and Ngũgĩ's ongoing concern with moving the center.

Ngũgĩ, in turn, has made relatively few references to the work of members of the troika though he widely acknowledges Fanon, who will be examined more fully in Chapter 3, and his recent statements on the intellectual appear to reinforce his egalitarian, grassroots validation for the intellectual who speaks clearly in works that "breathe distinctly" ("For Peace" 39). He displays his intellectual solidarity with the land-centered, grounded, concrete thinking of the world's aboriginal peoples and the expression of the Christian mythos in John's Gospel:

> Works of imagination and critical theories can only weaken themselves by pulling back from the challenge. Theory must always return to the earth to get recharged with new energy. For the word that breathes life is still needed to challenge the one that carries death and devastation. In rising to this challenge, the intellectual of our times would be working in the tradition of the first intellectual who made the word become flesh. ("For Peace" 39)

Maintaining that "God is the first intellectual" is a startling position for a thinker who discarded Christianity from his belief system nearly 50 years ago ("For Peace" 33). Despite his break with Christianity, however, he has continued to use biblical references in his work to respond to his Kenyan audience's frame of reference and expectations, and to acknowledge the radically adapted biblical reference in texts of revolutionary struggle. As he writes in *Penpoints, Gunpoints, and Dreams*, "where Christianity was meant to be a prison of African souls, it was often used as a key out of the colonial prison" (97). God as the world's first intellectual is also startling until we also consider the dramatic shifts in Ngũgĩ's thinking in over 50 years of vibrant artistic and critical production, and the surprising consistency in some of his views. John's Gospel is one of the "myths of creation," a mythic retelling of origins, one of the great religious-literary narratives of the earth. In this reconceptualization, the intellectual is intensely creative and is allied to and interconnected with other collective "human enterprise[s]." Ngũgĩ articulates a variation on Gramsci's view that all people are intellectuals:

> There is an intellectual dimension to every human enterprise. The transition of the human being from fruit gatherer and hunter to farmer and domesticator of animals must have been a great leap in the conceptual relation of the human to the natural. Intellectualizing as an autonomous area of human activity rose with greater material productivity and class differentiation to allow for the survival of the producer of the nonmaterial. An intellectual is a worker in ideas who uses words as the primary means of production. ("For Peace" 33)

In some of Ngũgĩ's other recent reflections on the intellectual, he returns to the perspective of some of his earliest critical interventions concerning Pan-African consciousness, but he also introduces the trope of memory. Similar to the notion of collective, community responsibility in "planetarity," which Spivak deploys to counter the ravages of enforced economic, cultural, and political globalization,[64] Ngũgĩ advances an oppositional "social integration of the globe" to check "the evolution of capitalist modernity" and create a new kind of "global intellectual community" ("Europhone" 155). In "Europhone or African Memory: The Challenge of the Pan-Africanist Intellectual in the Era of Globalization," a paper delivered at a conference in Dakar in December 2003 on the theme "Intellectuals, Nationalism and the Pan-African Idea," Ngũgĩ supports "a pan-African community of intellectual workers active in and connected to the continent, the accent being placed on the commitment to that connection" (156).

The African intellectual, the knowledge producer, or "worker in ideas" (*Penpoints* 95), he maintains, must resist the legacy of the colonial naming project, marking geography, people, and even culture. Here, Ngũgĩ employs the figure of the interpreter from Plato's allegory of the cave and Ayi Kwei Armah's deployment of that figure in a postcolonial context in *The Beautyful Ones Are Not Yet Born* (1968) (*Penpoints* 72–8). In Armah's version of Plato's allegory, "the intellectual is seen as an interpreter between [the] two realms" of darkness and light, but Armah's African intellectual, as Ngũgĩ points out, does not recognize the inability of his exhortations in the English language to reach the people to whom he speaks (77,78). Unlike Macaulay's "Minute" advocating that native intellectuals form a cadre and "stand as interpreters between them and the people they governed—a buffer between the real owners of the empire and the vast masses of the owned" ("Europhone" 158), Ngũgĩ's African intellectual must join forces with others and use African languages to advance science and technology. The African intellectual, however, perpetually must revisit the colonial legacy and interrogate the stance of native informant into which he or she has been forced which enables the archiving of the fruits of African knowledge, a process in which the intellectual participates with those who "anthropologize Africa" ("Europhone" 160). If all works by diasporic Africans could be made available through translation in all African languages, it would "create a common intellectual inheritance and become the common cultural basis for more intellectual productions with roots

---

[64] See Spivak's *Death of a Discipline* (96–7) and *An Aesthetic Education in the Era of Globalization: An Aesthetics of Education* (336–40).

in a common African memory" ("Europhone" 163). The role Ngũgĩ envisions for African intellectuals is formulated as a challenge: "African intellectuals must do for their languages and cultures what all other intellectuals in history have done for theirs" ("Europhone" 164).

Ngũgĩ refers to this responsibility as part of the intellectuals' "calling," and in the service of promoting access to a common cultural heritage—almost a quasi-mystical African collective consciousness—he elevates vocation and vocational solidarity, in a transhistorical, transcultural gesture, over and above political and historical divisions. The notion of African intellectuals as "keepers of memory" is one he reiterates here as he has done in *Penpoints* (95) and *Something Torn and New: An African Renaissance* (114, 121). He uses it to bolster a notion of collective Pan-African identity and to connect the contemporary intellectual with "the griot tradition, keepers of the word, keepers of memory of the family and the community, with orality as their means of communication" (*Penpoints* 95). In this elevation of a type of notional Pan-Africanism, he reiterates the artificiality of "colonial boundaries": "These borders were historically constituted, markers of European memory on Africa, to meet colonial needs, and there is no reason why they cannot be historically reconstituted to meet African needs and reconnect with African memory" ("Europhone" 162). Ngũgĩ suggests the model of shared border communities with common ethnic, linguistic, religious, and cultural practices as a model for a new postnational Africa, a subject explored in Chapter 6. He suggests, too, that African postcolonial intellectuals, through their use of African languages, may play a major role in making this happen.[65] In his challenge to African postcolonial intellectuals and in his recent theoretical works' tracing of the stages of the development of the traditions and misadventures of African intellectuals, Ngũgĩ is suggesting something much more fundamental: the decolonization of the African intellectual.

The Postcolonial Intellectual: Ngũgĩ wa Thiong'o in Context aims to show the significance of the consideration of the role of the intellectual within postcolonial studies, examining Ngũgĩ as the virtual type of the postcolonial intellectual, subaltern artist and theorist, and also as a postcolonial critic who has given ample attention in his own work to the location and role of the postcolonial intellectual.

---

[65] Ngũgĩ's promotion of Gĩkũyũ has been criticized as an outgrowth of Gĩkũyũ nationalism (Sicherman, *Ngũgĩ wa Thiong'o: The Making* 34), but he clearly encourages other African language publication and translation, recommending Swahili as a better candidate than English, or Gĩkũyũ, for a global language, because of English's ideological baggage, though overlooking Swahili's role in facilitating the slave trade. Ngũgĩ's conception of language has been more tellingly criticized as culturally essentialist, a fetishizing of language as an ahistorical repository of an innate, romantic cultural harmony (Arnove 284; Gikandi, "Ngũgĩ's Conversion" 133–43). In addition, as Harvey argues, elevating and isolating aspects of culture from political economy ignores "the forces constructing historical-geographical legacies, cultural forms, and distinctive ways of life" (*Spaces* 74). Ngũgĩ, nevertheless, historicizes his analysis, and his fetishization aims to establish a basis for national identity and material change.

Focusing on Ngũgĩ's largely overlooked early journalism and also his most recent critical and autobiographical writing, this book locates Ngũgĩ within the context of a consideration of the dilemma of the intellectual and some of his major theoretical influences. It argues for Ngũgĩ's position as a postcolonial theorist and not merely a novelist and dramatist who happens to do theory. It also argues for the vibrant development of his ideas over five decades as well as the surprising consistency of some of his core concerns. This first chapter ("The Postcolonial Intellectual") has attempted to introduce the perennial dilemma of the intellectual and the particularly fraught location of the postcolonial intellectual amid competing definitions and questions about utterance/voice. Examining primarily but not exclusively the three most prominent postcolonial intellectuals' views about the representation of the intellectual within some of their intellectual contexts, this chapter frames a closer study of Ngũgĩ as postcolonial intellectual.

"Chapter 2: The Decolonization of James Ngũgĩ: Early Journalism" considers Ngũgĩ's early, largely overlooked Nairobi journalism from the early 1960s. It analyses these articles and their site of articulation, that of the "abstract African," a type of native informant poised uneasily between a Kenyan colonial settler audience and a colonized audience on the eve of national independence. In the context of a consideration of Ngũgĩ's encounter with the colonial schoolhouse and the colonial university, this chapter looks at Ngũgĩ's first public articulations as a member of an emerging colonial elite, his vocation as one with a "right to write," his earliest desire to be a journalist, and perhaps his first encounter with censorship of his writing. These articles address the lingering psychological inferiority fostered by colonialism and the cultural degradation produced by anti–Mau Mau campaigns. They also show Ngũgĩ's own early quasi-colonial views of "tribalism" as a major national problem and of the Mau Mau period as one characterized by the profound bitterness, confusion, and disillusionment of a de facto civil war. They also display his confidence in education and literature, particularly drama, and the possibility of Afro-European hybrid genres, amid a widespread resistance to reading even among the emerging elite, as well as perhaps his earliest advocacy of the paramount importance of indigenous languages. While cautioning against exorbitant expectations after independence, some of the articles give enthusiastic support for Pan-Africanism. Ngũgĩ returns to the role of intellectuals and their significance and potential danger in the postcolony; though he voices a persistent impatience with what he calls "slogans," from "African socialism" to the "African personality," he also expresses some of his earliest, somewhat intemperate views on Négritude.

"Chapter 3: Diasporic Pan-Africanism: The Caribbean Connection" explores the influence on Ngũgĩ's ideas emanating from the crucible of intellectual ferment in Paris and especially London in the decades leading up to Kenyan independence. It gives particular attention to C.L.R. James, whose work is still not as widely recognized as it deserves to be and whose influence on Ngũgĩ has not been previously explored at length, focusing on James's ambivalent connection with European intellectual traditions and his writing of diasporic African history as a history of resistance, as well as his trickster-like genre-shifting and his works' innovative engagement with popular culture. The chapter also considers Fanon, whose work Ngũgĩ encountered at Leeds where he was a student of Marxist literary critic Arnold Kettle, a perceptive critic and also an influence. It focuses on the autobiographical inflections of Fanon's and James's works, their shared suspicion of intellectuals, and also their somewhat ambiguous status as Marxist intellectuals of the global left, all prominent features of Ngũgĩ's work.

"Chapter 4: Ngũgĩ's 'Aesthetics of Decolonization': Return to the Source" stresses the independence of Ngũgĩ's eight volumes of critical and theoretical essays from his novels, stories, and plays, as well as considering perhaps the major, underexplored influence on Ngũgĩ as a revolutionary intellectual in the work of Amílcar Cabral. It tackles Cabral's "Marxism," like that of James and Fanon, as an unorthodox innovation. In the context of a consideration of colonialism and late fascism in Portugal, it argues for Cabral's and later Ngũgĩ's view of culture as not merely an archive for a type of postcolonial necrophilia but as a preparation for and a constituent part of national liberation. As with Chapter 3's analysis of James and Fanon, it examines Cabral's suspicion of the intellectual's role in the revolutionary struggle, despite a near-total absence of a classically defined petty bourgeois class, but also the significant danger posed by intellectuals in the postcolony which Cabral held to be one of the main reasons for the failure of African independence. Cabral's much-discussed "return to the source" (*Return* 59) was predicated on an elevation of the peasantry, which is of such importance in Ngũgĩ's later work, but it was also predicated on the need for intellectuals' class suicide. Focusing on Ngũgĩ's *Penpoints, Gunpoints, and Dreams* and *Something Torn and New*, the chapter then examines Ngũgĩ's work on some of these concepts in his somewhat fetishistic view of language as cultural archive and his desire for the decolonization of education, as declared in his famous cowritten interdepartmental memo that launched a revolution and helped inaugurate the postcolonial project.

"Chapter 5: Postcolonial Intellectual Self-Fashioning" is divided into two parts. Part 1 examines the autobiographical imperative in much of Ngũgĩ's critical and theoretical writing or its autocritographic moments, in the context of an account of the emerging fields of auto/biography and postcolonial auto/biography studies. The chapter explores the autobiographical elements and especially the focus on the figure of the troubled intellectual in Ngũgĩ's early bildungs-narratives, his interviews, and his two recent memoirs, *Dreams in a Time of War* and *In the House of the Interpreter*. These works primarily show a relational self, whereas his prison diary *Detained*, examined in Part 2 in comparison with Wole Soyinka's *The Man Died* and Breyten Breytenbach's *The True Confessions of an Albino Terrorist*, shows a type of writing self resembling that found in "national autobiographies." Part 2 argues for the prison diary as a distinctly African genre. The role of intellectuals is a common concern in all of these genres of life writing, though in *Detained* Ngũgĩ most clearly comes to locate his voice within a history of national struggle.

"Chapter 6: The Global Intellectual: Conclusion" has three parts: "Multiple Ngũgĩs"; "Hybrid Nationalisms, the Postnation, and Globalization"; and "Globalectics." It considers the different public images of Ngũgĩ and his emergence as a global intellectual, a figure with elements of Gramsci's "new" intellectual, a collective intellectual, and a contemporary version of the griot in the cyberspace oral intellectual. Ngũgĩ is also an intellectual in political exile, in different ways like Lamming and Adorno, though he has perhaps come to regard language as his exilic home. In his most recent work, Ngũgĩ moves from a concern with Africa's holocaust—the latter increasingly concentrated in what is becoming known as Britain's gulag—to a focus on the hope of Africa's Renaissance, offering a select number of practical recommendations: the creation of an archive of diasporic Pan-African texts available in all African languages; the creation of a day of global mourning to re-member or reconstruct the anatomy of African memory, hijacked by colonialism, as well as to honor the victims of imperialism and the slave trade; a reconsideration of Pan-African alliances and associations of members of the global south in the wake of globalization to move in the direction of the African postnation (the focus of Part 2); and the decolonization of the postcolonial intellectual. The chapter finally considers Ngũgĩ's "globalectic" vision of a planetary conscience and aesthetic in the fields of culture and politics, taking back the world from cultural, economic, and political globalization.

Chapter 2
The Decolonization of James Ngũgĩ: Early Journalism

The decolonization of the postcolonial intellectual in an African context that Ngũgĩ's recent theoretical work addresses began in his own case nearly 50 years ago.[1] As a pupil at an elite colonial school, while his brother—like him from a landless, peasant background—was in the forest fighting against the colonial forces, Ngũgĩ was being trained to be the type of native intellectual famously advocated for colonial India by Macaulay in 1835:

> We must at present do our best to form a class who may be interpreters between us and the millions whom we govern, —a class of persons Indian in blood and colour, but English in tastes, in opinions, in morals and in intellect. To that class we may leave it to refine the vernacular dialects of the country, to enrich those dialects with terms of science borrowed from the Western nomenclature, and to render them by degrees fit vehicles for conveying knowledge to the great mass of the population.

Nearly 100 years later, at a London conference in 1931 on education in the British Commonwealth, renewed attention was directed to the relationship of colonizer and colonized in a changing imperial climate. As Gramsci noted, an account of this conference's discussion of language raised the problem of how "to decide if it was opportune to teach even the semi-savage population of Africa to read English instead of their native language, if it was better to maintain a bilingual approach or to aim at making the indigenous language disappear through the educational process" (Gramsci, *Selections* 286). Gramsci's attention to this discussion was part of his "interest in minority languages as forms of popular culture, of subaltern knowledge and resistance" (Young, "Il Gramsci meridionale" 18). Ngũgĩ was born and raised in a colonial atmosphere of diverse racial, linguistic, and educational hostility, with the option of linguicide always on the table for discussion.

Due to his facility with English, Ngũgĩ was elevated to a place at Alliance High School at Kikuyu near Nairobi and then later to Makerere University College in Uganda.[2] More ominously, Ngũgĩ's impressive scholastic achievements and

---

[1] Ngũgĩ changed his name legally from "James Ngugi" to "Ngũgĩ wa Thiong'o" in 1977. See Kamau Brathwaite's poem on the profound significance of receiving a new African name from Ngũgĩ's grandmother and reconnecting with a severed past ("*Limuru* and *Kinta Kunte*" 1–11).

[2] Makerere Professor of English Alan Warner noted in 1954 that "English is the chief hurdle in the path that leads to Makerere" (1).

their indication that he was a member of the new African elite secured his release from a false charge, exaggerated by jealousy, in the spring of 1959.[3] Moreover, Ngũgĩ's English education, the main subject of his most recent autobiographical memoir, *In the House of the Interpreter*, took place at Alliance, a school founded in 1926 by an alliance of Protestant churches that came to be based on the vision of Edward Carey Francis, the school's second principal from 1940 to 1962, an almost ruthless disciplinarian and simultaneously a beloved patriarch, who stressed high academic standards, with an emphasis on literary arts, sports, "post-racial" cooperation, and farming. Francis, in Ngũgĩ's estimation, was a rigorous supporter of the colonial regime, but also someone who "would turn out to be the most consistently subversive of the colonial order" (*In the House* 13). On the subject of Mau Mau, however, it appears that Francis's position was characterized by ambivalence, though he was certainly a "liberal" in the parlance of colonial authorities and settlers.[4] Regarding Africans' grievances in Kenya as "imaginary" and Mau Mau itself as "wholly wicked" (quoted in Greaves 108, 115), he felt that its defeat could be won "only by destroying the foundation on which the whole movement rests, by showing that we are not enemy invaders" and also by reining in the abuses of power by the security forces (110). His biographer maintains that he came to recognize Mau Mau as a "resistance movement" (109), but he was also somewhat dismissive of the significance of oathing, portrayed in colonial and settler propaganda as evidence of a return to barbarism, and of the integrity of many Mau Mau fighters. His account of peaceful school life amid the privations and terror of the Emergency resembles Ngũgĩ's memories of Alliance as an uneasy utopia at this time. Francis wrote in a letter, quoted by his biographer, combining a certain comic bravado and daring-do with an acknowledgment of disquiet abroad:

> Do not imagine that here at school we are living a life of fear, or setting our meals, as some do, with revolvers among the spoons. At present the school is an oasis in a grim desert, hardly affected by what is going on outside. ... Apart from this [intimidation of students] it would be difficult here to believe that there is any emergency at all; it seems almost indecent to be so happy and comfortable. ... We are as happy a family as ever, boys, masters, black, white, Kikuyu, non-Kikuyu. I sense no hostility whatever. (quoted in Greaves 111)

---

[3] This is a lengthy episode ending *In the House of the Interpreter* (189–240). He is released by the judge, who declines to "stand between you and Makerere" (239).

[4] In an interview in 1967, Ngũgĩ said,
> The Headmaster was said to be pro-African but he believed, and often told us so, that there was not a single African in the whole of Kenya, who on the basis of merit could qualify to Cambridge. As an African you could be taken in Cambridge, but not on the basis of merit, more as a gesture. Of course we protested, but inwardly we believed it, and unconsciously had a high regard for white boys. (Marcuson et al. 25–6)

Later, however, he was instrumental in investigating cases of abuse by colonial forces, though he declined to contact the British papers with his findings, anticipating reactions such as "You do not fight guerrilla warfare by the methods of the Y.M.C.A." (Greaves 119–22), perhaps inadvertently conjuring the famous remark of Mao Tse-tung on revolutions not resembling dinner parties. The main thrust of his objection appeared to be the undermining of the moral authority of the colonial forces if abuses were not punished (so that they resembled what he calls the "Mau Mau gangsters" [126]), rather than any recognition of the justice of the anticolonial resistance. However, Mau Mau fighters, including Ngũgĩ's brother, recognized the value of education in potentially overthrowing colonial dominance, and Ngũgĩ's initial travel to Alliance in fact was facilitated by nationalist forces (Sicherman, "Ngugi's Colonial" 19–20).

Makerere in the period when Ngũgĩ was a university student (1959–1964) was witnessing massive changes in the context of the tumultuous upheavals in Uganda itself, which would become independent on October 9, 1962, nine years before the coup of Idi Amin.[5] In the same period, Kenya would become independent: "I had entered Makerere as a colonial subject," Ngũgĩ recalls in *Globalectics*, "and emerged as a citizen of an independent country" (10). In the 1950s, Makerere had begun to operate as the University College of East Africa under an arrangement with the University of London that gave the English institution control of the curriculum as well as examinations.[6] In 1961, Makerere, with similar institutions in Nairobi and Dar es Salaam, sought to break from London and establish an independent identity as the University of East Africa, a move greeted with much hope by Ngũgĩ in his early journalistic articles, but the new institution was not a success. At Makerere, Ngũgĩ, who had graduated from an African school and hence lacked A-levels (a necessary qualification for university entrance), spent his first two years preparing three subjects at A-level to sit the London Preliminary Exam. As an Honours student, he then studied a single subject for three years; Ngũgĩ's subject was the novels of Joseph Conrad. Many changes were underway during these years. In 1961, 152 Americans arrived at Makerere to prepare to become educators in the Teachers for East Africa scheme, a precursor to the Peace Corps, but with different aims, and they aided the Makerere faculty to develop a lively theater program, in which Ngũgĩ's *The Black Hermit* was a notable achievement. He also actively participated as writer and editor in a number of other Makerere- and Kampala-based publications including *The Makererean*, *Penpoint*, and *Transition*. As the writer of two published short stories, he was eligible to participate in what would become the famous Conference of African Writers of English Expression at Makerere in June 1962, where he met and consulted with Achebe about his first

---

[5] For a full account of the history of Makerere, see Margaret Macpherson's *They Built for the Future: A Chronicle of Makerere University College 1922–1962* and Carol Sicherman's *Becoming an African University: Makerere 1922–2000*.

[6] I am indebted to Carol Sicherman's "Ngugi's Colonial Education" and *Becoming an African University* in the following account of Ngũgĩ's Makerere years.

novel, *Weep Not, Child*. As Obiajunwa Wali would write the following year in a critique of the conference that would become central to Ngũgĩ's work, "any true African literature must be written in African languages" (Wali 14).[7]

Despite the hothouse of almost exclusively English-language literary creativity that Makerere fostered, the institution also alienated its African students from their rural communities, and its unspoken aim was to Europeanize them and mould them into a "mandarinate" (Apthorpe quoted in Sicherman, "Ngugi's Colonial" 30). It inevitably had a psychologically debilitating effect. Kenyan students, in particular, may well have encountered suspicion in the aftermath of the Mau Mau struggle, because as one student remembered, he could not be sure if a staff member "regards you as a smartened up murderer, a sympathiser of the movement or what" (quoted in Sicherman, "Ngugi's Colonial" 31). Amid the widespread support for the development of African creative writing to match the cultural vibrancy of West Africa, so evident at the African Writers Conference, there was much anxiety if not outright antipathy toward the utilization of traditional African oral genres with which Ngũgĩ had been raised and that he had encountered at his first Gĩkũyũ Independent School before he entered Alliance. Carol Sicherman recounts a telling incident during the adjudication of the first short story contest in 1947 at Makerere when the judge, Elspeth Huxley, recommended that those writers who had submitted stories should study the work of "masters" like Somerset Maugham; she rejected a story that she considered to be the best in some ways because it drew on "the folk-lore and tradition of his [the writer's] people" and hence was merely "reportage" (Huxley quoted in Sicherman, "Ngugi's Colonial" 33).

Both Alliance and Makerere attempted with their student groups and extracurricular activities to homogenize ethnic and national differences and foster a Pan-Kenyan or even Pan–East African federation; Ngũgĩ noted in an article in the *Daily Nation* of August 19, 1964, that "most of the present African leaders served their political apprenticeship in their respective student organizations" (6). Both Alliance and Makerere also stressed the principles of F.R. Leavis,[8] whose pupils had carried his cultural program to the outposts of the colonial world. Leavis's "great tradition" of canonical English authors, including George Eliot,

---

[7] Not wanting "to discredit these writers" at the conference "who have achieved much in their individual rights within an extremely difficult and illogical situation," Wali nevertheless points out the sad contradiction that such a conference, intent on "defining African literature," excluded writers working in African languages; writing in European languages for Africans, he added, "can only lead to sterility, uncreativity, and frustration" (Wali 14).

[8] Ngũgĩ writes that his teachers at Leeds, including Kettle, "changed my approaches to reading texts" (*Globalectics* 20). In *Decolonising the Mind*, he recalls that Kettle and Raymond Williams "were studied, if at all, only remotely and fleetingly even in the time from 1959 to 1964" when he was at Makerere (90). In 1966, Ngũgĩ notes that at Makerere Karl Marx was read "only as an incidental rather eccentric figure" (Ngũgĩ quoted in Sicherman, "Ngugi's Colonial" 41 n28).

Charles Dickens, and Conrad, who would prove so important to Ngũgĩ,[9] was designed in part to act as a bulwark of Englishness against societal devolution and "cultural anarchy," in Matthew Arnold's phrase from the 1860s. Many colonial schools were also modeled on the public school Rugby, developed by Arnold's father, Thomas Arnold, an institution that he too regarded as a bulwark against political and social chaos, as C.L.R. James puts it in *Beyond a Boundary* (1963), his remarkable analysis of the mythology of cricket as an ideological expression of West Indian history and ideas that anticipates Roland Barthes's *Mythologies* as well as the best of cultural studies. For James, Thomas Arnold, like Macaulay, "aimed to create a body of educated men of the upper classes who would resist the crimes of Toryism and the greed and vulgarity of industrialists on the one hand, and the socialistic claims of the oppressed but uneducated masses on the other" (*Beyond a Boundary* 160); the same plan would obtain in the colonies because, "[n]o imperialist expatriates can rule an alien population alone" (220). In Arnold's school and eventually for all Victorians in James's assessment, games and particularly cricket became a vehicle for "character training and the inculcation of moral excellence" and "the basis of what can only be called a national culture" (163). At the center of Thomas Hughes's *Tom Brown's Schooldays* (1857), by an author James considers one of the three greatest Victorians, the Arnoldian public school is a totalitarian paradise in which a terrible veneration for the headmaster and a devotion to school rules and team spirit could almost supplant divine law. At the end of his life in 1840, Arnold was entertaining notions of traveling to New Zealand to establish a utopian society (161). In the elite Alliance school in Kenya, Ngũgĩ's once-devout Christian faith was tested. He later declared his renunciation of faith in "Church, Culture and Politics" read at the General Assembly of the Presbyterian Church of East Africa in March 1970 (Ngũgĩ, *Homecoming* 31–6),[10] but his early Makerere literary works often feature a messianic figure. *The River Between*, his first-written novel, was initially titled "The Black Messiah," for example. This striving toward national salvation through a messianic figure is also

---

[9] Ngũgĩ's *A Grain of Wheat* was composed at Leeds University, where he was working on a study of Conrad's *Under Western Eyes*.

[10] He is equally strident in "I Say Kenya's Missionaries Failed Badly" from the *Sunday Nation* of January 6, 1963:

> Christianity, whose basic doctrine is the equality of man, was an integral part of that colonialism which in Kenya was built on the inequality of man and the consequent subjection of one race to another. (5)

Moreover, Christianity aided in the destruction of traditional spirituality and the creation of "a people without spiritual roots which could anchor them to the soil":

> in face of [the] colour bar and race discrimination, the Church preached about heaven and the life to come. This, plus the reactionary political views of some missionaries who saw African nationalism as something akin to Communism and which was incompatible with the Christian faith, has left a bad legacy with some African Christians and Church leaders, who still see the religious life as that of a hermit divorced from the day-to-day problems affecting the whole country. (5)

directly associated with the line of prophets and seers in Gĩkũyũ tradition, though simultaneously the panacea for change is Western-style education. Ngũgĩ's more substantive moves away from the Christian and Leavisite faith of his early years came about during his study at Leeds and his encounter with the African diasporic literature of the Caribbean, the focus of the next chapter. A study of this material was one of his first major critical interventions—published as *Homecoming* in 1972—and anticipated his discovery of Fanon, Marx, and materialist history.

The importance of Alliance and particularly Makerere cannot be overestimated in Ngũgĩ's intellectual development, and for most of his career he has taught in universities. The importance of the idea of the African university, moreover, is central in considering the African postcolonial intellectual. Postcolonial intellectuals, even more than other intellectuals, indicates Kwame Anthony Appiah, are "almost entirely dependent for their support on two [powerful] institutions": the university and the Western publishing house (*In My Father's House* 149). These institutions mould and define this figure who in turn mediates images of the West in Africa, and also invents the image of Africa in the West.[11] Intellectuals, like Ngũgĩ, however, in Appiah's account, represent a notable resistance to this institutionalized definition in the arena of publishing and education. The colonial project of "[m]aking the African more like the European," in Lewis Nkosi's assessment, used the university as a tool, and as in Macaulay's India, authorities in Africa saw the "role of the African intellectual as an 'interpreter' and a collaborator, working essentially as a 'go-between' the coloniser and the colonised" (40). A historical narrative of the modern university in Africa as exclusively and homogeneously a foreign imposition, however, is incorrect in Nkosi's view. The African university instead is understood better as "the final terrain of struggle" (38), a space which functions for better or worse to allow a Kiplingesque meeting of East and West as well as potentially an engine for establishing and maintaining, or conversely for dismantling, neo-colonial structures (41–2). Apollo Obonyo Amoko's distinction of "universities in Africa in their capacity as 'African universities'" made within a preliminary discussion of the curricular revolution in Nairobi is useful in this context (11). He considers that African universities as well as the cultural expressions they produced in novels, for example, were conceived of in the postcolony as instruments with which to establish a distinctive national and continental identity (15–17). For Amoko, the now-canonical writers like Ngũgĩ, who were the product

---

[11] Appiah writes that
[p]ostcoloniality is the condition of what we might ungenerously call a comprador intelligentsia: of a relatively small, Western-style, Western-trained, group of writers and thinkers who mediate the trade in cultural commodities of world capitalism at the periphery. In the West they are known through the Africa they offer; their compatriots know them both through the West they present to Africa and through an Africa they have invented for the world, for each other, and for Africa. (*In My Father's House* 149)

of such institutions, as well as their works,[12] themselves aiding in the viability of such institutions, are perhaps fatally compromised by the institutional locus of their origin and development. This point about Anglo-African literature, of course, is one Ngũgĩ himself has been making for many years, repeating in the 1980s, for example, that "African literature" in European languages "has no right usurping the term 'African literature'" (Owusu 234), being at best a "hybrid" (Jaggi 272). Amoko goes on to maintain that some African universities' attempt to Africanize engaged them in a dance with invented traditions. Nkosi's assessment of African universities as locked in struggle on many fronts, with Amoko's caution, is valuable for understanding the context of Ngũgĩ's early encounters with this institution.

In his years at Makerere and before his departure for Leeds, Ngũgĩ was also engaged in writing newspaper articles for a number of Nairobi newspapers: the *Sunday Post, Sunday Nation*, and *Daily Nation* between May 1961 and August 1964.[13] It's unclear whether he considered extending these reflections into home thoughts from abroad when he reached Leeds. In retrospect, the bourgeois, settler-friendly context of these papers is indicated by the plethora of print ads surrounding Ngũgĩ's one- to two-page articles. There are ads for transformative Metamorphosa beauty soap, brandy, bras, electric shavers and razor blades, Morgan's Pomade, malaria prophylactics, cameras, American rubber truck tires, police automobile alarms, astrologers, Alka-Seltzer, Shell oil, the appearance of burlesque performers like Miss Fluffles at the Sombrero Night Club "in her romantic double role of tassel tossing and stripping" (*Sunday Nation* 12 May 1963, 9), and promotions for air and sea travel to South Africa and England. The assumption of a certain persona in Ngũgĩ's pieces and by extension their address to a certain audience may have been influenced by Alan Warner's *A Short Guide to English Style*, which is partly an anthology and also a promotion of good, plain style or "clean and clear English" (Warner v), a quality he maintains is sought after in writing in all genres from fiction to autobiography and journalism; it is also partly a text of instruction for students, including those "for whom English is not the mother tongue" (Warner vi).[14] Ngũgĩ recalls his first encounter with the rule of clean English in his memoir

---

[12] Amoko's remarks on the role of the study and production of literature in establishing a national cultural identity are significant in this context: "Despite, or in a paradoxical sense because of, the continent's obvious lack of technology and its material impoverishment, the study of literature—as well as the subsequent production of high canonical literature—cultural nationalists thought critical because of its perceived instrumentality in the establishment of appropriately nationalist postcolonial cultures" (16).

[13] A complete bibliography of these 80 articles is available in Bernth Lindfors's "Ngugi wa Thiong'o's Early Journalism" (38–41). I am most grateful to Professor Lindfors for providing me with access to this material.

[14] Warner writes: "Already there is much good English writing that has not been written by Englishmen or Americans, and I have no doubt that the English literature of the future will include books written by Asians and Africans" (*A Short Guide* vi).

of Alliance.[15] In a contemporary review of Warner's book, Roland Hindmarsh raises the spectre of the "social model" or authorial voice that a writer assumes. Hindmarsh celebrates Warner's advice on "how not to write," but he notes the difficulty of a contemporary writer in finding a persona: "There is perhaps no appropriate social model for the writer of clean English, since he is not acting a part but speaking his mind straight out. It may, however, be argued that clean English is a style which lends itself particularly to the rebel, the debunker, the enemy of hypocrisy, loftiness, atmosphere and enthusiasm" (33, 32).

Ngũgĩ's task in these articles was to represent an indigenous, African perspective on national affairs on the eve of independence. A notice in January 6, 1963's *Sunday Nation* has the byline "James Ngugi expresses another controversial and critical African viewpoint—this time on the part the missionaries have played in Kenya's development, and the future role of an African Church" (5). He thus was promoted as the embodiment of a representative, African point of view, that of a native informant or insider, that he would object to so sharply later. He was to be at least one version of the "abstract African" he later deplored (*Something Torn* 118). As a student at Makerere—which he frequently refers to in these articles as a type of educational utopia, cultural oasis,[16] and intellectual engine in East Africa, providing a space for a much-needed detached, objective, critical analysis—he was being fashioned as a member of the rising postindependence intellectual elite. However, in these articles, he was articulating his own version of the "license to write" that he refers to in his memoirs (*In the House* 24), and he was considering the best means of communication with his own intended African reader. This developing confidence is to an extent reflected in the tone of Ngũgĩ's articles, which becomes more strident in those published just before and just after independence. Ngũgĩ, moreover, must have recognized the vital role of journalism in fomenting the spread of information and coalescing a nationalist consciousness, as had happened in the decade leading up to independence in Ghana in C.L.R. James's recollection (*Nkrumah* 89). "To an intellectual in a highly developed country," James writes, "an article in a newspaper is just another article," whereas "among a colonial and largely illiterate population," an article can be of profound significance (122). James recalls Jomo Kenyatta's telling him how an article in the 1920s by someone like Marcus Garvey would be translated and then memorized by messengers in the bush who would run off to repeat it in distant centers; the idea that "Africa should belong to the Africans" could thus nourish "the illiterate Kenya native" (123, 124). In the Ghanian context, for James, the spread of inspirational

---

[15] Ngũgĩ recalls the advocacy of simple, direct style using Anglo-Saxon words, and a sentence worthy of Gradgrind's school in Charles Dickens's *Hard Times* held up as a negative example: "As I was perambulating on the road, I countenanced a red-garmented boots-appareled gentleman mounted on a humongous four-legged creature of bovine species" (*In the House* 22–3).

[16] See "The Oasis That Is Makerere," *Sunday Nation* 24 March 1963, 30. He notes, however, that "Makerere is still an island, isolated from the tides and waves around" (30).

ideas though journalism, and via the transfer of written, English text to indigenous oral messaging, was the dissemination of what he calls, in an Arnoldean phrase highly incongruous in this context, "the best that was being thought and said in the world" (124). In retrospect, however, Ngũgĩ would acknowledge the inadequacy of the journalistic medium to "order [the] chaos" of earlier colonial trauma and in particular the realities of a policy of terror in Kenya:

> The blood in the streets; the dead guerrillas hung on trees as a public spectacle; the horror stories of white officers collecting ears, noses, eyes, genitalia, or even heads of the vanquished as trophies! The tortures in the internment camps and concentration villages were symbolized by the horror at Hola where in 1959 eleven political internees were tortured to death in a couple of days. Fortunately, news of it somehow came out and reached the world. There were many horrors whose knowledge never went beyond the location of their commission. There was also the violence of the guerrilla army not always directed at the guilty party. Horror multiplied was still horror. (*Globalectics* 17)

Ngũgĩ was also moving toward one of the principles for which his later work would be most celebrated. Writing on the eve of and just after the declaration of independence on December 12, 1963, Ngũgĩ remarks on the need to repudiate the psychological inferiority inculcated by colonialism, as much as the need for political freedom and perhaps more importantly economic prosperity. In one of the articles he produced for the *Sunday Nation*, on March 17, 1963, he wrote that "[t]he worst colonialism was a colonialism of the mind, a colonialism that undermined one's dignity and confidence" ("Respect Will Come When We Are Self-Sufficient" 29). In October of the same year, in a discussion of many people's unrealistic aspirations for prosperity following independence in "The Three Levels of Independence" in the same newspaper, he refers to the "third level of independence" that should follow "political and economic security" though all of these developments may emerge "simultaneously." This third level is "psychological freedom," a condition that will enable "[o]ur personality [to] emerge" after decades of an enforced colonial "sense of inferiority," an early version of the decolonized mind (39). He also warns against the "live danger" of some type of reverse racism, condemning other races in Kenya "to live in the same state of insecurity and fear which was our lot in the colonial times" (39). He appeals for a type of post-racial as well as post-tribal and ultimately postnational Kenyan postcolonialism.

Ngũgĩ had wanted to be a journalist from the time when he was a student at Alliance, as he recounts in the second volume of his memoirs, *In the House of the Interpreter*, but he was unsuccessful in his application to the *East African Standard*, "the only major English daily in Kenya" (195). He was also pragmatic, however, acknowledging in 1964 that his early work in journalism was motivated at least partly by a need "to bring in some ready cash" (de Villiers 9), just as the writing of his first novel, *The River Between*, for a competition was, at least initially, "financially motivated" (Sander and Munro 47). However, he had already published a story in *Alliance High Magazine* in September 1957, inspired by Tolstoy's *Childhood, Youth, and Boyhood*, and a childhood belief about conjuring distant loved ones by whispering their names in an empty clay pot and the failure of this belief. The joy of first publication was exploded by a recognition of editorial license. The editors had changed Ngũgĩ's title from "My Childhood" to "I Try Witchcraft,"[17] inserting a declaration about Christianity's civilizing triumph over superstition and

> a condemnation of the pre-Christian life and beliefs of a whole community and, simultaneously, an ingratiating acknowledgment of the beneficial effects of enlightenment. I was turned into a prosecution witness for the imperial literary tradition from which I had been trying to escape. Although well intentioned, this editorial intrusion smothered the creative fire within me. (*In the House* 166–7)

It is unclear whether Ngũgĩ encountered extensive editorial intrusions when he wrote for Nairobi newspapers during the period when he was a student at Makerere, but at least once he objected to a title given to an article he wrote against naïve cultural atavism among educated Kenyans. The article makes a brief reference to Kenyatta's anthropological study *Facing Mount Kenya*, but the piece was given the title "African Culture: The Mistake that Kenyatta Made" and subtitled "There Is No Going Back to the Past." Given that this was published in the month that Kenyatta was granted political freedom following years of detention, the editors clearly wanted to position Ngũgĩ as a representative African voice standing in opposition to Kenyatta. The next week, the paper printed Ngũgĩ's letter of correction. As Bernth Lindfors writes of Ngũgĩ's response:

> He explained that he had not intended to suggest that "Kenyatta had at one time advocated a return to the past"; rather, he had stated that *Facing Mount Kenya* ... shared a widespread human tendency to "idealize the past." The book was a nostalgic view of Kikuyu culture, not an atavistic call for a regression to tribal traditions. Ngugi tried to make it clear that he admired Kenyatta "as an African writer who will for a long time remain in the forefront of those intellectuals who have tried to interpret their way of life to the world." He was applauding Kenyatta the anthropologist, not condemning Kenyatta the politician. (27)

Ngũgĩ does call for independent, high-quality, African-run and -financed English-language newspapers a year and a half later in an article of December 1962 in the *Sunday Nation* on the "Role of the Press" to cater to the expanding "African readership," which is an "increasing elite readership." He distinguishes this English-language newspaper for an elite African readership from "vernacular papers," which can potentially be dangerous:

---

[17] See Sicherman's revealing account of this story and Ngũgĩ's early writing in the context of his schooling in "Ngugi's British Education" (35–43) and "Ngugi's Colonial Education" (17–18).

> The Press in a developing country is called upon to exercise an even greater amount of responsibility. To most people the written word has a magical power. To them the printed word is the truth. It is even worse in a country where people are just beginning to read and write. In this respect, the vernacular papers have to be of a high quality for they have a large audience and they can do untold harm. (6)

In these articles, Ngũgĩ does tackle a wide range of worsening social and cultural problems. He considers the overcrowding and destitution in the new villages created during the Emergency and the resulting "moral degeneration" manifested in widespread prostitution and illegitimate births, as well as a related problem, an anticipated dissatisfaction when independence does not restore "paradise lost" or effect "a magic transformation over-night" ("Social Problems of the New Villages: A Challenge to African Leaders," *Sunday Post* 20 Aug. 1961, 12). He also deplores widespread drunkenness, especially among the very young, and in the same article, bribery and corruption, partly supporting his contentions with Shakespearean references ("In the Old Days It Was for the Old Men to Drink—Now Even Children Tread on the Toes of Their Fathers," *Sunday Nation* 12 May 1963, 9). He also warns about the effects of agricultural ignorance and a lack of agricultural education ("The Future and the African Farmer," *Sunday Nation* 3 June 1962, 33), as well as the consequences of short-term solutions such as distributing tiny parcels of land instead of creating large, cooperative farms ("Now the Emphasis Must Be on Co-ops," *Sunday Nation* 16 Aug. 1964, 6). He anticipates that such land distribution schemes were partly designed to tackle another social problem, the lack of old-age security measures ("Pensions—We Still Can't Rest Satisfied," *Sunday Nation* 14 June 1964, 3). The destitution of the elderly is matched by the problem of widespread unemployment among the young and even those with some education. Some professions, such as teaching, are underpaid ("Teachers, Too, Want Cash!," *Sunday Nation* 21 June 1964, 6), and the lack of teachers creates a continuing dependence on expatriate teachers who moreover "cannot help injecting the prejudices" of an alien ideology into students' minds (6). He adds that the education of women and girls needs more attention in order to foster gender equality and in particular to redress the widespread and growing imbalance between the rich and poor, the educated and uneducated ("Commentary," *Daily Nation* 18 Aug. 1964, 6). He also speaks out elsewhere against the practice of paying bride price as well as the still more culturally sensitive practice of female circumcision or genital mutilation, that would be at the center of his first novel, *The River Between*. The latter practice is an example of customs he calls "wholly uncivilised and repugnant to our sense of decency and progress" ("Let Us Be Careful about What We Take from the Past," *Sunday Nation* 5 Aug. 1962, 31). Rather than relying on its gradual eradication, Ngũgĩ calls unambiguously for broad-based, open condemnation of a "brutal" practice. His remarks have a certain anthropological frame of reference as if he is evoking the discussion of the subject by Kenyatta in *Facing Mount Kenya*:

> Let us take the circumcision of women. This custom could be defended in the traditional society. It had a useful function not only as a means of educating but also by serving as a cohesive force in the social structure of the tribe. But now the custom has completely outlived its purpose. It is brutal and shows a callousness to human suffering. It is quite nauseating to see some obviously very young girls being subjected to this, even on the verge of independence. And I am afraid that there are some, one would call them enlightened people, who condone the custom, who make the ordinary man feel that it has something special to do with his culture or with the more mystical "African Personality." Leaders of all shades of opinion must come out in the open and condemn this with one voice. It may win them unpopularity, as some Kikuyu are very touchy about the custom—but we cannot afford to turn our eyes from the problem. It must be attacked mercilessly from all sides. (31)

A number of articles address cultural problems, and Ngũgĩ maintains that a greater cultural awakening is a necessary part of genuine independence. Anticipating his own controversial work in community theater in the late 1970s, Ngũgĩ calls in 1962 for the development of "an indigenous drama rooted in the country" with an "amateur dramatic society" beginning in Nairobi ("Must We Drag Africanness Into Everything?," *Sunday Nation* 2 Sept. 1962, 30). In another article he again calls for a "touring [drama] company" ("A New Mood Prevails," *Sunday Nation* 24 Nov. 1963, 14). A year later, however, he writes of attending a dress rehearsal of a small theater company's performance of Ezekiel Mphahlele's *Pot of Tears*—"It is difficult to express the feelings going on inside me. So it was possible to take drama, no, to take the national theatre into the villages, into the African locations?" (7)—in the despairingly titled "I Hope This Theatre Group Won't Die, Too" (*Sunday Nation* 19 July 1964, 6–7). He also writes encouragingly to offer support to art centers, such as the Kibo Art Gallery, and arts and opinion magazines, like *Transition* ("Art Experiment Which Deserves to Succeed," *Sunday Nation* 29 Dec. 1963, 31). In all of these articles, he seeks an expanded, invigorated place for arts and culture in the new society so that political freedom and economic development will be matched by "a corresponding growth in our social institutions, drawing vitality from our past culture, and from the cultures of other people" ("Respect Will Come When We Are Self-Sufficient," *Sunday Nation* 17 Mar. 1963, 29).

One of the most marked differences in Ngũgĩ's early and later positions is evident in the interpretation of Kenyan history, and particularly the "Mau Mau" conflict, that forms the background narrative for his second volume of memoirs. He recalls being a member of an elite school which he regarded as a utopian refuge from the surrounding chaos as if his now-shattered domestic peace was being patrolled by bloodhounds (*In the House* 8, 35). It placed him in a conflicted position in which his perpetual anxiety was "that my connection with a guerrilla fighter might keep me from returning to Alliance" (78). "[T]he colonial state refused to see the Mau Mau as a legitimate anticolonial nationalist movement with political goals" (*In the House* 39). This statement from his 2012 memoir voices

Ngũgĩ's mature position on the Mau Mau struggle as an ideologically coherent, pan-Kenyan war against entrenched colonialism, apartheid, and injustice in Kenya, a necessary deployment of violence in an otherwise intractable situation, and one of the first blows against the England's colonial empire around the globe. This position stands in direct opposition to a statement he made in an 1962 article, "We Must Halt Spread of 'Freedom Army,'" in the *Sunday Nation*, in which he wrote that "[t]he Land Freedom Army cannot be seen by a majority of people as being a liberating force," though he is speaking of a rumoured "resurgence of secret societies and illegal oathing" of the Land Freedom Army at a time when "[t]here are many channels through which people's grievances can be voiced" rather than resorting to violent struggle (31). He speaks of such a resurgence as potentially disastrous. In the same article, he refers to the risk in the revival of "thug elements in their [Kikuyu] community" holding out the prospect of future chaos: "[u]nless we all co-operate the Land Freedom Army may spread" (31). However, he uses the threatening prospect of chaos to voice the need for channels to air grievances. In his early novels, and particularly *Weep Not, Child*, the Mau Mau struggle is presented as a virtual civil war, a fratricidal conflict that divides siblings, families, neighbours, and communities. On September 30, 1962, he can only consider this traumatic history as instructive: "The Mau Mau war will remain a bitter lesson to us" ("Why Don't These Two Leaders Learn From History?," *Sunday Nation* 30 Sept. 1962, 31). However, his overriding emphasis is on the trauma of the events rather than their justification or heroic nature:

> Those of us who lived under the insecurity of fear of what tomorrow might bring during those seven years are neurotically afraid of the phrase—a State of Emergency. We knew what this meant through our own flesh and blood. The shadows of many that we lost will haunt us even when we have crossed the river and gone to the opposite bank called independence. (31)

Approximately six months later, in the context of a condemnation of missionary activity and its alliance with economic and political exploitation, racism, and the promotion of a deferral of justice until "heaven and the life to come," Ngũgĩ briefly raises a question about Mau Mau as being an outcome or an exploitation of false traditionalism, though he may simply be referring to the Mau Mau practice of inserting revolutionary messages within conventional Christian hymns. He writes that "some religious aspects of Mau Mau are a direct result of the culture conflict initiated by missionary enterprise" ("I Say Kenya's Missionaries Failed Badly," *Sunday Nation* 6 Jan. 1963, 5). A later article makes this position clearer and places the discussion at the center of a debate about nationalism: "The African nationalist cannot forget that the white man used the Bible, the pen and the sword to take away the land. What is often forgotten however is that the African himself has taken those very instruments to hit back at the white man and claim his independence" ("Why Shakespeare in Africa?," *Daily Nation* 22 Apr. 1964, 6).

These articles' most extended reflection on Mau Mau occurs in a piece from June 1963, entitled "A Change Has Come Over the Land—A Sense of Destiny

Moves in Most People" (*Sunday Nation* 2 June 1963, 5) that continues the earlier emphasis on the traumatic legacy of the struggle but focuses more directly on the ambivalence of its outcome. In a passage with many echoes of Ngũgĩ's most accomplished early novel *A Grain of Wheat* (1967) with its title and epigraph from I Corinthians 15:36, Ngũgĩ articulates the ambivalence of the conflict and the weariness and even disillusionment of those involved. There is no call for public accountability or investigation, a 1960s version of the now much-imitated Truth and Reconciliation Commission in postapartheid South Africa, but there is a recognition of profound personal and collective change, an appreciation of having survived, and an expression of muted hope. This remarkable passage is worth quoting at some length:

> All these events have of necessity changed people's lives. People in this region feel that the battle, fought in the past, is now half-won. They now wait for the fruition of their struggle. They feel that political militancy is now unnecessary. They want to start living.
>
> But not the life as known before 1952. Now there is a greater sense of purpose and destiny. There is a job to be done. Let me do it. Now.
>
> This spirit, the spirit of work, is most remarkable in the men whose youth was spent in the detention camps. It is as if these men went to detention, uninitiated into the mysteries of life, its contradictions, stresses and hardships. They came back different.
>
> ...
>
> What then happened to some of these people in the camps? Long, and at times, lonely periods of contemplation had their effect. Then there was a sense of youth and time wasted. Some then came back determined to make up for the time lost. A sense of suffering too made others feel that they were saviours of a larger community outside themselves. So they could bear all. No revenge.
>
> One man came back, only to find family disintegration. His wife had had a child by another man. This is what he said to me a few months ago:
>
> "You see, there was no time for revenge. We had other things to do. The country was waiting for us and new horizons had opened before us. The scales in our eyes were broken. In the camps, there, we had a new vision. ... "
>
> What is that vision? I don't know. A change has come over the land. A sense of purpose and destiny moves in most people. They feel they are moving towards a point. And they are ready. But do they know the point, the destination, the purpose? Or is it a restless fumbling in the dark?
>
> Perhaps the new Government will give a sense of direction and give definition to the will to work and the desire to move.

> Whatever has happened, certain it is that there has been a change in the people's scale of values. What spiritual birth this will give rise to, is hard to tell. (5)

Ngũgĩ's final word on Mau Mau in these early articles is much less equivocal. This is perhaps the product of a greater assurance and authority in the postindependence period, a clarification of his own position, or a new willingness to state his deeply held beliefs. In his "Commentary" in the *Daily Nation* of August 8, 1964, one of his last articles, questioning the official reluctance to identify the reason for a former anti-Mau Mau fighter's deportation from Kenya, he writes that Mau Mau "is now regarded as a liberation movement that hastened Uhuru" (6).

Ngũgĩ's early journalism celebrates Pan-Africanism, and presents the divisions manifested by Mau Mau and naïve cultural atavism as potential threats to political, economic, and cultural unity. However, a number of these articles also point to a major problem that relates to these other concerns and a bugbear of settler attitudes: "tribalism." As Ngũgĩ writes in one of the last of these pieces, published in the *Sunday Nation* on July 5, 1964, on the eve of his departure for graduate study at Leeds University, entitled "How Do You Kill These Tribal Feelings?": "One of Kenya's biggest problems in nation-building is tribalism" (6). If the country's goal is a strongly marked national identity, then divisions of all kinds must end. As he wrote two years earlier just before independence was declared, on July 8, 1962, "[t]he immediate obstacle to the creation of a Kenya nation is now not so much racialism as tribalism" ("Let's See More School Integration," *Sunday Nation* 8 July 1962, 25). Two months later, on September 16, 1962, he reiterates the threat of "tribalism" to a newly independent national identity. At this sensitive time, "[t]ribal and other splinter groups can really frustrate the efforts of the new government" ("How Much Rope Should Opponents Be Given?," *Sunday Nation* 16 Sept. 1962, 9). "It's Time We Broke Up This Tribal Outlook," an article from the *Sunday Nation* of October 20, 1963, emphasizes still further the necessary severing of loyalty to "tribe" at the expense of nation. Ngũgĩ writes that "[t]he loyalty of the individual to the wider concept of the nation must transcend his loyalty to the local group. I see the movement toward the nation as a process operating on two planes. First, tribal cohesion must break up. Thus the individual becomes freed from tribal or communal dictatorship" (33). A post-tribal Kenya would be the first step toward a dramatically revisioned nation state. Ngũgĩ anticipates "the breaking-up process of the tribe" which would allow "a progressive realignment ... on the national basis" (33). Ngũgĩ envisions the demise of "tribalism," cultural atavism, and Mau Mau–like insurgency as enabling the establishment of national identity, but he also views this as a way station toward more broad-based alliances.

As in his first two novels, *The River Between* and *Weep Not, Child*, written while he was a student at Makerere, Ngũgĩ looks to education in his early journalism as the vehicle to foster national unity, though he also signals a related commitment to a common language to achieve the same end. Elevating the role of education was part of the philosophy he had absorbed at Alliance and Makerere, an outgrowth of the Victorian public school spirit promoted by Arnold, but it also responded to the devotion to education in traditional African society and also in colonial, settler communities. In an article condemning the betrayal of students enticed by corrupt private schools who rely on the widespread but somewhat naïve thirst for education, Ngũgĩ refers to education as "the African's God Number Two. Uhuru and Land were Number One" ("The Letter That Made My Heart Sink Inside Me," *Sunday Nation* 15 Sept. 1963, 15). As with his later use of Christian imagery, pointing to education as the national panacea was immediately acceptable to different sectors within the nation. He also anticipates that a union of national educational institutions into an East African University might begin the process of a broader East African Federation ("What Is Happening about Federation?," *Sunday Nation* 26 Aug. 1962, 30). To better "meet the needs and aspirations of an underdeveloped country," it must be a more flexible, pluralistic institution and while maintaining high international standards, it may need to sever Makerere's connection with the University of London ("Now Let's See More Flexibility from University Colleges," *Sunday Nation* 7 July 1963, 31). However, in an earlier article in the *Sunday Nation* (27 May 1962), Ngũgĩ warns about the neocolonial creation of "two nations in the same society" if the educated elite become alienated from their own cultural roots and develop a class loyalty at odds with "a national ideal" ("Can the Educated African Meet This Challenge?," 31). While promoting an egalitarian society based on shared values, Ngũgĩ advocates self-sufficiency but not at any expense. Given his later sympathy for the Eastern Bloc (Ngũgĩ's early masterpiece of socialist realism *Petals of Blood* [1977] was completed at the Soviet Writers Union's house in Yalta), it is interesting that he could remark in 1963 that in future "we hope that we shall not need to send our students to any obscure half-civilised country [like Bulgaria] that calls itself Communistic and Socialistic" ("Respect Will Come When We Are Self-Sufficient," *Sunday Nation* 17 March 1963, 29).

Mindful of the need for structural institutional change and the danger of the creation of an alienated elite of educated intellectuals as well as the cancer of unregulated, corrupt private schools, Ngũgĩ reiterates education's centrality in the project of decolonization. Tackling at once the aims of Macaulay's "Minute" and the absolutist, if somewhat distorted, "utilitarianism" of Dickens's Mr. Gradgrind and Mr. M'Choakumchild in *Hard Times* (1854)—a novel much admired by Leavis—Ngũgĩ advocates a curricular revolution, perhaps anticipating the far-more-extensive proposal in "On the Abolition of the English Department." In an article demanding proper remuneration for teachers, over and above any priestly "reward in heaven" offered to missionaries as "consolation when they get small salaries" (33) ("Mboya Is Right—Education Is an Investment," *Sunday Nation* 21 Apr. 1963, 10, 33), Ngũgĩ calls for curricular reform to decolonize history teaching: "In the past that system was designed to fit people into a colonial regime. It produced a whole group of people with a colonial mentality whose two facets were an inferiority complex that was ready to be apologetic of a people's past when not outright ashamed of it and an extreme dependency—a feeling that only the white man can do such things 'for us'" (10). In "Don't Forget Our Destination"

(*Sunday Nation* 10 Feb. 1963, 12, 35), he reiterates the need "to decolonise the education in the country" (12), by shifting the perspective on African history:

> The history of Africa is always taught as an extension of Europe and the African child for a long time thinks that he has no past, his past and the history beginning with the colonising mission of the Imperial powers.
>
> A civilising mission, no doubt, but at what spiritual cost to the colonised people and their mentality! (12)

However, while wishing to shrug off the patronizing, destructive attitude of colonial education, Ngũgĩ also rejects a "too 'utilitarian view' of education" in these articles ("Mboya Is Right" 10). National prosperity and material progress shouldn't become the sole aims of education. "Dickens was a prophet," Ngũgĩ declares in "Don't Forget Our Destination" (12), but while Ngũgĩ clearly advocates the promotion of arts, fancy, wonder, and the imagination as embodied in *Hard Times*'s organic and constantly moving circus, Dickens's utopian circus is contrasted with the mechanistic dystopia of Coketown and Gradgrind's Stone Lodge. Ngũgĩ no doubt would not support *Hard Times*'s ridicule of union organization, its mild poetic justice for perpetrators, or its apparent endorsement of Stephen Blackpool's view of the workers' agitation as a "muddle" for which a resolution is only available in heaven (Dickens 203, 204).

Ngũgĩ appears to have in mind something closer to the rejection of *Hard Times*'s utilitarian education presented in Alan Warner's *Shakespeare in the Tropics*, his inaugural address as the first Professor of English at Makerere College in 1954. Citing *Hard Times*, Warner rejects demands for only science and technology education in Africa, and the exclusion of literary study as one of the "cultural luxuries" (3) like Bounderby's "turtle soup and venison, with a gold spoon" (Dickens 57), because of the universal, transhistorical humanism embodied in the works of great English authors. Studying Shakespeare, Dickens, and Austen, for example, Warner asserts, will break the "stranglehold of the present" in African education as well as in the crisis management mode of handling social and political problems as Africans "advance towards ultimate self-government" (19, 3). Warner offers an Arnoldean defence and an injunction to his Makerere audience:

> Consider the best that has been thought and said in the world, before you follow what may be less than the best. The great writers write about themselves and their own times, but they can help you to understand more clearly your own selves and your own world. They will bring you a deeper awareness of the glory and terror of human existence. Through them you will inherit more fully the spirit, not of a white man or brown man or black man, but the spirit that has no colour, the spirit of man. (26)

In addition, he implies that studying the classics of English literature will mitigate against an angry rejection of all things English as well as an essentialist regionalism. Writers should strive to be global rather than national citizens. Rather than merely attempting to "anglicize their minds," he asserts that the study of English literature will model the production of African literature and he notes a plan to create a Department of African Languages at Makerere. Detailed analyses of English literature, despite the difficulty of Shakespeare's language, thus will enable the development of "[v]ernacular literatures ... only just emerging from oral and tribal traditions. They will need the stimulus of English ideas and forms if they are to develop successfully their own written literatures" (20). For writing literature and also writing about literature, Warner in *A Short Guide to English Style* (1961), presumably designed with Makerere students in mind, advocated an unadorned, "clean" style, though the distinction he draws between literature and orature is stark. This plain style was adopted by Ngũgĩ in his university essays on Conrad—one of which ("Why Nostromo?")[18] cites F.R. Leavis—as well as in his early journalism, but such a style may also be a weapon.[19]

While stressing the importance of English as a language "daily nearing what may be called a universal language," Ngũgĩ in an early statement of what will become one of his major themes insists on the health of African languages as a vital sign of true independence ("Swahili Must Have Its Rightful Place," *Sunday Nation* 23 Sept. 1962, 12). The small size of the audience for "vernacular language" creative writing is a result of the neglect of the study of African languages in schools and colleges: "This neglect of indigenous languages must remain a black spot in the whole of colonial education in Africa" (12). He presents one of his first versions of a challenge to African writers to write in African languages in order to grow their audience and to address the realities of being writers in a country in which "the great majority of the people cannot understand" English:

> This is ... a challenge to writers in general and African writers in particular, to produce more and more work in these languages so that there can be enough material for reading and study. African scholars must also be prepared to translate works in the other languages into indigenous languages. (12)

The consequences of neglect are particularly poignant on the eve of independence. He writes that "I do not think for a moment that we can ever be a nation of any importance unless we have a language of our own through which our national aspirations and spiritual growth can be expressed" (12). Following the example of Julius Nyerere and his anticipated East African Federation, Ngũgĩ promotes Swahili as a primary language, but he also maintains that all languages spoken in Kenya should be considered national languages. He also calls for the creation of indigenous drama companies. It would be Ngũgĩ's work with such an indigenous, grassroots company in the 1970s using indigenous languages, with this work's potential to raise the consciousness of community, rather than the deeply critical, anti-neocolonial stance of *Petals of Blood*, written in English, that probably was the last straw in arousing the ire of the authorities resulting in his year-long

---

[18] I am grateful to Peter Nazareth for sending me a copy of this unpublished essay.

[19] See the remarks of Roland Hindmarsh in his review of Warner's *Short Guide to English Style*.

detention without charge or trial. However, in this article from the early 1960s, he does not exclusively advocate African language theater. Moreover, to prepare for the East African Federation that he sees as the next major stage in a future political evolution, he suggests that French should be taught in East Africa. In one of his last articles, however, he sounds a note of warning, suggesting that "Lack of Communication May be a Barrier to an Africa United States" (*Sunday Nation* September 22, 1963, 14).

Ngũgĩ sees a threat to African language publication and publication in any language used by Kenyan intellectuals as a result of the limitations on audience and the potential hostility of the state. In an early essay on the fortunes of creative writing in Africa, he notes the small number of books published, as a consequence of the limitations of a "poor and illiterate" population, and a certain resistance to reading or abstaining from fiction among the educated ("The New Voices: Some Emerging African Writers," *Sunday Post*, June 4, 1961, 11). He notes two fundamental problems:

> The first one is the problem of language. One can write in vernacular but then for a small public. English, the obvious choice for the English-speaking Africans, is a foreign language and really to make it one's own will take some time. The other problem is that of the reading public. The small dialogue at the beginning of this article [regarding the impractical nature of creative writing when the people's material needs are not being met] shows the utilitarian approach to things like drama and poetry etc. by even the few educated Africans. Thus, reading a novel is a waste of time. Hence for an African writer, he has to look to Europe and America for his public. It was Europe and America which discovered Tutuola. It is Europe and America that is now welcoming Achebe. ... The solution is not simple. It is a question of time and the education of people especially in their tastes. For the struggling would-be writer the only thing one could say to him is, "Courage Brother, do not stumble." (11)

The Eurocentric focus of writing in Africa alienates creative writing from the country of its origin, almost as much as the threat of government sanction and misunderstanding. In "Why Not Let Us Be the Judges?" Ngũgĩ speaks about government censorship and book banning, and political hypersensitivity "to criticism through the printed word" (*Sunday Nation* July 29, 1962, 4). He notes the particular problems associated with misinterpretation of plays and novels, in words that would become ominously prophetic:

> The Government had better be even more careful when creative literature is concerned. A novel or a play is never a realistic mirror of life. The way we react to the characters in a play or in a novel is different from the way we would react to the same people if we had met them in the actual world. (4)

Ngũgĩ would know the foresight of these words in the late 1970s when he was detained due to his Gĩkũyũ plays and *Petals of Blood*, and later in the 1980s when a warrant for the arrest of one of his characters from *Matigari* was issued.

In these early journalistic articles, Ngũgĩ articulates a remarkably coherent Pan-African vision with a number of stages and refinements. For an undergraduate university student from a financially precarious background who had lived through nearly a decade of violent trauma on the eve of independence, such foresight, self-assurance, and authority are remarkable. However, he repeatedly cautions against deluded and exorbitant expectations for independence, when, as he writes, land still won't be free: "[c]rops do not hasten their growth at the fluttering of a flag; rains and droughts, plenty and famine, carry on their normal cycle. The ordinary man goes without shoes, without good shelter and sometimes without food" ("The Three Levels of Independence," *Sunday Nation* 27 Oct. 1963, 39). He regards a strong, self-sufficient national identity as a necessary precursor for an East African Federation. Such a Federation in turn would be a model for wider Pan-African union and a "test-case" for a United States of Africa ("Isn't It Time the Public Were Asked about Federation?" *Sunday Nation* 1 Sept. 1963, 31), that in turn could lead to still broader, international, intercontinental unions. In "What Do We Really Mean by Neutralism?" an article from the *Sunday Nation* of August 19, 1962, Ngũgĩ, a newly hired reporter, is remarkably bold in his hopes and dreams, though they are couched in a warning that almost appears prophetic in the dying days of globalization at the beginning of the twenty-first century:

> The consolidation of his [the African's] independence will be helped or accelerated by a progressive union with the other African States leading finally to the United States of Africa. This again is not a dream. The African countries have no choice. They must either unite, or singly sink to obscurity and insignificance in the world scene. Pan-African unity as a strategic position for the battle for world peace should transcend personality and national sovereignty. (30)

He went further in insisting on the nature of the connection between the members of an East African Federation half a year later. In "Co-operative Spirit Is Not Enough" from the *Sunday Nation* of February 3, 1963, he advances a somewhat more controversial proposal, given that "a loose spirit of co-operation without a form of political link-up will not do. The economic link-up of the East African countries must be made permanent through a political association" (4).

Ngũgĩ's promotion of regional and continental alliances partly stemmed from a recognition that colonial national models were obsolete and were founded on largely unexamined philosophical contradictions. He seeks a new, noncolonial or neocolonial basis for the nation and the postnation. While in 1962 he could be optimistic about the outcomes of the Lancaster House conference and the work of the Regional Boundaries Commission, saying that "[i]t looks as if the mistakes of the colonial powers who originally drew the provincial boundaries have been righted," he clearly regards this correction as a temporary measure ("Big Day for God's Children," *Sunday Nation* 30 Dec. 1962, 25). *In the House of the Interpreter* refers to an earlier, much smaller scale "land consolidation" during the anti-Mau Mau Emergency, when settlements were amalgamated into barbed-wire ringed concentration camps, during the policy of Villagization to cut off support to the fighters in the forest, as a "mass fraud" (36). However, in the early 1960s, while Ngũgĩ was still optimistic about the possibilities of independence and its aftermath, he was wary of colonial mimicry. A central problem in his estimation is the fundamental contradiction about the value of different races at the heart of the colonial project. In "Let's Get Out of the Dark and Take a Look at the Sun" from the *Sunday Nation* of June 17, 1962, he writes

> Colonialism was bound to fail. It was founded on contradictions. For it was those very nations whose culture was built on Christianity and the concept of rights and freedom of the individual, that denied the same things to the Africans. ... For if we are going to build our independence on contradictions as colonialism was, we are doomed to failure and spiritual destruction as a nation. (39)

Colonialism is founded on a strictly European notion of the nature of the human. This theme of humanity and race or "the colour of reason" to use Emmanuel C. Eze's phrase is one that would preoccupy Ngũgĩ increasingly in the twenty-first century.[20] It finds direct expression in the colonial reflections of influential Victorian philosophical sages and prophets such as J.S. Mill. Eze details the anthropological and racist basis of Immanuel Kant's understanding of reason, human nature, and moral agency, based in part on Jean-Jacques Rousseau's distinction between the primitive and civilized as well as on stereotypes spread in fiction and travel writing. For Eze, Kant's writing on anthropology was not marginal to his humanist metaphysics; on the contrary, "Kant's racial theories ... belong in an intimate way to Kant's transcendental philosophy" (449).[21]

The problem of how to understand Kenya's and Africa's pasts at the critical moment of the confrontation of past, present, and future on the eve of independence is the subject of a number of these articles. In an early article from 1961, Ngũgĩ is at pains to acknowledge the importance to him of European values and principles, and also like the youthful Fanon, to confront the betrayal embedded in these values as witnessed in the colonial encounter, perhaps the test case of the limitation of enlightenment rationalism and Modernist progress. In an examination of the work of French African intellectuals forced to attempt to reinvent lost traditions and lament the irretrievability of those traditions and that past due to the French colonial policy of assimilation, Ngũgĩ acknowledges his debts to European culture as one that recognizes the rights of individuals and forms a bulwark against totalitarianism:

> I like and cherish the basis of western culture. For this creed is Christianity which emphasises, the equality and dignity of each individual—that the one single lost sheep is as important as the rest of [the] 99 sheep. This in the end, is the best challenge to Communism or any form of totalitarianism. Seen in this light, the

---

[20] See, for example, Ngũgĩ's "Europhone" (159).

[21] As Eze puts it succinctly, "philosophical anthropology becomes the logocentric articulation of an ahistorical, universal, and unchanging essence of 'man'" (450).

> western culture, ceases to be a wholly European creation. It has [been] borrowed all over the world. Hence it is not to be confused with European prejudices, mannerisms or even fears. ("African Culture: The Mistake That Kenyatta Made. 'There Is No Going Back to the Past,'" *Sunday Post*, 6 Aug. 1961, 10)

However, in this article, Ngũgĩ also confronts the painful contradiction at the heart of these European ideals or their application. Admiring such ideals, the African

> at once sees a discrepancy between theory and practice, between that culture and the guardians of that culture. For that culture preaches about the equality and dignity of man, and about liberty, fraternity and the rights of man etc. etc. Yet the African, himself out of a colonial territory, sees all those beautiful things denied to him, or at least denied to the great mass of his people. (10)

Ngũgĩ's language here appears to mimic Caliban's, and the subject of *The Tempest* is one he considers in a later article ("Why Shakespeare in Africa?," *Daily Nation* 22 Apr. 1964, 6), in which he confronts the fatal contradiction of colonialism again. In the last gesture of this earlier article, Ngũgĩ will conjure a different approach to European culture, asserting that it was in its origins "borrowed" from the world and hence may be similarly borrowed and synthesized by others. In this call for a type of utopian synthesis, Ngũgĩ also alludes to the "common culture" of Matthew Arnold.[22] For Ngũgĩ the answer

> lies in a synthesis of the two ways of life. Thus Africa must be prepared to borrow a lot from the West, inasmuch as the West needs to borrow from Africa [especially to confront "the materialistic tendency"]. ... In conclusion, one might just say that what is needed is a culture that is not exclusive or inward-looking, but which is adaptable to changes, and above all, deep-rooted in the country. And what a splendid thing for Kenya! A common culture, created out of the three ways of life—European, African and Asian—would be a basis for unity. For only a people sharing the same culture and cultural outlook, can be united! ("African Culture" 10)

Gesturing to Hegel's notion of colonialism as the project marking the beginning of African history, Ngũgĩ reiterates the broader implications of national independence for historical understanding. In "Don't Forget Our Destination" from the *Sunday Nation* of February 10, 1963, he writes that "[t]he history of Africa is always taught as an extension of Europe and the African child for a long time thinks that he has no past, his past and history beginning with the colonising mission of the Imperial powers" (12). Ngũgĩ calls for state-operated schools in Uganda, which could develop a more Afrocentric curriculum. Ngũgĩ in this piece even somewhat facetiously suggests that Africa might save a decaying Europe, which in words echoing those of General William Booth (1829–1912) of

---

[22] See Gerald Graff's discussion of "the Common Culture Paradox" in "Arnold, Reason, and Common Culture" (192).

the Salvation Army, was a "dark continent": "The African nations, being young, should now assume the role of saviour to rescue a civilisation on the verge of decay. Their faith and optimism should act as the new beacons on top of Kilimanjaro to light not Africa alone but the Dark Continent of Europe as well" (35). Elsewhere, he suggests that Kenya's, an East African Federation's, and a United States of Africa's future lies not in Europe but in solidarity with the global south. The shared experience of colonialism would make a bridge between Africa and Asia, for example: "East and West might never meet, but Africa and Asia could" ("Even Brothers Can Cut Throats," *Sunday Nation* 17 Feb. 1963, 4). Ngũgĩ's rhetoric in this article becomes more starkly radical, and he suggests that a new species of solidarity might actively resist Western influence. Such global alliances would be based on common experience and would form a "bulwark against the imperialism of the West" (4).

For Ngũgĩ, this Pan-African advocacy in the early 1960s was undertaken with the acceptance that while broad community support would be valuable it would be politicians who must draft legislation. These articles frequently address the role and responsibility of Kenyan and African intellectuals, and they often do not discriminate between the educated elite, creative writers, artists, students, and in some cases politicians or scholar-artist political leaders, and presumably journalists. This diverse elite intellectual cadre shares a clearly defined, but not unnuanced and sometimes ambiguous social responsibility to the new and evolving national and Pan-African collective. Even students—and of course Ngũgĩ was writing as a student journalist—he insists, need "to give serious thought to the prevailing social, economic and political problems. Never before have African countries so much needed a cool, objective assessment of ideas, an honest appraisal of the conflicting forces at present rocking the continent" ("Commentary," *Daily Nation* 19 Aug. 1964, 6). Ngũgĩ insists on the intellectual's obligation to voice opinions, however unfavourable and unwelcome, and however easily misinterpreted. This stance is a particular necessity at the moment of independence when objective, cool, critical reflection is vital. He appears acutely aware of the hypersensitivity of politicians and of their readiness to distort critical opinions for political gain. A number of his remarks have great resonance nearly half a century later. For example, he refers, in an August 1964 article, to the support for East African Federation voiced by Mwai Kĩbaki, who in 2013 would be in the president of Kenya just about to complete his second term in office ("Commentary," *Daily Nation* 14 Aug. 1964, 6). In another article, from the same month, Ngũgĩ calls for greater government transparency in offering an explanation for the deportation of Ian Henderson, a decorated anti–Mau Mau fighter whose treatment may provide him "an aura of martyrdom" ("Commentary," *Daily Nation* 8 Aug. 1964, 6). He asks why this decision has been made by the minister of home affairs, Oginga Odinga, the father of 2013's prime minister Raila Odinga, who sought election as president in a closely fought contest pitting him against Uhuru Kenyatta, son of Kenya's first president, who, with his running mate William Ruto, faced charges of crimes against humanity for their roles in the 2007 election violence at the international criminal court (ICC) after the March 2013 election. While the ICC's ineffectiveness and paternalism in Africa has been faulted by some commentators like Binyavanga Wainaina (19), the charge represents a serious challenge to the country's governance. In a recent op-ed piece for the *New York Times*, "A Dictator's Last Laugh," Ngũgĩ suspects the hand of Daniel arap Moi behind the manipulations of the most recent election.

Intellectual leadership, a subject of increasing urgency in Ngũgĩ's most recent work, is stressed here for all intellectuals in the emerging country. "[E]merging writers" will have to tackle the "colonial paradox" that Shakespeare unfolds in *The Tempest*, confronting not just the "psychology of colonialism" but also the moral order of society so as "to give a sense of moral direction to our young countries in their search for order and stability" ("Why Shakespeare in Africa?," *Daily Nation* 22 Apr. 1964, 6).[23] Ngũgĩ also examined this issue in one of his first articles from 1962, pointing to the public's perceptions of intellectuals in different settings and hence their divergent responsibilities. There is a hint of paternalism in his assessment of the expectations of the intellectual:

> In the village, of course, he must be everything—moral teacher, adviser on social and economic activity, part psychiatrist. His every action is watched and quickly copied. At the national level, too, he is a hero—writer, politician, leader, interpreter of the social scene. The mass of the people leave things to the educated African, so his position in Kenya is one of strong influence and necessarily heavy responsibility. ("Can the Educated African Meet This Challenge?," *Sunday Nation* 27 May 1962, 31)

The artist in a developing country has an additional responsibility that, while he caters to the need for art production, he does not allow "his detachment" to "become an escape ... from the problems that are around him. People's agonies must be his agonies. A nation's joy must be his joy, too" ("Wanted—A Proper Place for Art," *Sunday Nation* 23 Dec. 1962, 11).

However, while stressing the intellectual's and particularly the creative writer's social responsibility, Ngũgĩ also finds a place for high Modernist aesthetic ideals, a tension creating a crisis of representation. An early article laments that writers of the calibre of Peter Abrahams "should spend all their talents engrossed with the Monster of colour prejudice" ("The New Voices: Some Emerging African Writers," *Sunday Post* 4 June 1961, 11). He takes up this question again half a year later. He laments that South African writers are "forced to resort to protest writing—to stories of violence, restlessness and hunger for freedom" ("African Writers Need a New Outlook," *Sunday Nation* 2 Dec. 1962, 29). The fraught political danger represents a "sharp difficulty" for the writer in that it strongly favors certain artistic choices such as the use of type characters and stock situations which cater to readers' expectations. In effect, the weight of political injustice

---

[23] James notes in the Preface to *Beyond a Boundary*: "To establish his own identity, Caliban, after three centuries, must himself pioneer into regions Caesar never knew" (n. pag.).

that the writer must tackle demands a type of aesthetic response which is bad for imaginative art. He elucidates another version of the crisis of representation: "Even before the writer has set his pen on the paper he has a public which is ready to sympathise with the situation. The battle is half done. It is easy to sit down and relax. No need to sweat. No need to examine and explore every corner of human experience" (29). The writer's danger lies in producing "mediocre ... social documentation, of interest only to students of politics and sociology," but this danger is also apparent in a different form to "the writer in the rest of the continent where there is political freedom." This danger is the easy assumption of what Ngũgĩ refers to repeatedly in these articles as "slogans" such as notions of the "African personality" and Négritude. Preindependence writers, he maintains, were obliged to offer optimistic assertions, but this mandate made for a "dilemma" that has changed with independence. The writer, however, is still obliged to voice "the aspirations, failures and successes of a nation on the move" and "[h]e has no tradition on which to hold" (29). In the face of this new dilemma, "[p]rotest writing and Negritude" are merely "poses and attitudes" (29).

In a later essay from 1964, "More Is Needed from Educated Africans" (*Sunday Nation* 7 June, 9), that begins with an endorsement of the new president Kenyatta's challenge to the new nation to "liberate 'our minds and souls from foreign ideas and thoughts'" and "the colonial mentality," Ngũgĩ expresses some dismay with calls for the creation of new hybrid art forms, as well as the redrafting of textbooks and even "evolving new architecture and songs based on African traditional forms and culture":

> This message raises many issues. What is colonial mentality and how is it affecting the growth of a nation? Can we ever get rid of foreign ideas and thoughts? In any case, would it be desirable to do so? What are African traditional forms in art? Are they to be re-created live side by side with European art forms, or can they be integrated with foreign traditions and influences to create a new dynamic whole? (9)

It is interesting to see Ngũgĩ struggling to meet this challenge to the European artistic forms that he had been studying so closely at Alliance and Makerere, when his own success had been a result of his ability to analyze these very forms at the moment when his own career as an artist was on the cusp of gaining international recognition. In many respects, his own Gĩkũyũ novels from the late 1970s and 1980s would be his most direct response to this challenge. They would embody his own version of a radically decolonized poetics.[24]

Ngũgĩ's discussion of the dilemma facing the artist intellectual of the newly independent African state relies on largely unexamined assumptions about the role of art and particularly its function in creating a new African. In an early article

---

[24] In a different context, Adrienne Rich writes: "Poetries are no more pure and simple than human histories are pure and simple. And there are colonised poetics and resilient poetics, transmissions across frontiers not easily traced" ("Legislators of the World").

from 1962, Ngũgĩ already evoked this notion of a new African who can "adopt a selective attitude and take from our past only those things which can keep in step with our progress to a higher and fuller humanity" ("Let Us Be Careful about What We Take from the Past," *Sunday Nation* 5 Aug. 1962, 31). Striving for an early version of mental decolonization through art, the artist is responsible for aiding in the creation of "a nation in which the individual finds fulfilment" ("More Is Needed from Educated Africans," *Sunday Nation* 7 June 1964, 9). The articles' notion of this new individual appears to be a type of ordinary heroism that relies heavily on humanist ideals.[25] A preindependence article outlining "the Kenya I want" has Ngũgĩ speaking of vanquishing "two forces of darkness" "[t]ribalism and racialism" so as to permit the new Kenyan individual to shuck off "shackles— material as well as spiritual—that prevent him from reaching the heights he is capable of" ("Here's the Kenya I Want," *Sunday Nation* 12 Aug. 1962, 28). He cites the Promethean actions celebrated in Shelley's *Prometheus Unbound*, Book III.iv: "Spectreless, free, uncircumscribed, but man / Equal, unclassed, tribeless, and nationless, / Exempt from awe, worship, degree, the king / Over himself; just, gentle, wise." He ends his quotation with an affirmation and a question: "This is the Kenya I want. What about you?" (28). Ngũgĩ celebrates here an elevation of the common person to a type of natural nobility, unconstrained by conventional political and religious limits. Ngũgĩ omits Shelley's references to absolute freedom from moral law and the law of the passions. He regards Prometheus as James did, writing about a decade earlier in the context of a comparison of Melville's heroism and Modernist intellectuals' self-indulgent angst. For James, the mythic figure embodies resistance and vigilance: "to this very day Prometheus is still the prototype of the revolutionary leader, benefactor of humanity, bold, defiant, confident" (*Mariners* 118), but James also contends that this type of heroic individual has vanished from literature, a contention that has significance for the potentially heroic but vacillating intellectual heroes of Ngũgĩ's first novels.[26] For James, Shelley, too, was a stalled revolutionary, a "genuine if frustrated democrat" (James, *American* 63). Ngũgĩ's reference to Prometheus also appears to invoke Shelley's notion of poets as "the unacknowledged legislators of the world" in *The Defence of Poetry*, those who can anticipate and bring into being a new order. The poet's work stimulates the imagination and "strengthens the faculty which is the organ of the moral nature of man," a passage Warner quotes in *Shakespeare in*

---

[25] Ngũgĩ's words appear to echo the conclusion of *The Wretched of the Earth* ("we must make a new start, develop a new way of thinking, and endeavour to create a new man" [2004, 239]), though Ngũgĩ had not yet encountered Fanon.

[26] While "Ahab is of the race of Prometheus," James contends that the Promethean hero is no longer possible as Melville recognized:
> that type was now doomed. Great men, leading their fellows from one stage of civilization to another, there have always been and will always be, but the Promethean individual, containing in himself, his ideas, his plans, the chart of the future, he seems finished. In the world of affairs he leads only to disaster, which is why perhaps in literature he no longer appears at all. (*Mariners* 119)

the Tropics (13). Shelley's *Defence*, however, anticipates only a glacial progress for the "savage," "for the savage is to ages what the child is to years" (ontogeny recapitulates phylogeny). For Shelley, in Adrienne Rich's interpretation, "there was no contradiction between poetry, political philosophy, and active confrontation with illegitimate authority"; moreover, poetry "has the capacity to remind us of something we are forbidden to see. A forgotten future." This notion of a future "African renaissance" where memory merges with realization would concern Ngũgĩ's most recent critical work.

Intellectual alienation is a subject Ngũgĩ addresses in a number of these essays, evoking the Victorian notion of the "two nations" theme ("Can the Educated African Meet This Challenge?," *Sunday Nation* 27 May 1962, 31). He stresses the separation between the mass of Kenyans and the educated intellectual elite, and also deplores the isolation or "hermit"-like existence of the writer ("Wanted—A Proper Place for Art," *Sunday Nation* 23 Dec. 1962, 11), a subject Ngũgĩ explored in a different context in his early play *The Black Hermit* published in 1968. There is a certain ambivalence in his discussion given that he seeks to conjure the educated intellectual's alienation from a traditional sense of identity and from the mass of the population, but also from other members of this African elite. In addition, he tends to accept as inevitable a degree of dominance in the relationship between the intellectual elite and the masses. The urgent need for a response to Kenyatta's call for more widespread cultural and psychological decolonization mentioned earlier, Ngũgĩ asserts, is one that "can only be thought out and thrashed [out] by the African elite" ("More Is Needed from Educated Africans," *Sunday Nation* 7 June 1964, 9). The "pity" of the situation in which this crisis must be confronted is that "when our nation cries for guidance," the elite has forfeited its guiding role (9). While political leaders "organised the masses into a successful weapon against colonial rule," moreover, "the intellectual stood aloof, caught in a dilemma he was unable to solve." Ostensibly concerned about the consequences of making public criticism in a period of political sensitivity, the intellectual merely complains and indulges in cynicism and apathy. Moreover, Ngũgĩ maintains that the alienation within the cadre of isolated intellectuals means they do not communicate with each other. In the face of this alienation, he calls for engagement and an acceptance of the responsibility to inspire and lead. In one of the most extended reflections on the role of the intellectual's encounter with postcolonialism, Ngũgĩ writes:

> [I]t is time the African elite came to the forefront. It is time they stopped living in this inward isolation, waiting for a chance that will never come. What is wanted is an intellectual community in which ideas will throb. These ideas will in turn animate the nation to new efforts and inculcate in us a sense of pride. For it is only through achievements in every field of human endeavour that even the rewriting of text books could be meaningful. It is true that the colonial theory rested on the basic assumption that the ruled had no culture or a past with any significance. But the redefinition of that past is surely not enough. In the final analysis we shall have to reckon with the present endeavour, with present concrete achievements, realising all the time that we shall have to judge

ourselves by the highest standards possible. We want Kenyans in the forefront of science. We want many Kenyans in the forefront of art. We shall borrow from heaven or hell for we can only shut ourselves from outside influences to our sorrow. Our culture, a dynamic force, not still, always in the process of change, will be the sum total of our achievements in every aspect. ("More Is Needed" 9)

Interestingly, at the end of this injunction to the elite, evoking a Promethean resolve, Ngũgĩ repositions the intellectuals in relationship to politicians and the masses who he maintains are performing their role in revitalizing culture. He concludes with a reiteration of the social and ideological alienation of the intellectual: "The peasant is as much part of that culture as the politician. The two have accepted their role and [are] making something of it. It is only the intellectual, the university product, who continues to live in splendid isolation" (9).

The African intellectual movement called Négritude is one of the subjects, with the African personality, African socialism,[27] and African nationalism, that Ngũgĩ repeatedly dismisses in these articles as "slogans." He targets a regressive essentialism in such notions that carries with it marks of a wounded "colonial mentality." He writes in "Must We Drag Africanness into Everything?":

I am now tired of the talk about African culture: I am tired of the talk about "African Socialism." Why must I always try to discover something inherently "African" in every system of thought ranging from democracy to culture—as if none of these things could be really useful to me unless they were prefaced by the word "African?" To me this is a colonial mentality and as we are now getting rid of colonialism in all its manifestations, we should also try to get rid of this. Not that I mean to under-rate any genuine contributions to thought and culture by Africans. But be it far from me to go about looking for an "Africanness" in everything before I can value it. (*Sunday Nation* 2 Sept. 1962, 30)

Ngũgĩ is particularly weary of talk about the "African personality," a concept that arises, as he says with mock piety, "wherever two or three African students and politicians are gathered together" ("An African Says 'The African Personality Is a Delusion': Do Tigers Have 'Tigritude'?," *Sunday Post* 7 May 1961, 12). In this respect, Ngũgĩ appears to belong to those who, as Abiola Irele puts it, dismiss Négritude as the expression of "a kind of black narcissism" ("Négritude" 48).[28] French intellectuals, like the scholar-poet-politician Senghor, merit the youthful Ngũgĩ's admiration, but he appears to perceive a tragic loss at the heart of all of the work of Négritude and its poets. In a later article from 1964, Ngũgĩ comments

---

[27] See "African Socialism: Two Views," *Daily Nation* 9 May 1964, 6.

[28] Irele credits the value of Négritude in pointing out, however unconsciously, its own internal contradictions: "Senghor's négritude, for example, is an anti-intellectualism mediated by the intellect, and the whole movement is expressed through a Western mould which absorbs African realities" ("Négritude" 48). In an earlier "Defence of Negritude," Irele credits Sartre's influence on the movement from its inception, noting that Négritude's focus on emotion does not exclude the intellect (9–11).

that Senghor's poetry is moving, but lacks the specifics of individual experience, instead offering only vague generalizations about Africa or some unremembered past ("He's Africa's Poet-Statesman," *Daily Nation* 10 July 1964, 6). Ngũgĩ does not comment on the Négritude poets' gender politics or pervasive sexism, or on the association of Négritude itself with the ideology of Pan-Africanism.

Négritude and Ngũgĩ's dismissal of it in his early journalism warrant additional attention because they synthesize a number of Ngũgĩ's early ideas and indicate the dramatic shift in his thinking over five decades. Négritude ostensibly provides a distinctive ideology and aesthetics for African writers and those in the African diaspora, but Ngũgĩ strongly suggests in these articles that it is founded on the devastation and attempted annihilation resulting from the French colonial policy of assimilation, even though C.L.R. James claims it as distinctively West Indian in origin and character (*Black Jacobins* 394). Négritude is nostalgic and idealistic, and it attempts to link the corporeal with the creative and the numinous in opposing the reification of the African body used as an object of exchange in the slave trade. In Ngũgĩ's view, however, and far more problematically, it is culturally atavistic and also hopelessly cerebral, despite its celebrated sensuality and vitalism, and also solidly entrenched in a type of narcissistic intellectualism, divorced from common peasant culture.

Writers like Senghor, Césaire, and Léon Gontran Damas, "'French' Africans," Ngũgĩ contends, "have tended to see themselves as exiles in a foreign culture. They look back and see an Ideal African culture—now lost. They want to revive it—revive the culture of their ancestors" ("African Culture: The Mistake That Kenyatta Made. 'There Is No Going Back to the Past,'" *Sunday Post* 6 Aug. 1961, 10). While self-fashioned as a positive expression of identity politics, Négritude for Ngũgĩ is a desperate attempt to establish uniqueness, but it reduces a collective heritage to race, geography, and shared grievances, though Ngũgĩ insists that the Négritude poets' ideology of African vitalism merely echoes that of Modernist writers like D.H. Lawrence and trades on a lamentable "racial stereotyping," as he points out in the first of his articles focused on Négritude ("An African Says 'The African Personality Is a Delusion': Do Tigers Have 'Tigritude'?," *Sunday Post* 7 May 1961, 12). He takes particular umbrage at Césaire's famous *Cahier d'un retour au pays natal* (*Notebook of a Return to My Native Land*)—a poem written on holiday in Yugoslavia in 1935 about memories of Martinique, while Césaire was completing a thesis in Paris on the Harlem Renaissance—and its apparent embrace of absolute self-sufficiency experienced as triumphant failure: "Hoorah for those who never invented anything, / for those who never explored anything, / for those who never mastered anything."[29] Ngũgĩ would later come to reverse

---

[29] This is James's translation of one of his favourite poems, one of the finest expressions of Césaire's notion "that salvation for the West Indies lies in Africa" (*The Black Jacobins* 399–400): "It is the desperate cry of a Europeanised West Indian poet for reintegration with his own people" ("The Artist in the Caribbean" 189). Lamming quotes from the poem in an epigraph to *The Pleasures of Exile* first published in 1960, calling Césaire "perhaps the greatest of all Caribbean poets" (95, 49). Despite his admiring yet suspicious attitude to

his opinion, even regarding this poem as one that "held for all time the monopoly of beauty, intelligence and knowledge" (*Moving* 10). Finally, in this early article on Négritude, he rejects replacing racial inferiority with superiority, questioning whether "it is not an unconscious confession of an inferiority complex or an attempt to kill that feeling of inferiority" ("An African Says" 12) and similarly whether "recent attempts to 're-discover' the African history and culture (or 'create' or 'mould' one where nothing is clear) is an attempt to answer the above accusation, i.e. that one has no culture or history" (12). This stolid unwillingness to idealize the precolonial past may go a long way to explain the absence of a *Things Fall Apart*–like attempt to evoke a distinct history, even one based on colonial-era anthropological models,[30] in Ngũgĩ's early novels, over and above a frequent reference to a shared mythology of genesis and a lineage of seers and prophets.

Ngũgĩ credits Achebe in an address at Makerere with Wole Soyinka's famous remark about Négritude that "a tiger does not sing about its 'tigritude'" (12). The youthful, brash Ngũgĩ might be accused of being an example of those who "underestimated or belittled" the "vision of Negritude" in Soyinka's own later terms (*Myth, Literature* 126). This assessment might have staying power save that Ngũgĩ's views are not totally dismissive and that they echo Soyinka's own remarks from his famous and often misunderstood 1967 essay, "The Writer in a Modern African State,"[31] delivered on the eve of the Nigerian civil war and shortly before Soyinka's imprisonment, in which he refers to Négritude's "myth of irrational nobility, of a racial essence that must come to the rescue of the white depravity" (Soyinka, "The Writer" 20). Ngũgĩ also anticipates Soyinka's further objections in his essays from the early 1970s in *Myth, Literature and the African World*:

> Negritude trapped itself in what was primarily a defensive role, even though its accents were strident, its syntax hyperbolic and its strategy aggressive. It accepted one of the most commonplace blasphemies of racism, that the black man has nothing between his ears, and proceeded to subvert the power of poetry to glorify this fabricated justification of European cultural domination. Suddenly, we were exhorted to give a cheer for those who never invented anything, a cheer for those who never explored the oceans. The truth, however, is that there isn't any such creature. (129)

Négritude in *Black Skin, White Masks*, Fanon gives this poem considerable attention (21, 123–4, 195–7). In 1964, Irele wrote that "Aimé Césaire seems to me to be Black Orpheus par excellence" ("In Defence" 11).

[30] See Lovesey's "Making Use of the Past in *Things Fall Apart*" (273–99).

[31] Soyinka is a famous trickster, and in at least some of his critical remarks on Soyinka's essay, Ngũgĩ may have misread Soyinka's facetious, self-directed irony. See Ngũgĩ's comments about the reality of material poverty in Africa (in the face of the indifference of "we, the black intellectuals, the black bourgeoisie" [25]) and the necessity for armed insurrection in "From the Discussion" following Soyinka's lecture in the proceedings of the Writer in Modern Africa conference, Stockholm, in 1967 (Wästberg 25–6), and the later clarification by Dennis Brutus and Soyinka himself (Wästberg 49–51). For a discussion of the reception of this essay, including Ngũgĩ's remarks, see Biodun Jeyifo (x, xxi).

Soyinka's most recent work, the continental reflection *Of Africa*, continues his later reassessment of Négritude, which he now sees as "a concept that advanced beyond racial separatism to propose the eventuality of a universal synthesis of humanistic values," a vision of "African humanism" (19). Soyinka would go on to critique another attempt to revive an essentialist African ideology.[32] However, some of Soyinka's early remarks on the African writer's innate and shared sense of social responsibility, a responsibility voiced by Ngũgĩ, appear to gesture to a transcendental notion, one "in-built" and "intuitive," and one seemingly co-opted by colonialism. Colonialism's force has undercut this sense of responsibility and the consequence has been the construction of the African writer in 1967 as a "prop of the state machinery" and the very "crystallization … of the Establishment" (Soyinka, "The Writer" 15, 18). For Ngũgĩ, writing a few years earlier, the danger for the writer is social isolation, though he shares Soyinka's later dismay at the African writer's failure of vision and abdication of responsibility to him- or herself and "his roots" (17). In a later essay, inadvertently tracing the sweeping influence of Négritude in the African diaspora, Ngũgĩ discusses James Baldwin and the danger of the "race myth," reiterating the dangers of replacing the "bigotry of white supremacy with the bigotry of black supremacy" ("The Negro Is a Myth," *Daily Nation* 9 Apr. 1964, 6).

Ngũgĩ would come to a profoundly different and much more nuanced assessment of Négritude in his recent work, claiming in *Globalectics*, for example, that it was "an attempt to complete Marx" (22),[33] almost as if to make amends with his earlier dismissal. He also reflects that *Discours* would help him understand the experience of returning to find his home and clan village destroyed (*Globalectics* 18). He would thus return to the source of this statement in Césaire's famous *Discours sur le Colonialism* [*Discourse on Colonialism*], which was first published in 1950 and then revised and republished in 1955, a work that anticipates a number of the assertions regarding historiography made by Fanon in *The Wretched of the Earth* as Moore-Gilbert suggests (*Postcolonial Theory* 172). Césaire's work contains a clear position on the origins of Négritude as resistance to the psychological damage of colonialism, the pressure for assimilation particularly in the French colonial world, and the pervasive colonial and precolonial myths about Africa and Africans. "Négritude" itself, moreover, was used as a "term of defiance" as Césaire remembers ("Interview" 89),[34] designed to direct a type of intentionally offensive assault to the sensibilities and to provoke a shocked reaction by taking

---

[32] See Soyinka's account of the troika in "Neo-Tarzanism: The Poetics of a Pseudo-Tradition" (38–44).

[33] In *Culture and Imperialism*, Said made a similar reflection in his discussion of James's assessment of Négritude in Césaire's *Cahier d'un retour au pays natal*: "it would be the most vulgar racism not to see here a poetic incarnation of Marx's famous sentence, 'The real history of humanity will begin'" (280–281).

[34] See Richard Philcox's account of the challenge of translating Fanon's "Nègre" and its complex of meanings in a Caribbean context ("On Retranslating Fanon" 247–8).

back or assuming agency over a shameful, demeaning term, as might be said many decades later of the deployment of "queer" in the gay community and "nigger" in the Afro-American hip hop community. He refers to the collective creation of the notion, though he was first to deploy the term:

> It was really a resistance to the politics of assimilation. Until that time, until my generation, the French and the English—but especially the French—had followed the politics of assimilation unrestrainedly. We didn't know what Africa was. Europeans despised everything about Africa, and in France people spoke of a civilized world and a barbarian world. The barbarian world was Africa, and the civilized world was Europe. Therefore the best thing one could do with an African was to assimilate him: the ideal was to turn him into a Frenchman with black skin. (88)

In effect, then, in its origins, Négritude was a kind of African dreaming or dreaming of Africa by Afro-Caribbeans who had never known their motherland because of slavery and the betrayals of history as well as by Senghor from Senegal, displaced in Paris. The reassessments of Négritude by Soyinka and Ngũgĩ may have been partly the new perspective brought about by African intellectuals reflecting on memories of Africa from a condition of exile in America.

Césaire refers, in his interview with René Depestre appended to *Discourse on Colonialism*, to the resistance among Communists to considering the significance of race: "Communists would reproach me for speaking of the Negro problem—they called it my racism. But I would answer: Marx is all right, but we need to complete Marx. I felt that the emancipation of the Negro consisted of more than just a political emancipation" (85–6). What he has in mind in particular is the "coming to consciousness among Negroes" (86), the decolonization of the African consciousness, manifested in the vibrant cultural expressions of the Harlem Renaissance, the utilization of African iconography in the neoexoticist work of the French and Spanish Modernist painters, and the work of C.L.R. James and Marcus Garvey. As we shall see in the next chapter, this challenging of the disregard for race in politics and an emphasis on an emancipation of consciousness would preoccupy a number of the Caribbean intellectuals that Ngũgĩ would study after his departure from Makerere. This would lead to his eventual return to exploring much further his early interests in African diasporan ideologies and a type of diasporic Pan-Africanism.

Chapter 3
Diasporic Pan-Africanism: The Caribbean Connection

Ngũgĩ's early view of colonialism in Africa was tremendously influenced by C.L.R. James's examinations of diasporic Pan-African history as a history of resistance and Frantz Fanon's stress on psychic liberation. Central to the re-visioning and reconceptualizing of African history as one of active struggle against imperialism, colonialism, and capitalism was James's account of the first rebellion against colonial rule in eighteenth-century Haiti in his enormously influential *The Black Jacobins* (1938) and the parallels it draws between this historical moment of armed struggle and the twentieth century's tumultuous history. While he would probably not have read James's 1969 "update" detailing the "history of African Revolt" added to his 1938 monograph *A History of Negro Revolt*, republished in 1969 as *A History of Pan-African Revolt*, the Ngũgĩ of *Homecoming*, his first collection of critical essays, was aware of the ferment of Caribbean literature and theory and its influence on Kenya and more generally on Africa's cultural, political, and literary growth when he was a student at Leeds University beginning in October 1964. At Leeds he would encounter the work of Fanon, whose views of the global south and of Africa were so astute that "it was as if Fanon had been born and raised in Kenya" (*Globalectics* 42). The writing of Fanon and others of the "Caribbean literary renaissance" would provide Ngũgĩ a bridge between the close textual studies of Alliance and Makerere and the world (*Globalectics* 15). Ngũgĩ's evolving historiography and intellectual understanding of cultural engagement hence would be positioned against the "myth" of Africa and Africans that fueled imperialism.[1] It was also positioned against Hegel's and later Hugh Trevor-Roper's denial of the

---

[1] James elucidates the myth of Africa:
Africans are, and always have been, a backward and barbarous people who have never been able to establish any civilised society of their own. Some of the more liberal would qualify this by saying that this backwardness was due not to any natural inferiority but to the circumstances of their environment, the climate or the soil or the forests, or something of the kind. These barbarous people were brought in contact with civilisation by the brutalities of the slave trade. ... The British government has by and large aimed at bringing these peoples to the stage where they would be able to exercise self-government, despite certain lapses from principle to which all nations, all peoples and all individuals are of course subject, human nature being what it is. It was always a *principle* of the British colonial system, but within recent years with the rise of the colonial peoples, it has been clearly understood and is being carried out. (*Nkrumah and the Ghana Revolution* 29–30)

existence of African history (and even African humanity) and the dismissal of oral history as unreliable and archaeological evidence as inconclusive. It is perhaps yet more directly positioned against the downplaying of anti-imperial revolt by the "disinherited and downtrodden" in the work of philosophers of the history of ideas like Hannah Arendt (Arendt, *On Violence* 21). Arendt would also have occasion to refer to "African literature" as well as Swahili as "nonexistent subjects" (96 n32).[2]

Leeds was in the process of establishing itself in the mid-1960s, through the influence of towering figures like Arthur Ravenscroft and Norman Jeffares, as a major center for the creation of the emerging "Commonwealth" literary studies that would evolve into postcolonial studies, though Ngũgĩ would come to regard Fanon as "the original theorist of the postcolonial" (*Globalectics* 55). Ngũgĩ appreciated the "strong radical tradition" at Leeds, despite what he saw as the oppressiveness of its industrial environment, and he preferred it to Oxford or Cambridge (Marcuson et al. 29). Ngũgĩ studied at Leeds with Arnold Kettle, a member of the Communist Party who was, in his literary criticism, an advocate of a quasi-Leavisite, socialist humanism.[3] While Ngũgĩ was ostensibly working on a dissertation about Conrad's *Under Western Eyes*,[4] he was gaining an awareness of James's sweeping reconceptualization of Pan-African history and the imperial

---

[2] See Hegel's *The Philosophy of History* (93, 99) and Trevor-Roper's remarks (quoted in Appiah, "Africa" 1). Arendt reflects a tendency to discount subaltern resistance: "The rarity of slave rebellions and of uprisings among the disinherited and downtrodden is notorious; on the few occasions when they occurred it was precisely 'mad fury' that turned dreams into nightmares for everybody" (*On Violence* 21). In her reference to African literature, Arendt also cites Swahili as "a nineteenth-century kind of no-language spoken by the Arab ivory and slave caravans, a hybrid mixture of a Bantu dialect with an enormous vocabulary of Arab borrowings" (96 n32).

[3] See Martin Kettle's account of reading MI5's files on his father, Arnold Kettle, revealing that organization's knowledge of his party membership from 1936 till his death, his opposition to the Soviet invasion of Hungary, the party's criticism of his "Leavis critical approach," and the passage of "many Indian and African students" who "appeared to be intellectual types" through the family home in Leeds. The files also note Kettle's "homosexual tendencies," a "secret" his son claims was well-known to the family. Lessing, who knew Kettle when she was a party member, claims that Kettle did not leave the party despite the horrors of Stalinism simply because the party in England accepted his homosexuality (*Walking* 76). Kettle questioned Lessing's criticism of limitations on open critique within the party in passing in "The Artist and Politics" (39–40). In an interview with Asha S. Kanwar, Kettle says that in works like his two-volume *An Introduction to the English Novel*, a text cited by Ngũgĩ (*Globalectics* 20), "[t]he last thing I had in mind was to write Marxist literary criticism—it would be a pretentious thing to do" (58).

[4] Personal communication with Andrew Gurr, February 2013. Sicherman refers to this novel as being much more closely related to Ngũgĩ's academic work: "The most evident proof of the Conradian pudding was to lie in *A Grain of Wheat*, in which he transmuted *Under Western Eyes* into a tale of Kenya at the moment of independence, on the model already exemplified in Kironde's transposition of Synge" (Sicherman, "Ngugi's Colonial" 24).

assault on a transhistorical African consciousness, and his graduate work would focus on Caribbean literature. At Leeds, Ngũgĩ entered the one-year Postgraduate Diploma course in English studies, which included a course on the nineteenth-century novel taught by Kettle. Kettle would impress Ngũgĩ and other African students who formed a tight-knit socially conscious group with his sensitivity, generosity, and materialist literary analysis, inspiring close reading of texts that opened to the possibility of transforming society.[5] Kettle exemplified a critic from English left-wing intellectual circles that had witnessed two world wars. While exercising a type of atheoretical or nondoctrinaire lucidity, his critical writing possessed the characteristic of his milieu that Raymond Williams called "radical populism" (quoted in Nandy 13):

> If we are to seek for the sources of the lucidity and economy of his style, or of the absence, so notable and so easily unnoticed, of any irritable reaching after theory in his work, it is in that milieu that we shall find them. The eschewing of theoretical pretensions is a positive force which is too easily unacknowledged. In contrast to a definitive critical "explanation" grounded in some as yet undiscovered critical theory, Arnold Kettle's critical practice holds out the prospect of an alternative role for the critic—the role of a participant, better informed and trained perhaps but no more infallible than the rest of us, in a process which, far from being conclusive, demands instead to be performed afresh for each new generation of readers. It is a profoundly egalitarian, democratic conception of the critic. (Nandy 14)

Ngũgĩ first acknowledged the "formative" influence of the West Indies in "Africa's political and literary consciousness" in *Homecoming* (81).[6] Part 3 of *Homecoming* was based on the academic work he completed for his graduate thesis, "A Study of the Theme of Alienation in the Fiction of the West Indies, with Particular Reference to the Novels of George Lamming," one that was never formally submitted at Leeds before his departure.[7] In this period, Ngũgĩ was also reading widely beyond the curriculum, and works that influenced him included the plays of Bertolt Brecht, Maxim Gorky's *Mother*, Robert Tressell's *Ragged Trousered Philanthropists*, Marx's *Communist Manifesto*, and Lenin's *Imperialism, The Highest Stage of Capitalism*, but perhaps most of all Fanon's *The Wretched of the Earth*, which became "a kind of Bible" for Leeds's African students as Ngũgĩ later put it (*Moving* 2).

---

[5] See Sicherman's detailed account of Ngũgĩ's years at Leeds in "The Leeds-Makerere Connection and Ngugi's Intellectual Development," to which I am indebted in the following (3–20).

[6] He was also becoming aware that "Africa's presence in the [Black] West Indian consciousness" was central to the quest in so much Caribbean fiction "for an identity in an essentially colonial situation" (*Homecoming* 83, 89).

[7] It appears that John Hearne felt the work required significant revision (Sicherman, "Leeds-Makerere Connection" 8).

The change in political awareness that Ngũgĩ witnessed in this period, however, may have been influenced less by his reading or his reflection on African realities than by his shock at the condition of England. He was appalled by the racism, inequality, and poverty he encountered after the image of the imperial center he had received through his colonial education. As his Leeds colleague Ime Ikiddeh wrote, "Ngugi's Marxist thinking" as it appears in *Homecoming* was ironically the product of the disillusionment of encountering England after the utopian atmosphere of Makerere: "it was the experience of social and economic relations in Britain, more than in Kenya, that actually settled Ngugi's socialist conviction" (Ikiddeh, "Foreword" xii, xiii). In an interview, Ngũgĩ recalled that his introduction to Leeds was not auspicious:

> I found Leeds absolutely depressing. All those houses crouching like old men and women hidden in the mist! Then there is the question of what I had expected. … [C]olonial education made you think of England as the ideal. Well, I was not here for long before I realized that things were not so rosy, that all this idle talk about freedom of the press and freedom of speech, etc., has to be seen in the context of an economic and political life dominated by a few rich men. The whole system is basically wrong. (Marcuson et al. 28)

Peter Nazareth, Ngũgĩ's student colleague at Leeds, had a similar reaction:

> Deep disillusionment. The first big shock was when I got to Leeds. I had never really imagined an industrial city like that. I'd read about it in Lawrence and Dickens but could not imagine an England as nasty as that. Colonialism had persuaded us that England was a perfect place, a developed country where everybody was happy, had perfect knowledge, had good houses. … Otherwise, how were they ruling us? When I got there, it was a real shock to see Leeds. The buildings looked like giant cockroach shells. People used to say that Leeds was a place where you woke up to the sound of birds coughing. The city hall was completely blackened with soot. Before I left, they were cleaning it up so there was this very black building guarded by white lions. Symbolic, perhaps. (quoted in Lovesey, *Ngũgĩ* 14)

The group of Caribbean intellectuals like James and Fanon of such importance to Ngũgĩ were united by "their unapologetic claim to Africa as their roots" (Ngũgĩ, *Writers in Politics*, rev. ed., 134), and some had a similar reaction to England.[8] These West Indians shared with African intellectuals the same "bio-geographic roots," a common history of slavery, colonialism, and resistance, as well as Pan-African aspirations (Ngũgĩ, *Decolonising the Mind* 98). While researching Caribbean novels during his study at Leeds, Ngũgĩ discovered "Africa's dominant

---

[8] Walter Rodney's reaction is not atypical: "There are a host of emotions and fears, phobias and illusions and disillusionments that come from looking at that very, very cold society: the cold buildings, the cold people, the cold food, and everything else that one has to come up against" (*Walter Rodney Speaks* 20).

presence in the West Indian consciousness" and noted "the writers' agonizing sense of exile and persistent groping for some form of cultural identity" (Ikiddeh, "Foreword" xiv). In this period, Ngũgĩ was perhaps primarily focused on writing his lengthy novel set on the eve of Kenyan independence, *A Grain of Wheat*, which has a complex intertextual relationship with Conrad's *Under Western Eyes* but also *Nostromo*,[9] a novel he would say later he appreciated for its multilayered focalization and deferred thematic closure (*Decolonising* 76).[10] He was beginning to be disillusioned, however, with what he would come to describe as Conrad's "moral ambivalence ... towards British imperialism," and the absence in Conrad's novels of "any possibility of redemption arising from the energy of the oppressed" (*Moving* 6), which is so central in James's historical and literary critical work. Under the influence of novelists like Lamming, who had learned the technique from James, and especially Lamming's autobiographical novel *In the Castle of My Skin*,[11] Ngũgĩ was moving in his novelistic work from a focus on a central, flawed protagonist to a broader consideration of a handful of central characters, which would eventually evolve further, in his Gĩkũyũ novels, into a single central character but one who embodied the creative aspirations of the masses. He was searching for a narrative mode that would take him away from the limitations and Eurocentrism of the bildungsroman that he had largely used in his first two novels. In Ngũgĩ's extensive engagement with the literature of the Caribbean, James was a provocative and also synthesizing force, offering a material history, and in his other works an ongoing engagement with cultural forms and also the legacy of his own internalized colonial education and attitudes. James's work, like Said's—and for Said, James is an exemplary figure of the oppositional cultural intellectual—would anticipate postcolonial,[12] trans-Atlantic, and cultural studies. Like Ngũgĩ, James was wary of totalizing systems, though for James these were primarily state capitalism, Stalinism, or fascism, and for Ngũgĩ neocolonialism and, later, globalization. Both James and Ngũgĩ would take advantage of a freedom from state repression and censorship in an otherwise tragic exile to write some of

---

[9] See Nazareth's analysis of the relationship between *A Grain of Wheat* and *Nostromo* as well as *Under Western Eyes* in "Is *A Grain of Wheat* a Socialist Novel?" (247–9) and "Teaching *A Grain of Wheat* as a Dialogue with Conrad" (165–70). See, too, Bronstein (411–37).

[10] Ngũgĩ's position resembles Kettle's: "*Nostromo* is, from the technical point of view, an amazing *tour de force*" (*An Introduction to the English Novel* 2: 71).

[11] Lamming notes in an interview that it was from James that he learned to employ in his narratives "the creative power of mass, the central character is usually the mass more than the individual" (Lamming, "C.L.R. James" 29, 35).

[12] "Writing across the cultural geographies of Europe, Asia, the Caribbean and the United States, C.L.R. James provides a postcolonial revision of the ideas of modernity. He is a secular intellectual, practiced in the magic arts of interpretation; a revolutionary thinker who looks to the future and frees the past" writes Bhabha in the paperback jacket promotion for James's *American Civilization*.

their major works.[13] There is a marked autobiographical cast to the work of both writers,[14] which is explored further in Chapter 5, and a similar acknowledgment of the legacy of a colonized mentality. Both were deeply read in Victorian classics and the Bible, both were products of elite colonial schools, and both had a profoundly disillusioning encounter with the imperial center, to which cricket was James's passport and English Ngũgĩ's. Both writers have been marked forever by certain positions they took early in their careers, however much their ideas changed over the many decades of a tumultuous century. It might even be said that James saved Ngũgĩ's life by warning him in London not to return to Kenya after the release of *Detained*, examined in Chapter 5: "They will kill you in six months, the way they did Walter Rodney" (Ngũgĩ, *Moving* 103). James's words were the first of a number of stark warnings culminating in Ngũgĩ's decision to accept exile.

As Sylvia Wynter puts it, James "lived all the contradictions" of his colonial and postcolonial condition and his "pluri-consciousness" (70, 69). He was

> a Negro yet British, a colonial native yet culturally a part of the public school code, attached to the cause of the proletariat yet a member of the middle class, a Marxian yet a Puritan, an intellectual who plays cricket, of African descent yet Western, a Trotskyist and Pan-Africanist, a Marxist yet a supporter of black studies, a West Indian majority black yet an American minority black. (69)

James was often referred to as a "Renaissance man" or even the "Black Plato" (Cudjoe and Cain, *C.L.R. James: His Intellectual Legacies* 7; Buhle, *C.L.R. James: The Artist* 1). He would become "the grand patriarch of contemporary West Indian culture" establishing a creative and critical heritage for "many Caribbean intellectuals and artists" (Said, *Culture* 257, 313), but he was also a figure of enormous importance for Ngũgĩ and Said. Like Wynter, Said lists James's diverse achievements and identities, his autodidacticism and protean imagination, pointing out that "above all he was a revolutionary steeped in African, Caribbean, and Black nationalism" (*Culture* 248). Meeting in Brixton, London, when James was 86, Said remembers an elder statesman who was still "the precocious schoolboy, with the revolutionary's interest in history, politics, and theory, and the intellectual's attentiveness to ideas, contradictions, and the sheer sporty adventurousness of

---

[13] Walcott notes "the irony that the freedom James sought he could find perhaps only in England, which is a great place of exiled everythings" (34). Ngũgĩ remarked in 1989 that discussions he engages in freely in an American classroom would land him in jail in Kenya (*Moving* 157).

[14] Grimshaw remarks on James's autobiographical project:
> In a sense, then, both *Mariners, Renegades and Castaways* and the longer, unfinished work, *American Civilization*, can be understood as the first stage in James's attempt to place himself in history, an autobiographical project which occupied him intermittently in his final years. This was so not just because together they contain the fullest statement of his political position as he reached the peak of his creative powers; but also because they have at their heart the excavation of the intellectual tradition to which James himself was so closely bound. (Anna Grimshaw and Keith Hart, "*American Civilization*: An Introduction" 16-17)

good literature, music, and conversation" (247). For Said, James is an exemplary oppositional scholar and cultural intellectual who addressed a broad metropolitan and "Third World" audience from the ambivalent, audacious hybrid position of both insider and outsider. In Said's estimation, James, with his immersion in European culture, is a figure much like Said himself, a type of Caribbean Edward Said. Just as Said was ambivalent about the postcolonial, James resisted studying the legacy of empire in narrow disciplinary silos as well as the formation of new disciplines.[15] While entertaining no illusions about the ruthless self-interest behind imperialism, James was for Said, like Fanon and Cabral, a revolutionary cultural figure whose work challenged "the unity forged between imperialism and culture" (277). Hence, James provides a central illustration of one of Said's main themes in *Culture and Imperialism*. Said traces a creative narrative pattern in James's history of resistance: "his basic metaphor is that of a voyage taken by ideas and people; those who were slaves and subservient classes could first become the immigrants and then the principal intellectuals of a diverse new society" (253). What might be read as the triumphalism of this narrative is overshadowed in Said's analysis by the pervasive sense of disappointment in and exclusion from the European intellectual tradition that was of such importance in James's intellectual history.

James was unapologetic about his own embedding in Englishness—sometimes appearing almost as if he were the last Victorian—and he was acutely aware, like Lamming, of his own detachment from his Caribbean and African origins, while maintaining a clear commitment to revolutionary politics. As Derek Walcott points out, "Much criticism of Caribbean achievement is based on 'despite,'" but there is no "despite" in James whatsoever (Walcott, "A Tribute" 35). James's celebration of Caribbean culture and Caribbean futures was sometimes, for Walcott, too "oratorical," "prophetic," and even "ecclesiastical" and sometimes "hectoring" (36, 38, 44). He did not entertain false modesty. In one of his autobiographical fragments, James implies, for example, that it was in his reading of Victorian novels in Trinidad that he first encountered the ideas of Marx (Grimshaw, "Preface" vii). He accepted the absence or obliteration of an indigenous Caribbean identity, but he focused "less on the losses that resulted from de-Africanization" than the "potential gains of Europeanization" (Henry and Buhle, "Preface" x). This is what Lamming in an interview from 1987 refers to as "the problem of what we would call the Euro-centered James" (32). While it was the site of a tragic history, James's Caribbean was open to modernism and pluralism, and its intellectuals were exposed to a possibly volatile but strengthening ideological challenge (Lazarus, "Cricket" 102; Lai 180). Hence, James did not regard the overwhelming influence of European civilization in the Caribbean or, importantly, the legacy of the English language—something of crucial significance for Ngũgĩ in the African context—as problematic.

Moreover, James, the son of a schoolteacher and himself briefly a teacher and a patriarch who was regarded by many, including Lamming, Rodney, and Walcott, in

---

[15] James was particularly impatient with "Black Studies" or what he called "intellectual sloth in the name of 'Blackness'" (quoted in Buhle, *C.L.R. James: The Artist* 155).

this role, considered that due to its "uniqueness" the Caribbean could be a teacher or mentor and influence the fate of Africa.[16] The "double consciousness of the Caribbean," for James, in the assessment of Stuart Hall, "was not a burden, but a gift" (Hall quoted in Schwarz 271). On the other hand, for James, there was always something theoretical or perhaps utopian about Africa; Africa, for James, was, in Farrukh Dhondy's formulation, an "abstract concept" (155).[17] James, however, may have shared this alienation from Africa with many West Indians, who, as Lamming would write in the late 1950s, still suffered from a residual historical "amnesia" concerning Africa and "still have to learn that Africa existed ... as a home where men were alive and engaged in a human struggle with nature" (*Pleasures* 224, 155). Like Césaire's dream of Africa—Césaire being a poet for whom a knowledge of Africa was a matter of interactions in Paris with Africans as well as "ethnographic studies" (Césaire, "An Interview" 87)—James's Africa was initially a scholarly archive in France. One of those unusual Caribbean expatriates in England, also James's student, who saw the mythic return to Africa only as a by-road to the ultimate return to the true homeland in the Caribbean, was Walter Rodney (Rodney, *Walter* 33). Rodney's most famous book, *How Europe Underdeveloped Africa*, is a Jamesean counterdiscourse aimed partly at the historical masternarratives of "bourgeois scholars" and European apologists for empire whose work had contributed to underdevelopment and a yet more destructive dependency (Rodney, *How Europe* 20, 104). Like James, Rodney would return to the Caribbean and its politics, having discovered a way of being a "revolutionary intellectual," a phrase his teachers considered oxymoronic as he reflected in *Walter Rodney Speaks: The Making of an African Intellectual*, but he would later advocate the figure of the institutionally embedded but oppositional "guerrilla intellectual" (19, 112–14).[18] Rodney's work was terminated by political assassination, and hence we have James's warning to Ngũgĩ. James's nearly evangelical zeal for the power of ideas and his "overwhelming confidence in his capacity to make ideas function as a force" in fact may have jeopardized his effectiveness as a political organizer (Lamming, "C.L.R. James" 31).[19] James entertained grand schemes for political action. In particular, James believed that "a federated Caribbean ... would have

---

[16] Elaine Savory discusses the immense, worldwide influence of Caribbean intellectuals under the rubric of her term "logo/rhythms" ("Postcolonialism" 219–20).

[17] Per Wästberg evoked the notion of an "abstract Africa" in 1967 at the African-Scandinavian Writers' Conference in Stockholm (12), in which he stresses the conference's focus on continental, and not diasporic Pan-African, writing (9).

[18] Sited primarily in universities and struggling against "white thought, white institutions, and white learning" but also "expropriating bourgeois knowledge," this figure is a type of Che Guevara who has not taken up a gun (*Walter Rodney Speaks* 112, 113).

[19] James's optimism about the inevitability of revolution never waned. As Martin Glaberman notes of scholars' impatience with the pace of political change within a study of James's Marxism: "In American sociology there is the myth that workers are plagued with the desire for instant gratification. In reality, it is the petty bourgeois intellectual who needs instant political gratification" (307).

had the intellectual resources that could have been very decisive in its influence on African leadership" (Lamming 33). James was fated to be more effective as an intellectual and one who inspired others to action, though as Lamming recalls, there was some resistance to James's Eurocentrism and his somewhat patronizing notion of Caribbean mentoring for Africa, holding that "the evolution of the African intellectual has its own interpretation of Europe" (33).

James notes that as a schoolboy and young man, he lived "according to the tenets of Matthew Arnold"[20] and that while raised in Trinidad, "[i]ntellectually I lived abroad, chiefly in England" (*Beyond* 71). When, in 1932, he boarded a boat for England, he writes, "[t]he British intellectual was going to Britain" (114). His alienation from his identity as a Caribbean was fostered by his schooling and especially its colonial history curriculum:

> It was only long years after that I understood the limitation on spirit, vision and self-respect which was imposed on us by the fact that our masters, our curriculum, our code of morals, *everything* began from the basis that Britain was the source of all light and leading, and our business was to admire, wonder, imitate, learn. (38–9)

Like Ngũgĩ at Alliance, however, James considered his school "our little Eden" (39), a perception influenced by his love for cricket as well as his wide personal reading. The seeds of his future counterhegemonic incursion into Caribbean history were planted in this school and his dawning awareness of exclusion:

> when reading elementary English history books, I became resentful of the fact that the English always won all, or nearly all of the battles. ... as far back as I can trace my consciousness the original found itself and came to maturity within a system that was the result of centuries of development in another land, was transplanted as a hot-house flower is transplanted and bore some strange fruit. (49–50)

London provided an intellectual vortex, a school for anticolonial revolution, and a site for dreaming a Pan-African future (a notion that had been revived by James in the 1920s) in the mid-twentieth century[21] with a collection of emerging African national voices, eventually including Nkrumah's and Kenyatta's, gathering around the organization founded by West Indian and Afro-American theorists, activists, and intellectuals like James, George Padmore, and Du Bois.

---

[20] See Kenneth Surin's discussion of the Arnoldean influence in James (187–90). As Anna Grimshaw and Keith Hart point out, James styled one of his last major, unpublished works, *American Civilization*, around binaries of civilization and barbarism, democracy and totalitarianism (19), and this may well have been an unconscious borrowing from Arnold.

[21] In this period, London was also "indisputably the West Indian literary capital" as Kenneth Ramchand noted in his 1969 introduction to a republication of James's 1936 novel *Minty Alley* (5).

The West Indians in this group encountered their distinctly Caribbean identity in some cases for the first time by interacting with others from their home in this milieu. "In this sense," as Lamming writes, "most West Indians of my generation were born in England" (*Pleasures* 214). Padmore brought to the African Bureau in London his disillusionment with Stalinism as a model for Africa after his work for the Comintern in Soviet Russia, and he would finally be honored as the "Father of African Emancipation" in Ghana. Padmore's work drew on the Pan-Africanism of Du Bois who, like James, brought his historical knowledge of the slave trade and the American civil war to this Pan-African organizational work.[22] They debated whether anticolonial movements in Africa in the postwar period could evolve independent from anti-imperial agitation in Europe or the rest of the world, and they wondered if primarily illiterate peasant societies possessed the required revolutionary vanguard. There was, however, another significant point of contention.

James broke with Trotsky and Padmore broke with the Soviets mainly due to the Russians' view of race as peripheral or "incidental" to class struggle—a notion of profound importance to Ngũgĩ[23]—remaining adamant that the issue of race would melt away in postrevolutionary societies.[24] For Padmore, and also Fanon, who would be skeptical about what he saw as Pan-Africanism's elitism and conservatism, the Communist failure to support black liberation struggles led to a decisive rupture (Srivastava, "Travels of the Organic Intellectual" 55–79).[25] James and Padmore further considered the role of general strikes, boycotts, and violence, as well as the effects such shifts in theory, planning, and practice would have on classic Marxist theory (James, *Nkrumah* 74). As James recalls, it was the

---

[22] James's account of nineteenth-century abolitionist intellectuals like Frederick Douglass in *American Civilization* is informed by contemporary reflections on America in the 1940s. For James, "The Negro question in the United States is the No. 1 minority problem in the modern world" and the situation is worse than European fascism because it is enforced not only by state violence but also by "the mass of the white population" (201, 202). In addition, a "Negro intelligentsia" is being prepared to function as Macaulay's native interpreter in the economy (206).

[23] Ngũgĩ refers to the mistaken notion of making race "incidental" to politics in *Something Torn and New* (110) and *Globalectics* (22). It was articulated in Césaire's *Discours sur le Colonialisme* [*Discourse on Colonialism*] published in 1955 when Césaire recalls "criticiz[ing] the Communists for forgetting our Negro characteristics. They ... acted like abstract Communists. I maintained that the political question could not do away with our condition as Negroes. We are Negroes, with a great number of historical peculiarities" (85).

[24] The same issue, along with shock over the excesses of Stalinism, would provoke Césaire's break from the Communist Party in Trinidad in 1956.

[25] Srivastava, in "The Travels of the Organic Intellectual: The Black Colonized Intellectual in George Padmore and Frantz Fanon," provides a valuable account of the notion of the intellectual in Padmore, Fanon, and Gramsci, and their shared emphasis on the solidarity of the intellectual and the people (55–79).

nearly absolute alienation from Africa in the experience of these West Indians that galvanized their fervor for independence. In addition, they were the products of colonial education:

> They had had the benefit of the excellent, if rather academic, system of secondary education which existed in the islands. Having no native culture, no native language, no native religion and being raised entirely in the British tradition, they mixed easily in English intellectual and left-wing political circles. In the political thirties they participated fully in the intense discussions and activities of the time, and few in England, except European refugees, had had more actual inside experience of revolutionary politics than Padmore. It was to this circle with its accumulated knowledge, experience and wide contacts that Nkrumah was introduced in June 1945. (76–7)

James's historical work on the revolution in San Domingo in *The Black Jacobins* almost single-handedly reconceptualized the understanding of revolutionary historical change, and would later inflect his comprehension of the "reasonable madness" that was revolution in Ghana (130). James in this period was becoming somewhat disillusioned with doctrinaire Marxist assumptions that world revolution would begin in Europe within the industrial working class, and he would later begin to associate with a group of radical socialists, the Johnson-Forest Tendency, whose vision for change lay in small, casually organized, autonomous collectives, and not all-powerful, dictatorial, Soviet-style state structures or the actions of a vanguard party led by an intellectual elite. However, Ghanaian independence and later the anticolonial struggle in Kenya led him to rethink his own historiography. As he came to recognize, *The Black Jacobins* "implied that the African revolution would be similarly contingent upon the socialist revolution in Europe. It did not envisage independent movement of Africans as being able to succeed in face of the enormous military power that a stable imperialist government would be able to bring to bear" (James, *Nkrumah* 68–9). He anticipates with great prescience that Africa's future will be "violent and strange" as well as "unpredictable" (69).

A History of Pan-African Revolt is in a sense a sequel to *The Black Jacobins* and it "embraces the whole scope of revolts ... in the Pan-African world since the time of the San Domingo Revolution" (Holloway viii). James writes the history of revolution as engaged revolutionary history, and he always seeks to link past events with those of the present, *The Black Jacobins* concluding, for example, with a lengthy appendix extending its analysis of the revolutionary leader Toussaint L'Ouverture to include Fidel Castro.[26] As he states emphatically in *Nkrumah and the Ghana Revolution*, "it is the present, and not researches into archives which

---

[26] Said remarks perceptively that James answers a vital question in this chapter: "How can a non- or post-imperial history be written that is not naively utopian or hopelessly pessimistic, given the continuing embroiled actuality of domination in the Third World? This is a methodological and meta-historical aporia, and James's swift resolution of it is brilliantly imaginative" (Said, *Culture* 280).

determine our understanding of the past" (107). For James, the expansion of imperial control in Africa provoked "a series of revolts, which have never ceased" (*History of Pan-African* 41), and he ever seeks to update his analysis to include current developments. This examination of linkages or "counterpoint" is partly, too, a consequence of recognizing imperialism as a project that requires at least two parties.[27] He distinguishes in his history of Pan-African revolt between resource and settler colonies, maintaining that the latter, as in South Africa, Rhodesia, and Kenya, based on a wholesale appropriation of land, could only be operated through a system of state terrorism. Despite regional variations and distinctions between French, Italian, German, Belgian, and English colonial methods, "imperialism remains imperialism" (44). James's history is an account of intellectual leaders, whether politician-philosophers turned presidents such as Nyerere or Nkrumah or activist organizers like Marcus Garvey. James is careful to include an account of Afro-American resistance in his survey of Pan-African revolts.

As in Ngũgĩ's journalistic dismissals of Négritude and "slogans" about the "African personality" considered in the last chapter, James is largely contemptuous of Garvey though he credits him with a major accomplishment in reconnecting Afro-Americans with their African roots. James considers the rise of Garvey in a period when Southern whites in America reasserted the values that had administered slavery using the myth of Afro-American male desire for white women as "propaganda ... to cover the naked economic exploitation" (76). Garvey had come from Jamaica to the United States, which in that period was "the Mecca of all West Indian Negroes" and would be so important to other writers like Lamming and to James himself (78). Garvey's Back to Africa campaign James calls "pitiable rubbish" (79), a scheme promoted by an unscrupulous man whose ideas were based on a type of internalized racial inferiority and an acceptance of essential race-based psychological naïveté that in turn evoked in Garvey a desire for mimicry. Soon Garvey "appointed himself President, Emperor, King and what not, of Africa, and created a string of Negro nobility, and titled followers, from Dukes to plain baronets" (80–81). However, while in James's estimation, Garvey's "movement was in many respects absurd and in others thoroughly dishonest," it was of great importance for making "the American Negro conscious of his African origin and [it] created for the first time a feeling of international solidarity among Africans and people of African descent" (82).

In his update on the history of African revolt from 1939 to 1969, James gives close attention to Kenya and Tanzania, as would Ngũgĩ in his early theoretical

---

[27] Said presents this caution in reading James: "If these ideas of counterpoint, intertwining, and integration have anything more to them than a blandly uplifting suggestion for catholicity of vision, it is that they reaffirm the historical experience of imperialism as a matter first of interdependent histories, overlapping domains, second of something requiring intellectual and political choices" (Said, *Culture* 259).

works. He offers an incisive examination of the "myth of Mau Mau"[28] in which he makes clear that "[n]ot African beliefs and tribal practices but land and white settlers on the land were to be decisive in shaping the character of the black revolt in Kenya" (109). Significantly, he notes that anticolonial and antisettler resistance did not begin in the 1940s or 1950s, but were "continuous" from the earliest attempts to appropriate land and to make Kenya into "white man's country" (110). In tracing some of the developments during the Emergency, James seeks to elevate certain nationalist leaders, including Dedan Kimathi and Stanley Mathenge, a desire that would inform a good deal of Ngũgĩ's work and particularly his cowritten play on Kimathi and his later allegorical treatment of Mathenge in *Matigari*, in order to point to the intellectual leadership of the movement, its organization, and its clearly defined goals. The aim of those, like Kimathi, who continued their struggle to the end was, over and above bare survival and the goals of land and freedom, "to attract international attention to their cause. No outside help was forthcoming, and the Emergency did not give rise to a major political investigating commission from Britain" (111). James gives significant attention to this call for international attention and to the concentration camps established to terrorize and repress the movement that would themselves eventually lead to the scandal that galvanized international, and particularly English parliamentary attention. The conditions of what Elkins calls "Britain's gulag," as mentioned earlier, would be thoroughly investigated in Elkins's own *Imperial Reckoning: The Untold Story of Britain's Gulag in Kenya*, Anderson's *Histories of the Hanged: The Dirty War in Kenya and the End of Empire*, and Cobain's *Cruel Britannia: A Secret History of Torture*. More than half a century after these events, survivors seek redress in British courts. James notes, "Some 50,000 Kikuyu and other revolutionaries were detained in special camps to undergo special training to cure them of the mental disease which the British authorities discovered as the cause of their refusal to submit" (112). These assessments of the role of international outrage at the atrocities and the concern of the British about the effect of such practices on the perpetrators, while of vital importance, tend to minimize the impact of Kenyan resistance in effecting the departure of the colonizers.

James outlines the rapid succession of independent African states in the 1950s and 1960s as well as the rise of military dictatorships. He targets "the continued exploitation by the industrial and finance-capital of Europe and the United States," the catastrophic reduction in commodity prices and escalation in costs for manufactured items, as well as the tainted legacy of the colonial states themselves. Citing Fanon, James notes that often "the newly independent African state was

---

[28] James notes that
what was (by the British) labelled as Mau Mau was an ad hoc body of beliefs, oaths, disciplines newly created for the specific purpose of gathering and strengthening the struggle against British imperialism, its military, political and economic domination and, in particular, the Christianity it sought to inject and impose. (*History of Pan-African* 112–13)

little more than the old imperialist state only now administered and controlled by black nationalists" (116). The model is reflected in the Caribbean where, despite a modernized population that has produced internationally recognized intellectual giants such as Garvey, Fanon, Padmore, and Césaire, "black men administer the imperialist interests" and "the economy continues to be a colonialist economy of the seventeenth century, completely dominated by foreign powers" (129). In contrast, James points to the example of Tanzania and the leadership of Nyerere as being "one of the foremost political phenomena of the twentieth century" (117), a state organized on cooperative principles that James maintains incorporated some of the late realizations of Lenin. Its brand of "African socialism," a term he despises due to its use in the "bureaucratic balderdash" of certain repressive African regimes and its association with "what exists in Russia and Eastern Europe" (137, 136), is potentially revolutionary. For James, the experiments in Tanzania and Zambia offer a "new African conception of the future of Africa [that] lays claim not only to a future, but also to deep roots in the past" (139), an optimism that would be severely tested in the next decades.[29]

James's praise for Nyerere and Kaunda in particular, however, would appear to overstrain even James's resilient optimism and contradict his unreserved faith in the masses. As Paul Buhle notes, James's celebration of these presidents "seemed to close observers altogether too representative of the elder thinker's desperation at finding hope, most uncharacteristically for him, in the wrong place—among the leaders rather than the mass"; moreover, his criticism of these leaders and his faith in the viability of intellectual leadership from the Caribbean—"that the West Indian legacy from Europe could serve as an international-theoretical guide in the Third World"—in turn would test these leaders' reliance on James's words of advice (Buhle, *C.L.R. James: The Artist* 141). But in the late 1960s, James could still predict that these two countries in particular "can initiate a new road for Africa—the mobilisation of the African people to build an African society in an African way" (140). In addition, these experiments in creating a new type of state "can fertilise and reawaken the mortuary that is socialist theory and practice in the advanced countries" (143). Tanzania, Zambia, and the West Indies are points of light indicating the possibility of a Pan-African renaissance, a phrase to which Ngũgĩ's recent writing returns. As James says of the West Indies: "Small as they are, their historical origin and development have been such that these Caribbean islands can make highly significant contributions to the economics and politics of a world in torment" (131). James is primarily focused on reversing a reductive, evolutionary understanding of Pan-African history that on a national and global scale is based on the model by which ontology replicates phylogeny: "African achievement, discoveries and creations [are treated] as if Western civilisation was the norm and the African people spent their years in imitating, trying to reach or,

---

[29] See, for example, René Dumont and Marie-France Mottin's *Stranglehold on Africa* and Dumont's *False Start in Africa*.

worse still, if necessary going through the primitive early stages of the Western world" (131).

"If I could make every black person read one book on the history of black people in the West," Ngũgĩ wrote in *Moving the Center*, "that would have to be C.L.R. James's *The Black Jacobins*" (142).[30] In *The Black Jacobins*, James recounts the dramatic story of the revolution in San Domingo (Haiti) in the eighteenth century, "the only successful slave revolt in history" and "one of the great epics of revolutionary struggle and achievement" ("Preface" ix). James's account reads like a historical novel, with the heroic figure of Toussaint L'Ouverture at its center. It is the history of a great man[31] informed by the analyses of Marx and Engels as well as Lenin and Trotsky, and comparisons with subsequent revolutionary movements to show the operation of an underlying masternarrative of history.[32] It ends with a lengthy appendix extending James's study of great men from L'Ouverture to Fidel Castro. For Ngũgĩ, the book was "written with Africa in mind," proposing that the Haitians' struggle against slavery and imperialism "could be replicated in Africa and the entire Caribbean region in the twentieth century" (Ngũgĩ, *Something Torn* 73). James's account is also driven by an awareness of Aristotelian and Shakespearean tragedy (252–92), perhaps a residue of his work's origins as a play performed by Paul Robeson under the auspices of the League for the Protection of Abyssinia after Italy's invasion of Ethiopia, itself the image of a heroic African past (Hall, "C.L.R. James" 8). Designed as counterhistory, as James writes in the Foreword of 1980, the study was a reaction to his irritation with "reading and hearing about Africans being persecuted and oppressed in Africa, in the Middle Passage, in the USA and all over the Caribbean" ([v]). This was the legacy of historians like James Anthony Froude who, in *The English in the West Indies* (1888), produced after what he admits was a "flying visit" to the region (127), dismissed the possibility of independence in the Caribbean being achieved by former slaves.[33]

---

[30] Lamming in 1960 wrote similarly that "*Black Jacobins* should be Bible-reading for every boy who would be acquainted with the period in question" and he points to the significance of its being out-of-print for decades (*Pleasures* 119).

[31] Writing in 1938, James notes the present tendency
to a personification of the social forces, [with] great men being merely or nearly instruments in the hands of economic destiny. ... Great men make history, but only such history as it is possible for them to make. Their freedom of achievement is limited by the necessities of their environment. To portray the limits of those necessities and the realisation, complete or partial, of all possibilities, that is the true business of the historian. ("Preface to the First Edition" x)

[32] As James puts in *Nkrumah and the Ghana Revolution*: "The theoretical basis of the book [*The Black Jacobins*] ... is that in a period of world-wide revolutionary change ... the revolutionary crisis lifts backward peoples over centuries and projects them into the very forefront of the advanced movement of the day" (66).

[33] "[W]eak nations" may only gain freedom, he maintains, "when they are subject to the rule of others who are at once powerful and just. This was the duty which fell to the

In James's narrative, L'Ouverture is a visionary and a brilliant strategist and diplomat, as well as being courteous and learned, but he was also a man of his time and place who was flawed by a certain arrogance and a fatal "neglect of his own people" shown in his distrust of their capacities to help him realize his desire to create a post-revolutionary society without racial discrimination (240). As a result, he was overly conciliatory toward white colonists, which provoked sustained suspicion toward him among the majority of the population, and he was also somewhat naïve about the ruthlessness of European hostility to a state in the Caribbean that had outlawed slavery. To train a second generation of "black and Mulatto" children to be an intellectual elite in the new society, he even sent them to be educated in France. He also harbored a dream of ending slavery by freeing Africa itself:

> He cherished a project of sailing to Africa ... and there conquering vast tracts of country, putting an end to the slave-trade, and making millions of blacks "free and French," as his Constitution had made the blacks of San Domingo. It was no dream. ... What spirit was it that moved him? Ideas do not fall from heaven. The great revolution had propelled him out of his humble joys and obscure destiny, and the trumpets of its heroic period rang ever in his ears. In him, born a slave and the leader of slaves, the concrete realisation of liberty, equality and fraternity was the womb of ideas and the springs of power, which overflowed their narrow environment and embraced the whole of the world. But for the revolution, this extraordinary man and his band of gifted associates would have lived their lives as slaves, serving the commonplace creatures who owned them, standing barefooted and in rags to watch inflated little governors and mediocre

---

Latin race two thousand years ago. In these modern times it has fallen to ours, and in the discharge of it the highest features in the English character have displayed themselves" (Froude 207). After emancipation of the slaves in the West Indies,

> [t]he blacks could not be trusted, with the equally dangerous supremacy which their numbers would insure them. ... If you choose to take a race like the Irish or like the negroes whom you have forced into an unwilling subjection and ... strike the fetters off them, and arm them at once with all the powers and privileges of loyal citizens, you ought not to be surprised if they attribute your concessions to fear, and if they turn again and rend you. (208)

Froude comments on former slaves:

> Nature has made us unequal, and Acts of Parliament cannot make us equal. Some must lead and some must follow, and the question is only of degree and kind. ... The negroes of the West Indies are children, and not yet disobedient children. They have their dreams, but for the present they are dreams only. If you enforce self-government upon them when they are not asking for it, you may turn the dream into a reality, and wilfully drive them back into the condition of their ancestors, from which the slave trade was the beginning of their emancipation. (235–6)

Later, he concludes, "[t]he generality [of "the blacks"] are mere good-natured animals" (348).

officials from Europe pass by, as many a talented African stands in Africa to-day [as James wrote in 1938]. (265)

He was unable to accept, however, that "a population of slaves recently landed from Africa could ... attain to civilisation by 'going it alone'" and he was fatally attracted to the ideals of the French revolution[34] and to a belief in the absolute necessity of maintaining ties with France to access the principles and technologies of modernity (289–90). As Hall maintains, James shows that L'Ouverture became his own phantom double, the autocratic Napoleon, a precursor of Stalin (Hall, "C.L.R. James" 9). Ultimately, in the face of a French force of 20,000 dedicated to the restoration of slavery and a violent insurrection in his own ranks, L'Ouverture enacted harsh repression against his own people, and caught between contending forces he became "the embodiment of vacillation" (290). He hoped for a reconciliation with France until the final fight with its set battles, sieges, exterminations of civilians and soldiers on both sides along racial lines, guerrilla war, and diplomatic treachery. Ultimately, in James's assessment, though Napoleon would come to recognize that he should have ruled the colony by proxy through L'Ouverture, the failure of L'Ouverture's leadership doomed the campaign: "The black revolution had passed him by" (321, 373).

Ngũgĩ interprets James's account of leadership and its failure as an early example of the development of the native intellectual interpreter:

> The leader of a revolution ... is often one of those who have taken advantage of the language and culture of the oppressor. This is because he knows all the contradictions inside the language and culture of his captors. He was being trained to be a good Macaulay's man, carrying the mind of the English in his black body, but instead he is translating reality from the standpoint of the minds of the dwellers in the cave. He is a double spy. The assimilated begins to curse in exquisite French. ... By this time he has already become a traitor to his historical calling as a conveyor of messages from the West and a spy for the West among his people. So words like "traitor," "ungrateful," "uppity," are often used against this kind of interpreter. (*Penpoints* 84)

For Ngũgĩ, the heroic rebel leader of eighteenth-century Haiti is the type of the intellectual elite in colonial and presumably neocolonial societies. In a characteristically Jamesian gesture, Ngũgĩ projects James's insights onto later historical developments.

---

[34] James qualifies L'Ouverture's admiration, however:
It is Toussaint's supreme merit that while he saw European civilisation as a valuable and necessary thing, and strove to lay its foundations among his people, he never had the illusion that it conferred any moral superiority. He knew French, British, and Spanish imperialists for the insatiable gangsters that they were, that there is no oath too sacred for them to break, no crime, deception, treachery, cruelty, destruction of human life and property which they would not commit against those who could not defend themselves. (*Black Jacobins* 271)

In *Nkrumah and the Ghana Revolution,* a discussion of the profound importance of Ghanaian independence "which had struck imperialism in Africa the blow from which it would never recover" (7), James considers with dismay the developing crisis in the country. In many respects his account of independence in Ghana, like *The Black Jacobins,* is an extended reflection on leadership and particularly the relationship between the moment of revolutionary crisis and the tactics of individual leaders. James's studies of revolutionary leaders also seek to reignite a fervor for "the genuinely revolutionary process" with which "our age has lost contact" due to the distortions of "parliamentary fetishism and the falsifications and bureaucratisation of the concept of leadership by Stalinism" (James, *Nkrumah* 100). While considering the somewhat deterministic statements of theorists such as Engels and Trotsky about the leader's fortuitous wisdom at the moment of revolutionary crisis, James subscribes to the dictum of Jules Michelet: "The chief actor is the people" (quoted on 105),[35] but he also claims that Nkrumah "was able to give the unverbalised desires of an unexpressed people a concrete form which could satisfy their highest aspirations and open out always widening vistas" (112), and that he embodied symbolically "the will of the people" (134). James holds to this principle of the people as somehow embodied in the revolutionary leviathan when assessing Nkrumah's reception in Ghana as if it were the Second Coming but also the varied support offered his organizations. He deplores many of the problems that assaulted Nkrumah's new nation: rampant corruption, the leader's own messianic megalomania and paranoia, and the illegal suppression of oppositional voices, representative of the all-too-frequent postindependence "African degeneration" (11). In this context, he considers the position of the intellectual who is "at the helm":

> He succeeds—or independent Africa sinks: unlike Britain in the seventeenth and France in the eighteenth centuries, there is no class on which the nation falls back after the intellectuals have led the revolution as far as it can go. ... As in Russia after the 1917 revolution, it is the intellectuals who will lead the continent. Yet Western racial prejudice is so much a part of the Western outlook on life that the African intellectual continues to be looked upon as some kind of primitive barbarian climbing the sharp and slippery slope to civilisation. (15)

For James, "the African intellectual is a modern type, and will never be understood except as a type of Western intellectual" (James, *Nkrumah* 16), largely as a consequence of colonial education.[36] As a result, in James's estimation, this intellectual is necessarily alienated. In a gesture anticipating one aspect of Said's view of the intellectual, but in a radically different cultural and political context, James maintains that the African intellectual is perpetually in exile, self-

---

[35] James remained an unapologetic student of the French Revolution and Michelet (Foot 99–101).

[36] James's biographer Kent Worcester notes that he "openly rejected the category of 'intellectual'" (xii).

alienated, and sunk in endless vacillation. This vacillation defines "the crisis of the intellectuals of all the underdeveloped countries and African peoples" (James, *Nkrumah* 18). For Nkrumah, however, African intellectuals had a duty as "the intellectual vanguard" to overcome this inherited lassitude and exercise their revolutionary role. The acknowledgment that this vanguard would be created through an educational process was made with an understanding of the limitations placed on education by colonial authorities. As Nkrumah writes in one of his manifestoes on Pan-Africanism,[37] *Africa Must Unite*: "The history of human achievement illustrates that when an awakened intelligentsia emerges from a subject people it becomes the vanguard of the struggle against alien rule. There is a direct relation between this fact and the neglect of the imperial powers to provide for the proper growth of educational facilities in their colonies" (43). Nkrumah cites an estimate from 1939 that at the current rate of school expansion it would take 700 years before universal literacy could be achieved in the Gold Coast, and he regards the pace and nature of educational development to be at the root of the postindependence shortage of skilled labor in all sectors and the continuing desire among many of those educated in the liberal arts for a sinecure in the civil service (45). The root of the problem lies in colonial policy:

> Our pattern of education has been aligned hitherto to the demands of British examination councils. Above all, it was formulated and administered by an alien administration desirous of extending its dominant ideas and thought processes to us. We were trained to be inferior copies of Englishmen, caricatures to be laughed at with our pretensions to British bourgeois gentility, our grammatical faultiness and distorted standards betraying us at every turn. We were neither fish nor fowl. We were denied the knowledge of our African past and informed that we had no present. What future could there be for us? We were taught to regard our culture and traditions as barbarous and primitive. Our text-books were English text-books, telling us about English history, English geography, English ways of living, English customs, English ideas, English weather. Many of these manuals had not been altered since 1895. (Nkrumah, *Africa Must Unite* 49)

As in James's view of the need for a certain species of leadership, Nkrumah acknowledges the role of intellectuals in the large task of educational development, because "it is vital that we should nurture our own culture and history if we are to develop that African personality which must provide the educational and intellectual foundations of our Pan-African future" (49).

---

[37] In "Continental Government for Africa" from *Africa Must Unite*, Nkrumah calls for continental African union in all areas, a demand that would inform his work to create the Organization of African Unity: "It is for us to grasp what is a golden opportunity to prove that the genius of the African people can surmount the separatist tendencies in sovereign nationhood by coming together speedily, for the sake of Africa's greater glory and infinite well-being, into a Union of African states" (222).

In a paper delivered in 1959, "The Artist in the Caribbean," James discusses the role of art and artists in developing the national consciousness. The "supreme artist" is both "created by" and in turn influences the national consciousness, but there must be a "long and deeply rooted national tradition" from which this artist can draw (185), and in general James finds this lacking in the Caribbean. There is no artistic leader or heritage in the region with which emerging artists can contend: "There is no Donne in our ancestry for us to rediscover and stimulate the invention of new forms and new symbols" (184–5). In particular, there is no medium that is unique to the region, "so native to the Caribbean, so rooted in the tight association … between national surroundings, historical development and artistic tradition" (184). The closest to a viable, unique indigenous form for James is calypso in the work of practitioners such as the Mighty Sparrow (188),[38] because in James's opinion even novelists such as V.S. Naipaul are somewhat disappointing, and Lamming, whose work was so important to Ngũgĩ, is "objectively circumscribed" as a result of working in an alien narrative form (187). James appears to be calling for a type of hybrid art that has evolved from indigenous forms that voice the experience of the masses: "In dance, in the innovation in musical instruments, in popular ballad singing unrivalled anywhere in the world, the mass of the people are not seeking a national identity, they are expressing one" (*The Black Jacobins* 417). As Lazarus has argued, for James, unlike Adorno, art is not autonomous and separate from the life of the society in which it was created (Lazarus, "Cricket" 97–108). James does not distinguish high and popular art which for Adorno was a vehicle for state repression and control via commodification. Moreover, in James's view, popular culture can bridge the gap between intellectuals and the people (Idahosa 394). For James, the artist is not a figure in the vanguard leading the society but rather the embodiment or representation of popular aspirations.

James's *Mariners, Renegades and Castaways: The Story of Herman Melville and the World We Live In* is a book James presented to Ngũgĩ in London when he warned him not to risk returning to Kenya, and Ngũgĩ began what would become more than three decades in exile after being "shipwrecked" (*Moving* 104). Ngũgĩ recalled the ostensible subject of James's book as "a novel we used to read as an exam text in Kenya in the fifties" (103). *Mariners*, however, is a much broader study of Melville and in particular *Moby Dick* as an allegorical socialist epic that anticipates the rise of totalitarianism, "great mass labour movements and colonial revolts," and the twentieth-century crisis among intellectuals (3). It is an extraordinary book with a distinctly autobiographical cast partly because of the circumstances of its composition. It is an example of literary criticism as citizenship application, a display of the writer's cultural knowledge demonstrating worthiness or eligibility, because it was composed when James was a prisoner on Ellis Island awaiting a decision on his claim for American citizenship. This

---

[38] See James's "The Mighty Sparrow" (191–201).

book on the classic American epic was designed to advance James's claim.[39] The lengthy final chapter is an autobiographical account of James's case and his detention, under the provisions of the McCarran Immigration Bill of 1952, concluding with his assertion that his knowledge of American life, popular culture, and intellectual malaise qualified him to be a citizen of a country "unburdened by the weight of the past which hangs so heavily on Europe" (160). He denounces the poisonous rottenness of the "culture" of "European intellectuals," as well as the alienation and defensiveness of "American intellectuals apologizing for their 'Coca-Cola civilization'" (159). In a sweeping linkage of totalizing institutions that is his claim for citizenship and his analysis of Melville's prophecy, James associates the prison of Ellis Island, itself a microcosm of American and also world civilization—a compound of "aliens, mariners, renegades and castaways" (145)—with *Moby Dick*'s floating utopia/dystopia. James argues that "Melville intends to make the crew [the "mariners, renegades and castaways" of his title] the real heroes of his book, but he is afraid of criticism" (18), though Melville's plan is evident in the scenes of meaningful communal labor on board. James's book and especially its long-suppressed final chapter have had a troubled critical reception, with James being blamed by critics of both the left and the right in an ongoing interpretative war about his political stance in this text, a strange re-creation of the legal battle in which James was enmeshed on Ellis Island, as Donald E. Pease explains (xv–xvi). Pease focuses on James's subversive association of the American state security apparatus and the institution of American literary studies in his reading of *Mariners*, a work in which "James produced a fictive retroactivity whereby he represented the experiences he underwent on Ellis Island as having 'realized' in historical time one of the national futures Melville had imagined a century earlier" (xxviii). Pease concludes that James helped inaugurate a vibrant and innovative "Transnational Americas Studies" (xxxi).

The modern intellectual's class alienation is represented by Ishmael in James's reading of *Moby Dick*. Ishmael is a double of Ahab, in fact "an intellectual Ahab" (41), but he is alienated from his own labor—as if he were a worker in a modern factory—and from the crew: "What keeps them apart is his intellectualism, his inability to embrace reality spontaneously, the doubt and fear and guilt and isolation from people, which compel him at all times to seek to find out what is happening to him in relation to the world" (43). James suggests that *Moby Dick* includes "elements of a new reorganization of society" in this crew (54),[40] and especially its "savage" harpooners, but it is subordinated to his concern with

---

[39] Fanon, in *Black Skin, White Masks*, would recall an incident during his first period in France when his reference to a literary parallel conferred on him an "honorary citizenship" (38).

[40] As James explains: "Melville worked out an entirely new conception of society, not dealing with profits and the rights of private property ... but with new conceptions of the relations between man and man, between man and his technology and between man and Nature" (88).

Ahab's and Fadallah's mutually supportive dictatorship. Ishmael, the "dissatisfied intellectual," survives to tell the tale after the catastrophic encounter with the white whale, though James is surprisingly myopic about the narrative's racial politics. In a chapter entitled "Neurosis and the Intellectuals," James points to an "intellectual disease" manifested in Ishmael and in the hero of Melville's next novel *Pierre* (91, 103). This disease, afflicting both nineteenth- and twentieth-century intellectuals—and perhaps James himself[41]—results from an inability to confront "social crisis" and to "decide what attitude they should take to a changing society" (91). They are too preoccupied with personal anxieties and complexes to make decisions, and they focus instead on their own inability to solve problems. The doomed nature of their predicament, itself illustrative of the oppressiveness of the dehumanizing bureaucracy and surveillance of the modern state, is exemplified in Pierre's method of "reconciling irreconcilable worlds" (104). Some of the classics of Modernist literature, a "mountain of self-examination and self-pity," produced by "intellectuals without vision," display the "diseased stamp" of their authors (113, 114). In James's estimation, Melville is "the unsurpassed interpreter of the age in which we live, its past, its present and its uncertain future" (124).

As he makes clear in his magisterial quasi-autobiographical memoir of cricket, *Beyond a Boundary*, James wanted to go to England from Trinidad to become a writer, and this book traces his intellectual history. His notion of sport as cultural myth anticipates the work of Roland Barthes but perhaps originates in the work of William Hazlitt.[42] His book is an account of cricket in the West Indies as an ideological spectacle. In its scope, it anticipates the best work of cultural studies, and it comes, in Shandyesque phrase, to resemble another anticipated "book such as had never yet been written" that "would tell us as much about the past and the future of the people of the West Indies as about cricket" (148). However, James does celebrate cricket as a beautiful, almost mystical game, a product of the rise of a sports culture in eighteenth- and nineteenth-century England and contemporaneous with the rise of democracy. It also recalls the veneration of sport in Greek culture and the view of games as "a centre for the intellectual life of Greece" (154). He notes that it was Trotsky's view of sport as a distraction from politics that began his questioning of the Russian revolutionary (151). *Beyond a Boundary* makes it very clear, however, that colonialism just isn't cricket (163). James exposes a strain of hypocrisy poisoning the valuable European legacy and

---

[41] For Hall, "Ishmael is a figure of James himself, an intellectual with a tendency to be pulled toward abstractions, to watch things from the side, and to think about them in theoretical terms but not become involved" ("C.L.R. James" 11).

[42] See Lazarus's "Cricket and National Culture in the Writings of C.L.R. James" (109.n.6) and Surin's "Future Anterior" (200). See Michael Foot on James's debt to Hazlitt who "introduced him to the England he most loved and honoured" (103–4), and Andrew Ross's account of James's approach to popular culture derived from the Frankfurt School (78).

undermining the possibility of anticolonial victory on the much-vaunted level playing ground. As Hall notes, James

> redefined the game as one of the civilized ways in which the anti-imperialist struggle is played out through sports. James often remarked that the British said that the Empire was won on the playing fields of Eton and would be lost on the playing fields of Lord's Cricket Ground. Just as the British had trained themselves to create the Empire on the playing fields, so on the playing fields they would symbolically lose the Empire. ("C.L.R. James" 13)

Colonialism's manifest hypocrisy never makes James question the spiritual aspects of the game, but he has few illusions about the system that brought it to the West Indies.

The "abolition of intellectuals" was always part of James's political program, as Anna Grimshaw maintains in *Popular Democracy and the Creative Imagination*. Moreover, he was convinced that intellectuals should take the lead in their own abolition. In particular, James sought "to break the hold of the intellectuals over political and cultural life, thus clearing the way for his assertion of the decisive role to be played by ordinary people in the creation of a new society" (Grimshaw, *Popular Democracy* 16). James's genealogy of the intellectual tradition emerges in one of his posthumously published works from the late 1940s, *American Civilization*, that ends with this wish to abolish, exterminate, or liquidate intellectuals. Four of the chapters, "The American Intellectuals of the Nineteenth Century," "[Negroes, Women and the Intellectuals]," "The Transition," and "Conclusions" tackle this figure, informed by James's intense discomfiture with the vacillation of Western intellectuals after World War I. Working through binaries of European and American intellectuals, including present and past intellectuals as well as individual intellectuals and intellectuals as a class, he articulates his both dismissive and also ambiguous understanding of the intellectual's role in society and his somewhat rhapsodic vision of a utopian future.

Emerging "from the very genius of the country" (James, *American* 91), intellectuals for James should embody, represent, and voice the will of the people, but they fail to recognize their social construction and the nature of their role. However, intellectuals, including "abolitionist intellectuals" such as William Garrison and Frederick Douglass, always "were only anticipations, an eruption in a crisis" (92), and not solely responsible for provoking the creative crisis. The situation of mid-twentieth-century American intellectuals indeed is especially critical because for James they are totally dependent on European theory while simultaneously ignoring "the creative power inherent in the masses of the American people" (225). They also participated in the creation of a totalizing bureaucracy, which itself provokes a need for more technocrats, and then they "drown themselves and their doubts and hesitations" or escape into the impotent narcissism of existentialism or psychoanalysis (226, 233–4). James appears to anticipate a role for intellectuals in the vanguard of change, however, while he laments their failure, particularly in America, "to give leadership to the masses" (260). However, in "The Transition,"

James maintains that "the complete bankruptcy of the intellectuals" is a function of their devotion to serving the machine and being alienated from meaningful political organizations and the specific demands of their own time and place (261). His conclusion is that intellectuals are "a social grouping *for which the world no longer has any use*" (261). They were always

> the product of a great intellectual ferment, of social conditions, the high peak of thousands of lesser men and connected by a thousand threads with the active life of their time. Even the superb Pascal, priest and religious maniac as he was, took religious controversy from the cloisters of the church and carried it to the people. They explained society to itself, were its conscience, the organizers of its ideas, they charted the new discoveries, they resisted and endured, were heroic or subservient, but they filled a role, and an independent role within the social limitations of their particular time. (262)

Intellectuals have become slaves of the system they helped devise, and cannot recognize that they are out of step with a changed and changing world. They lack the conviction, direction, and purpose that can only be restored by joining a unified movement in which "the worker as such and the thinker as such will disappear" (276). He suggests the inevitability of a type of "class suicide" for intellectuals that will be explored in the next chapter. In contrast with intellectuals' increasing redundancy, James points in somewhat rhapsodic fashion to the creativity of the masses:

> the primary creative force will be the collective actions of the mass seeking to solve the great social problems which face them in their daily lives. Intellect will play a high role, higher than ever, but it will be the intellectual activities of millions of men, dealing with realities. Intellectuals will be of use to the extent that they recognize the new forces but as a class they will recognize it only when they see and feel the new force. The role that they played between 1200 and today will be over, because the condition of that role, the passive subordinate mass, will be undergoing liquidation in the very action of the mass which will be creating a totally new society, an active integrated humanism. (276)

James cites Lenin on the inevitability of diverse forms of violence driving this lengthy transformation, and he predicts that the violent upheavals of the first half of the twentieth century already are inaugurating this new society.

James shared some views about the role of intellectuals with his far more famous Caribbean colleague Fanon. James and Fanon were both briefly creative writers, though James published only a single novel and none of Fanon's early plays survive. Both men were intellectual exiles who shared a disillusionment with the political passivity of the Caribbean.[43] Albert Memmi contends that Fanon's

---

[43] Fanon referred to a moment of historic unrest in his native Martinique in 1959 as merely a "wet dream," a fantasy of revolution after which complacency returned (Philcox, "On Retranslating Fanon" 243–4). Fanon resembled the innovative, politically-committed

"impossible life" in particular exemplifies the predicament of the colonial subject (Memmi 9–39). Fanon's romantic embrace of the heroic and hypermasculine struggle in Algeria, Third World solidarity and Pan-Africanism, and finally, universalist humanism, Memmi argues, was the product of his disillusioned rejection of Martinique, Césaire's Négritude, and the philosophical ideals of the French enlightenment, and his disdain for his own position as a "professional revolutionary" or dissident intellectual, as he said to Beauvoir shortly before his death (*Force of Circumstance* 609). James and Fanon shared a "conceptualization of the intelligentsia's role in the operation of popular and democratic organizations," and they recognized, as Paul Idahosa puts it, that "[b]eing clear as to *who* makes decisions, or who—amongst the 'people'—are the principal agents or agencies of political and social change, becomes integral to disputes about achieving the aims of a democratic society and political system" (388–9). Fanon, however, was perhaps more successful in mobilizing intellectuals, like Ngũgĩ, through his writing, and in addressing the pragmatics of revolutionary change. While never an avowed Marxist, many of his ideas were in general accord (Gilly 2–3). He was prepared to "stretch" Marxism to accommodate the situation of the global south (Macey 479–81), and, like Mao, he focused on the role of the peasantry, of a somewhat homogenized and romantic character, in revolution. While Fanon shared with James a commitment to global, and not merely regional or national, revolutionary goals, James lacked a clear organization that would allow the people's struggle to succeed, and his is "an intelligentsia in search of an apt form" (Idahosa 389–90, 400). Fanon stressed the intellectual's moral responsibility to participate in and encourage the progress of the struggle, but he also expressed, in the words of Ngũgĩ's fellow student at Makerere Grant Kamenju, a "withering contempt for the westernised nationalist bourgeoisie" who in some cases lack legitimacy even as a bourgeoisie (Kamenju 51, 52). If Fanon articulated a clearer sense of the organizational divisions necessary for the struggle to succeed and set out the stages for the intellectuals' evolving role, he was not adverse to questioning their ultimate importance. In fact, both Fanon and James at different moments in their writing expressed a desire to "efface the role of intellectuals" "as a distinct group, agency, or class" (Idahosa 400–401).

Everywhere in his critical and theoretical work, Ngũgĩ acknowledges the vital significance of Fanon. His first collection of essays, *Homecoming*, begins with Fanon's critique and prophecy about "national culture" (3), and his most recent *Globalectics* extends his analysis of Fanon's works to consider Fanon's transformation of the Hegelian master-slave dialectic and the distortion of referring to Fanon as "the apostle of violence" (25). "Fanonism," he writes in a

---

Canadian doctor Norman Bethune (1890–1939) who sought a more heroic, engaged life and possibly an early grave first in Spain and later in China, where he would become a hero of the revolution thanks to a brief hagiography by Chairman Mao that was required reading during the cultural revolution.

consideration of Fanon's central importance to him and other students from the "colonies and former colonies,"

> was a combination of psychoanalysis and Marxian-cum-Hegelian dialects applied to the colonial situation from inside the colony by a student of philosophy, a practicing psychiatrist, and an active revolutionary. Where in *Black Skin, White Masks* Fanon had used the combination, particularly the dialectic of master and slave, to analyze white and black largely as metaphysical and psychological entities, in *The Wretched of the Earth* the combination is turned on the concrete material situation. (*Globalectics* 23–4)

In Ngũgĩ's view, Fanon contributed to the development of African literary culture, and just before his detention he instructed his students at the University of Nairobi about to embark on a study of the novels of Achebe to read *The Wretched of the Earth* and particularly "The Pitfalls of National Consciousness" "without which I believe it is impossible to understand what informs African writing, particularly novels written by Africans" (*Decolonising the Mind* 63). Central to Ngũgĩ's recognition of Fanon's importance is his acknowledgment that Fanon's view of African literature belongs to the corpus of diasporic Pan-African literature (*Globalectics* 55). Furthermore, Fanon embodied the potential of the postcolonial intellectual raised in a colonial environment and especially in colonial schools to formulate an analysis of the nature of colonialism in the global south and to engage with the theory and practice of its dissolution.

Fanon's *The Wretched of the Earth* offers a perennially compelling psychopathology of colonialism—a personal and national trauma not ending with independence—and a prescription for recovery through political and cultural action. Ngũgĩ would recall that *The Wretched of the Earth* had the status of "a kind of Bible among the African students from West and East Africa then [in the mid-1960s] at Leeds" (*Moving the Centre* 2). It is a book that has the urgency, rage, poetic frenzy, and pentecostal fire of a dying revolutionary's last words, a dramatic oral narrative marked by digression and repetition, dictated by Fanon to his wife in the year of his death from leukemia.[44] This oral narrative offers a somewhat homogenized approach to revolutionary struggle in the global south and especially Africa, Latin America, and Asia, but it draws numerous examples from Kenya's Mau Mau insurrection, pointing in particular to the betrayal of the Mau Mau fighters as "extremists" in the negotiations between the nationalist leaders and the colonial power.[45] Fanon's Oedipalization of the colonized offers a way out only

---

[44] *Black Skin, White Masks* was also composed through dictation, and this oral style of composition may partly explain the passionate tone of both books as well as their sometimes jarring shifts in subject and focus.

[45] In what would appear prophetic of the negotiations prior to independence in Kenya, Fanon writes:
> The political cadres hole up in the towns and make it clear to the colonial authorities they have no connections with the rebels, or else leave the country.

via a violent outbreak, both psychic and physical. Ngũgĩ would eventually come to tire of Fanon's emphasis on psychological victimhood, though on first encounter he readily accepted and came to advocate Fanon's prescriptions. His early zeal for Fanon perhaps approximates the truth behind Hall's remark that *The Wretched of the Earth* is the "Bible of decolonisation" (quoted in Bhabha, "Foreword" xvi) and François Maspero's reference to it as the "Bible of Third Worldism" (quoted in Macey 450)—remarks hinting at Sartre's recognition of the poetry of Négritude in "Black Orpheus" of 1948 (20)—and the myriad ways in which Fanon and particularly his last work have been read and interpreted, and perhaps distorted, and this interpretive history has become part of his work's critical reception.

The Wretched of the Earth's "On National Culture" is almost an instructional manual for alienated colonial and postcolonial artist-intellectuals, in addition to its other concerns, and it is no wonder Ngũgĩ felt Fanon was speaking directly to him and responded accordingly. Reading *The Wretched of the Earth* just a few years after its composition and publication in 1961 in the crucible of the Algerian conflict with its seismic repercussions being felt among students in Europe, Ngũgĩ reacted to the poetic urgency of Fanon's wildfire pronouncements, injunctions, prescriptions, warnings, and prophecies. In its compact Grove Press English translation, which Ngũgĩ would have read at Leeds in 1965, *The Wretched of the Earth* would soon become a Western backpackers' classic, a kind of political *On the Road* or *Siddhartha* for 1960s adventurers on their journeys to the east. As Bhabha notes, this text had a very direct personal appeal for dissident thinkers in Europe, Africa, and America (Bhabha, "Foreword" xxviii–xxxi), and its emotional, even sensual, address, rather than a dispassionate setting out of an abstruse series of doctrinal propositions, was part of Fanon's plan (Philcox 246). In his famous "Preface," Sartre stresses that Fanon's text is addressed to the colonized, not Europeans, but he interprets the implications of its doomed message for Europeans in such a way that it might provoke a style of healing and in effect decolonize the colonizer (xlix, lvii). No doubt stimulated by the righteous wrath of Fanon's book and its author's attractive and unambiguously heroic intellectual posture, Sartre writes an almost ecstatic account that is by turns a confession, a warning, and a prophecy: his text confesses collective European guilt over colonialism and hypocrisy, warns of apocalyptic retribution, and predicts a reversal, the last stage of the dialectic, in which colonizer becomes colonized. Famously he asserts that the colonized establish or reconstruct their humanity and gain self-knowledge through the purifying initiation of violence which "can heal the wounds it has inflicted" (lii–lv, lxii).[46]

Seldom do they join forces with the people in the mountains. In Kenya, for example, during the Mau-Mau insurrection no known nationalist claimed he was a member of the movement or attempted to defend it. (*Wretched* 2004, 71)

[46] This preface, initially provoking violent reactions referring to it as a textual bomb or "verbal masturbation" (461), took on a life of its own in the following years until Sartre's death (Macey 458–64).

Ngũgĩ's first encounter with Fanon's "The Pitfalls of National Consciousness," in Constance Farrington's translation, and Fanon's precise, clinical analysis of the fledgling national bourgeoisie in colonized countries of the global south in which Fanon pins the colonial and neocolonial intellectual elite to the wall, must have resembled a moment of revelation like Fanon's own account of Lacan's mirror stage (*Black Skin* 161–4 n25). For Ngũgĩ this prophetic analysis encapsulates a central and still-unresolved problem in postcolonial culture, education, and political life, and he makes at least a brief reference to Fanon's chapter in all eight of his critical and theoretical works.[47] Instead of renouncing bourgeois attitudes, loyalties, and values, intellectuals in Kenya, he writes in 1983's *Barrel of a Pen: Resistance to Repression in Neo-Colonial Kenya*, sought compromises with colonial power to continue their narcissistic existence, appropriate settler lands, and finally, succumb to decadence (10–22). He continues the theme a decade later in 1993's *Moving the Centre: The Struggle for Cultural Freedoms*:

> The class that took over power after independence was an underdeveloped middle class which was not interested in putting the national economy on a new footing, but in becoming an intermediary between Western interests and the people, a handsomely paid business agent of the Western bourgeoisie. ... I have always argued that literature written by Africans, and particularly the literature of this period, cannot really be understood without a proper and thorough reading of the chapter "Pitfalls of National Consciousness." ... The literature of this period was really a series of imaginative footnotes to Frantz Fanon. (65–6)

Ngũgĩ's own position on the responsibility of the postcolonial intellectual has remained remarkably consistent in over five decades. While acknowledging recently that Fanon had recognized that "the colonial order of knowledge" of the 1960s eventually produced "the postcolonial literary intellectual" (*Globalectics* 41), he also stresses that this figure's responsibility is clear. As he wrote in his 1972 work *Homecoming*: "I believe that African intellectuals must align themselves with the struggle of the African masses for a meaningful national ideal. ... Perhaps in a small way, the African writer can help in articulating the feelings behind this struggle" (50).

The Wretched of the Earth anticipates and even guides cultural revolution in colonized nations, and Ngũgĩ himself, as he readily accepts, had been just the sort of colonized artist-intellectual that Fanon portrays whose internal colonization and ambivalent relationship to colonial educational and political authorities were witnessed in the formal mimicry of his first two novels. Fanon articulates the crisis of representation that must face someone like Ngũgĩ when his perception of his own ideological positioning and his understanding of his audience change:

---

[47] See *Homecoming* (75), *Writers in Politics* (rev. ed., 18), *Barrel of a Pen* (96–7), *Decolonising the Mind* (63), *Moving the Center* (65–6), *Penpoints, Gunpoints, and Dreams* (93), *Something Torn and New* (55–6), and *Globalectics* (41–2).

> The colonized intellectual, at the very moment when he undertakes a work of art, fails to realize he is using techniques and a language borrowed from the occupier. He is content to cloak these instruments in a style that is meant to be national but which is strangely reminiscent of exoticism. The colonized intellectual who returns to his people through works of art behaves in fact like a foreigner. (2004, 160)

He has unknowingly become an imitation foreign devil of the sort described by Lu Xun before China's revolution. Fanon diagnoses the symptoms of the colonized, assimilated, alienated intellectuals' attempts to combat the psychopathology of colonialism. They must reclaim their past from colonial myths about the superiority of European culture and the savagery and stasis of African culture, a myth repeatedly voiced by James. Fanon also notes colonialism's attempt to distort or destroy precolonial history, remarks to which Ngũgĩ turns in his two most recent theoretical works (*Something Torn* 40; *Globalectics* 34, 38), but Ngũgĩ overlooks Fanon's warnings about the seduction of a desire "to return" to "unknown roots" in this connection (2004, 155). Fanon also cautions about the seductions of a naïve, essentialist, race-based Pan-Africanism and the pseudo-traditionalism of Négritude. He dismisses the search for a precolonial past, either as a model for the future nation or as a text for cultural expression. Anticolonial resistance, not race-based neonativism, for Fanon, bonds Africans. Such psychic maneuvers may appear to be needed to arrest "serious psycho-affective mutations," but they ultimately only produce violence directed inwards toward the self: "how necessary it is for the intellectual to inflict injury on himself, to actually bleed red blood and free himself from that part of his being already contaminated by the germs of decay" (2004, 157). For Ngũgĩ, the recognition of the self-destructiveness of his alienated artistic expression was partly an acceptance of his work's address to an almost exclusively European or elite African audience. Fanon had articulated the colonized intellectual's movement from addressing the oppressor to the people (2004, 173).

The work Ngũgĩ was undertaking when he first read Fanon, *A Grain of Wheat*, was a formal innovation, but it bore a distinct intertextual relationship to Conrad's *Nostromo* and *Under Western Eyes* as noted in the last chapter and while it moved away from the novel with a hero, it stayed within the confines of the classic realist text. While *A Grain of Wheat* abandons the heroic protagonist of *Weep Not, Child* and *The River Between* in favor of a collective hero and it thematizes a requiem for a traditional past, its conclusion offers muted hope and somewhat conventional renewal but not the prospect of continuing struggle leading to a transformed national consciousness. Speaking of "l'intellectuel colonisé" (*Les Damnés de la Terre* 143) translated as "the native intellectual" in Constance Farrington's Grove Press edition (*Wretched* 1968, 209), Fanon offers cautions against intellectual detachment:

> When the colonized intellectual writing for his people uses the past he must do so with the intention of opening up the future, of spurring them into action and

fostering hope. But in order to secure hope, in order to give it substance, he must take part in the action and commit himself body and soul to the national struggle. (*Wretched* 2004, 167)

Ngũgĩ was struggling to find a new narrative form that would rally and galvanize the folk, and he found it in the formal departure of his most ambitious early career novel *Petals of Blood*, though that too had a marked intertextual relationship to another novel, Sembene Ousmane's African socialist epic *God's Bits of Wood*. He may have been responding very specifically to Fanon's articulation of "a combat stage where the colonized writer, after having tried to lose himself among the people, with the people, will rouse the people. Instead of letting the people's lethargy prevail, he turns into a galvanizer of the people. Combat literature, revolutionary literature, national literature emerges" (2004, 159). Having lost or at least recognized the alienation and stagnation of a colonized mentality, Fanon's artist intellectual becomes a "galvanizer of the people," a voice and "spokesperson of a new reality in action" (159). In *Petals of Blood*, it appears that Ngũgĩ was responding to Fanon's prophetic words about the reemergence of the epic, the "new song of heroic deeds," within the stage in which "combat literature" begins to flower (173–4).

At the same time as Ngũgĩ was completing *Petals of Blood*, however, he was also contemplating his intervention in collectively written and produced communal theater, another development anticipated by Fanon. As if analyzing Ngũgĩ's movement from his student play *The Black Hermit* to his Gĩkũyũ plays, *Ngaahika Ndeenda* (*I Will Marry When I Want*), cowritten with Ngũgĩ wa Mĩriĩ, and *Maitũ Njugĩra* (*Mother, Sing For Me*) performed at Kamĩrĩĩthũ Community Educational and Cultural Centre, Fanon in 1961 recognizes drama's explosive character in the period of combat literature. Drama, he says, is "no longer the domain of the intellectual's tormented conscience … it has become the people's daily lot, it has become part of an action in the making or already in progress" (*Wretched* 2004, 175). Perhaps the most striking expression of Ngũgĩ's creative work seemingly responding directly to Fanon's articulation of the development of combat literature arises in Ngũgĩ's embrace of orature in his first Gĩkũyũ novels translated as *Devil on the Cross* and *Matigari*. At such a moment, "[t]he storyteller … searches for new models, national models, apparently on his own, but in fact with the support of his audience" (174–5). Fanon says that in the zone of combat literature the oral changes from the descriptive and documentary modes to the anticipatory: "What I am going to tell you happened somewhere else, but it could happen here today or perhaps tomorrow" (174). Fanon articulates a pivotal role for the colonized intellectual in embodying popular aspirations and propelling forward the struggle, but he also elevates culture itself in a range of artistic media as a prime mover in the task of raising national consciousness.

Fanon's emphasis on the need for psychological liberation that would inform Ngũgĩ's notion of mental decolonization derived in part from Fanon's studies in phenomenology and particularly Négritude, and its poets' attempt to evolve a mode of representation for alienated identities and aspirations. In "Orphée Noir" ("Black Orpheus"), his preface to Senghor's 1948 *Anthologie de la Nouvelle Poésie Nègre et Malgache de Langue Française* (*Anthology of the New Negro and Malagasy Poetry in French*), a preface which came to be almost more famous than the book it introduced and whose interpretation both defined and delimited Négritude and particularly the position of Fanon, Sartre refers to surrealist methodology and aesthetics permitting a recovery of lost memory, but he isolates the problem of language in his account of the work of these doubly exiled diasporic African poet intellectuals. For Sartre, Négritude mediates between an inaccessible past in a "mystical" "imaginary" Africa and an unknowable future (21), and in his emphasis on its poetic, even elegiac character, he depoliticizes Négritude. Négritude poetry contains a collective memory of slavery, an erotic, intuitive response to nature, and the bare suggestion of a racial allegory of capitalist relations of power, but it is conveyed in the oppressor's language. Due to this replacement of lost African languages with the oppressor's language, the Négritude writer deploys the genre of poetry to resist the analytical guise of prose and importantly to destroy the "European knowledge he has acquired" (22), to reject or eject an internalized identity as subhuman, to destroy the oppressor's language, and to obliterate the very category of Négritude itself. The Négritude poet hence performs a liberating type of linguistic genocide. The poet-intellectual of Négritude strives to be "both a beacon and a mirror ... the herald—half prophet and half follower" (20), though this figure must first liberate himself from self-exile:

> The herald of the black soul has gone through white schools, in accordance with a brazen law which forbids the oppressed man to possess any arms except those he himself has stolen from the oppressor; it is through having had some contact with white culture that his blackness has passed from the immediacy of existence to the meditative state. But at the same time, he has more or less ceased to live his negritude. In choosing to see what he is, he has become split, he no longer co-incides with himself. And on the other hand, it is because he was already exiled from himself that he discovered this need to reveal himself. He therefore begins by exile. It is a double exile. (20)

That colonialism is violence in its origins and Manichaean attitudes and methods, and colonialism can only be countered by violence are two of the central maxims commonly associated with Fanon. This position underlies much of *The Wretched of the Earth*, but its assertion is not unqualified. The counterviolence called for, like the antagonistic relationship of colonizer and colonized, is inherently symbiotic and reciprocal, a "cohabitation" itself defined and policed by violence (2004, 2, 46). Colonialism cannot be overcome by "the wave of a magic wand, a natural cataclysm, or a gentleman's agreement" (2004, 2). Raising the specter of another form of violence, Fanon notes that "we do not expect this colonialism to commit suicide" (*Toward* 105), and he dismisses the notion that in the operation of a Hegelian dialectic, colonialism will simply pass away of its own accord. Anticolonial counterviolence itself, however, nurtures an atmosphere of violence, an atmosphere that, with the dissatisfaction of newly liberated populations and the paranoia of new, independent leaders, rapidly can become an endlessly repeated cycle. As Fanon with characteristic prescience points out, this legacy of violence and the threat of future violence are exploited by the new capitalist enforcers, such as America, for whom the ex-colonies have become important markets in a period when the superpowers fight proxy wars in the global south. Tensions are heightened in the postcolony by media reports and exacerbated by a burgeoning demographic of teenagers (*Wretched* 2004, 41).

Fanon's remarks on violence emerged from his own lived experience and from a very specific historical and political context, which he regarded as a harbinger of seismic continental shifts. "On Violence," the opening salvo of *The Wretched of the Earth*, was first delivered powerfully at the All Africa People's Conference in Accra, December 8–12, 1958, in the presence of advocates of nonviolence such as Nkrumah and Kenya's Tom Mboya, and shortly before the majority of African colonies, save for settler colonies such as Kenya and South Africa, gained independence; the Algerian war drew France's fire away from other French African colonies where agitation for independence was fomenting (Young, *Postcolonialism* 280; Macey 368–71). Fanon's acceptance of anticolonial violence was contingent, moreover, on his view of the vanguard position of the Algerian conflict in the struggle for African liberation. Ngũgĩ in hindsight would come to interpret the Mau Mau anticolonial conflict in Kenya in the same light, an awareness made especially poignant by his own somewhat muffled contemporary awareness of the conflict as a schoolboy in Kenya and by his growing outrage with the opposition of the neocolonial political elite to acknowledging the conflict's role and its combatants' sacrifices in fighting colonialism. For Fanon, the vanguard position of the Algerian war was a consequence of its long history and of the severity of the conflict itself (Fanon, *Toward* 114–15, 129, 146). As Fanon's biographer David Macey puts it, "In Algeria, violence was not just the midwife of history. Violence was Algeria's father and mother" (473). Fanon in Algeria witnessed extreme terror, and he was a military strategist and a participant in attempting to heal the trauma of those who suffered torture's effects as both victims and perpetrators, and he advised military personnel on methods to endure torture. Moreover, as he argues in his essays written from 1952 to 1961 collected in *Pour la Révolution Africaine* (*Toward the African Revolution*), decolonization is not just the work of "an objective dialectic" operating independent of human engagement (170). He suggests further that even if a political solution can be achieved, some cathartic violence may be needed to forestall a movement toward civil war amid the intense emotional expectations immediately following independence (187). In this respect, liberating violence may allow the entire populace to let off steam as it were, particularly given the instability of the would-be bourgeois intelligentsia for whom the notion of nonviolence is seductive. Fanon's especial concern for the immediate aftermath of decolonization belongs to his aspirations for establishing a Pan-African union before the entrenchment of independent postcolonial nation states drawn along colonial lines:

I have been trying to bring the misty idea of African Unity out of the subjectivist bogs of the majority of its supporters. African Unity is a principle on the basis of which it is proposed to achieve the United States of Africa without passing through the middle-class chauvinistic national phase with its procession of wars and death-tolls. (*Toward* 187)

For Fanon, this violence is also symbolic, epistemic, and psychic in nature, as much a part of the inferiority and dependence fostered by colonialism as of the violent confrontation needed to end the intellectual elite's alienation. This is necessary because the colonized intellectual has become "a kind of mimic man" (*Wretched* 2004, 13) who seeks a compromise with the colonizer and the neocolonial successor:

The intellectual who, for his part, has adopted the abstract, universal values of the colonizer is prepared to fight so that colonist and colonized can live in peace in a new world. But what he does not see, because precisely colonialism and all its modes of thought have seeped into him, is that the colonist is no longer interested in staying on and coexisting once the colonial context has disappeared. (2004, 9)

The secret saboteur in the anticolonial and anti-neocolonial struggle, Fanon makes clear, is the colonial school-educated intellectual class, the fraternal hypocrite betrayer who suggests nonviolent compromise at the critical juncture. In Kenya, the national bourgeoisie even offers to mediate in the Mau Mau conflict and negotiate with white settler forces (2004, 24, 44). Distinguishing the class, party, ethnic, leadership, regional, religious, and gender conflicts in the postcolony, Fanon isolates the main cause of conflict in the gap stretching between the elite national bourgeoisie struggling to emerge and the people who are for the intellectual a type of terra incognita. For this national bourgeoisie, the postcolony in neocolonial guise becomes a career. In its Western mimicry, it is narcissistic, cynical, and greedy, and its actions aim at transforming "its country virtually into a bordello for Europe" (2004, 102). The colonial inheritance ensures that the elite joins the burgeoning independent state's bureaucracy and by intention or indirection attempts to create "a dictatorship of civil servants" fighting to entrench its power (2004, 123). Fanon calls for reparatory violence to be directed by this emerging national bourgeoisie against itself via self-mutilation, self-repudiation, and self-betrayal (2004, 98–9)—a version of Cabral's "class suicide" examined in the next chapter—in order to avail the people of "the intellectual and technical capital it culled from its time in colonial universities" (2004, 99).

Fanon and particularly his treatment of violence have had a varied reception among the philosophers, and as noted earlier Ngũgĩ objects to the conception of Fanon as "the apostle of violence" (*Globalectics* 25). Due to its "great influence on the present student generation" in the late 1960s, Arendt discusses Fanon's *The Wretched of the Earth* in her *On Violence*, but a study of violence published in 2009 by the wildly popular "punk philosopher" Slavoj Žižek makes no reference to Fanon, which may be at least one measure of his currency.[48] Both philosophers consider qualifications on what Žižek calls the "endorsement of emancipatory violence," referring to Walter Benjamin's work on divine violence (Žižek, *Violence* 174). Žižek points out that Benjamin acknowledges that it is difficult to know when revolutionary violence has achieved its aim (168–9), a qualification Arendt also finds in Fanon's work. Fanon, she maintains, was "more doubtful about violence than his admirers" (Arendt, *On Violence* 14 n19), chief among them Sartre whom Arendt singles out for an irresponsible, grandiose glorification of violence.[49] In a recent assessment of Sartre's infamous, inflammatory preface to *The Wretched of the Earth*, Wolin points to Sartre's abstraction of violence and counterviolence from the specifics of the Algerian crisis (208), as if the real goal of his "revolutionary romanticism" was "to legitimate a new categorical imperative appropriate to an age of anticolonial collective struggle" and hence to offer a critique of Kant rather than an understanding of contemporary upheavals (Wolin 209). Sartre's zeal for revolutionary violence in his preface, Wolin contends, may also have been a reaction to his reemergence as a vital thinker in a chaotic world leading up to May 1968, after having become by the 1950s a highly respected irrelevance—exactly the type of moribund universal intellectual he despised—subject to attacks from Althusser, Lévi-Strauss, and Foucault (Wolin 179–91).

While Fanon's endorsement of violence appears unambiguous, he notes at least once that it is a necessary notional or interpretive tool, "the key for the masses to decipher social reality" (*Wretched* 2004, 96). As Bhabha points out, apparently reading *The Wretched of the Earth* in light of Fanon's account of racial alterity in *Black Skin, White Masks*, Fanon's discussion of violence has to be regarded in connection with its author's bifurcated position as both a colonial French citizen and a dehumanized other; violence hence originates at least partly in "the realm of psycho-affective conflict" (xxv), and it expresses the colonized subject's psychic struggle for identity (Bhabha, "Foreword" xxi–xxxvi). While never contending that there are numerous Fanons, Bhabha points to Fanon's "rich variety of readers" of different generations and in different ages who seek to make use of and create their own mythic if "opaque" Fanon (xli). Beauvoir remembered Fanon's suspicion—even horror—of violence, but also his apprehension that his reaction was the expression of his innate incapacity as a colonized intellectual:

> He attributed this repugnance to his intellectual conditioning; everything he had written against the intellectuals had been written against himself as well. His

---

[48] Philcox's energetic new translation of Fanon's text in 2004 was designed to reinvigorate the "rather heavy, pompous style and language of the 1950s" so as to make the work appeal to a "young reader" in the twenty-first century (Philcox, "On Retranslating Fanon" 246). Bhabha's 2004 Foreword to *The Wretched of the Earth* regards the text as overlooked (ix–xi), but Macey's authoritative biography points to Fanon's vital contemporary relevance, concluding that Fanon endures: "*Fanon, pas mort*" (xvii).

[49] She associates him with those who distort Marx and locate justifications for violence in anarchism and "pre-Marxian utopian socialism" (*On Violence* 89 n17).

origin made this inner conflict even worse; Martinique was not yet ready for a rising. Anything gained in Africa serves to advance the cause of the Antilles as well, yet it was evident that he found it distressing not to be fighting the battle on his native soil, and even more so not to be an Algerian-born. "Above all, I don't want to become a professional revolutionary," he told us anxiously; theoretically there was no reason why he shouldn't work for the revolution in one place rather than in another, but—and this is what made his situation so pathetic—he had a passionate desire to send down roots. (*Force of Circumstance* 609)

Arendt cites Barbara Deming's claim that Fanon's endorsements of violence could be interpreted as calls for nonviolent action, and Arendt even claims that Georges Sorel's *Réflexions sur la violence* (1908), which influenced Fanon, and Sorel's advocacy of quasi-military class struggle eventually became merely another call for a general strike (Arendt, *On Violence* 71, 12). In *The Wretched of the Earth*, Fanon does warn of the danger of the intoxication of violence that can lead to civil war after independence, and he cautions that revolutionary forces require political education to forestall a cycle of destructive violence without end (2004, 86). Arendt's analysis of violence equally concerns power, and she considers that Sorel and presumably Fanon could not have foreseen the growth in technology that enabled the emergence of intellectuals as the elite of a new technocracy (72). Noting Noam Chomsky's dismay at the rise of these "new mandarins" (*On Violence* 100 n99), Arendt maintains that intellectuals lack organization to seek power, they cling to social status, and in their reactionary thinking they sustain "categories of the past that prevent them from understanding the present and their own role in it" (73). Rumors about the domination of the intellectuals are exaggerated, even in the wake of expanding student protest and threats of nuclear war and ecocide.[50]

A number of interpretive sites open in some of Fanon's other texts that also have direct resonance for Ngũgĩ's works, but there is everywhere a focus on the psychological and cultural liberation of the colonized individual. In *Toward the African Revolution*, Fanon states that national liberation only arrives when the individual is independent, and when colonial culture—including "the pre-eminence of the language of the oppressor"—is destroyed (101–3, 105). In "Algeria Unveiled" from his 1959 collection *L'An Cinq de la Révolution Algérienne* (*A Dying Colonialism*), Fanon extends his interpretive analysis to consider the role of gender and particularly the ideological and cultural significance of the French colonial attack on the veil and Algerian women's renewed adherence to this traditional cultural practice in the face of colonial opposition as an expression of resistance. As in Ngũgĩ's account of missionary attacks on traditional Gĩkũyũ cultural practices, and particularly female genital mutilation, and its linkage to access to education in *The River Between* (historically a vital impetus behind the

---

[50] Arendt writes: "For better or worse—and I think there is every reason to be fearful as well as hopeful—the really new and potentially revolutionary class in society will consist of intellectuals" (*On Violence* 73).

formation of the Gĩkũyũ Independent Schools Association),[51] Fanon points to Algerian women's centrality in the struggle. Colonial and anticolonial violence and control were enacted on the bodies of women, and while Ngũgĩ's novel's position on the practice of female genital mutilation is at best ambivalent—holding that it is a potentially deadly practice, with a narrowly defined cultural significance, that will naturally die out—it does point to what would become in his later novels, and particularly *Devil on the Cross* and *Wizard of the Crow*, a dramatic assertion of women's revolutionary agency.[52] A scene of anti–Mau Mau torture, practiced on an innocent school boy, in *Weep Not, Child*, in a small way reflects the extensive account of torture practices in *The Wretched of the Earth* and *Toward the African Revolution*. In the latter, Fanon maintains that torture is "a fundamental necessity of the colonial world," and he deplores the silence or complicity of French intellectuals (66, 67–71). Fanon in "This Is the Voice of Algeria" from *A Dying Colonialism* raises the question of information capital, media, and communication as weapons in the war of resistance, which anticipates Ngũgĩ's satire on the official "Voice of Truth" in *Matigari* and his endorsement of the Internet and cyberspace orature in *Penpoints*. However, Ngũgĩ had long been an advocate of radio and film and other media technology as democratic means of reaching a largely illiterate, rural audience (rather than an elite, Western-oriented one), dissolving national and other boundaries, and circulating cultural knowledge (*Homecoming* 19). He makes his case most forcefully in *Barrel of a Pen* written at a time when he was actively exploring film making:

> [F]ar from destroying tradition, modern technology (e.g. video, cinema, television, radio) should make it possible to actually reclaim the positive aspects of tradition and peasant cultures which are withering away under the pressures of the economic exploitation. Africa, for instance, has a rich tradition of oral literature. ... African peasant theater relied heavily on song, dance and mime, and these can now be permanently captured on the screen. Thus not only is it possible to use modern science and technology to democratize access to this heritage—more people can be told the tale at the same time—but even more crucial, it is possible to use it to integrate the cultures of the different nationalities within the geographic state into a national whole. Through video, T.V. or cinema, the tales from the different nationalities become mutually accessible and comprehensible. (78)

There are virtually no white characters in Ngũgĩ's novels, save for cipher-like caricatures like Fraudsham and Winterbottom, and discussion of racism is notably sidelined in his early Nairobi journalism, though the underpinning of colonial

---

[51] See Theodore Natsoulas's "The Politicization of the Ban on Female Circumcision and the Rise of the Independent School Movement in Kenya: The KCA, the Missions and Government, 1929–1932" (137–58). See, too, Gikandi's reflection on these events and their impact on his reading of Ngũgĩ's literary works ("Moments of Melancholy" 70–2).

[52] See Brendon Nicholls' insightful reading of gender politics in these novels in *Ngugi wa Thiong'o, Gender, and the Ethics of Postcolonial Reading* (159–89).

dehumanization is everywhere acknowledged. A notable exception is *Wizard of the Crow*'s recurrent motif of a skin lightening obsession, and more specifically the ruling elite's pathological obsession with becoming white. In *Moving the Centre*'s chapter "The Ideology of Racism," Ngũgĩ writes that racism is "not some disembodied abstraction"—possibly thinking of Fanon's dialectic of racial binaries as "metaphysical and psychological entities" (*Globalectics* 24)—but "an ideology founded on an economic system of exploitation and social oppression" (*Moving* 122). Internalized racist phobia, however, Ngũgĩ allows, is debilitating to the intellectual elite who have been "imbued with an almost pathological self-hatred and contempt through years of racist cultural engineering. Racism has thus produced an elite endowed with what Frantz Fanon once described as an incurable wish for the permanent identification with the West" (*Moving* 120). In *Peau Noire, Masques Blancs* (*Black Skin, White Masks*), first published in 1952, which may have begun, but was later rejected, as a dissertation (Macey 136–8, 140–141), Fanon examines the phenomenology, psychosexual mythology, as well as the lived experience of race in a colonial context. Racism underpins colonialism, but "epidermalization" has the effect of internalizing inferiority in the colonized (11). As in Du Bois's *The Souls of Black Folk*, in which the figure of the veil is deployed to express the lived experience of a divided, double consciousness and white blindness to the existence of Afro-Americans, Fanon discusses the Afro-Caribbean's race-based self-alienation, self-masking, and body dysmorphia provoked by colonialism.[53] Fanon's starting point for his sweeping, harrowing account of race relations and mythologies particularly in the Antilles is Sartre's analysis of Jews and anti-Semitism, though Fanon also gives significant attention to Freud, Lacan, Hegel, Jaspers, and Jung as well as Sartre's account of Négritude in "Black Orpheus." In effect, Fanon "postcolonializes" European anti-Semitism in a Caribbean context. Fanon concludes with an assertion of humanity. It is a response to the Cartesian question, an assertion of existential freedom and contingent but radical independence. His analysis is based on his own experience and in some respects resembles an autobiography (Macey 161) and a species of self-analysis if not self-psychoanalysis. Its critical moment is Fanon's departure from Martinique and his arrival in France only to discover for the first time that he was black.[54] It is the equivalent of Lacan's mirror stage in his own self-perception

---

[53] On the connection between Du Bois's and Fanon's view of the black intellectual, and the notion of "whitening" in racial, cultural, and other terms as necessary in the black intellectual's creation, see Ross Posnock's "How It Feels to Be a Problem: Du Bois, Fanon, and the 'Impossible Life' of the Black Intellectual" (323-49). In this context, see Gikandi's discussion of race and identity, in light of Du Bois, in "Obama as Text: The Crisis of Double-Consciousness." Obama's "blackness is considered incomplete ostensibly because it fails a surreptitious test of authenticity, the one that insists that to be truly black in America one must be connected to a past of slavery and its violence" (215).

[54] A similar revelation occurs in Chimamanda Ngozi Adichie's recent *Americanah* in which Adichie's character Ifemelu writes a "race blog" including the notion, "I only became black when I came to America."

and his awareness of the shadow of racist assumptions and stereotypes lying behind others' perceptions of him, as he suggests in a lengthy footnote (161–4 n25), detailing the psychotic break and the self-reproduction that occurs when "the black man makes his entry into the phenomenal world of the white man" (160); Fanon later expresses his aim that his book "will be a mirror ... in which it will be possible to discern the Negro on the road to disalienation" (184). His object is as much psychotherapy as philosophy, aimed at freeing "the black man [from] ... the arsenal of complexes that has been developed by the colonial environment" (30) rather than an attempt to conjure an abstract, collective, cathartic "metaphysical guilt" in all people (89 n9). He clearly identifies his species of alienation and self-alienation as the particular province of the intellectual immersed in European culture. Aside from his general aim of effecting "the liberation of the man of colour from himself" (8), he appears to seek to purge his own internalized and intellectualized "Negrophobia" (155, 160).

Learning the colonial language or studying Montesquieu in Martinique was a type of skin-whitening technique (18, 193), and a similar effect could be achieved, Fanon maintains, through acquisition of money (44). Fanon appears well-aware of the paradox of his intellectual analysis and his own intellectual authority, steeped as he is in the European philosophical and psychological traditions but convinced of the inability to effect change through intellectual means because prejudice is imprinted through popular culture and other influences by the age of six or eight. As he points out, "[i]n the Antilles, the young Negro identifies himself *de facto* with Tarzan against the Negroes" (152 n15), and later, "the Antillean who goes to France in order to convince himself that he is white will find his real face there" (153 n16). To effect meaningful change, however, Fanon does suggest the creation of an affirmative children's literature and a children's history for children of the African diaspora, just as Ngũgĩ wrote his Njamba Nene stories of childhood heroism set during the Mau Mau conflict (148).[55]

However, Fanon's suspicion of his own abstract intellectual orientation and the nature and direction of his own philosophical, psychological, and historical/cultural analysis remains. Just as "philosophy has never saved anyone," so intelligence has been deployed both to proclaim equality and justify genocide (29). He persistently questions the application of notions like the Oedipal complex, the collective unconscious, or "neurotic homosexuality" to Martinique or more generally the global south (180). He also resists the study of the past merely "to avenge the Negro of the seventeenth century" and to recover a glorious heritage, a critique in which he is possibly thinking of *The Black Jacobins* (228). In particular, he refers to the "unhappy romanticism" of Négritude (135), that, while inspirational, cannot nurture genuine culture in the absence of basic human rights and respect for human dignity. Anticipating the material focus of *The Wretched of the Earth* and his later movement into direct action, he maintains that diasporic African

---

[55] See Lovesey's "'Initiation for the Nation': Ngũgĩ wa Thiong'o's Writing for Children" (193–210).

intellectual history is almost a species of self-indulgence or self-therapy despite the imperative of "[m]oral anguish in the face of the massiveness of the Past" given present realities:

> I am convinced that it would be of the greatest interest to be able to have contact with a Negro literature or architecture of the third century before Christ. I should be very happy to know that a correspondence had flourished between some Negro philosopher and Plato. But I can absolutely not see how this fact would change anything in the lives of the eight-year-old children who labor in the cane fields of Martinique or Guadeloupe. (230)

The implication is to deflect white "manicheism delirium" as just one symptom of a persistent pathology subject to "the conflicts of a tortured conscience, a vacillating intellect, and a frustrated instinct" (*Black Skin* 183, 171 n32). As we shall see in the next chapter, a less despairing but still sharply suspicious view of intellectuals was developing elsewhere in Africa that would have a profound effect on Ngũgĩ.

Chapter 4
Ngũgĩ's "Aesthetics of Decolonization": Return to the Source

Ngũgĩ's first five collections of essays were written while he was most actively engaged in writing novels, and Jacqueline Bardolph has argued for their symbiotic relationship with this creative work. However, while Ngũgĩ has acknowledged that his early novels and the essays in *Homecoming* "have been products of the same moods and touch on similar questions and problems" (xv), the essays are not contingent on the novels. The essays are not merely diagrams for the novels' stories, or, still worse, "answer keys" to the issues raised in the novels, of the sort that Achebe famously deplored in "The Novelist as Teacher." Moreover, their concerns go well beyond the often narrowly defined national focus of the fiction, so often fixated on the cataclysmic Mau Mau period in Kenya and its insufficiently historicized and unresolved legacy, though this has recently changed in dramatic ways. As Ngũgĩ asserts in his most recent volume, all of his work may be considered an engagement with the "aesthetics of decolonization" (*Globalectics* 8), considering cultural work vital to liberation. However, while the early essays were often written to respond to contemporary events or for particular public occasions, or even to satisfy academic degree requirements, they do return again and again to core values and key autobiographical events by way of illustration. In addition, over and above the obvious focus of *Writers in Politics* on cultural engagement, *Decolonising the Mind* on language, and *Moving the Centre* on diasporic identities, there is a certain amount of repetition as some of the collections readily admit, and Ngũgĩ has been an inveterate reviser of his own work. Ngũgĩ's three most recent works, *Penpoints, Gunpoints, and Dreams*; *Something Torn and New*; and *Globalectics* are each more focused on particular subjects, partly because they were all delivered as separate series of lectures. *Penpoints*, in particular, tackles performance and the state, *Something Torn* examines Modernism's incestuous relationship with colonialism, and *Globalectics* advances a new, global, planetary theory. Moreover, these three recent works all engage with memory and the future as well as with African spirituality.

Ngũgĩ suggests that Africa is needed to revive a moribund globe, and he returns to Africa's centrality in global events of the last century: Africa's "discovery" enabling Modernism, African colonialism functioning as a dry run for worldwide fascism, and African decolonization inaugurating the end of one stage of imperialism in the global south, and specifically in the case of Guinea-Bissau forcing the hand of a lingering fascist dictatorship in Portugal. This reevaluation, moreover, is not the type of what we might call "postcolonial necrophilia" that Ngũgĩ deplores in W.B. Yeats's use of the archive of Celtic culture remaining in a state of suspended animation to provide a type of cultural *spiritus mundi* from which new Irish artists could draw sustenance (*Something* 42–3, 52, 53). In fact, Ngũgĩ would conjecture in 2003 that as an African writing in English, he had been performing just this type of necrophilic or cannibalistic exploitation "to enrich English" (Trivedi with Wangui 403).[1] However, often for Ngũgĩ, as for Amílcar Cabral, a postindependence "return to the source" is essential. Like James, Ngũgĩ celebrates a still-vibrant African culture with direct roots to its past—"the real beginning of the history of humanity" (James, *Nkrumah* 20)—accessible through memory and cultural acts, the spirit of which exemplifies and can inspire a planetary transformation.[2] Citing Césaire, James refers to "the way of life which the African has not lost which will restore to a new humanity what has been lost by modern life" (*Nkrumah* 23). Ngũgĩ's access to the source is via language and memory, because he is not from the Caribbean and hence separated from indigenous culture and language. He has almost been fated to return to his early dismissal of Négritude, no doubt with the wisdom of age and an acute appreciation of the natal alienation that generated this movement among the doubly dispossessed Afro-Caribbean intellectuals in Paris after his own nearly three decades long exile: a kind of neoexilic Négritude, a fondness for the lost object of desire.

One of the major non-Caribbean influences on the ideas articulated in Ngũgĩ's eight volumes of critical and theoretical essays, the extent of which has not been sufficiently recognized, lies in the work of the charismatic Guinea-Bissauan and Cape Verdean revolutionary theorist, military tactician, professional agronomist, and poet[3] Amílcar Cabral. Cabral is one of those, in Ngũgĩ's terms, like Fanon, Kimathi, and Nkrumah, whose "dreams" inspire the ongoing struggle in Africa and hence "have not really died" (Martini et al 127). Cabral has influenced Ngũgĩ's views on the relationship between culture and genuine liberation (not merely independence), the importance of the peasantry, and the role of the postcolonial intellectual. A concern with the position of the intellectual in the postcolony is central to Cabral's thinking on class suicide and the return to the source, as we shall see. Ngũgĩ's focus on Kenya and especially the Mau Mau period—like Fanon's Algeria and Cabral's Guinea-Bissau—is the result of his knowledge and lived experience, but, as he makes clear, it is part of a much broader consideration

---

[1] Ngũgĩ might say that such exploitation treats the African language as if it were dead, and the very process is dangerous for its survival. He said in this interview that "As an African when I'm writing in the English language, I'm actually—ironically—also drawing on that experience of my language equally. And what I'm doing in reality is taking away from the Gikuyu language to enrich English. So when I'm writing in Gikuyu, I'm really exploiting the possibilities of that language and I have found it very, very liberating for me in expressing my environment" (Trivedi with Wangui 403).

[2] Horace Campbell has written more recently on the role of spiritual values in the Pan-African ideal, whose core he maintains is the "spiritual and cultural renewal of the African peoples" (226).

[3] See Gerald Moser's account of Cabral's poetry, which provides a selection of the poems themselves (176–97).

of events in Africa, the Pan-African world, and the global south. Like Cabral, Ngũgĩ encounters in the colonial creation of the Kenyan state, a complex of diverse communities and historical tensions, as well as a large peasant population that does not conform readily to conventional class analysis. Like Fanon and Cabral, Ngũgĩ's analysis of the role of the postcolonial intellectual is inflected by his personal understanding of the colonial petty bourgeoisie—educated in colonial schools and universities as well as in the colonial mother country—and the neocolonial seductions it faces. Ngũgĩ clearly regards part of his own role as broadly educational in consciousness-raising among the peasantry via the indigenous-language mediums of popular plays, films, and folktale-influenced novels, though more recently he has taken to addressing other postcolonial intellectuals directly.

In his early and mid-career essays, Ngũgĩ cites Cabral as an authority on imperialism and neocolonialism (*Moving* 70), but he also draws on Cabral to express the effects of colonialism on the history of the colonized and to declare armed struggle as well as national liberation itself an "*act of culture*" (Ngũgĩ, *Barrel* 87; Cabral, *Unity* 142–3). In all of Ngũgĩ's critical and theoretical essays, moreover, he deploys Cabral's effortless merging of theoretical insights— often with a certain impatience for received conceptual niceties—and concrete illustrations, sometimes taken from local orature or his own autobiography. Cabral's discursive style may be the product of his extensive educational work in training cadres to raise popular awareness of the economic exploitation of agricultural production (price fixing and taxation without returns or representation), and like Ngũgĩ he was briefly a school teacher with multilingual expertise. Both were raised in conditions in which food shortages were a frequent hardship (Rabaka 229). Ngũgĩ's first reference to Cabral's work, however, in *Homecoming*, cites Cabral's remarks on "tribalism" in an article published in September 1968 as "Determined to Resist," and later reprinted under the title "Practical Problems and Tactics." This is a subject given considerable attention in Ngũgĩ's early newspaper articles considered in Chapter 2. Cabral refers to the decimation of tribal, ethnic allegiances before the arrival of the colonial forces due to the slave trade, but he also acknowledges the further dismantling of the "existing remnants of tribalism" as one of the only possible benefits of colonialism (quoted in Ngũgĩ, *Homecoming* 19; Cabral, *Revolution* 144–5). In Kenya, as eminent African historian John Lonsdale argues, and Ngũgĩ would agree, tribalism was virtually created by colonialism and exploited increasingly in its dying days, one of its most toxic bequests to the emerging independent nation ("Kenya" 1–3). *Homecoming* refers to "tribe" as "a special creation of the colonial regimes" (xvii). Ngũgĩ omits reference to Cabral's later assertion that tribalism—like racism and bribery of traditional chiefs—was exploited by "political opportunists" some of whom "attended European universities ... who are completely removed from the problems of their own people [and] ... who at times even look down on their own people" (Cabral, *Revolution* 139, 145). In *Writers in Politics*, Ngũgĩ refers to Cabral's influential position on the history of the colonized in "National Liberation and Culture," citing Cabral to the effect that colonialism is "the negation of the historical process of the dominated people through the violent usurpation of the freedom of the development of the national productive forces" (quoted in Ngũgĩ, *Writers in Politics*, rev. ed., 19). This statement is part of a theoretical elaboration of three historical stages Cabral presented at a conference in Havana, Cuba in January 1966 entitled "The Weapon of Theory" (*Revolution* 90–111). In this influential speech, Cabral argued that history's motivating force lies—not in the origins of class or class struggle itself as in Marxist dogma—but instead in "the development of the productive forces in conjunction with the pattern of ownership of the means of production" (Cabral, *Revolution* 95).

In his writings on revolutionary struggle, a major part of his international diplomatic offensive, Cabral emphasizes the uniqueness of each geopolitical struggle in Africa and around the globe, stressing the impossibility of following to the letter the theories of Marx, Lenin, Mao, or even Che Guevara, though he is clearly exercised to justify his positions. Necessity forces him to be realistic and pragmatic as he reiterates on many occasions, allowing that "only in stories is it possible to cross the river on the shoulders of the crocodile's friend" (*Return* 24). This pragmatic and apparently untheoretical emphasis may also have been a calculated maneuver to distance his stance from Marxist-Leninism that was so much reviled in government and diplomatic circles in the West during the Vietnam war, and Cabral was perpetually seeking diplomatic support and material aid for the liberation movement. Cabral's writings engaged him in an academic, even semantic debate on two fronts: the readiness of a unified Guinea-Bissau and Cape Verde for independence (a question perpetually raised by Portugal) and the political correctness of his class analysis (of concern to textbook revolutionaries and party stalwarts). He faced opposition from both the reactionary right and the ultra-orthodox left. What appears to be Cabral's hostility to theory is an impatience with enforced Soviet conformity, the apparent extravagance of theoretical maneuvers for their own sake at a time of material crisis, and the Eurocentrism and inherent racism of some "First World" theory, including Marxism.[4] "Cabral's work," Jock McCulloch points out, "represents a dis-Europeanisation of revolutionary theory" (135). Moreover, while he was drafting his speeches and essays and then traveling the globe to deliver them in order to attract international condemnation of Portuguese oppression (even engaging for artists to document the realities of life in the liberated areas [*Return* 21–2]), to appeal for support in particular from Europe's intellectuals, and to acquire financial and military aid, he was a charismatic revolutionary intellectual simultaneously conducting a guerrilla ground war in very difficult topography against a well-supplied, ruthless enemy and attempting to maintain discipline within the movement without violating his own humanitarian principles or attracting foreign censure.

Guinea-Bissau was a colonial creation, acquired by Portugal at the Berlin Conference of 1885 through the influence of Britain who sought to contain France's sphere of influence in West Africa. Guinea-Bissau was a resource,

---

[4] See McCulloch (131–5).

not a settler, colony of Portugal, which claimed the region as its overseas "province"; in a similar fashion, Italy had claimed Libya as part of greater Italy, a consideration of importance in Gramsci's postcolonial views. Portugal had an unusual status in Europe in the 1950s and 1960s, being a virtual colony of Britain with a repressive fascist government. Cape Verde and Guinea-Bissau, however, were of vital importance for Portugal because its own ailing economy required a captive colonial consumer market there as well as in Angola and Mozambique. The strategic significance of these colonies, moreover, guaranteed the support of Britain, America, the other North Atlantic Treaty Organization (NATO) countries, and South Africa. In a discussion in America not long before his death, Cabral said "Portugal is an underdeveloped country—the most backward in Western Europe. It is a country that doesn't even produce toy planes—that is not a joke, it's true" (*Return* 82). Cabral pointed out elsewhere that Portugal even disregarded European Modernism's fascination with African art and artifacts (*Revolution* 156), which had raised Africa's status in Europe, even if in a neoexoticist guise. In effect, Cabral's Portugal is Europe's "Third World" and unworthy even as a colonizer. He anticipated that the anticolonial war in Guinea-Bissau would strike a blow against fascism in Portugal, an early instance of Africa's assisting in the decolonization of Europe—or its liberation from fascism—that would be a theme in Ngũgĩ's later work. Cabral's murder, orchestrated by Portugal's secret police in 1973, was a consequence of the very success of Cabral's mission of liberation, because it was an attempt to silence the growing domestic opposition in Portugal to the costly colonial wars and the policy of conscription that supplied them (Chabal 133–4).

As Cabral repeated in different contexts, responding to his critics on the right and the left, Guinea-Bissau did not present a conventional picture of revolutionary readiness: "the peasantry is not a revolutionary force," "we ... did not have a proletariat," "we looked for the working class in Guinea and did not find it" (*Revolution* 61, 65–6). Cabral was not an orthodox Marxist-Leninist, though as he aimed to achieve socialism in nonaligned Guinea-Bissau, his military support came mainly from the Soviet Bloc and the Organization of African Unity (OAU), and NATO supplied his enemies. Cognizant of "the retreat of the revolution in Europe [and] of a certain apathy" there (*Revolution* 73), Cabral connects the armed struggle in "Portuguese" Guinea to the anti-imperialist movement in the socialist world of the global left and the global south generally but primarily to the goal of Pan-African liberation.[5] While not discounting nonviolence, he is skeptical of its effectiveness, partly as a result of witnessing his own movement's early metropolitan demonstrations and strikes being viciously suppressed by massacres (most notoriously the 1959 massacre at the Pidjiguiti docks [*Unity* 166]) and incarceration in concentration camps supplied in some cases with Nazi-trained torturers. Portugal's stubborn refusal even to consider decolonization outside of violent confrontation was demonstrated by its attempts in the face of

---

[5] Moreover, while he generally avoids the "argot of the super-left" (McCulloch 130), his writing does show a certain fondness for phrases like the "colonial yoke," "class struggle," and "lackeys of international imperialism."

growing international condemnation to accelerate Portuguese settlement to justify occupation and to offer "fictive" citizenship to colonial subjects to placate some members of the petty bourgeoisie.

Importantly, for Cabral, the anticolonial struggle targeted the colonist but also aimed to raise the awareness of the majority of the people (99 percent of whom were illiterate [*Revolution* 143]) about the material nature of their oppression, to foster meaningful economic development in liberated zones, and to prepare the necessary social and material infrastructure for independence. He calls for the publication of new educational materials and the establishment of a radio station, and he anticipates the need after independence to develop writing systems for local languages and dialects (*Revolution* 173). It was for Cabral a battle for hearts and minds as much as a series of guerrilla operations destroying lines of communication and military posts, ending destructive incursions into liberated areas, downing planes and armed helicopters, withstanding napalm attacks and manufactured famine, and bringing to a close a condition of virtual slavery and a policy of genocide (*Revolution* 114, 128, 132). For Cabral, the struggle is an educational opportunity, formative of its own culture, and enabling the people's active reentry into their own history. As he said in a speech in Tanzania in 1965:

> [W]e do not possess today the special weapons which others possess, we have no big factories, we don't even have for our children the toys which other children have, but we do have our own hearts, our own heads, our own history. It is this history which the colonialists have taken from us. The colonialists usually say that it was they who brought us into history: today we show that this is not so. They made us leave history, our history, to follow them, right at the back, to follow the progress of their history. Today, in taking up arms to liberate ourselves ... we want to return to our history, on our own feet, by our own means and through our own sacrifices. (*Revolution* 77–8)

While forcing colonized peoples into an historical endgame is not an atypical colonial sleight of hand, Guinea-Bissau was a unique colonial situation in Cabral's analysis in large part because of the difficulty of demarcating its social stratification and particularly because of its underdeveloped intellectual class.[6] By his own admission, Cabral belonged to a group of revolutionary intellectuals within Guinea-Bissau's petty bourgeoisie, the "*Guiné assimilados*" with some European experience and education, who were inspired by events in Africa and elsewhere (*Revolution* 66–7; McCulloch 131). He belonged to the "revolutionary petty bourgeoisie ... the part of the petty bourgeoisie which is nationalist and which was the source of the idea of the national liberation struggle in Guinea" (*Revolution* 62). He accepts the apparent contradiction that a united "revolutionary vanguard" is indispensable for the revolution (*Revolution* 105), while acknowledging this

---

[6] The difficulty of demarcating Guinea's classes is repeated by the former revolutionary leaders interviewed by Ronald Chilcote over and above a designation of the great majority of peasants and a generalized desire to build a classless society in future based on a new vision of humanity (97–177).

vanguard's colonial creation and believing, to an extent like Gramsci, that "all men are philosophers and political actors" (McCulloch 132–3). This is the "paradox of colonial domination" (*Return* 69). In some respects the gap between Cabral's acceptance of the need for strong leadership and his idealistic view of humanity allowed for the conditions that facilitated his assassination as we shall see, just as Ngũgĩ's desire to return to his homeland and the source of his inspiration in 1982 nearly led to his murder. The bourgeoisie in Cabral's estimation is a colonial creation, naturally allied with and desirous of the style of living of the international capitalist bourgeoisie—preoccupied with retaining their salaries, cars, and refrigerators; luxuries Cabral acknowledges possessing (*Unity* 33–6)—and thereby naturally and unnaturally alienated from family, ethnic groupings, and its own identity (*Return* 62). Cabral was deeply conscious of the particular alienation of Portuguese colonial subjects, though his account resembles those of Ngũgĩ and James from other very different colonial contexts:

> All Portuguese education disparages the African, his culture and civilization. African languages are forbidden in schools. The white man is always presented as a superior being and the African as an inferior. The colonial "conquistadores" are shown as saints and heroes. As soon as African children enter elementary schools, they develop an inferiority complex. They learn to fear the white man and to feel ashamed of being Africans. African geography, history and culture are either ignored or distorted, and children are forced to study Portuguese geography and history (*Unity* 25–6).

The alienation of colonial education was compounded in those who, like Cabral himself, attended university in Lisbon, though this experience allowed him to connect with individuals such as Agostinho Neto from other Portuguese colonies in Africa. Together, they

> [b]egan to seek how to *re-become* Africans, for the cunning of the Portuguese had always lain in not allowing us to be Africans in order to turn us into second-class Portuguese. Anyone who had the luck to go to school was used by the Portuguese as an agent, as an individual who would disown Africa to serve the colonialists. So our work lay in searching out again our African roots. (de Andrade xxv)

Due to their isolation and alienation in their quest to "*re-become* Africans," colonized intellectuals sought out a sense of identity in Négritude and Du Bois's Pan-Africanism, Cabral stressing that many of the originators of these concepts were Afro-American and Afro-Caribbean members of the "African diasporas" "outside black Africa" (*Return* 62–3).

Guinea-Bissau's petty bourgeoisie was made up of two groups in Cabral's analysis, though his later work refers to a three-part division. The first of his two groups is a small, somewhat diverse collection of European-educated intellectuals, civil servants, officials, professionals, and business employees:

> We ... looked for intellectuals, but there were none, because the Portuguese did not educate people. In any case, what is an intellectual in our country? It could probably be someone who knew the general situation very well, who had some knowledge, not profound theoretical knowledge, but concrete knowledge of the country itself and of its life, as well as of our enemy. We, the people I have talked about, the engineers, doctors, bank clerks and so on, joined together to form a group of *interlocuteurs valables*. (*Revolution* 66)

The second group "for which we have not yet found any precise classification" "play[s] a very important role" (*Revolution* 62, 59).[7] This is a dynamic, self-confident assemblage of unemployed youth from the countryside who have lived with relatives in the metropolitan areas, and bring a diverse linguistic capacity and an intuitive grasp of the material inequality and injustice of the colonial system. Many individuals from this group were trained as cadres by Cabral and others, and sent to raise the consciousness of the peasantry. Importantly, "they knew how to read and write (which makes a person an intellectual in our country)" (*Revolution* 67). The future of this collective petty bourgeoisie after independence, however, is problematic and potentially catastrophic. As Cabral notes, "in colonial conditions it is the petty bourgeoisie which is the inheritor of state power (though I wish we could be wrong). The moment national liberation comes and the petty bourgeoisie takes power we enter, or rather return to history, and thus the internal contradictions break out again" (*Revolution* 69).

Confident of its "honesty" and presumably sincerity of revolutionary purpose, in one of his most daring assertions, Cabral expresses a hope that after independence the petty bourgeoisie will "commit suicide" as a class and "abandon power to the workers and the peasants and cease to exist qua petty bourgeoisie"; he optimistically anticipates, however, that this group "will not lose; by sacrificing itself it can reincarnate itself, but in the condition of workers or peasants" (*Revolution* 110, 70, 72). Cabral's notion of class suicide was an attempt to anticipate and defuse what he dreaded as an almost inevitable and destructive postcolonial class conflict. The startling, even outrageous, nature of Cabral's suicide proposal points as much to the somewhat naive confidence of Cabral himself as to the intractability of the problem (the problem of postcolonial intellectuals), and the sheer unlikeliness of such an outcome: the petty bourgeoisie's voluntarily drinking poisoned Kool-Aid, even symbolically, for the greater good. In his preface to Marx's *Capital*, Louis Althusser refers to this perennial problem of the intractability of petty bourgeois intellectuals, a problem for which he elsewhere advocated "a long, painful and difficult re-education. An endless external and *internal* struggle" (*Lenin and Philosophy* 16). While he does not refer to Cabral's solution, Althusser stresses the violence of the difficult shift in allegiance and provides salient illustrations. Intellectuals, he writes, must

---

[7] McCulloch refers to this group as the "lumpenproletariat" and cites Gerald Chaliand who defines it as "a temporary proletariat with a middle-class mentality" (McCulloch 74).

make a real *rupture*, a real *revolution* in their consciousness, in order to move from their necessarily bourgeois or petty-bourgeois class instinct to proletarian class positions. It is extremely difficult, but not absolutely impossible. The proof: Marx himself, who was the scion of a good liberal bourgeoisie (his father was a lawyer), and Engels, who came from the big capitalist bourgeoisie and was himself a capitalist in Manchester for twenty years. Marx's whole intellectual history can and must be understood in this way: as a long, difficult and painful rupture by which he moved from his petty-bourgeois class instinct to proletarian class positions, to whose definitions he contributed decisively in *Capital*. (*Lenin and Philosophy* 96)

Althusser also includes Lenin as a further example. As Young suggests, Cabral probably derived the notion of class suicide from a number of sources: Lenin's pronouncement about the ruling class's reluctance to renounce power, the Cuban government's ostensible willingness for the disaffected to emigrate, and the Chinese government's campaigns of enforced reeducation through labor (Young, *Postcolonialism* 288). Cabral would not live to see this post-suicide rebirth or the alternative he dreaded: the creation of a neocolonial bourgeoisie who would work via international aid "to put a brake on the revolution and to enlarge the possibilities of the petty bourgeoisie as a neutraliser of the revolution" (*Revolution* 73).

Suspicions about the role of postcolonial intellectuals in the postcolony preoccupied Cabral in what would be the last months of his life. Cognizant of the fate of friends like Nkrumah in Ghana, Cabral calls the social stratification of the postcolony "*the most important problem in the liberation movement*" and "*perhaps the secret of the failure of African independence*" (*Return* 84). He returns in other speeches delivered in late 1972 to the conundrum of the petty bourgeoisie and its loyalties, and he offers three subdivisions of this class within Guinea-Bissau to clarify the diversity of problems presented by this class. He distinguishes first a minority opposing independence; a second silent majority who are "hesitant and indecisive"; and a third minority working for liberation who still do not "truly identify with" the people (*Return* 63–4). Within this last group develops the revolutionary vanguard and examples of artist-intellectuals who resemble Ngũgĩ in the period after Kenyan independence. The artist-intellectual employs foreign literary and artistic forms to express personal alienation and the discovery of an emergent identity, but still fails "to express the hopes and sufferings of the masses. And precisely because he uses the language and speech of the minority colonial power, he only occasionally manages to influence the masses, generally illiterate and familiar with other forms of artistic expression" (*Return* 68).

While Cabral's tragic—possibly inadvertent—assassination on January 20, 1973,[8] on the eve of the independence for which he had dedicated his life,

---

[8] Davidson notes that Cabral's belief in human goodness facilitated his murder (Davidson, "Remembering Cabral" 81). While aware of a conspiracy, Cabral was unwilling to discipline the plotters partly because of its potentially disastrous international perception. His confidence in his own ability to rehabilitate offenders meant that in his final days he

kept him from the very different challenges of the administration of a new state amid rampant popular expectations as well as what would become the pressures of globalization, transnationalism, and ecological degradation; he had already begun to plan for a postrevolutionary, independent future even while fighting the Portuguese. However, Cabral may have underestimated the relentlessness and ruthlessness of his Portuguese opponents, and in one of his last addresses, weeks before his assassination, he calls finally for the targeting of colonial businesses and subjects in metropolitan areas (*Return* 98), something from which he had always turned away before. He would not live to witness what his mentor Basil Davidson referred to in the 1990s as the "banditries and corruptions and vile external interventions [that] have gone far to wreck or utterly destroy the harvests of progress that Cabral and his companions were able to promote and produce" ("Remembering" 85).

After independence, Cabral anticipated his country's active re-entry into history, and its people's renewed assertion of their historical identity through culture, a process in which postcolonial intellectuals were to have a vital role. In one of his last addresses, "Identity and Dignity in the Context of the National Liberation Struggle," delivered at Lincoln University in America in October 1972, he developed his influential concept of the "return to the source" (*Return* 57–69). This return was to be of particular importance for the colonial petty bourgeoisie, the "colonized intellectuals" or "assimilated intellectuals" who most needed a "spiritual reconversion—of mentalities" or a "re-Africanization of minds" (*Unity* 145, 146; de Andrade xxiii) resembling Ngũgĩ's "decolonizing the mind" with his late-career focus on the still-necessary decolonization of postcolonial intellectuals. In fact, McCulloch contends that all of Cabral's "analysis of culture is essentially an account of the situation, experience and aspirations of the petty bourgeoisie" (89). For Cabral, the source of culture, as well as identity and dignity, lies in the peasantry, and particularly that sector of the peasantry least affected by colonialism as a result of limited contact or remoteness or through active cultural resistance to assimilation. The people's culture in general, however, has not been significantly affected by colonialism, he maintains, and it "acts as a bulwark in preserving their *identity*"; they do not require a postindependence "return to the source" or a "cultural renaissance" because "it is they who are the repository of the culture and at the same time the only social sector who can preserve and build it up and *make history*" (*Return* 61).

Cabral's notion of culture rooted in the peasantry, while of vital importance in his theory of history and the state, is primarily static—almost atrophied—and the

---

inadvertently enabled his own assassination by having the plotters near him. Moreover, his charisma meant that other leaders were reluctant to oppose his unwillingness to be accompanied by personal security. The Portuguese who orchestrated the assassination had attempted to foster a split between the mainly Cape Verdean leadership and the Guinean rank and file, and this perception of a split was given credence by the success of the assassination. For a full account of the background and implications of the assassination, see Patrick Chabal (132–43).

human embodiment of this commodity is nearly totally stagnant in his analysis. Culture for Cabral is a sweeping category entailing "the fruit of a people's history" and a legacy expressed "in works of art as in oral and written traditions, in cosmogony as in music and dances, in religions and creeds" (*Unity* 141, 148). His evocation of a pure repository of culture residing in the people may be part of his "subliminal involvement with negritude" as McCulloch contends (105), an involvement that is certainly apparent in some of Cabral's early poems. Cabral's notion of the people as a cultural archive also carries residual traces of narodism (McCulloch 91), narodism being the reactionary idealization or mythologizing of the peasant, which Lenin addressed in 1897's *The Heritage We Renounce*. Lenin refers to a view of the peasant as exceptional, and hence opposed to and outside the course of change, a figure who represents a critique of the role of class struggle in history and historical change. While Cabral does allow that postcolonial culture may "take on new forms" and while he resists a postcolonial "return to traditions" (*Return* 60, 63), which suggests that his notion of culture is not absolutely fixed, he does hold to the essential truth of the cultural purity of the peasantry as a repository of integrity from which the petty bourgeoisie in particular may draw and into which it may merge after its collective class suicide. This somewhat romantic, essentialist notion of the peasantry as a living repository similarly poses problems for Ngũgĩ's elevation of the masses in much of his critical and theoretical work.

There are a number of connections to consider finally between Cabral's nemesis, the Portuguese dictator António de Oliveira Salazar and his neo-Salazarian successor Marcelo Caetano, on the one hand, and Ngũgĩ's nemesis, Kenya's Daniel arap Moi and his descendants (see Ngũgĩ's "A Dictator's Last Laugh"), on the other. Salazar said "Africa does not exist" (*Unity* 140), claiming Guinea and Cape Verde as part of the project he adopted of Lusotropicalism, celebrating Portugal's 500-year history as a multicontinental state whose "national" independence depended on maintaining this diverse empire. Salazar, however, while defiant in the face of calls for reform, was unsettled by the events in Paris in May 1968 (de Meneses 599). After his brain hemorrhage that year, followed by a performance of the last rites and the planning of a state funeral, Salazar was replaced by Caetano who maintained a policy of "neo-Salazarism" (*Return* 27), introducing a devious scheme of concessions and repression in Guinea-Bissau that Cabral referred to as his "policy of smiling and bloodshed" (*Return* 27; *Unity* 181, 191). However, Salazar survived, and he even regained lucidity, living a phantom life as supreme ruler in private, supported in this fantasy by his aides until July 1970. In a sympathetic portrait in *Salazar and Modern Portugal*, Hugh Kay pointed out with somewhat macabre and also chilling overtones that "it is a measure of his indomitable will that he has simply refused to relinquish his life" (425). A report in *Time* magazine in late 1969 explained the bizarre court drama that indirectly illustrates the dictator's power and his isolation from the realities of his extensive empire:

> Austere old Dictator António de Oliveira Salazar is still unaware that he was replaced 15 months ago ... and he may never find out. No-one in Portugal has so far been able to summon up the nerve to tell the old man that his 36-year reign is over. The task of preventing Salazar from finding out has fallen chiefly to his housekeeper, *Dona* Maria de Jesus Caetano Freire, and his physician. ... On several occasions, Rear Admiral Américo de Deus Rodrigues Tomás, Portugal's figurehead President since 1958, has tried to break the news gently to Salazar, who at 80 is lucid but semi-paralyzed. Each time, *Dona* Maria recently told a friend, Tomás approached the old Premier's Lisbon quarters "with the firm intention of telling the truth. But he can't find the words." (quoted in de Meneses 608)

Cabral survived Salazar, and he could claim that "Africa was the sickness that killed Salazar," but Cabral would eventually be assassinated through the actions of Salazar's successor (*Return* 26). Ngũgĩ was imprisoned by Moi who claimed to be following in the footsteps of his political mentor Kenyatta. In addition, Ngũgĩ has claimed that recent elections in which Kenyatta's son, Uhuru Kenyatta, has won the Presidency despite being wanted on charges of crimes against humanity by the International Criminal Court in the Hague, are the reincarnation of Moi's dictatorship. In his most recent novel, *Wizard of the Crow*, Ngũgĩ portrays an African dictator who is driven by fantasies of paranoia and envy to the extent that he lives in an unreal world in which all those around him support his delusions.

Like Cabral and also Fanon, Ngũgĩ does not express an orthodox Marxist-Leninist position in most of his critical and theoretical writing, though more than these other revolutionary theorists Ngũgĩ has been labelled and also lamentably even dismissed as an old Iron-Curtain era Soviet. In a period when Marxist-Leninism appears in decline—the era of "post-Marxism" beginning probably in the 1970s—particularly due to the crises in communist states like China and the USSR (Hobsbawm 385–98), and the work of Marx is relegated to the province of things "academic" or "intellectual" in the worst sense with the consequent loss of the power of seriously engaged Marxist critique especially in the wake of the post-9/11 "war on terror," Ngũgĩ continues to be seen as a revolutionary rebel of the old guard.[9] Rampant speculation about his direct antigovernment political activism has been trumpeted by neocolonial governments in Kenya where at times he has been a convenient bogey man. In the period of *Writers in Politics*, he did cite Marx extensively with a somewhat unsubtle application of moral binaries and deployed "the argot of the super-left."[10] One example of this exasperated criticism appears in John Povey's otherwise sympathetic 1981 review of *Writers in Politics*:

---

[9] Surveying the "retreat" from Marx and Marxism between 1980 and 2000, Hobsbawm writes that "in the greater part of the world Marxism was reduced to little more than the set of ideas of a slowly eroding corps of middle-aged and elderly survivors" (385). Writing in 1997, Williams noted that Ngũgĩ "remains ... unfashionable in his refusal to renounce Marxism" ("'Like wounded birds'?" 218), and in 2011, Lazarus could still claim categorically that "Ngugi is a Marxist" (*Postcolonial* 34).

[10] To use McCulloch's phrase from his discussion of Cabral (130).

Those tired clichés exemplify what is so dismaying about this book. No matter what one's general sympathy for much of Ngugi's view, his diction is banal, and that is a devastating accusation to launch at a writer. But use of secondhand phrases from socialist tracts, as George Orwell properly reminded us, is not accidental but is clear evidence of avoiding original thought. There are excellent reasons to teach Kenyan children in Swahili rather than in English, as Ngugi advocates. His recommendation carries less credence when couched in slogans such as "Neocolonial profit hunting adventures" or "imperialist cultural domination in the cultural struggle." The only familiar animal I missed was the legendary "fascist hyena." (717)

Ngũgĩ's revised version of this text in 1997, however, removed a number of Marxist references, though his stance remains strident. In a revealing interview with Amooti wa Irumba conducted in 1979, Ngũgĩ set out, chapter and verse, some of the most influential Marxist texts in his estimation that he first encountered at Leeds. As elsewhere, he stresses what he considers the central importance of Lenin's *Imperialism: The Highest Stage of Capitalism* for understanding neocolonial imperialism.[11] For Lenin, colonialism is a necessary outcome of "high" capitalism's accelerating hegemonic appetite for "economic territory" in raw materials and geopolitical influence:

When the colonies of the European powers in Africa, for instance, comprised only one-tenth of that territory (as was the case in 1876), colonial policy was able to develop by methods other than those of monopoly—by the "free grabbing" of territories, so to speak. But when nine-tenths of Africa had been seized (approximately by 1900), when the whole world had been divided up, there was inevitably ushered in a period of colonial monopoly and, consequently, a period of particularly intense struggle for the division and the redivision of the world. (124)

While the cogency of this text would remain for Ngũgĩ, over time the work of Marx and Engels would eclipse that of Fanon or at least it would help, as Ngũgĩ said to Amooti wa Irumba,

to reveal the serious weaknesses and limitations of Frantz Fanon, and especially his own petit bourgeois idealism that led him into a mechanical overemphasis on psychology and violence, and his inabilities to see the significance of the rising and growing African proletariat. I avidly read Engels' *Socialism: Scientific and Utopian*; Marx's preface to his *Introduction to Political Economy*; some sections of *The German Ideology*; Engels' *Anti-Duhring* and the first volume of Marx's

---

[11] Lenin defines this phrase in the following terms:
Imperialism is capitalism in that stage of development in which the dominance of monopolies and finance capital has established itself; in which the export of capital has acquired pronounced importance; in which the division of the world among the international trusts has begun; in which the division of all territories of the globe among the great capitalist powers has been completed. (89)

> *Capital*, as well as Marx's two studies on class struggles: *Class Struggles in France* and *The 18th Brumaire of Louis Napoleon*. I could not always understand all these writings ... but nevertheless they opened a new world to me. Or rather, they made me look at the old one differently. (xxxiii)

Gikandi refers to Ngũgĩ's "orthodox Marxist phase in the 1970s and 1980s," stressing its relative brevity in his lengthy career and the unwillingness of some critics to perceive the connection between Ngũgĩ's "ideological dilemma" and his "aesthetic problems" (*Ngugi* 11). In his most recent work, Ngũgĩ is more likely to cite Foucault, Lao Tze, Plato, or even the Bible. In *Something Torn and New*, it appears Ngũgĩ has both simplified his utterance and deleted the language of Marxism, as if he is acutely conscious of the fact that he is directly addressing an American audience who may be unfamiliar with some of his core ideas and also instinctively and rabidly hostile to the "s-word" (socialism) if not "Marxism." This recognition of audience may also lie behind his initial primer on colonialism which extrapolates on the theme of Rodney's *How Europe Underdeveloped Africa*, a text he cites in the third lecture. However, in these lectures, his central interest remains history and its transformation. To quote Marx as the English historian Eric Hobsbawm does in the title of his recent *How to Change the World: Marx and Marxism, 1840–2011* and as Ngũgĩ himself does at the end of *Penpoints, Gunpoints and Dreams*: "It was ... Marx who talked about the point of philosophy not being so much to explain the world, as had been the trend hitherto, but to change it" (*Penpoints* 132). Ngũgĩ's most recent *Globalectics* does return to and cite Marx, though Ngũgĩ refers more extensively to Hegel in light of Fanon's account of the master-slave dialectic in *Black Skin, White Masks* (*Globalectics* 24). Ngũgĩ's references to Marx primarily illustrate historical and cultural insights and Marx's anticipation of globalization, but they ignore class struggle. In his seventh decade, Ngũgĩ becomes a grand old man of African letters if still an amazingly energetic, productive, and passionate one, a man full of years like Du Bois, James, or even Sartre near the end of their careers, and further in some ways from those charismatic intellectual activists who died young like Fanon, Rodney, or Cabral. As Rodney recognized, not every intellectual activist can be Che Guevara (*Walter Rodney Speaks* 113). While he is sometimes regarded as an extremist or fetishist in his insistence that African literature must be written in African languages and that European-language literature about Africa is a multinational version of "Afro-Saxon" literature, Ngũgĩ has mainly utilized English for his essays and even his autobiographical writing, and he increasingly addresses an audience of postcolonial and other intellectuals in these works. While it is a mark of the impact of his early theoretical work that it still to an extent defines him, Ngũgĩ has broadened his perceptions considerably to address memories of the past and dreams of an African renaissance in the future.

Where Ngũgĩ does embrace politics most explicitly is in his view, following Cabral, that political and national liberation is a cultural act, and that cultural ferment itself provokes material change. For Ngũgĩ in the Kenyan situation, these connections are most clearly demonstrated in the figure of Dedan Kimathi, general of the Kenya Land and Freedom Army, and first prime minister of the Kenya parliament in internal exile, who was also the organizer of the Gichamu theater group in the 1940s that held secret performances in locations such as Karunaini and Ihururu. Cultural renewal for Kimathi, as for Cabral and Ngũgĩ, was a vital component of the armed struggle. The practice of the artist-intellectual-activist was perhaps most clearly brought home to Ngũgĩ during his involvement with the Kamĩrĩĩthũ Community Educational and Cultural Centre in the late 1970s. This was a community theater project that began as an educational endeavor, teaching literacy through the raising of political awareness, an approach based on the theories of Paulo Freire. The sensitive nature of this center's communally produced Gĩkũyũ-language plays for the neocolonial government and its subsequent brutal suppression would be an object lesson for Ngũgĩ in the political nature of all art and especially that using indigenous languages as a medium. The African artist-intellectual engaged in creative work in the local community is necessarily engaged in politics, and an awareness of this relationship is vital and vitally connected to ending material poverty.

Ngũgĩ, moreover, has always been wary of evocations of cultural purity for its own sake as well as Modernist assertions of the artist's detachment. In his introduction to Okot p'Bitek's *Africa's Cultural Revolution*, for example, he suggests that the great oral poet was "in danger of emphasizing culture as if it could be divorced from its political and economic basis" (xii). Moreover, in *Homecoming*, Ngũgĩ rejects "the cult of the artist with its bohemian priests" (6), and in *Barrel of a Pen*, he distinguishes the "people's artist" from "the poet laureate or the court singer to the status quo" (61). Later in *Homecoming*, he criticizes Soyinka's glorification of the artist as a figure standing aloof from material concerns and more generally his failure to identify uncritically with the masses or to herald radical political action, though Ngũgĩ does concur with Soyinka's censure of intellectuals' "moral atrophy" (*Homecoming* 61). Ngũgĩ's views accord with those of his Leeds professor Arnold Kettle who in 1965's *Communism and the Intellectuals* noted the relatively recent fondness of intellectuals for social detachment and "retreat into idealism" (17), to the point where at present "the more 'intellectual' the intellectual the less likely is he to be much concerned with ... the more down-to-earth aspects of professional responsibility," even artist-intellectuals maintaining they have "no specific social responsibilities at all except perhaps in the light of eternity" (19). Kettle asserts that intellectuals only hold moral power or can claim to act as "the conscience of society," asserting their "unique claim to social leadership," so far as they "identify themselves in practice with the needs and struggles of the people as a whole" (24). In one of his early strident proclamations on the responsibility of African artist-intellectuals, Ngũgĩ, like Kettle, says the writer should investigate the "revolutionary struggle" and contribute "moral direction and vision" to the cause (*Homecoming* 66). In particular, he writes: "I believe that African intellectuals must align themselves with the struggle of the African masses for a meaningful national ideal" (*Homecoming* 50). These statements point to a certain tension in

Ngũgĩ's works between a view of the postcolonial artist-intellectual as director and visionary, positioned in the vanguard of the struggle and a criticism of such a placement as elitist, in favor of a Gramscian view of intellectual workers existing for a time in every class and a perception of the intellectual as merely a member of the masses.

Ngũgĩ comes closest to advocating something like class suicide for neocolonial artist-intellectuals, the survival of Cabral's hybrid petty bourgeoisie, in *Writers in Politics*, a text that displays a certain hardening of attitudes. The African writer must

> recognize the global character of imperialism and the global character and dimension of the forces struggling against it to build a new world. He must reject, repudiate, and negate his roots in the native bourgeoisie and its spokesmen, and find his true creative links with the pan-African masses over the earth in alliance with all the socialistic forces of the world. He must of course be very particular, very involved in a grain of sand, but must also see the world past, present, and future in that grain. He must write with all the vibrations and tremors of the struggles of all the working people in Africa, America, Asia and Europe behind him. Yes, he must actively support and in his writing reflect the struggle of the African working class and its class allies for the total liberation of their labour power. (*Writers*, rev. ed., 75)[12]

Though this injunction to "reject, repudiate, and negate" signifies the severing of bourgeois ties and the forging of popular solidarity (the first edition refers to the "peasant class" as the group to which the "working class" must adhere [*Writers*, 1st ed., 80]), it also universalizes the writer's role, conjuring the phrases from Blake's "Auguries of Innocence"[13] to which Ngũgĩ returns again in his recent writing (*Globalectics* 2) and to which he will attribute some of the characteristics of globalectics. This injunction from *Writers in Politics* also conjures the hyperbolic assertions of the philosopher Imlac, who seeks admission and then escape from the pleasure palace of the Happy Valley and finally resolves to assist others with the search for meaning, in Samuel Johnson's *Rasselas*. In his lengthy account of the vocation and the training of the poet who is the "legislator of mankind,"[14] not obsessed with "number[ing] the streaks of the tulip" (61–2), Imlac is a parody of the enthusiast. Johnson, like Swift, one of Said's model intellectuals, was also a citizen of a colonized country (Scotland).

Kwame Appiah would question whether Ngũgĩ's view of the writer in politics is not "avant-garde" and Western, maintaining that "African intellectuals"

---

[12] An almost identical version of this strident injunction appears in the first edition (79–80).

[13] "To see a World in a Grain of Sand, / And a Heaven in a Wild Flower, / Hold Infinity in the palm of your hand, / And Eternity in an hour" (403).

[14] *Rasselas*'s phrase anticipates Shelley's final declaration in *A Defence of Poetry* that "Poets are the unacknowledged legislators of the world" (1087).

are inexorably entangled in "the intellectual life of Europe and the Americas" accepting at the same time that a "conflictual," "antagonistic" relationship between discourses and ideologies is itself a large part of the postcolonial project (*In My Father's House* 149, 68, 72). Ngũgĩ proceeds, however, in *Writers and Politics* to name Sembene Ousmane as the writer and filmmaker who best embodies the features of the engaged postcolonial artist-intellectual, with particularly an assured sense of solidarity against "the imperialist idol and his band of white and black angels" (*Writers*, rev. ed., 77). Far from anxieties about "this dreadful indulgence called fiction," as Ngũgĩ sometimes thought of the activity of telling stories while drafting *Petals of Blood* (*Writers*, rev. ed., 87), African and Afro-American literature is itself the story of resistance to imperial hegemony, and he calls on "writers and all cultural workers" to accept their position "at the forefront of this struggle" (*Writers*, rev. ed., 131) even while they are living within an oppressive state. Even writers such as those in Plato's Republic, he maintains in *Penpoints*, while admitted solely to praise the emperor, may still embed oppositional attitudes within their works (*Penpoints* 31–5).

Ngũgĩ's well-known manipulation of the pen-gun analogy in *Barrel of a Pen* and *Penpoints, Gunpoints and Dreams*, while probably originally derived from Bulwer-Lytton's phrase about the pen being mightier than the sword or Mao's about truth issuing from the barrel of a gun, encapsulates Ngũgĩ's mid-career assertion of cultural work's relationship to politics and the engaged intellectual's responsibility. In the postcolony, the artist should voice the new national culture, even using new media, and not simply reproducing "petrified museum culture" (*Barrel* 81), and Ngũgĩ would experiment with film making in this period.[15] By the time of *Moving the Center*, while still enjoining intellectuals to ally with the peasantry and use African languages as a means of accomplishing this alliance, Ngũgĩ expresses more sympathy for the widespread intellectual despair of the late 1960s and 1970s after the intoxicating optimism of independence and the slow recognition that true independence—not merely political independence—required more than notional support.[16] The failure or unwillingness of post- and neocolonial states to overcome their distrust of intellectual truth telling and of intellectuals as a group may be one of the central weaknesses of many African governments in the assessment of Thandika Mkandawire (10–55), a concern indirectly anticipated by Cabral. Even when not in despair, the intellectual in the neocolony may still internalize the oppression of the state's surveillance, through an awareness of spectacles of terror or through internal or external exile. At this point in *Penpoints*, as in his most recent *Globalectics*, Ngũgĩ conjures the images of Plato's cave and Armah's house of the interpreter. The postcolonial intellectual, Ngũgĩ contends,

---

[15] See Lovesey's *Ngũgĩ wa Thiong'o* (99–103).

[16] As Bill Schwarz puts it, "Becoming postcolonial is not only a protracted, uneven transformation, pitting colony against metropolis; it also has its subjective dimensions, in which that which is 'already the past' and that which is the present never quite seem to stay in place" (268).

must be either a neocolonial native informant for those outside the cave, a narcissistic lamenter of personal bondage, or a rebel interpreter working as the people's guide, using African languages like the traditional Gĩkũyũ griot or "oral intellectual" (*Penpoints* 96).

The knowledge tools of the traditional oral intellectual in African society were public property, Ngũgĩ maintains (*Writers*, rev. ed., 150), but the neocolonial intellectual is doubly alienated: both self-alienated and alienated from the community by a Western orientation,[17] a desire to maintain material privileges and status, and especially by language, a growing unfamiliarity with the mother tongue and a resistance to using it in intellectual work. This linguistic divorce would come to preoccupy Ngũgĩ's view of the postcolonial intellectual in his most famous theoretical work, that is powerfully inflected with autobiographical reflections, *Decolonising the Mind*. He would also posit language—to some extent distinct from the peasantry—as the repository or archive of culture in Cabral's terms. He would also in his later work advocate for Swahili as a universal language, for translation to allow knowledge flows within the Pan-African diaspora, and for multilingualism to overthrow what he has recently called "the dictatorship of monolingualism" ("A Multi-Centered Globe" 122). Ngũgĩ acknowledges a certain repetition in his insistence on the importance of language in many of his works, but justifies it with an echo of Cabral's "return to the source": "[T]he responsibility of Africa's artists and intellectuals to return to the languages of the people ... has been my theme in books, and in my talks, over the last ten years. This is because I do not want the issue to be forgotten" (*Penpoints* 128). In *Something Torn and New*, published shortly before Ngũgĩ's memoir of childhood (*Dreams in a Time of War*) when clearly remembering was on his mind, his career-long concern with language appears to shift to a focus on memory, or the relationship between language and memory. He suggests that memory—not language alone—embodies the storehouse of personal and collective culture.

---

[17] This sense of intellectual alienation is noted in diasporic Pan-African studies by Cornel West and Paul Gilroy. Both see it as a consequence of Eurocentric education and the resulting divorce from cultural community. West in works like "The Dilemma of the Black Intellectuals" regards the alienation and hence impotence of African-American intellectuals as the product of their alliance with European intellectual traditions and the resulting separation from the nurturing spiritual and musical sources of African-American humanistic intellectual inspiration. For West, in Clarence Shole Johnson's assessment, the black intellectual falls into the fatal impasse of Gramsci's traditional intellectual (325), and hence does not resemble Gramsci's organic or new intellectuals. West's assessment is echoed to some degree by Gilroy's *Darker Than Blue* which traces in black popular culture a denial of community identity and responsibility. Gilroy's slam-dance of popular culture, theory, history, and politics in *Postcolonial Melancholia* stresses the imperative of remembering the imperial legacy (also part of *The Black Atlantic*'s account of black intellectual history) but it also calls for a planetary debate about the necessity but also the impossibility of conceptualizing a postracial Britain.

Appiah questions the "fetishistic attitude" of colonized intellectuals toward "the customs, folklore, and vernacular traditions of their people" (*In My Father's House* 61). In a study of Ngũgĩ's theory of language, Gikandi extends this critique, maintaining that it fetishizes language as an ahistorical repository of an innate, romantic cultural harmony ("Ngugi's Conversion" 133–43), and other critics like Arnove (284) and William Slaymaker (95–6) would agree. Moreover, language itself, particularly in the medium of orature, is a dynamic, inherently unstable category. There is an apparent acknowledgement of this critique of Ngũgĩ's theory of language, particularly when he has lived in a type of linguistic exile for over three decades, in *Wizard of the Crow* that incorporates a heteroglossic mixture of languages and dialects including Sheng.[18] Moreover, in *Globalectics*, he accepts that semantic instability "applies more appropriately to the spoken" (*Globalectics* 84). Language, too, as he has recently developed this theme, is not merely a communication system or a cultural archive, but a commodity, an export within the grid of "intellectual production," and also a weapon of control (*Globalectics* 53). Ngũgĩ's movement in the direction of memory in some of his most recent theoretical work, over and above its connections with both the historical imaginary and African spirituality, may indicate a recognition of the problem of a homogeneous language theory.

Ngũgĩ first called for the study of African languages and the acceptance of language as a vital medium of culture in *Homecoming*'s "Towards a National Culture," but a more lengthy and powerful statement about the politics of language, prior to *Decolonising the Mind*, appears in *Writers in Politics*' "Return to the Roots." This essay begins with a consideration of the debate among African writers in the early 1960s about the relative merits of writing in African languages or in the languages of the colonizers. In particular, Ngũgĩ cites the virulent reaction against Obiajunwa Wali's now famous pronouncement in 1963, a year after the Conference of African Writers of English Expression at Makerere, that writing in European languages was a dead end for African culture and that true African literature could be written only in African languages. Proponents of African writing in English of the time suggested that colonial languages, like English, in fact had united members of diverse linguistic and ethnic groups against colonialism. Even Ngũgĩ, at one time, advocated this position, but at least by 1979 he declared categorically that he regarded Kenyan novels written in English as belonging not to African but to "Afro-saxon literature" (*Writers*, rev. ed., 57). Language, he asserted, is the basis of a people's material and cultural life, and the repository of historical memory. Ngũgĩ traced the repression of Kenya's languages to the 1940s, the period of increasing opposition to colonial rule, when English was promoted in schools, and theaters and cinemas were erected to assimilate an elite class of Kenyans who would assume the mantle of neocolonial power. Independent Kenya

---

[18] See Evan Mwangi's discussion of Ngũgĩ's discourse in this novel in "Contextualizing Untranslated Moments in Ngũgĩ's Prose and Drama" (104-6) and *Africa Writes Back to Self: Metafiction, Gender, Sexuality* (41).

has maintained and even encouraged such a policy. The colonial authorities banned the Gĩkũyũ edition of Kenyatta's *Facing Mount Kenya* and neocolonial authorities have suppressed Ngũgĩ's Gĩkũyũ texts, while their English translations are readily available. Such practices result from internalized linguistic inferiority and distrust of the people. Years later, in *Decolonising the Mind*, Ngũgĩ is struck by remembering how the Makerere conference organizers and he personally had so blithely overlooked the program's omission of many famous African-language writers, whose form of expression he had come to accept as genuinely African.

Decolonising the Mind is almost certainly Ngũgĩ's best-known and most widely cited critical/theoretical work, a sustained synthesis of his argument on the politics of language and a powerful, autobiographical account, his own story of growing up in Gĩkũyũ. Near the beginning of the volume, Ngũgĩ announces his "farewell to English as a vehicle for any of my writings" (xiv). However, only 2 of the 21 essays in his subsequent 1993 collection, *Moving the Center*, were originally published in Gĩkũyũ, and in that volume's preface, Ngũgĩ laments the shortage of African-language translation and the total absence of journals or newspapers in Gĩkũyũ, a situation rectified to some extent with the launch of the Gĩkũyũ journal *Mũtiiri* at New York University in 1994 and soon to go online. The policing of English in colonial schools that Ngũgĩ relates in *Decolonising the Mind* is powerfully evoked: "[O]ne of the most humiliating experiences was to be caught speaking Gĩkũyũ in the vicinity of the school. The culprit was given corporal punishment—three to five strokes of the cane on bare buttocks—or was made to carry a metal plate around the neck with inscriptions such as I AM STUPID or I AM A DONKEY" (11). Ngũgĩ adds to this catalogue of horrors in *Moving the Centre*: "In some cases, our mouths were stuffed with pieces of paper picked from the wastepaper basket, which were then passed from one mouth to that of the latest offender" (*Moving* 33). Exposure of native speakers was encouraged by a system of informers. The effects of this linguistic apartheid were more far-reaching. Colonial English in particular accelerated alienation among colonized intellectuals trained in such schools. While some postcolonial African writers began using traditional forms and a more direct address in their writing, they were often ambivalent about writing in African languages, though these remained vibrant among the peasantry and were championed by "organic vernacular intellectual[s]" such as Gakaara wa Wanjau (Pugliese, "Organic" 177). Ngũgĩ reiterates that "African literature can only be written in African languages," and only in this way can such cultural forms foster mental decolonization (*Decolonising* 27).

Such pronouncements would become part of Ngũgĩ's lived experience through his work in Gĩkũyũ at Kamĩrĩĩthũ and within the walls of a maximum-security prison writing *Devil on the Cross*. At Kamĩrĩĩthũ the main theatrical language was Gĩkũyũ, a language connecting the village performers and audience members with their own history. Linguistic and historical authenticity were maintained through ongoing dialogues between everyone in the theater and the village, the living archive of Gĩkũyũ linguistic expertise. The success and then annihilation of the theater driven by the politically sensitive nature of using indigenous languages partly inspired Ngũgĩ's first fiction in Gĩkũyũ. Detained without charge or trial after the launch of *Petals of Blood* and Kamĩrĩĩthũ's destruction, within the walls of the prison in which Kimathi had been hanged, Ngũgĩ saw his cultural work in Gĩkũyũ as connecting him directly with a tradition of resistance. He acquired improvised writing materials—a pen for writing an appeal to the authorities and rough toilet paper—and tackled the difficulty of Gĩkũyũ orthography and the question of finding a fictional form to reach a peasant audience. Ngũgĩ chose a pared-down story with a highly dramatic and suspenseful plot, incorporating elements of Gĩkũyũ fable, parable, praise song, and myth. Writing about a country in which outrageous occurrences had become commonplace, Ngũgĩ introduced fantastic satire to escalate the narrative interest of actual events to incendiary levels.

Ngũgĩ's work at Kamĩrĩĩthũ was undertaken when he was teaching at the University of Nairobi, where he was also involved in what would come to be regarded as a major intervention in cultural liberation, beginning with the now-famous memo that launched a revolution. This intervention can make a claim for originating postcolonial studies. Before this intervention, however, Ngũgĩ had entertained other radical educational notions. In *Homecoming*, written while many Western intellectuals were still caught in a love affair with the Chinese cultural revolution,[19] Ngũgĩ recommends a type of Maoist sending down of students and intellectuals to the rural areas to learn from the peasants.[20] He writes that "[t]he universities and our schools should go to the countryside; there must be total involvement with the creative struggle of the peasants and workers. The present dangerous, unhealthy gap between intellectual and practical labour, between the rural and urban centres, would be bridged" (*Homecoming* 18). This combination of literary and vocational education, however, was also part of the mix he had encountered at Alliance, though its origin at that school was Protestant and American segregationist, rather than communist, as Ngũgĩ explains in his memoir *In the House of the Interpreter* (9–11). The event that appears increasingly significant in hindsight for Ngũgĩ was the outcome of discussions in the English Department at the University in 1968 and 1969.[21] Ngũgĩ, Taban

---

[19] See Wolin's *The Wind from the East: French Intellectuals, the Cultural Revolution, and the Legacy of the 1960s.*

[20] In *Red China Blues*, Canadian journalist Jan Wong recounts her experience as an overseas student in Beijing of being sent down to the countryside and the drafting of new, revolutionary history textbooks for Beijing University:

> Our professors were supposed to be ideologically bankrupt. The more book learning they had, the more polluted their thinking. In contrast, we were pure. Our ignorance was a virtue. To ensure the textbook would have the correct revolutionary spin, we would show our draft not to our teachers but to the local peasants, the motherlode of political correctness. (128)

[21] See Amoko's *Postcolonialism in the Wake of the Nairobi Revolution: Ngugi wa Thiong'o and the Idea of African Literature*, a work that explores the sweeping implications of this seemingly localized event.

Lo Liyong, and Henry Owuor-Anyumba wrote the memo "On the Abolition of the English Department," included as an appendix in *Homecoming* (145–50). The writers argue that Kenyan, East African, and African literatures must be the focus of the department, which should be renamed a department of literature, and that orature must be the core of the curriculum. They dismiss as absurd the elevation of European literature as having universal application and the deflation of African literature as having only local application. The university debate continued at the September 1974 conference on the teaching of African literatures in Kenyan schools, a conference that recommended the centrality of Swahili literature in a national school curriculum.

"An African Renaissance" is the subtitle of Ngũgĩ's recent volume *Something Torn and New* which offers a sweeping examination of Africa's potential in the twenty-first century from the perspective of an artist-visionary that extends the sweep of his reforming gaze to the global, cyberspace classroom and a renewed connection with African spirituality. Ngũgĩ had referred to the possibility of a "cultural renaissance" in *Homecoming* derived from the decolonization of the English Department and the liberation of colonized minds via the study of indigenous languages (16). His more recent optimism in *Something Torn and New* is related to the potential for diasporic Pan-Africanism and the alliance of the global south to combat transnational globalization. *Penpoints* is framed with the hope that the potentially oppressive machinery of the state will wither away (131). In achieving this end, "art" performs "the role of a John the Baptist," and its "mission" is "dreaming to change the conditions that confine human life" (131, 132). *Penpoints* identifies cyberspace as a new medium for performative orature, a hybrid considered further in *Globalectics*' improvisations on "cyberture" (77). While Ngũgi is drawing on a revolutionary Romantic view of the power and potential of art and the artist, and evoking the role of John the Baptist in the Gospels, he is also increasingly donning the prophetic mantle of the griot, and the utilization of the instruments of the unconscious (hypnosis, narcotherapy) to which Fanon refers as well as a type of African spirituality. Ngũgĩ may be conjuring a mode of reconnecting with the past, via dreams and memory, that resembles Césaire's use of surrealism to evoke a type of prenatal memory of a lost homeland and identity. In his account of Césaire's "Cahier d'un retour au pays natal," James writes,

> In this poem Césaire makes a place for the spiritual realities of the African way of life in any review and reconstruction of the life of modern man. Césaire's whole emphasis is upon the fact that the African way of life is not an anachronism, a primitive survival of history, even of prehistoric ages, which needs to be nursed by unlimited quantities of aid into the means and ways of the supersonic plane, television, the Beatles and accommodation to the nuclear peril. Césaire means exactly the opposite. It is the way of life which the African has not lost which will restore to a new humanity what has been lost by modern life. (James, *Nkrumah* 23)

Ngũgĩ's new prophetic dreaming of an African renaissance may thus be regarded as a return to a type of neoexilic-Négritude, a sustained fondness for the lost object of desire.

Ngũgĩ's *Something Torn and New* also expands the range of the postcolonial imaginary to encompass Ireland and hence to conceptualize a new metropolitan and even global postcolonial. In his account of anticolonial resistance in Ireland, he examines the English Renaissance's attempt to eliminate Irish linguistic and national identity, desiring merely to preserve the corpse of a dead culture as a reservoir to supply the spiritual inspiration, when needed, for the development of an Anglo-Irish identity. Ngũgĩ considers that Yeats sought just such a cultural reservoir from which to feed—the type of postcolonial necrophilia, mentioned earlier—in a modernizing, postcolonial Ireland. The suggestion of postcolonial necrophilia that Ngũgĩ deplores in his discussion of Yeats, he may have first encountered in *Black Skin, White Masks*. Fanon variously identifies the uses made of racial stereotypes and the deep-seated desire for their maintenance. In general, he suggests the African is a repository of organic, libidinal, and cultural authenticity necessary in the Manichean economy of colonialism to balance the excess of mechanization, impotence, and cultural stasis. Perversely, Fanon argues in words that suggest some of the thoughts of James (James, *Nkrumah* 20–23), that Africans represent for whites "an insurance policy on humanness. When the whites feel that they have become too mechanized, they turn to the men of colour and ask them for a little human sustenance" (*Black Skin* 129). One of the voices in Fanon's dialogue on racial identity—a type of psychomachia—proclaims:

> [W]hen we are worn out by our lives in big buildings, we will turn to you as we do to our children—to the innocent, the ingenuous, the spontaneous. We will turn to you as to the childhood of the world. You are so real in your life—so funny, that is. Let us run away for a little while from our ritualized, polite civilization and let us relax, bend to those heads, those adorably expressive faces. In a way, you reconcile us with ourselves. (*Black Skin* 132)

The creation of mythic proportions in Fanon's racial other, propelled by an anxiety about the cost of "intellectual gain," enables the projection of fantasies of completeness and excess in a libidinal economy without limits: "The civilized white man retains an irrational longing for unusual eras of sexual license, of orgiastic scenes, of unpunished rapes, of unrepressed incest. ... Projecting his own desires onto the Negro, the white man behaves 'as if' the Negro really had them" (165). However, inadvertently, Fanon appears to utilize this binary. Despite an inability to "understand Louis Armstrong and the music of the Congo," Fanon writes, for example, the "white man ... identifies himself with the Negro: white 'hot jazz' orchestras, white blues and spiritual singers, white authors writing novels in which the Negro proclaims his grievances, whites in blackface" (45, 177).

In *Something Torn and New*, Ngũgĩ moves beyond a broadening of the scope of the postcolonial and of the notion of merely dreaming the future that ends *Penpoints*. He wants, instead, to move the focus from "African holocaust" to

"Africa's Renaissance," and in so doing he advances a more methodical inquiry into African intellectual history of which he clearly sees himself as a part, as we shall see in the next chapter. His notion of celebration for rebirth, indicated in the title of *Something Torn and New*, conjures the idea of remembering as in putting together the anatomy of a dismembered idea and identity, that of the body of Africa itself. In Ngũgĩ's most recent work, moreover, there is a reengagement with spirituality and quietude which might not have been anticipated when considering his early scathing indictment of the Christian Church in Kenya. The Church oppressed the poor, allied with the forces of Caesar, and opposed the struggle for independence. Ngũgĩ concludes, conjuring the spectacle of the lynching of Christ in Waco, Texas, in Du Bois's *Darkwater* (1920), "if Christ had lived in Kenya in 1952 ... he would have been crucified" (*Homecoming* 34). While *Penpoints* refers to John the Baptist, in 2006's "For Peace, Justice, and Culture: The Intellectual in the Twenty-First Century," Ngũgĩ refers to "God" as the "first intellectual" (33), and finally to "the first intellectual who made the word become flesh" (39). *Globalectics* begins with the model of Taoism, and its embrace of apparent weakness, poverty, and vulnerability. In Ngũgĩ's most recent autobiographical work, the cave of exile becomes the house of the interpreter.

Chapter 5
Postcolonial Intellectual Self-Fashioning

Part 1: Ngũgĩ and Postcolonial Auto/biography

Ngũgĩ has not published an "autobiography" in name but much of his work engages with the autobiographical impulse, evident in the personal anecdotes in his critical and theoretical essays (particularly in his most influential *Decolonising the Mind*), his prison diary, two recent volumes of memoirs, and personal reflections in myriad interviews, as well as his early deployment of the *bildungs*-narrative in his first novels. Moreover, his early "As I See It" journalistic pieces gave a distinctly personal cast to his observations as a type of "abstract African" (as considered in Chapter 2), and early in his career he was approached to write a biography of Kenyatta, whose own style of autoethnography in *Facing Mount Kenya* and whose own biographies have been examined extensively by Gikandi in terms of the creation of the African autobiographical subject ("Cultural Translation" 355–75). Ngũgĩ's work exemplifies elements of "classic" autobiography,[1] broadly conceived, and also the anecdotal gestures of theorists, and particularly postcolonial theorists, who use autobiographical reflections or "auto-critographic" moments in their theoretical work.[2]

The field of auto/biography studies has witnessed a great expansion in recent decades, and may in its contentiousness almost rival postcolonial studies. Much of the contentiousness of auto/biography studies follows from debates about assumptions relating to a unitary, stable, constructed self embedded within some of the historical constructions of the genre. This written, autographed self or "ideological subject" in Paul Smith's phrase (105), moreover, carries traces of the diverse heterogeneity of the Eurocentric, modern, bourgeois, humanist, paternalistic, all-knowing and universal, "Enlightenment 'self'" in Julia Watson and Sidonie Smith's influential formulation ("De/Colonization" xvii). The "Enlightenment 'self'" was not female and it also certainly was not African. In addition to misogyny and racism, the genre also may carry traces of the homophobic and xenophobic. Interest in postcolonial autobiography has witnessed a significant

---

[1] Moore-Gilbert provides a concise overview of the genre in *Postcolonial Life-Writing* (xi–xx).

[2] H. Aram Veeser's *Confessions of the Critics* collects examples of "autocritography" and autobiographical and confessional criticism, analysis, and reflection, by a wide range of critics, including Spivak (Veeser, "Introduction" xxiii). In his wide-ranging deconstructive account of postcolonial critics' (including Derrida's) self-constructions, Huddart also refers to such work as "autocritography" (20); he later calls it in a different context "the strange, non-theoretical theoretical moment that is the autobiographical moment" (87).

leap in recent years, partly due to Smith and Watson's influential *De/Colonizing the Subject: The Politics of Gender in Women's Autobiography*, and its task of decolonizing a genre. Their interest in autographic representations of the other "dark continent" has been enormously influential (Smith, "The Other Woman" 411).[3] One of the major results of their text's influence is a careful attention to gender in considerations of the colonized and "postcolonized" subject in much recent criticism. Some of this work is at pains to show that postcolonial auto/biography studies are not merely accounts of non-Western life writing with colonization and race replacing gender, or of merely reading the colonial subject in the most hackneyed terms as the "feminized" other. Additionally, a danger has been isolated of merely reversing the binary and hence universalizing and fetishizing the position of the diasporic postcolonial intellectual (Holden 21), and the related temptation for the postcolonial critical gaze to re-create the world and its selves in its own image.[4] Moore-Gilbert maintains that postcolonial auto/biography is a distinct subgenre with a discrete poetics (multiple, relational, locational, and embodied), an inter- and multidisciplinary openness, and often a stance of political engagement.[5]

Postcolonial auto/biographical writing is partly a reclamation of the narrative of the self or a described postcolonial subjectivity from colonialism but also from the discourses of ethnography and Christian confession. The colonized subject is perhaps inevitably afflicted by what Du Bois termed "double consciousness," a bifurcated locational and bodily self-awareness at the center of Fanon's work in *Black Skin, White Masks*, a text that Moore-Gilbert upholds as providing a "template" for postcolonial auto/biography writing (*Postcolonial Life-Writing* 53). African diasporic writers like Fanon were alienated from a natal awareness of African language or culture, and while a writer like Ngũgĩ shared their colonial alienation and he uses the colonizer's language in his memoirs, his autobiographical self-construction is differently inflected. In particular, in his two volumes of memoirs, Ngũgĩ shares the intellectual and cultural capital of his own personal experience, though he is less obviously engaged, than Said, for example,

---

[3] Sidonie Smith contributes an essay on the romantic fantasies of two white women in Kenya, Beryl Markham and Isak Dinesen. In light of Freud's assessment of "the inscrutability of female sexuality" ("The Other Woman" 411), Smith writes that "Dinesen's fictive 'Africa' becomes an imaginative map on which we see projected a white woman's desire for an irrecoverable past of empowered subjectivity" (430).

[4] See, for example, Dirlik's "The Postcolonial Aura" (328–56).

[5] See Moore-Gilbert's remarkably comprehensive *Postcolonial Life-Writing: Culture, Politics and Self-Representation*, which despite its brevity offers a valuable historical overview of the field, an insightful poetics of the subgenre, and cogent close readings of representative autobiographies. In *Postcolonial Nostalgia*, Dennis Walder also addresses the growth in the number of works poised in the "uncertain zone between memory and history" in which writers "express their relationship with the recalled or remembered pasts they identify with," though critical work tends to overlook "memories of the dispossession, trauma, and genocide associated with colonialism" (2, 3, 5).

in an exercise of self-understanding or "self-location." Said pointed out that he wrote *Out of Place* because "I felt that I had something to understand about a peculiar past" (Said quoted in Huddart 45). While Said's words were also partly designed to counter challenges to his legitimacy—though they subsequently fostered additional questions about his truth telling—Ngũgĩ had different concerns. Inevitably the writing self of Ngũgĩ's memoirs has absorbed the legacy of the native elite's construction of agency. This agency, however, is constructed amid myriad pressures, desires, and assumed identities, including the myth, identified by Gikandi in his account of Kenyatta, that colonialism itself allows or forces the colonial subject out of a vague, collectivized, irrational ontology into history and modernity, or that colonialism creates subjective, individual identity ("Cultural Translation" 357–60). Ngũgĩ's memoirs may be seen to violate a social code prohibiting or inhibiting full revelation or disclosure of community secrets. As the Gĩcaandĩ Player, the Prophet of Justice, says at the beginning of *Devil on the Cross*, "The secrets of the homestead are not for the ears of strangers" (7).[6] Ngũgĩ, however, does not appear to consider any sanction on acting as a native informant, disclosing insider knowledge or opening the community to the outsider's interpretation, perhaps partly as a result of his own personal perception of his outsider status within this community as we shall see. Unlike Kenyatta who gives the subject considerable attention in his ethnographic account of the Gĩkũyũ, *Facing Mount Kenya*, or even Nelson Mandela, Ngũgĩ is quite circumspect on the subject of initiation or circumcision, a subject of considerable attention in his first written novel *The River Between*. Moreover, unlike Kenyatta, who maintained his connections with the Christian church, Ngũgĩ appears to have little to no concern with the Christian examination of conscience or confession as self-renunciation, the Christian "technology of the self," in Foucault's terms, designed for the disclosure, renunciation, and ultimate murder or suicide of the self ("Technologies of the Self" 16–49).

While postmodern hybridity may be the default mode for categorizing postcolonial auto/biographies to avoid the problems associated with an understanding of the genre as the "master narrative of Western hegemony in its celebration of the sovereign individual" that is "inimical to people whose modes of expression were formerly oral and collective" (Smith and Watson, *Reading* 45),[7] Ngũgĩ's auto/biographical work is both less obviously postmodern while having at its center a conception of the self as fundamentally relational.[8] A significant

---

[6] This statement in the novel, however, is part of a stylized pattern of beseeching and refusal, a type of discursive apology, that is shortly afterwards countered with the speaker's being admonished by the "voice of the people" which is "the voice of God": "Who has told you that prophecy is yours alone, to keep to yourself? Why are you furnishing yourself with empty excuses?" (8).

[7] See Holden's account of this tendency (21).

[8] Moore-Gilbert considers the relational self in postcolonial auto/biography, but he does not examine Ngũgĩ (*Postcolonial Life-Writing* 17–33).

voice in the discourse of the relational in postcolonial auto/biography is Édouard Glissant and particularly his *Poétique de la Relation* (1990) (*Poetics of Relation*) in which he refers to "[i]dentity as a system of relation ... [that] challenges the generalizing universal," with the understanding that such a "generalizing universal is always ethnocentric" (142, 117). Glissant's relational identity, resembling to some extent Martin Carter's poetics of "affinity,"[9] is a product of the experience of being conquered, visited, exiled, or subjected to nomadism. Glissant is referring mainly to the Caribbean experience and more generally the cultural politics of multilingualism broadly interpreted, but his model has application for the world of mass migration of the twenty-first century and for Ngũgĩ's auto/biographical works. Such experiences of conquest, colonization, and exile, for example, force the colonized

> into a long and painful quest after an identity whose first task will be opposition to the denaturing process introduced by the conqueror. A tragic variation of a search for identity. For more than two centuries whole populations have had to assert their identity in opposition to the processes of identification or annihilation triggered by these invaders. (17)

While Glissant uses the notion of relation as a defining characteristic of "the creolizing cultures of the Caribbean" and also of the broader oceanic narrative of the middle passage, he also considers it to have broader application (142). His poetics of relation, a concept with distinct similarities to Ngũgĩ's globalectics, as we shall see in the next chapter, is a sweeping, mythopoeic formulation based on multilinguistic, creolized relations in the global south but its application extends to an understanding of world literature—"reconciling Homer and Plato, Hegel and the African griot" (21)—the oral and the written, history, ecology, and national formations, as well as creolized, relational identity (103–9).[10] In the case of Ngũgĩ's work, the poetics of relation is central to the account of his extended family and its complex interconnections and disruptions, his village community, his membership within a tiny Kenyan intellectual elite, and later his location or institutionalization within the neocolonial prison and its links with a legacy of resistance fighters, as well as his dominant concerns with diasporic Pan-Africanism, globalization and postglobalization, and multilingualism and the politics of language.

Like a number of African writers who began writing on the eve of national independence, such as Achebe and Soyinka, Ngũgĩ has always been concerned with the question of the nation and the state, though he has declined running for elected position. His lived experience and his life writing, like those of Kenyatta,

---

[9] See Carter's *Poems of Affinity* (1980), included in *University of Hunger* (145–63).

[10] Glissant accepts the dangers of his concept: "This cultural relativism has not always come without a tinge of essentialism, which has coloured even the concepts that contributed to challenging the domination of conquering cultures. The idea of *one* Africa, conceived of as undivided, and the theory of Negritude (among French speakers) are two examples of this frequently debated for that very reason" (135).

Nkrumah (*Ghana: The Autobiography of Kwame Nkrumah*), Oginga Odinga (*Not Yet Uhuru, An Autobiography*), and Kenneth Kaunda (*Zambia Shall Be Free*), have been twinned with the emergence of his nation, though none of his auto/biographical works is a "national autobiography" of the type examined by Philip Holden's *Autobiography and Decolonization*. "National autobiography," as Holden defines it, displays through the life writing of a "representative individual who is paradoxically also an exceptional leader, the nation's entry into modernity" (5). As Ngũgĩ and Soyinka demonstrate, however, not only statesmen or stateswomen can write themselves into the nation's history, and often they become by accident or design, not only engaged witnesses, but embodiments or microcosms of the national story. In the case of Said, the intellectual writes his autobiography in part as the story of the displaced or disappeared nation to which he cannot go home. This resembles Ngũgĩ's and Soyinka's experience, when like Nkrumah and Mandela, they write diaries from inside the walls of their states' prisons as political prisoners. Ngũgĩ's *Detained, A Writer's Prison Diary* ironically is the sole example in his life writing of a text that was not written in exile, a type of home thoughts or memories from abroad. Moreover, while *Detained* is partly a manifesto of his movement into writing novels in Gĩkũyũ and of seeing his place in a cultural history of struggle, this prison diary and Ngũgĩ's other auto/biographical texts were written in English, the colonizer's language, though they may have been "mental translations" as he says of his early work (Trivedi with Wangui 403). While he does not consider Ngũgĩ's auto/biographical writings, Moore-Gilbert cites Ngũgĩ's remarks on the significance of language as a cultural transmitter in his consideration of other examples of life writing; Moore-Gilbert writes that "any narration of Self in European languages could be deemed a form of subservience to and reproduction of western cultural authority" (*Postcolonial Life-Writing* xxv).

The vagaries of postcolonial theory as it relates to postcolonial identity politics[11] are markedly different from the material realities of anticolonial political resistance. The extravagances of "self-subalternization" caught up in careerism and disciplinary boundary markings appear particularly self-indulgent in the face of real hardship and suffering in the struggle for and the period following independence as David Huddart acknowledges (Huddart 14–15). However, autobiography is not an apolitical genre, and postcolonial autobiographers in particular are often politically astute and their work, while partly engaged in constructing a usable past, is often "future-oriented" and constructive of postcolonial agency (Moore-Gilbert, *Postcolonial Life-Writing* 112). Autobiography itself may constitute "a potential site of decolonization" (Smith and Watson, "De/Colonizing" xxii). As Foucault points out in "Technologies of the Self," the ancients'—particularly Plato's and Marcus Aurelius's—concern with attending to, caring for, administering, examining, or recovering the self through writing, and acquiring self-knowledge

---

[11] James Clifford presents a persuasive argument on the importance of "taking identity politics 'seriously'" (94–112).

by becoming a "self-interpreter" was not incompatible with political activity. In his most extensive consideration of the place of the artist within the state in *Penpoints*, a text heavily inflected with autobiographical reminiscences, Ngũgĩ cites Plato extensively and in particular the allegory of the cave, to which he returns in *Globalectics*.

In what amounts to a type of autobiographical reflection in "Between Roots and Routes," Gikandi addresses the construction of postcolonial identity within the present-day cosmopolitan condition, and how its elite origins jive with the hard realities faced by migrants, refugees, and outcasts who are rootless and stateless by necessity. He considers the paradox of the comfortable, culturally enriched existence of the postcolonial elite and that of their "subject," the deeply unhappy mass of subaltern humanity forced into migration. He points to the "inherent tension between the self-identity of postcolonial elites and the people they claim to represent," when in some cases they "profited (directly or indirectly) from the inequalities and corruption of the postcolonial state" though resisting any identification with the social elite of their originary country ("Between Roots" 29). In metropolitan centers in the global south, he feels that he is "suspended between the rank of the insider and the detachment of the tourist," his location divorced from that of the migrants, refugees, and outcasts who are "caught in the cracks of the failed state" (22, 23). It is the responsibility of postcolonial intellectuals to bridge the boundaries of states, languages, and cultures, and not to seek solace in the postcolonial claim to free-floating authority via "a certain claim to displacement as the essential condition of modern subjectivity" (24), embracing a metaphysical, transcendental exile as did postwar exiles like Arendt and Adorno (27). For cosmopolitan, postcolonial intellectuals to delight in the amorphous movement between states, classes, and cultures is to ignore the fact that "global cultural flows are still dominated by those coerced migrants rather than the free-willing cosmopolitan subjects" (28).[12] They have a responsibility to use their knowledge capital, a mastery of Euro-American high culture, and an awareness of privileged access to "re-route the postcolonial" as themed in the collection in which Gikandi's essay appears.

---

[12] Gikandi reiterates this point in the powerful ending of this essay:
If the postcolonial elite has become a major component of American and European high culture, it is precisely because of its mastery of this culture as a tool for cultivating a reliable postcolonial identity. To invoke postcoloniality is to claim to be a citizen of many cultures and nations; but it is to claim rootlessness in order to position oneself in multiple cultural spaces and to have access to the goods that come with them. But by positioning itself as the stand-in for both metropolis and ex-colony, postcolonial cosmopolitanism conceals its own peculiar, particular, and often privileged entry into the world cultural system. By claiming to speak for others, postcolonial elites elide the circumstances by which the majority of the ex-colonial enters the world system, as refugees or illegal aliens, and how the process of entry and its terms of engagement generate a different narrative of global cultural flows. (33–4)

It may be useful at this point to offer a brief overview of Ngũgĩ's life so as to situate the autobiographical moments, often highly traumatic, to which he returns by way of illustration in his fiction, interviews, and memoirs, and more generally in his critical and theoretical work. Ngũgĩ's personal experience has informed his own creative and critical writing, and it plays an important part in much critical commentary about his works. Ngũgĩ would universalize the autobiographical impulse in writing ("Every writer's books are autobiographical—that is, you write about your experience, your immediate experience" [quoted in Marcuson et al., "James Ngugi" 27]), but he also saw it as distinct in his creative process, as when he referred to his collected stories, *Secret Lives*, as "my creative autobiography" ("Preface," [xii]). The traumatic events of his personal experience in many ways have paralleled what we might call Kenya's national trauma, and particularly its colonial and neocolonial narratives. Ngũgĩ is, moreover, a writer whose home thoughts have often been written abroad. Ngũgĩ's novels *The River Between* and *Weep Not, Child* were written in Uganda; *A Grain of Wheat* was written in England, and *Petals of Blood* in England, America, the Soviet Union, and Kenya. *Matigari Ma Njirũũngi* (*Matigari*) was written in England and *Mũrogi wa Kagogo* (*Wizard of the Crow*) in America. *Caitaani Mũtharaba-inĩ* (*Devil on the Cross*) was produced in Ngũgĩ's homeland, but within the walls of a maximum-security prison. The location of the act of writing may account in part for the fondness for home, and the anguish of exile and return, so prevalent in his fiction.

Ngũgĩ was born on January 5, 1938, in Kamĩrĩĩthũ, Limuru, Kenya. His mother was the third of his father's four wives, and he was one of 28 siblings. His father was a tenant farmer who farmed some of the land of an African landowner, land of which he may have been the rightful owner. He attended both independent Gĩkũyũ and mission schools at a time when the country's anticolonial Mau Mau struggle enveloped his family: a stepbrother or *muru-wa-ithe* in Gĩkũyũ (or "belonging to the same father") by the name of Gitogo was killed; a brother, Wallace Mwangi (Good Wallace in *In the House of the Interpreter*), fought in the forest; and his own mother was detained and tortured. His skill in English propelled his academic success for, as he explains in his long essay *Decolonising the Mind*, colonial authorities were training an elite to manage their bureaucracy, and facility in the colonial language was rewarded disproportionately. He entered prestigious Alliance High School in 1955. The irony of his position as the child of a displaced peasant family enjoying the fruits of academic success within an institution of the repressive colonial regime was made clear when he returned from school to discover his home and village obliterated as part of the colonial government's "villagization" policy, an event he reflects on at length in the second volume of his memoirs, *In the House of the Interpreter*. This policy was designed to enclose or destroy villages to prevent villagers from aiding the rebel fighters in the forest, but it effectively imprisoned, starved, and terrorized an entire community.

After briefly teaching in a primary school, Ngũgĩ entered Makerere University College in Uganda where the special subject for his BA was Joseph Conrad. One of his professors at Makerere was the future president of Kenya Mwai Kĩbaki, "a brilliant young lecturer" who inspired Ngũgĩ's interest in economic theory and history, including the all-important notion of the fictional nature of some economic pronouncements (*Writers in Politics*, rev. ed., 88). He wrote "The Black Messiah" in 1961 and over the next four years revised the manuscript of what would be published as *The River Between*. He also wrote newspaper articles for various Nairobi newspapers (*Sunday Post*, *Sunday Nation*, *Daily Nation*) as discussed in Chapter 2, in the period before his departure for graduate study at Leeds University. Ngũgĩ's precocious energy fired his formidable productivity while he was a student: in addition to editing the journals *Penpoint* (1963–1964) and *Zuka* (1965–1970), he wrote the accomplished *Weep Not, Child* in 1962, and his play *The Black Hermit* was performed in Uganda's independence celebrations; his Leeds University research on Caribbean literature was published in his essay collection *Homecoming* in 1972, and he began writing *A Grain of Wheat*. In 1967, the year of the publication of his third novel, Ngũgĩ joined the English Department of University College, Nairobi as its first African faculty member; by 1973, he was its first African department head, and under his direction the department's curriculum was transformed to focus on African languages and literatures, as a result of the famous memo that launched a revolution as discussed in Chapter 4. In 1970, *This Time Tomorrow*, a collection of his early plays, was published, his last book to appear under the name "James Ngugi," though he did not change his name legally till 1977.

Petals of Blood was completed at the Yalta guest house of the Soviet Writers' Union in 1976—"my contribution to 'détente'" (Parker 57)—and Ngũgĩ's former teacher, Mwai Kĩbaki, attended its launch in Nairobi (*Writers in Politics*, rev. ed., 89), and Ngũgĩ began work with the Kamĩrĩĩthũ Community and Cultural Centre where his coauthored plays were performed. This was one of the climactic experiences of Ngũgĩ's life, a cultural, political, and linguistic reeducation.[13] While continuing to work at the University of Nairobi, he began writing, in English, the novel that would become *Devil on the Cross*. In December 1977, Ngũgĩ was detained for one year without charge or trial in Kamĩtĩ Maximum Security Prison, the order signed by Daniel arap Moi, Kenyan vice president and minister for home affairs. In prison, he wrote, on toilet paper, his first novel in Gĩkũyũ, *Caitaani Mũtharaba-inĩ* (*Devil on the Cross*). Upon release, Ngũgĩ was denied employment at the University of Nairobi, and he declined job offers from abroad with "fantastic salaries" (Margaretta wa Gacheru 96), and he was briefly imprisoned again in 1981 and in 1982 on trumped-up charges after which he went into exile in London, aware of the danger of politically motivated assassination should he return to his homeland in the political turmoil after an attempted coup. His next novel *Matigari ma Njirũũngi* (translated as *Matigari*) was published in 1986. In "A Statement" from the beginning of *Decolonising the Mind: The Politics of Language in African Literature* (1986), Ngũgĩ formally announced his "farewell to English as a vehicle

---

[13] See Gĩchingiri Ndĩgĩrĩgĩ's authoritative *Ngũgĩ wa Thiong'o's Drama and the Kamĩrĩĩthũ Popular Theater Experiment*.

for any of my writings" (xiv). He worked for the release of prisoners of conscience in 1987, and chaired Umoja, an organization of Kenyan dissident groups. Kenya's president Moi was convinced that Matigari was a living person and a threat to his political security, and he issued a warrant for his arrest. Learning that he was a character in a novel, he had all bookstores in the country raided and arrested the books instead (*Moving the Centre* 159), keeping the title out of circulation for a decade. In 1993, *Moving the Centre* and in 1998 *Penpoints, Gunpoints, and Dreams* appeared, the latter a series of lectures delivered at Oxford University in 1996. In 1999 he gave the Ashby Lecture at Cambridge University, and mentions that he had "just finished the fourth draft of a one thousand one hundred and forty-two page novel in the Gikuyu language tentatively titled *Mugori wa Kagogo*, in English *The Wizard of the Crow*" (quoted in Sander and Lindfors, "Chronology" xxv).

Ngũgĩ began using film as a vehicle in the mid-1980s and film technique figures in the structure of *Matigari*. Like Sembene Ousmane, Ngũgĩ would consider film a more accessible medium for an illiterate mass audience in Africa. Between 1985 and 1986, he took a film course at the Dramatiska Institute, Stockholm, Sweden, completing a short feature about antiapartheid sanctions entitled *Blood-Grapes and Black Diamonds*, presented at the 1986 Edinburgh Film Festival. He also made another film with students from Tanzania and Mozambique entitled *Africa in Sweden* that focused on Western media images and European stereotypes of Africa.[14] With Manthia Diawara, Ngũgĩ codirected *Sembene: The Making of African Cinema* (1994).[15] Ngũgĩ's exile has continued in America, where he has taught at Yale (1989–1992), Smith, Amherst, and New York University, where from 1992 to 2002 he was Professor of Performance Studies and Erich Maria Remarque Professor of Comparative Literature, having declined an offer of tenure at Yale. Since 1994, he and his wife, Njeeri, have cofounded *Mũtiiri*, a Gĩkũyũ-language journal of literature and culture in which some of Ngũgĩ's poems appear, and in early April 1994, Ngũgĩ was the subject of a huge international conference organized by Ngũgĩ scholar Charles Cantalupo. He is the recipient of seven honorary doctorates as well as many awards, including the Nonino International Prize for Literature and the Medal of the Presidency of the Italian Cabinet.

Ngũgĩ had begun *Wizard of the Crow* well before his took up his present position as Distinguished Professor of English and Comparative Literature in the School of Humanities at the University of California, Irvine, in 2002, where he has also been the director of the International Center for Writing and Translation. The Kenyan launch for the novel in August 2004 coincided with another traumatic and nearly fatal episode, though it signaled Ngũgĩ's triumphant and courageous return to Kenya after decades of exile. In Nairobi, Ngũgĩ and his wife were viciously

---

[14] It appears that the only remaining copies of these films were lost when Channel 4 in England was preparing a documentary on Ngũgĩ, as Patrick Williams has informed me.

[15] An account of this film and of other film projects in which Ngũgĩ was involved appears in Lovesey's *Ngũgĩ wa Thiong'o* (99–103).

attacked (Njeeri was raped and Ngũgĩ was beaten and his face was burned with cigarettes) during an ostensible robbery attempt that Ngũgĩ was convinced was politically motivated and may have been provoked by the old regime's response to *Wizard of the Crow*.[16] Another incident, this time racially motivated, when Ngũgĩ was harassed and ejected from a San Francisco hotel in November 2006 while he was promoting *Wizard of the Crow*, received international condemnation, one of a number of famous incidents highlighting the prematurity and naïveté of announcements of a postracial America.[17] Amid the violence that erupted in the events surrounding the 2007 Kenyan election, Ngũgĩ publically endorsed his former teacher Mwai Kĩbaki in his bid for the Kenyan Presidency and spoke of his guarded hope for the future. Ngũgĩ and his coeditor, his wife Njeeri, are working to move their Gĩkũyũ-language journal *Mũtiiri* to an African Writing and Translation Center that he is cofounding with his publisher Henry Chakava in Nairobi, where there are plans to have the journal translated into many different African languages; it should soon go online. Ngũgĩ's American-born son Mukoma wa Ngũgĩ, a poet and also political columnist for the BBC *Focus on Africa* magazine, published a novel in 2009 entitled *Nairobi Heat*. In early 2009, Ngũgĩ published a collection of essays based primarily on his 2006 McMillan-Stewart Lectures at Harvard University: *Something Torn and New: An African Renaissance*. *Globalectics: Theory and the Politics of Knowing* (2012) is the outcome of Ngũgĩ's delivery of the Wellek Library Lectures in Critical Theory in May 2010 at the University of California, Irvine.

In his often-autobiographical fiction writing, Ngũgĩ was initially influenced by Leo Tolstoy's fictional autobiography, *Childhood, Boyhood, and Youth*. The moralistic, somewhat humorless Russian patriarch, with his massive celebrity cult, whose own country assumed aspects of his projected image, might be considered an unexpected writer model for Ngũgĩ, though his own eventual status as the *éminence grise* of Kenyan letters would bear similarities to Tolstoy's place in his homeland. Moreover, Tolstoy was a lifelong writer of personal diaries, and his long epic novels, so much admired by the mature Ngũgĩ, are composed of well-crafted individual chapters. *Childhood, Boyhood, and Youth* is a series of vignettes of parents and friends with a concentration on education, moments of guilt, and intimations of a vocation for writing. Tolstoy's evocation of blissful childhood,

---

[16] In a review of *Wizard of the Crow*, Gikandi refers to rumors that the attack "was an act of revenge for the way the novelist had represented the old regime in his fiction. There has even been speculation that an early manuscript found its way to the regime and that the attack was financed and planned by its supporters" (Gikandi, "The Postcolonial Wizard" 165).

[17] This type of racial profiling has targeted prominent African-American intellectuals, as in the incident involving Henry Louis Gates Jr. and Sergeant James Crowley that led to July 2009's "beer summit" with president Obama, and another earlier incident involving Cornel West. West recalls: "Years ago, while driving from New York to teach at Williams College, I was stopped on fake charges of trafficking cocaine. When I told the police officer I was a professor of religion, he replied 'Yeh, and I'm the flying Nun. Let's go, nigger!'" (quoted in Yancy, "Vanguard" 3).

however, is markedly different from Ngũgĩ's representations of boyhood in his novels or in his memoirs. Tolstoy writes: "Happy, happy, never-returning time of childhood! How can we help loving and dwelling upon its recollections? They cheer and elevate the soul, and become to one a source of higher joys" (40). As Ngũgĩ points out in his second memoir, *In the House of the Interpreter*, this text inspired him with an intense desire "to write about my childhood":

> Before, such feelings had been vague and fleeting, not calling for immediate action. This new desire was insistent. ... The story that came out of me was based on a belief we held as children that we could summon a loved one from wherever they were, by whispering their name into an empty clay pot. In the story, the fictional but autobiographical narrator's first whisper works. (*In the House* 165)

The magic soon ends in the story, and this fictional disappointment is related to Ngũgĩ's first experience with editorial intrusion before his experience in journalism, examined in Chapter 2. He had submitted the story, "My Childhood," to the student magazine who published it as "I Try Witchcraft" with an additional sentence added about the superiority of Christianity to superstition:

> A simple story, in which I had poked fun at our childhood beliefs and superstitions, had been turned into a condemnation of the pre-Christian life and beliefs of a whole community and, simultaneously, an ingratiating acknowledgment of the beneficial effects of enlightenment. I was turned into a prosecution witness for the imperial literary tradition from which I had been trying to escape. Although well intentioned, this editorial intrusion smothered the creative fire within me. (*In the House* 166–7)

The story introduces him personally to literary interpretation and particularly one friend's biographical literary analysis which has unintended consequences, making him recognize his longing for home and his occasional speculation about "what it had felt like to be in my mother's womb" (169). His writing is a manifestation of inner insecurity and trauma at least according to his friend's gospel of Dale Carnegie.

Ngũgĩ's early stories and novels contain a number of potentially heroic but vacillating intellectuals who may have some autobiographical resonance, reflecting the myriad ambivalences of the postcolonial predicament. As he wrote in the preface to his collection of short stories *Secret Lives* mentioned briefly earlier, the stories "form my creative autobiography over the last twelve years and touch on ideas and moods affecting me over the same period. My writing is really an attempt to understand myself and my situation in society and in history" (xii). In an interview in 1967, however, he universalized this position, holding that "[e]very writer's books are autobiographical—that is, you write about your experience, your immediate experience" (Marcuson et al 27). A number of the early fictional works evoke a figure with heroic aspirations to serve his people but caught in what is presented as the binary of tradition and modernity. A very early short story, "Mugumo," raises the prospect of a savior or messiah who will liberate the people from all forms of oppression. In interviews Ngũgĩ appears uncomfortable with this interpretation, relating the apparent savior figures in his early fiction to symbolic embodiments of abstract forces within society; he argues that in these works the people

> invest someone with this symbolic significance, but he himself is not inherently a savior—he is invested to be so symbolically. I'd be more in line with Tolstoy when he sees in the country the social forces creating certain individuals—individuals as such do not create situations, situations create these individuals. Of course, certain individuals are very important too. But the people create the individual. (Sander and Munro 50)

This shift, however, would have to wait for *Petals of Blood* to be represented effectively.

In "A Meeting in the Dark," a short story that may be an early version of Ngũgĩ's first-written novel *The River Between*, the central character, John, once again is torn between tradition, in terms of family expectations for marriage, and modernity, in his ambition for education. In his irritated, frustrating indecision, John, like Njoroge in *Weep Not, Child*, is troubled shortly before the catastrophe at the story's end by dreams of angels wrestling, and he feels that all gods have failed him. *The River Between* focuses on a young man, Waiyaki, who aspires to be his people's savior, in the line of traditional prophets, but whose career falters in moral compromise, frustration, and fatal indecision. He may be "the human 'River Between'" (Nnolim 141). In the form of an economical bildungsroman, the novel sets out both a social narrative of Waiyaki's yearning to develop education in his district in the face of traditional opposition, on the one hand, and a conflicted love story, a type of *Romeo and Juliet* beside the Great Rift Valley, on the other. He is torn between his respect for tradition, his love for Nyambura, and his appreciation for Gĩkũyũ and Christian prophecy, an early instance of Ngũgĩ's attempt to create a new, hybrid mythos, "a common body of assumptions" (Sander and Munro 52), that could respond to the expectations of different readers. Convinced he is the savior, the "black messiah" that his father prophesied and also the bridge between the ridges, tradition, and modernity, he is unbalanced by the appearance of a rival to his leadership in the community. His colonial education leads him away from his prophesied destiny, and his indecision causes him to neglect opportunities to preach reconciliation when something more militant is required. He may be defeated by his share in the ineffectiveness of all prophets or simply by his appetite for compromise which satisfies no one. Waiyaki is finally given over to the justice of the traditional council and probably executed, and it appears he is fashioned as a kind of sacrificial Christ. Reacting to interpretations of this closure as a failure, Ngũgĩ commented in 1966 that "personally, I think the person who undergoes a martyrdom is not the loser" (Nagenda and Serumaga 23). However, Ngũgĩ's apparent message of unity and reconciliation cannot be conveyed by a weak, internally divided leader, pulled between commitments to both traditional values and Western education. The account of his existential crisis of identity at his campaign's critical moment is complicated further by his personal relationship and by portentous biblical parallels. Waiyaki is a modern, Westernized intellectual tortured by personal angst and middle-class choices.

Weep Not, Child, like *The River Between*, is both an historical and also an autobiographical, coming-of-age novel with a mythic dimension. Much of the narrative traces Njoroge's educational career, beginning with his delight at entering primary school and later the elite Siriana, a school that as in *The River Between*, resembles Ngũgĩ's own Alliance. He considers the school a utopian retreat until the violence of the anti–Mau Mau forces finds him. This is a story that Ngũgĩ would later address from a strictly personal perspective in *In the House of the Interprete*r. Njoroge, like Waiyaki, begins to feel that his intimations of having a "vital role in the country" may signal his election as "the instrument of His Divine Service" (94, 95). His messianic delusions, full of potential but leading nowhere, reveal only his narcissism. His final attempt to take his own life after the virtual destruction of his family and his utter disillusionment with education, Christianity, love, and even prophets, at the sacred mugumo tree, represents the near annihilation of a people.

A Grain of Wheat, unlike *The River Between* and *Weep Not, Child*, is a novel without a hero, a series of interrelated autobiographical narratives, personal stories or confessions triggered by accidents. One of four central characters, Mugo, has entertained grand illusions of founding and leading a mission, and regarded himself as a member of God's elect, a Moses, though later he identifies more closely with Judas. The quest for a heroic, prophetic figure in this novel is undermined by Mugo's fatal compromise and his final exposure. Munira in *Petals of Blood* is closest to being that novel's central character, and he is another of Ngũgĩ's vacillating intellectuals, tormented by guilt over an early sexual indiscretion, his rejection by his wealthy, hypocritical father, and his awareness of being a spectator of his own life.[18] Much of the narrative may be understood to be Munira's extensive written confession as he reflects on and tries to understand his past. The reader of his confession is police inspector Godfrey who is Munira's Conradean double, alter ego, or conscience, but Munira is also engaged in a dialogue with himself, an expression of his perception of being an outsider. He reflects on his 12 wasted years of oscillation, indecision, and compromise. The novel's teacher of history, Karega, comes to reject an African history merely focused on great empires and heroes of the past and to embrace a transformative, engaged history of resistance as a result of an active engagement with trade unionism. He embodies the social

---

[18] Ngũgĩ however has said that "I think there is this shift in *Petals of Blood* from a concentration on the vacillating psychology of the petite bourgeoisie to the position of the worker and the peasant, the one alliance of classes which has changed the history of Africa"; in the same interview, he explains that writers "from a petit bourgeois class position . . . have tended in the past to create peasant and worker characters with all the mentality of the petit bourgeois. You create a peasant or worker character but inject into him or invest him with the particular mentality and outlook of the petit bourgeois class" (Martini et al. 123, 124).

forces that Ngũgĩ had hoped to foster in his earlier intellectual saviors, but he is a less psychologically nuanced figure.

While Ngũgĩ had expressed dissatisfaction with writing novels in English as early as 1967, the year of *A Grain of Wheat*'s publication (Marcuson et al 32), he would only finally make the break in 1980's *Caitaani Mũtharaba-inĩ*, its translation, *Devil on the Cross*, appearing in 1982. Like *Petals of Blood* and also *A Grain of Wheat*, *Devil on the Cross* has four central characters, one of whom, Gatuĩria, is a petit bourgeois intellectual of the timid, vacillating type often encountered in Ngũgĩ's earlier fiction. He is the beloved of Warĩĩnga, who has been sexually exploited by a rich older man, Gatuĩria's father, as we learn later. Gatuĩria is an artist-intellectual but he is starkly different from the novel's narrator, who acknowledges that his tale is communal property and his voice the expression of a collective call for justice. Gatuĩria plans a national oratorio in praise of heroic deeds of the past like Karega before his revolutionary transformation in *Petals of Blood*. He has spent 15 years overseas, and like Munira in *Petals of Blood* he enjoys traditional circumcision ceremonies, but is a wooden dancer unfamiliar with traditional songs, and he becomes confused when participating in ritualized erotic cross talk. He also has difficulty writing African music because its notation is insufficiently differentiated from Western forms. Perhaps most significantly, he cannot speak Gĩkũyũ without breaking into English, a sign of "the slavery of the mind" (*Devil* 56), a particularly debilitating inadequacy for a would-be artist of the nation in a Gĩkũyũ novel. His inability to communicate in his mother tongue is especially catastrophic because hearing is a metaphor in the novel for correct understanding. Keen hearing assuages mental "deafness," debilitating self-questioning, and the dread of listening to the echo of one's own voice betraying community secrets (7). At the end of the novel, Gatuĩria hears "in his mind music that lead[s] him nowhere" (254). His directionlessness is critical in a novel that ends with an emphasis on the imperative of choice leading to action. His national commitment and his love for Warĩĩnga stop at the point of hatred, which Warĩĩnga insists must be intertwined with true love. He reaches the same impasse as Waiyaki at the end of *The River Between* who refuses to take revenge on his enemies and instead dies at their hands.

Matigari is a unified myth of return, and it lacks the wayward, dithering intellectuals of Ngũgĩ's earlier works. Matigari is a leviathan-like embodiment of the people and of history itself, and his story resembles the myth of the return of the undefeated Mau Mau leader Stanley Mathenge, but he is not obviously a traditional oral or organic intellectual. In his next and longest novel, Ngũgĩ returns to this figure, but now with significant differences. *Wizard of the Crow*'s dual protagonists, Kamĩtĩ and Nyawĩra, meet by accident and become polyglot, New Age sorcerers and healers by chance, though their apparent sorcery is demythologized in the text. Kamĩtĩ belongs to a family of revolutionary figures and a line of seers, but despite his Indian MBA, he is unemployed and quickly falls into despair and vacillates like many of Ngũgĩ's earlier intellectuals. Unlike the cynical, corrupted artist Kaniũrũ, Kamĩtĩ cannot decide on any course of action.

His divided consciousness is represented by his own initial disembodiment. He is torn between retreating to the life of a hermit, "a hazy notion of becoming a physician of wounded souls," or accepting a role in the struggle (210). He requires the encouragement of the more skeptical, pragmatic, and socially committed Nyawĩra, who is directly inspired by heroic female figures she reads about in world literature, including *Devil on the Cross*'s powerful Warĩĩnga. As Gikandi points out, "Nyawĩra and Kamĩtĩ, the woman revolutionary and the hesitant male idealist, rehearse the story not only of Warĩĩnga and Gatuĩria in *Devil on the Cross*, but also that of Wanja and Karega in *Petals of Blood*" ("Postcolonial Wizard" 168). Eventually, everyone, including the dictator, is off to see the wizard for a cure for some version of the pervasive "white-ache," the debilitating manifestation of internalized racism and colonized consciousness whose poisonous influence can only effectively be cured by accessing the powerful heritage of "black people the world over" (494). Kamĩtĩ is perhaps an appropriate, modern hero—and perhaps a sort of postcolonial intellectual—in what Gikandi calls a lengthy but "incomplete epic" that ends, not with a grand, utopian gesture of coherence and significance, but with the minor miracles of love and personal freedom within a dictatorship (169).[19] At the center of the novel is the dictator's desire for and anxiety about the powers of the trickster wizard which he wants to control or eliminate, much as was to be the fate of the Ngũgĩ's fictional Matigari whom state authorities in 1987 sought to arrest as a troublemaker, in response to rumors that he was roaming the countryside demanding truth and justice.

Ngũgĩ has given many interviews over the course of his five-decade long career, and he is very generous with his time, due to his commitment to open dialogue, hearing readers' reactions, promoting his core ideas, and introducing new readers to his growing corpus of texts. However, Ngũgĩ is not the prominent "celebrity-type of intellectual" or media or multimedia personality perhaps most famously embodied by Cornel West and the late Christopher Hitchens, though there are similarities in these intellectuals' commitment to communicating their ideas.[20] In some cases, Ngũgĩ's interviews at their best offer a type of dictated or mediated autobiography and a reflection on his work that has an autobiographical cast. As he said in a revealing interview from 1964, "[w]riting, I take to be a kind of confession where the writer is almost confessing his own private reactions to various individuals, to various problems; you know the feeling of shame here, the

---

[19] For a study of representations of this dictator figure in African literature, see Gĩchingiri Ndĩgĩrĩgĩ's collection *Unmasking the African Dictator: Essays on Postcolonial African Literature*, including my essay, "The Last King of Africa: The Representation of Idi Amin in Ugandan Dictatorship Novels."

[20] Clarence Shole Johnson cites Lewis Gordon's view of the celebrity intellectual (327), and West freely admits that he takes his vocal, public role from the traditions of the Black American church and Afro-American music, accepting that "speaking outweighs writing in my intellectual praxis" (West 360). James Cone maintains that "West perceives himself as an intellectual freedom fighter" "who uses his intellect as a weapon against oppression in all its forms and to inspire ordinary people to believe in themselves" (108, 109).

feeling of inadequacy there, the love-hatred" (Abdullahi 15). The interview itself can be a form of "conversation" or "translation" of his ideas of the sort involved in the interchange of the best translation from one language to another (Trivedi with Wangui 405). There is a certain amount of repetition in these "conversations" due to the homogeneity of the questions and Ngũgĩ's own increasing tendency to highlight certain episodes in his life (schooling, the curricular revolution at Nairobi, community theater, detention, and exile) as well as to emphasize his preoccupation with history, resistance, language, the artist, the peasantry, and the state. He also inevitably rehearses his literary and theoretical influences, noting particularly Tolstoy, Brecht, Shakespeare, Stevenson, Lawrence, Conrad, Lamming, Fanon, Cabral, Marx, Engels, Lenin, and Plato. In some cases, these "schooled" responses, frequently involving self-quotation or paraphrase, give his utterance a certain hectoring quality as he reiterates, rephrases, and repeats his core positions that inevitably become more inflexible and almost formulaic through being so often rehearsed. Moreover, he inevitably, despite his frequently noted desire to allow readers to form their own opinions, becomes a major interpreter of his own words and of the stages of his work's development. The tendency to refer to Ngũgĩ's own words as definitive is a feature of much criticism of his work. In these interviews, a number of which are collected in Reinhard Sander and Bernth Lindfors's valuable *Ngũgĩ wa Thiong'o Speaks*, there is a remarkably consistent return to the question of the role of the writer and intellectual in postcolonial Kenya and the global south. Taken together, these interviews "trace the trajectory of his intellectual engagement with his ideas" and show his "evolution as a thinker" (Sander and Lindfors, "Introduction" xii, xi).

Ngũgĩ frequently returns to questions of social organization and class relations in the postcolony and the role of intellectuals in producing but not sharing cultural and intellectual capital. As he said in 1971, after "formal independence" there is a need to rationalize inherited colonial institutions, economic systems, and land distribution, but also the postcolony's social structure: "What shall we do about the differences between the educated or elite class and the masses of peasants and workers? What is the best form of social organization which might release the tremendous energy in the people of East Africa?" (Sander and Munro 54–5). In his understanding of these issues, language is a fundamental component. He clearly regards his experiences at Kamĩrĩĩthũ and also in detention as demarcating his own liberation from his acquired class position, partly as both experiences, however harrowing and also educational in different ways, were based on his reengagement with Gĩkũyũ. The peasants at Kamĩrĩĩthũ guaranteed the linguistic authenticity of the communally produced plays, and even some of the warders at the maximum-security prison gave assistance in his search for Gĩkũyũ words and structures for his first Gĩkũyũ novel (Wilkinson 202; Granqvist 170). He laments the separation of the intellectual elite and the people, and the sequestering of the intellectuals' knowledge capital in an inaccessible foreign language (Schwerdt 285). Linguistic alienation is as much a symptom of neocolonialism as the democratic deficit that follows when "most Africans are made foreigners in their own countries at the level of cultural practices" (Msimang 328), and feel impotent in the political process. While, like Gramsci, he acknowledges differences within the body of intellectuals, he takes a firm stance on intellectual responsibility:

> An intellectual is not a neutral figure in society. In fact, intellectuals have their different class biases and inclinations. In a class-structured society intellectuals also reflect different class positions and outlook in that society. They are often spokesmen of this or that class position. They articulate a world outlook which is in harmony with this or that class. There are some Kenyan intellectuals who do not see anything wrong with imperialism. To such, therefore, collaboration with imperialism was not necessarily evil. (Omari 130)

Ngũgĩ is adamant that intellectuals tackle "present needs" in their writing (Friedberger 41), and in a related but legislative vein he says that literature is good only if it addresses "the people's struggle" (Parker 61) and that historians must produce a type of inspirational, heroic history; in fact, he says provocatively, "I feel that Kenyan history, either precolonial or colonial, has not yet been written" (*Weekly Review* 87). He is also adamant that critics of African literature must know African languages, and he refers to his own work in promoting criticism in African languages:

> What becomes important is that authors, writers and academics must start responding to African languages. For example, in the United States, and all over the world, there are experts on Africa—historians, philosophers and so on—who do not know a single African language. It is only with regard to Africa where, once again, the continent is taken so much for granted that people assume they can become experts on the region without having to concern themselves with African languages. It is inconceivable the other way round, that there could be a scholar on, say, French history or French philosophy, who could not be bothered to learn the French language. (Jaggi 271)

The primary responsibility, however, lies with domestic intellectuals and presumably even those in exile, because if they "do not do anything about those languages, who else can?" (Kumar 173).

Ngũgĩ's strictly autobiographical work in his two memoirs is the accomplishment of his senior years though it follows on the emphasis on memory and dreams in some of his more recent critical and theoretical works. His first memoir, however, is in some respects an expansion of a surprisingly detailed personal interview, conducted in Ngũgĩ's home in his village of Limuru over two days in January 1979, included as an 85-page appendix in Amooti wa Irumba's graduate dissertation. The poignancy of this domestic setting after his year-long detention may have facilitated the detailed reflections on Ngũgĩ's early life in his most revealing interview.[21] Asked about his family background and particularly his father's separation from his mother, one of his four wives, in 1946 or 47, leaving her with six children to raise, he recalls that,

---

[21] An accessible abridgement of this interview is contained in Sander and Lindfors's *Ngũgĩ wa Thiong'o Speaks* (99–108).

> my mother ... initially suggested that I go to school. I remember those nights when I would come back home from school, and not knowing that she could not read or write, I would tell her everything that I had learnt in school, or read to her something and she would listen very keenly, and so on, and give me a word of advice here and there. So my mother is a remarkable peasant woman in every way. (Amooti iv)

Asked whether he retains any residual bitterness towards his father, he responds,

> You see, in a peasant polygamous family it is the woman anyway who looks after the children and takes care of her immediate house, so to speak. But I later understood the deep frustrations and psychological violence brought about by the indignity and exploitation of virtual serfdom that was my father's lot. Family breakdown results from such a social situation of exploitation and oppression. Family breakdown is very common in Kenya and it is getting worse. (vi)

Ngũgĩ's tendency to generalize from the particular and the personal, and to extract a lesson or piece of proverbial wisdom from moments of suffering that appear so often in his school memoir—in effect to use the narrative of personal experience as a teaching occasion, and perhaps by so doing to distance the event from himself and to disguise a reluctance to reveal the self as somehow unseemly—is already apparent. However, the words of his mother in his second memoir perhaps offer an explanation for Ngũgĩ's response to Amooti's question, when she cautions Ngũgĩ's younger brother: "He is still your father. Don't you judge him. Let him judge himself" (*In the House* 99).

Dreams in a Time of War, A Childhood Memoir is an autobiographical work that seems poised to become one of the most celebrated postcolonial autobiographies of childhood. It details Ngũgĩ's childhood like the first of Soyinka's autobiographical works, *Aké: The Years of Childhood*, and the early sections of Said's *Out of Place*. It contains the stark power of Goretti Kyomuhendo's Ugandan war novel *Waiting* in its account of the realities of rural poverty and the incursions of distant terror into domestic life, evoked with what Lazarus calls in a different context, a powerful "representation of subaltern consciousness" (Lazarus, *Postcolonial* 145). While its focus is remembering rather than explaining or justifying, its retrospective perspective is balanced with the intensity of reliving experience. While it details the progress of a major artist and postcolonial intellectual, it also displays the everyday material realities of the lives of many of the poorest Africans, lives in which illness can be catastrophic and lack of food is a frequent fact of life. It also displays the yet more catastrophic entry of colonial history into an extended family as the Mau Mau conflict makes a harsh material existence still harder. The memoir extends homage to those who offered support and encouragement, and at its center is a divided self.

Dreams in a Time of War's narrative overlaps with some of the scenes and relationships in Ngũgĩ's early novels. The memoir and *Weep Not, Child*, for example, both contain the incident of going to the landlord's house for a children's party, a happy occasion due to an abundance of food disrupted by laughter during grace. In the memoir, the landlord's wife deplores the disruption explaining it as the result of Ngũgĩ coming from a family of "heathens" ignorant of "Christian etiquette" (82), and in *Weep Not, Child* they are from "primitive homes" (18–19); Ngũgĩ also recounts this incident in his interview with Amooti wa Irumba (iv–v). In all accounts, there is a recognition of the conflict between missionary converts' and traditional cultural values, but in the novel the scene enables the protagonist to connect with his beloved Mwihaki, whereas in the memoir motives and reactions are more complex and conflicted. Ngũgĩ leaves without eating. He feels ashamed after his first direct encounter with the marriage of Christianity and class differences, though his reaction is conflicted due to the landlord's earlier aid with a serious eye problem. In the early fiction and the memoir, education is held out as a panacea which can "keep dreams alive even in times of war" (*Dreams* 195). There are also echoes of later texts such as the story of murdering the home guard in hospital which recalls the scene ending Ngũgĩ's children's story *Njamba Nene and the Cruel Chief*, and Ngũgĩ's perception that one needs a "license to write" or risk arrest and imprisonment that seems to anticipate the state censorship underlying *Detained* (220). There is an intertextual or more specifically Dickensian element to the memoir, to which Ngũgĩ gestures with his references to *Oliver Twist* and *Great Expectations* and more generally the scenes of childhood poverty, hunger, abandonment, and neglect. It does demonstrate the importance of hearing stories and later of reading to escape the relentless oppression of poverty and particularly foodless lunches as well as in forming the self and fostering an ambition to write. His accounts of orature and of performative rituals like his cousin's precircumcision ritual of rebirth largely disappear after his discovery of reading, and particularly reading the Old Testament and its stories of heroic figures like David. Ngũgĩ also shows again and again how stories, even those about World War II or local crime, quickly get embellished and enter communally circulating gossip.

It is a highly episodic account, and as often mundane or ordinary as unusual, though the very ordinariness of accounts of sibling rivalry or thefts of candy are powerfully evoked, and Ngũgĩ gives attention to the cruelties and bullying he witnessed in his childhood, and also his own moments of intense shame, often the consequence of a lack of modest clothing or food. He remembers a frequent reference to proverbial wisdom as a method for enduring the harsh realities of life. Ngũgĩ's education is his mother's "dream and her entire doing," and though she is illiterate she closely monitors his progress. However, while he is soon caught by a love of learning, he is initially enraptured by the promise of a school uniform, so unlike his usual clothing, a "single piece of rectangular cotton cloth, one side under my left armpit and with the two corners tied into a knot over the right shoulder. No shorts, no underwear. When my younger brother and I ran down the ridge, playing our games, the wind would transform our garments into wings trailing our naked bodies" (*Dreams* 60, 59). Pride in the new clothes slowly changes as he must remove the uniform on arrival home, and "I soon found embarrassment increasingly creeping into my awareness of the world, especially when I encountered the other kids who had simply changed into regular shorts and shirts" (62).

The first half of the memoir offers a very personal, though never really intimate, account of his early life in his extended family, after which his narrative of schooling supersedes his family stories and his growing "pantheon of mythical heroes" (141). Increasingly, too, accounts of acting as a scribe to his maternal grandfather, success in a school essay contest, reputation as a singer, and various schemes to earn money, are punctuated by historic events (the return of Kenyatta, Mau Mau, and the murder of Chief Waruhiu). Increasingly, the focus of the narrative changes to accounts of others, from his teacher, the "itinerant scholar" Ngandi Njuguna (135), Mbiyu Koinange, Waiyaki, Makhan Singh, his bitter grandmother Gathoni, who wants his circumcision, his mentor Ngandi, and his beloved English teacher Samuel Kibicho, and all those who become surrogate parents in the absence of his father. It becomes a work of homage, of paying respect, and perhaps its most intense homage is to his mother, a woman of great wisdom and skillful strategy, and also few words, after whom he is named in the home compound (Ngũgĩ wa Wanjikũ); he is named "Ngũgĩ" after his maternal grandfather and "wa Thiong'o" after his father; Ngũgĩ wa Thiong'o is his school name (61).

About midway through the account of the "dreams" of personal ambition, "the time of war" and the national story take over and Ngũgĩ shifts into retelling Kenya's story as if he doesn't feel his own story is that important or, more likely, he is still somewhat reluctant to tell all due to his discomfort over his outsider status. This self-perception may be especially acute in one who is regarded in postcolonial studies as the ultimate insider, the native informant, the subaltern speaking. His memoir's recounting of history, filtered through his personal experience of seeing a firing squad and recounting the "split loyalties" regarding Mau Mau even in his own family, is in turn punctuated by intensely described mini-scenes, including his grandmother's stories about a curse and finding pieces of glass in her body as well as his circumcision and recovery. The latter is an event somewhat drained of its traditional significance, but it is one he undergoes as "I hoped it would contribute to my self-identity and the sense of belonging that I had always sought" (197). It appears that Ngũgĩ's exile and his perception of his outsider status began very early. He offers repeated accounts of his sense of this outsider status and perception of internal exile. This aspect of the autobiographical account may explain why Ngũgĩ gives no precolonial portraits in his narratives of Gĩkũyũ life,[22] and perhaps why he particularly resents the appellation of "Gĩkũyũ nationalist,"

---

[22] Ngũgĩ appears reluctant to delve deeply into the myriad legal complexities of his father's landless status in colonial Kenya, for example, and the relations between traditional, colonial, and neocolonial society. Daniel Branch's recent account of the complexity of this history, *Defeating Mau Mau, Creating Kenya*, while focusing on Mau Mau as a type of civil rather than simply an anticolonial war, indicates the great complexity of events leading up to this period. Branch points out that "[n]ineteenth-century Kikuyuland was no outpost of 'Merrie Africa'" (28).

and also why his championship of the Gĩkũyũ language as a means of direct access to the source of cultural integrity may seem so ironic. His paternal grandfather was Maasai, not Gĩkũyũ, and Ngũgĩ's own father had to learn Gĩkũyũ and his was not ancestral land, but land purchased via traditional means, an arrangement that was not recognized later when the unscrupulous seller resold the property to the new African landlord. Moreover, Ngũgĩ's immediate extended family was composed of his father, who identified with modernity and the urban life of Nairobi, his uncle, who hated modernity and kept his children from attending school but participated in all traditional rituals, and even the African landlord who took Ngũgĩ and his mother to Nairobi to see a doctor but also allowed his son to escape responsibility for a pregnancy. After he is abandoned by his father, and driven out of his father's compound to seek refuge in his maternal grandfather's home with his mother, and after his brother Wallace joins the "nationalist guerrilla army," Ngũgĩ discovers that his mother's house has become "a menace to others," and he is again reminded of his status as an outsider (211, 217). Like Achebe in researching his novel *Things Fall Apart*, Ngũgĩ may be paying a certain debt for his father's rejection of traditional ritual and lore.[23] Ngũgĩ refers to himself as having a divided perception of the values of tradition and modernity, and in this resembling his father.

The constructed self in *Dreams in a Time of War* is somewhat divided. The writer is both remembering and re-membering, or reassembling the anatomy of his past, but also simultaneously reliving this past. He shifts from narrative present tense, as if reliving events, to simple past, as if simply re-creating a past retrospectively. There are only occasional comments on this reflection, often of a somewhat formulaic variety ("A human normalizes the unusual in order to survive. I could still count my blessings" 209), denoting a certain discomfort with the process of writing the self. He strives to give a truthful, balanced account—presenting the rich landlord's kindness in taking him to hospital, his father's aloofness and violence towards his mother and then his abandonment, and his family's rich linguistic environment but also a persistent family reluctance to uncover all of the details of the past. Moreover, his account is punctuated with reflections on his dislike of others' teasing and his happiness to be, however briefly, identified with his father and not always and only his mother. He elaborates the stories of his extended family and kinship relations, but he also points out that he cannot explain all of the connections because they are complex and everyone is not forthcoming. We do not have tales of sexual awakening conventional in Western accounts, though there is a reference to rivalry with his brother to be near his mother's breasts when they all sleep together on the same sleeping platform. As a subjective account, it lacks a certain emotional detail: events are stated, and then the narrative moves forward, as if the speaker is somewhat uncomfortable with the "confessional" mode or that he has learned through a variety of hardships not to dwell on unhappiness, however unjustified. Moreover, given the number of scenes of illness or dismemberment,

---

[23] See Lovesey's "Making Use of the Past in *Things Fall Apart*" (275–82).

the memoir sometimes resembles a disability narrative (Ngũgĩ's eye troubles, his foot lacerated by barbed wire, his sister and brother's paralysis, sight and hearing loss, his grandmother's limp arm). Traditional treatments, such as the cutting of the eyelid to restore sight, are presently as being mostly ineffective, and there is no local hospital, clinic or nursing station. It does appear that his grandmother's healer is able to restore her health by easing the broken pieces of glass from her body, the result of a curse. She suspects her husband's youngest wife as the evil-doer. There is a good deal of anxiety about curses, which impels Ngũgĩ's father's departure. However, the accounts of disability are always exacerbated by the harsh material realities of the lives of subsistence farmers, and the oppressive actions of those with land and money, such as the Reverend Kahahu and his wife.

Ngũgĩ's life as a colonial student in a time of war[24] is the focus of *In the House of the Interpreter*, the second volume of his memoirs. Its title, taken from *The Pilgrim's Progress*, indicates the author's gradual awareness of "double consciousness" arising from European-style intellectual training in the house of the colonizer, and also the role of Alliance school as both window on and filter of momentous national and international events just outside its walls. It begins with a moment of alienation, when Ngũgĩ returns home to the trauma of finding his family's home razed to the ground. This destruction he learns was part of the anti–Mau Mau policy of villagization,[25] placing over 1 million Africans, especially in Gĩkũyũ areas, into compounds (Elkins 235), sometimes surrounded by moats and barbed wire ostensibly to prevent their offering material support to the guerrilla

---

[24] David Sandgren offers a different account of schooling in this period for children outside elite boarding schools, detailing the conflict's complexity, the general atmosphere of terror with spectacles of horrifying violence, the shifting of allegiances for bare survival, the targeting of schools, and the postconflict legacy of inequality, injustice, and silence (18–39). The discussion of the differently motivated, politically enforced silence following 1978 in which "conflict, instability, and vicious ethnic politics" reigned is valuable for an understanding of Ngũgĩ's position in this period (13, 132–46).

[25] In an Appendix to *Mau Mau Author in Detention*, Gakaara wa Wanjaũ provides the very different colonial explanation of the policy. The following appeared in a Press Office of the Department of Information circular from August 11, 1954:

> The Kikuyu in their 2,000 square miles of highland country have never lived in villages. Each family occupies its own piece of land and lives in family or clan units, in many cases widely separated from neighbours. This, coupled with the lack of roads and communications in the Reserve, enabled terrorists to intimidate the ordinary Kikuyu. By concentrating these scattered tribesmen into villages, protected by Kikuyu Guard posts, the Government is not only dealing a severe blow to the gangs but is also making a great step forward in matters such as education, health and local government. Each new village will eventually have its own school, health centre, women's welfare centre and village council. Already there are hundreds of villages in the Fort Hall, Nyeri and Embu districts, and each of them has resulted in the creation of a much happier and a more co-operative attitude among the villagers now free from the fear of murder and terrorist brutality. (245)

fighters. As near the beginning of *Dreams in a Time of War*, this initial disruption is also accompanied by a change of clothing, as the return of the prodigal, educated son is not celebrated; instead, he is asked to change his school clothes to participate in building new huts. He has been transformed into a "stranger" or "outsider" in his own home (8, 48), partly from a desire to keep him removed from the brutalities of his mother's and sister-in-law's detention. In effect, his real home has become the peaceful, utopian Alliance under the paternalistic control of Edward Carey Francis who regards the school "as a grand opportunity to morally and intellectually mold a future leadership" of the country (11), an elite schooled in ethnic equality but separated from the African majority who should retain respect for the whites' superiority. Unlike his own remote father who makes a single, brief appearance in the memoir, Carey Francis seems omnipresent to Ngũgĩ, and while a Christian Anglophile, he is the uncanny interpreter who reveres Winston Churchill, fosters the egalitarian ethic at Alliance, and importantly recognizes the legitimacy of Mau Mau's nationalist aspirations as well as the counterproductive consequences of the colony's ineffective anti–Mau Mau strategy. He is a strict, even brutal disciplinarian,[26] but he also has an aptitude for performing magic shows, and Ngũgĩ's portrait is notably even-handed and generous. A good deal of Ngũgĩ's memoir records his own intellectual development, and like *Dreams* offers homage to mentors, from his teachers and fellow pupils, to the authors he reveres, as well as political figures like Nkrumah, Padmore, Du Bois, and Mboya. While Ngũgĩ's constructed identity in the memoir is that of the teachable self, he takes pains to show that schooling did not interfere with his education from the street and the community, as when he is struck by "passing comments and fleeting images" (27), such as seeing a teacher holding a copy of Peter Abrahams's autobiographical *Tell Freedom*, hearing an old woman dismiss ethnic divisions in the country, and recalling his mother's spare words under the sacred mugumo tree.

Despite an air of being the product of archival research, unlike the more spontaneous *Dreams in a Time of War*, and a certain, quasi-Victorian quality of being "Ngũgĩ wa Thiong'o's Schooldays," reminiscent of the Thomas Hughes text much loved by James, in *In the House of the Interpreter* Ngũgĩ is acutely conscious of the colonial inflection of all of his boarding school experiences which may be the clearest sign of the text's retrospective interpretation of people and events. The Victorian quality of the memoir is also partly a consequence of the school's being modeled on, not only an English school, but a nineteenth-century English public school—"an African Hogwarts, without the magic," said Hector Tobar in the *Los Angeles Times*—and Ngũgĩ's own tendency to regard all events as life lessons. With the many photographs accompanying the text, the memoir has a documentary quality as if it is a biography of the life of Alliance school, with details of chapel, classroom, and sports field, and a rehearsal of momentous first

---

[26] This is confirmed in the experience of Gakaara wa Wanjaũ who is perhaps more uncompromising than Ngũgĩ in his promotion of national languages. He was expelled from Alliance after a student protest (Pugliese, *Author, Publisher* 28–9).

encounters with prefects, debating teams, chess, Scouts, Shakespeare ("an integral part of my intellectual formation" [177]), and Christianity. Ngũgĩ describes himself as having been an evangelical Christian, converted by watching the Billy Graham film *Souls in Conflict*, though he is struck by the performative nature of public confession: "[a]s if borrowing from the *Confessions of Saint Augustine*, one dramatized the depth of one's depravity in the previous existence, before the Lord had felt pity and showed him or her the way of the Cross" (90). Amusingly, he recalls that "[w]hen my turn came, I found, to my dismay, that I had no sins to confess" (91). However, he is as much self-doubting as assured of his faith, recounting disputes about God's color and language, though he intimates at the end of the memoir that he makes a convert, just prior to a sexual encounter, and this knowledge inspires him to accuse his accuser in the courtroom scene that terminates an arbitrary arrest motivated by jealousy.

Alliance was an introduction to wide reading in the colonial library for Ngũgĩ, and he acknowledges again the influence of the King James Version of the Bible for its narratives, heroes, and plain style, as well as his more popular reading. While Tolstoy's *Childhood, Boyhood, and Youth* inspired him to write, as noted earlier, Ngũgĩ also learns the power of dramatic suspense from reading popular fiction, eliciting his retrospective comment: "Looking back, I can see that Haggard and other popular writers, when it come to my continent, were penning from the same dictum: imperialism was normal, resistance to it immoral," and that there is no such thing as ideologically "untainted fiction" (161). He enjoys the Biggles stories, for example, until he remembers that Royal Air Force (RAF) fighters were bombing his brother in the mountains, a moment of awareness he recounts at greater length in *Moving the Center*'s autobiographical essay "Biggles, Mau Mau and I" (136–41). He explains that "[his] first autobiography" was Booker T. Washington's *Up from Slavery*, but he was disconcerted by "his statements that black people had gotten more out of slavery than the whites" (*In the House* 163). Comparing the autobiographical instincts of Albert Schweitzer and Carey Francis, the latter who left no autobiography, Ngũgĩ points out admiringly that Francis disliked anything "that drew attention to himself," an indication of a reluctance to reveal too much private information that Ngũgĩ seems to share (176). Save for the brief mention of the unnamed girl who inspired his defense in court at the end of the memoir, Ngũgĩ is very modest, though seemingly surrounded by friends who actively pursue girls and women. He refers to unwed pregnancy using the distinctly old-fashioned euphemism, "getting in the family way."

Ngũgĩ instructs the reader in drawing parallels between events at home or Alliance and incidents in his stories and novels, such as the importance of his mother's mugumo tree and his first story "Mugumo" (99), a conversation about tolerance with a white student in *Weep Not, Child* (146), and the significance of running in *A Grain of Wheat* (141). However, perhaps inevitably for an autobiographical writer, there are many other links, as with his brother's "[b]urying his gun under a Mugumo tree" in his story of near capture and the beginning of *Matigari* (83) and the final discussions of the prisoners at the remand prison and the talk among imprisoned characters in *Devil on the Cross* (206–29). He notes the appeal of detective fiction and the impression made on him by the multiple narrators of *Wuthering Heights*, but he does not refer to his use of these genres and techniques in novels like *A Grain of Wheat*. The memoir ends with a powerfully told account shortly before his departure for Makerere in Uganda, which he names "A Tale of the Hounds at the Gate" (187–240). It tells of his arbitrary arrest; a number of nights spent in a crowded, fetid prison; an encounter with a white man his own age with similar school experiences and postsecondary aspirations whose part-time job in the anti–Mau Mau forces gives him almost supreme power over Ngũgĩ; the prisoners' shared stories of crime, justice, and folk wisdom; his trial on trumped-up charges of resisting arrest and assaulting a police officer; and his final, debating-style, cross-examination of the accusing police officer witness. He is accused by the police out of jealousy of his academic success, and despite his final eloquence, pointed cross-examination, and obvious innocence, it appears he is released because he is an Alliance graduate en route to Makerere, and not because the accusation against him lacks foundation. The fate of his accusers in the house of the colonial interpreter is unrecorded. As he says ominously, "Little did I know that this ordeal would turn out to be a rehearsal for others ahead" (240).

Part 2: Ngũgĩ's *Detained* and African Prison Diaries[27]

The colonial prison was the school for national leaders from Nkrumah and Kaunda to Kenyatta; Robben Island is referred to as "Mandela University." The prison diary confronts the realities of colonialism's definition of the African nation, created by colonial cartographers as a result of global imperialism and industrial capitalism, from within its very center. The connection between this literature and nationhood appears in an examination of the linguistic, cultural, and ideological constraints faced by African writers imprisoned or "institutionalized" within their own countries.

Soyinka was detained in Nigeria for 27 months between August 1967 and October 1969 for his political activities, in the tense atmosphere leading up to the Nigerian Civil War. Ngũgĩ was detained in Kenya between December 1977 and December 1978 after the enormous success of his Gĩkũyũ dramas. Breyten Breytenbach was imprisoned in South Africa for seven and a half years, under the terms of the Terrorism Act, from November 25, 1975 to December 29, 1983. These writers were imprisoned by African leaders—in *Detained*, Ngũgĩ calls

---

[27] This section is a shortened version of "Chained Letters," which appeared in *Research in African Literatures*. Earlier versions were read at the European Association for Commonwealth Literature and Language Studies (EACLALS) conference at the University of Graz, Austria, June 1993, and at the Modern Language Association (MLA) conference in Toronto, Canada, December 1993.

them "Africa's tin gods" (142)[28]—whose suspicion of artistic expression resulted from their own mental colonization: "[L]ike their colonial counterparts, they had become mortally afraid of the slightest manifestation of a people's culture" (*Detained* 71). Many African writers have been imprisoned by neocolonial governments, and left their "smudges on / the blank page of this nation," in the words of Jack Mapanje in "Where Dissent Is Meat for Crocodiles" (80).[29] It is a tragic historical irony that Ngũgĩ read Dennis Brutus's *Letters to Martha* and requested *The Man Died* while himself in political prison. He even joked to his jailer about writing to the man responsible for his detention, "Jomo Kenyatta in his capacity as an ex-detainee" (4).

The imprisonment of African writers, particularly those who are politically engaged, is the incarceration of the creative national spirit seeking to define and celebrate national freedom.[30] The writer's detention is, in Ngũgĩ's words, "an admission by the detaining authorities" that their acts and words are "an immoral sale and mortgage of a whole country and its people" (*Detained* 12–3). The imprisoned writer confronts the linguistic debasement of the prison environment, the unwillingness to define the conditions of imprisonment, and the offer of release in exchange for silence. The prison diary writes the story of the nation's contradictions from within its very center, the state institution par excellence. Examining Ngũgĩ's *Detained*, Soyinka's *The Man Died*, and Breytenbach's *The*

---

[28] Ngũgĩ has recently written about the reluctance of African heads of state to cede authority to a unified Africa: "I have a feeling that most of these leaders would rather remain tin gods than have a God who can make tins" ("Unity" 19).

[29] Jacobs's taxonomy of African prison writing comprising five categories ranging from "Biographical works with accounts of detention or imprisonment" to "Poetry and drama dealing with detention, imprisonment, and interrogation" ("Breyten Breytenbach" 96–7) is useful, although its attempt to delineate a schematic range from history to fiction is problematic, as "historical" works like Breytenbach's *True Confessions* self-consciously use fictional techniques, and collections of poetry such as Dennis Brutus's *Letters to Martha* and Jack Mapanje's *The Chattering Wagtails of Mikuyu Prison* are autobiographical. Here and in "Confession, Interrogation and Self-interrogation in the New South African Prison Writing," Jacobs usefully lists various prison writings. The attempts at definition in Jane Wilkinson's "African Diaries" and Mineke Schipper's *Beyond the Boundaries: Text and Context in African Literature* (see especially 114–18) are also valuable. Ngũgĩ discusses African (and especially Kenyan) prison writing in a number of places (*Barrel* 65–6; *Moving* 45, 72, 93–4), and Sicherman documents specific cases in *Ngugi wa Thiong'o: The Making of a Rebel* (424–8).

[30] The African prison diary has a number of the elements of Jameson's problematic but highly evocative and influential formulation of "third-world literature" as "national allegory." It allegorizes the individual's imprisonment, and the denial of history and truth contained in it, relating personal and national detention. As Ahmad has pointed out, in an essay that is often read as the essential companion piece to Jameson's article, the "national allegory" formulation is essentialist in its claims of universality, simplistic in its "first" and "third" world binary construction, and almost romantic in theorizing a synthesis of "public and private" in non-Western cultures ("Jameson's" 79).

True Confessions of an Albino Terrorist, the discussion that follows considers the prison diary as one of the defining genres of postcolonial African literature.

The tag "self-writing" or "fictionalized version of oneself" (Davies 120) seems inadequate to define the genre of the African prison diary. J.U. Jacobs has suggested "confessional narrative" (125) and Govind N. Sharma has offered "consolation" (520–8) for some examples of the form. Distinguishing autobiography and diary writing by their retrospective or simultaneous handling of the temporal, we may define *The Man Died* and *Detained* as diaries. *True Confessions*, however, is a retrospective autobiography, written "from hindsight, beginning from the certainty of a known end" (Egan 90).[31] These works are rooted in the assertion of individual identity in the face of brutal dehumanization, although in *True Confessions* the "self" functions discursively as well as referentially. These works violate the convention of private, introspective "self-writing" in their insistence on the typicality of experience, and its social and political context. Moreover, they are clearly mixed genres, with broken chronology, signs of extensive editing, and numerous additions.

"Life in prison," Ngũgĩ writes, "is basically a cliché: dull, mundane, monotonous, repetitious, torturous in its intended animal rhythm of eating, defecating, sleeping," and not "a story of sentimental heroism" (116, 97). "A narration of prison life is, in fact, nothing more than an account of oppressive measures in varying degrees of intensity and one's individual or collective responses to them" (100). In general, Ngũgĩ's method seems to be to "let impressions form in my mind until they accumulate into a composite picture" (127). In terms of genre, *Detained* is a hybrid; it collates an account of his routine at Kamĩtĩ Maximum Security Prison; essays on Kenyan colonial history; colonial aesthetics; letters written in prison; and a meta-critical account of the production of his work in progress. In *Detained*, Ngũgĩ theorizes his narrative practice in his allegorical works, which arises from what we may call his "Mau Mau aesthetics."[32] Like the seventeenth-century Puritan revolutionary John Bunyan, whose work Ngũgĩ refers to in *Decolonising the Mind* and from which he takes the title of his second volume of memoirs, a writer who evolved the allegorical poetics of *The Pilgrim's Progress* in his spiritual autobiography *Grace Abounding to the Chief of Sinners*, Ngũgĩ discovered the potential of transformative narrative allegory in the crucible of prison experience. His political detention forced him to confront the postcolonial "crisis of representation" (Jameson, "Third-World" 81). Like the Mau Mau freedom fighters, Ngũgĩ uses Christian narrative, transforming it into a cultural weapon issued from the barrel of a pen. The liberation movement, Ngũgĩ explains in the first edition of *Writers in Politics*,

> rejected the culture of the oppressor and created a popular oral literature embodying anti-exploitation values. They took Christian songs; they took even

---

[31] Shirley Neuman's call for a "poetics of differences" (225) in the drive to define the genre of autobiography is useful in this context.

[32] See my discussion of this concept in *Ngũgĩ wa Thiong'o* (64–5).

> the Bible and gave these meanings and values in harmony with the aspirations of their struggle. Christians had often sung about heaven and angels, and a spiritual journey into a spiritual intangible universe where metaphysical disembodied evil and good were locked in perpetual spiritual warfare. ... The Mau Mau revolutionaries took up the same song and tune and turned it into a song of actual political, visible material freedom and struggle for land. The battle was no longer in heaven but here on earth, in Kenya. (27)

This movement took "[t]he Christian universe and spiritual idealism ... [and] made them stand firmly on the ground, our earth, instead of standing on their head" (29). The themes of Ngũgĩ's new narrative project, engendered in political prison, are celebration of national culture and resistance to foreign exploitation. Ngũgĩ sees a connection between his diary of neocolonial detention and the accounts written by "Mau Mau and pre-Mau Mau detainees" [xii], because Kenya's laws have a "colonial basis" and "Detention was an instrument for colonial domination" (44).

The Man Died was written between lines of volumes such as Soyinka's own *Idanre* and on toilet paper and cigarette packages. Soyinka's editing decisions were "all influenced by ... my continuing capacity to affect events in my country, of effecting the very revolutionary changes to which I have become more than ever dedicated" (12). Obi Maduakor argues that "Soyinka had hoped to forge a new literary technique in *The Man Died*, a technique of 'brutal realism'" (168). Soyinka felt that "a book if necessary should be a hammer, a handgrenade which you detonate under a stagnant way of looking at the world" (168). The prison notes document his struggle in a combination of forms ranging from reportage, testimony, and stream of consciousness, to creation myth. Soyinka interrupts the relentless, deterministic narrative logic of the prison diary genre—the "indestructible continuum of ordeal-survival-affirmation" (11)—with an extended meditation on Nigerian national identity (154–83), in light of its degrading colonial legacy. This somber essay, ending with the affirmation that a nation is a people, "a unit of humanity bound together by a common ideology" (183), informs the rest of Soyinka's account of day-to-day drudgery and anguish. Soyinka survives through his faith in the "ethical base" of the nation (182), despite his wariness about the consequences of civil war. He never forgets the colonial stamp on the nation's identity:

> the artificiality, the cavalier arrogance, the exploitive motivations which went into the disposal of African peoples into nationalities. One overcomes the sense of humiliation which accompanies the recollection of such a genesis by establishing his essential identity as that which goes into creating the entity of a people. (175)

Soyinka's meditation on the nation disrupts the plot of the prison diary narrative and allows him to recover from his captors' control over his story, to connect this history to the nation's story, and to consider the future.

Breytenbach suggests the prison diary is a distinct genre, the story of "four walls, a floor and a light bulb on high" (339, 253). His "confessions" are an edited transcription of tapes completed in Paris in August 1983, a process which "defined the inner structure and tone of the book" (338). The account is driven by the "necessity to confess" and addressed to a shadowy implied reader, referred to as "Mr. Investigator" (14), a comrade and traitor, who resembles Baudelaire's ambiguous narratee in *Les Fleurs du Mal*. Mr. Investigator is so well-informed that he resembles "Mr. Interrogator" and another imaginary figure who "took shape in" Breytenbach shortly before his arrest for whom he gains "affection" (101, 118, 244). Breytenbach refers to this figure variously as "my dear dead I," "my dark mirror-brother," and "[y]ou old voyeur" (255, 260, 329). The nature of this figure's construction indicates the reader's complicity produced by the act of reading Breytenbach's revelations. This formal metafictional frame and the text's self-conscious reference to diegetic levels follow from Breytenbach's beginning his "confessions" by reliving the experience of endlessly rewriting accounts of himself and his activities upon his initial arrest and interrogation. He felt that he became the interrogator's creation. Telling the fictionalized account of the actant named Galant, Breytenbach begins to write himself. Because, in his imprisonment, "[w]ords have replaced my life" (28) as he says, he now wishes to write himself back to life. Nevertheless, he is ever aware of the sweet treachery of words and of how his writing is a "labyrinth" and "truth is a convention" (36). He perpetually reevaluates his own motivations, even suspecting, during one police interrogation, that the underground political activity leading to his arrest might have been merely "an elaborate form of self-delusion" (88). The image of the chaotic labyrinth—Brutus refers to "the labyrinth of self" in *Letters to Martha* (6)—provides Breytenbach with one of his work's central organizing metaphors, the other being the mirror. These metaphors allow the representation of the prison warders's "world of make-believe where fact and fancy mix," where "your personality is broken down, to be reassembled" (48, 129). Breytenbach tells "everything, hodge-podge ... whichever way it comes" in a "book of et ceteras" like the record of incidents kept by the sergeant or warrant officer (151, 279). *True Confessions* is a Taoist or Buddhist spiritual autobiography, the revelation of a bungled attempt at underground work, a sociological and political document about the apartheid prison system, and a poet's account of psychological deterioration.

Confronting prison's debasement of language is one of the common features of survival literature, such as Primo Levi's *Survival in Auschwitz*. The prison diary allegorizes linguistic colonialism, in which language becomes a prison house. The idiom of expression in these works is English, the discursive medium of the colonizer. The linguistic debasement of colonialism—the abbreviation and perversion of words into the utterance of the servant and slave, and the colonial association of indigenous linguistic expression with the demonic—is mimicked in the prison environment. Soyinka's warders babble meaningless phrases, and Ngũgĩ is irritated by the "voices of warders" which "would grate on my nerves" and oppressed by the language of incarceration: "Abusive language, innuendos, gibes, outright denunciation" (22, 126). He realizes that any place acquires "its own ... special vocabulary" (131). However, the real prison language is silence. On admission Ngũgĩ loses his name. He is never charged or told for how long he is detained. He believes his detention results from his revolt against the "colonial ... aesthetic of submissive silence" (93). In prison he struggles to find a new language of resistance, although he refuses the "entirely different language," "sprinkled of course, with occasional nationalistic slogans borrowed from past memories" (87), spoken upon release by those former revolutionaries (like Kenyatta) broken by detention. Ngũgĩ is schooled by his detention: "the walls ... have become my dictionary" (166). He begins his novel in Gĩkũyũ, translated as *Devil on the Cross*, after a jailer's lecture about being one of the educated elite who despises his own language. Through writing in Gĩkũyũ, Ngũgĩ is able to escape the isolation of detention and to connect with national issues, as he later refers to African languages as "the collective memory bank of a people's experience in history" (*Decolonising* 15). Writing *Devil on the Cross*, Ngũgĩ affirms his "faith in the possibilities of the languages of all the different Kenyan nationalities" (*Detained* 8). Cultural expression has become his weapon of resistance and means of survival.

Soyinka's inability to talk, read, and write freely is "torture"; it condemns him to a "flotsam existence," creating doubts about "his human identity" (278). Writing the prison notes "rescues words from a debasement to which they were constantly subjected by my gaolers, a debasement which ... constituted one of the gravest challenges to my egoist survival" (14). Most demoralizing to Soyinka are the fabricated public reports of his "chronic syphilis" (291), the publication of a mock confession, and a report of an attempted escape. He imagines his own obituary: "the dramatist over-dramatizes himself once too often" (77). For Breytenbach, imprisoned in what he refers to as "No Man's Land"—the ironic counterpoint to "paradise," his other term for South Africa/Azania—confinement is death, and as a result his account is the self-consciously fictionalized process of creating "the fragmentary scenario of my identities" (331). He becomes, as he says in a different context, "a weaver of shrouds" (308). For Breytenbach, prison is a distinct world in which language is institutionalized and dehumanized. Prison language emphasizes abusive categories. Breytenbach traces "the evolution of prison language" (177), but primarily demonstrates how this penchant for categories (from "Big Fives," or informers, and "grocery rabbits," or prisoners who sell their bodies for food, to "misters," prisoners with "illusions about being human" [191]), mimics the structure of apartheid, and the way apartheid has debased Afrikaans, rendering it "the language of oppression and of humiliation" (354). Significantly, for a famous Afrikaans poet permitted to write in prison due to pressure from intellectuals who considered his facility with the language a national treasure, Breytenbach denounces Afrikaans's ideological encoding: "In its present sociological context and political impact Afrikaans bears the stigma of being identified with the policeman, the warder, the judge and the White politician" (353–4). For Breytenbach, the chronicle of this linguistic universe attempts to overcome "the filth—the degradation of human relationships imposed on one within the interrogator-detainee or warder-prisoner context" (337). In order to purge himself of the experience, he must "vomit" up and "exteriorize" the debasement of the prison experience and its language (337, 155).

The prison diary is a detailed psychological account of a mind in sensory and emotional deprivation, an intense moral self-examination, and a forum on national issues. The individual's isolation from the community is linked to the nation's traumatized self-alienation. Ngũgĩ realizes that detention is designed to make him "feel that he has been completely cut off from the people and hence from that group solidarity—the sense of being one with the people—which alone keeps men and women going even when menaced by truncheons, nailed boots, tear-gas and deathly whistling bullets" (20). However, he comes to define his detention in terms of national struggle, and to regard acts of noncooperation with the absurd humiliation of imprisonment as taking "a principled stand on national issues" (140).

Soyinka discovers in the complex power relations within the prison community a microcosm of the national dilemma. He recognizes the residue of deep-seated colonial psychological inferiority, a process that allows the jailers to rationalize their participation in injustice as "acts of self-preservation" (70). Soyinka refuses to sacrifice any of his commitment to national issues and social justice, in exchange for freedom from trauma or increased chances of survival. As a result, he confronts warders and refuses cooperation. He resists the notion that prison is off-bounds, outside history, a moral wild zone in which only considerations of personal survival are legitimate. He agrees with "those who acknowledge that prison is only a new state from which the struggle must be waged, that prison, especially political prison is an artificial erection in more senses than one whose bluff must be called and whose impotence must be demonstrated" (69). He must "fight for an equitable society" from within the jaws of oppressive power (70). Therefore, protest against the inhumane treatment of other prisoners becomes an act of great courage with wider political consequences. He resists the robbery of citizenship which the neocolonial prison, like the colonial state, performs on its subject. As a result Soyinka connects individual and collective detention.

Similarly, Breytenbach acknowledges "the need to be able to contribute something to life outside" prison during his incarceration (157). While his "confessions" are a mythopoeic account of a journey into hell, a meditation on this experience in Buddhist terms, and a major work of sociological documentation, they are also an anatomy of the apartheid prison and in a sense a dialogue with it, written to enable "national liberation," through a class-based, anticolonial, anti-imperialist struggle (384). Breytenbach's confessions, nevertheless, explain in detail how an individual may dwell in the prison without ending in "psycho city" (188), the special wing for psychiatric cases. Breytenbach makes clear from the outset that part of him died in prison, and that dehumanization results from knowledge of degradation. Bare survival is "made up of a million little compromises and humiliations" (258). Breytenbach learns that "if you want to remain whole, recognize the humanity of your enemy" (360). The confessions acknowledge that "violator and victim ... are linked forever perhaps, by the obscenity of what has been revealed to you, by the sad knowledge of what people are capable of. We are all guilty" (343). However, Breytenbach regards such knowledge as essential for the revolutionary militant, who must never ignore the dedication and the humanity of the opponent and must not violate fundamental principles, such as the sacredness of life. The prison account reveals Breytenbach as a type of Buddhist revolutionary, for whom right thinking and right action compel recognition of South African realities.

The African prison diary brushes against the grain of official histories of the prisoner's activities; it rewrites the official version of national history. In this sense Soyinka's meditation on his imprisonment and its writing, and his self-conscious reflection about the fate of the nation become an historical metanarrative. The writer reflects on the process by which official and unofficial, colonial, postcolonial, and neocolonial histories are encoded. The progress of his personal humiliation recalls that of the "humiliated nation" to use Mangakis's phrase (quoted in *The Man Died* 19), under colonialism. This is most clearly shown in his awareness of how certain aspects of imprisonment encapsulate national history. For example, Soyinka is chained in heavy manacles "the like of which I had seen only in museums of the slave-trade" (38).

Ngũgĩ's *Detained* is an extended rewriting of Kenyan colonial and neocolonial history and aesthetics, characterized as a struggle against domestic and foreign oppression. Ngũgĩ reinserts those nationalist fighters and "the millions of dead and detained [who] had been wiped off the face of known and written [neocolonial] history" (89). Central to his project is the notion that in the struggle for national independence "the various nationalities" in Kenya acted together (64). He rejects the "tribal" determinism of colonial historians. He comes to regard his involvement in the Kamĩrĩĩthũ Community Education and Culture Centre's theater production as a continuation of the cultural program of Dedan Kimathi, whose remains lie in Ngũgĩ's prison. Significantly, too, he implies that the Centre's communal "creation" of plays was a distinctively African mode of production (*Barrel* 43–5). His period of working with this collective, "the most exciting in my life and the true beginning of my education" (*Detained* 76)—allowing him to assert his peasant origins and his family's involvement in Mau Mau, and to repudiate his alienating colonial education—enables the intellectual to declare "I felt one with the people" (78). He regards the logical consequence of the government's terror at the group's success as the desire to "[d]etain a whole community" (80). In default, he is detained and left "in cell 16 wrestling with multifarious demons in the dry wilderness of Kamiti Prison, contemplating the two dialectically opposed traditions of Kenyan history, culture and aesthetics" (80). Ngũgĩ will either be one of those who resists or is broken by detention and becomes a "colonial zombie" (83). Meditating on these options, he learns that the other detainees "fall into groups that span the whole history of post-independence upheavals in Kenya" (123). His own imprisonment and his writing in Gĩkũyũ, therefore, are phases in revolutionary struggle. Ngũgĩ exults: "I am part of a living history of struggle" (124). Therefore, writing about detention represents the culmination of his own narrative of postcolonial history. Through his defiant detention and his revolutionary aesthetics and practice, Ngũgĩ writes himself into history.

In *True Confessions*, Breytenbach also must position himself historically before he can write himself back to life. He is trapped in the official "warped history of the Afrikaner," part of a system which is itself "anti-historical" (54, 116). South Africa for him is "No Man's Land. Another world. A world of genteel manners and old-fashioned picnics. And a vicious world. A land of harsh, dream-like beauty. Where you can feel your skin crawling. Ever on that last lip of annihilation" (93). His confessions begin "with an appreciation of the political situation which ... I still subscribe to," and his recruitment in "the early 1970s for the specific purpose of creating forms of aid to militant White opposition to the Apartheid regime in the country" (73, 77). Therefore, the history of his imprisonment is part of the history of apartheid and the global struggle for national liberation. Underground political work, like his own entry into South Africa to recruit for Okhela, "inserts itself in a long and glorious line of historical struggle" (83). Similarly, specific parts of the confessions allegorize South African history, such as, for example, when, after his release, Breytenbach apocalyptically emerges from a swim in the ocean into an integrated South Africa.

Accepting conditions for release in these prison diaries is directly related to the country's future: the closure of the prison diary, if the integrity of the writer has not been destroyed in the prison house, must be a possible future for the nation. Created between iron brackets, the prison diary genre and prison itself would appear to enforce their own closure on writing, the closure of "either death or freedom" (*Detained* 146). Ngũgĩ's *Detained* begins, after his release from prison, with an account of charges and accusations in the media, culminating in a "call for self-censorship" (xix). Like *Matigari*, the beginning of *Detained* is a somewhat disillusioning homecoming after release. The narrative order of Ngũgĩ's diary resists the logic of the genre, problematizing the relationship of beginning and ending, detention and freedom. Ngugi's prison diary, however, rejects the inevitability of release or of the definite ending of torment upon release, although he admits that "dreams of freedom start at the very minute of arrest" (146). Just as he envisions his detention as part of repressive national imprisonment—and so, in this sense, he is caged in a "double prison" (Davies 220)—he connects genuine release with the nation's liberation, so that "prison [should not be] our destiny as a Kenyan people" (63). The prison diary's narrative closure is therefore directly related to the destiny of the national narrative and especially to Ngũgĩ's desire for "a truly democratic Kenya in which the different ... nationalities would freely debate the past, present and future of our country," as when the political detainees talk of rights and justice and "the walls of nationality break asunder" (113, 130). Ngũgĩ postulates what he terms "progressive nationalism" for the future (159).[33]

In his views about release, Soyinka furiously denies the eschatology of the Victorian classic realist novels he is briefly permitted to read in prison: the belief that genuine social justice only exists in heaven. Instead, he speculates that in some mythical future, the cartographer's pen may redraw Africa's nations and override the injunction,

---

[33] See Lovesey's discussion of Ngũgĩ's nationalism in "Initiation for the Nation" and "Ngũgĩ wa Thiong'o's Postnation."

> What God (white man) has put together, let no black man put asunder. The complications of neo-colonial politics of interference compel one to accept such a damnable catechism for now, as a pragmatic necessity. Later perhaps, the black nations will themselves sit down together, and, by agreement, set compass and square rule to paper and reformulate the life-expending, stultifying, constrictive imposition of this divine authority. (181)

As in Ngũgĩ's allegorical rewriting of biblical myth in *Matigari*, the sound of the horn of justice for both Soyinka and Ngũgĩ must echo on earth. In *Detained* he also rejects the quasi-religious colonial/neocolonial injunction: "any awakening of a people to their historic mission of liberating themselves from external and internal exploitation and repression is always seen in terms of 'sin' and it is often denounced with the religious rhetoric of a wronged, self-righteous god" (13). Breytenbach, writing in 1983 and drawing on biblical parallels, narrowly avoids the dangers of making predictions. As he notes, "The temptation, when writing about No Man's Land/Azania, is to pour forth visions of apocalypse. Or to give way to the temptation of trying to be a prophet. Or both" (358).

All three writers began nondocumentary writing projects while imprisoned. *Devil on the Cross*, *Season of Anomy*, *A Shuttle in the Crypt*, and *Mouroir: Mirrornotes of a Novel* bear the marks of their prison genesis. Paradoxically, national imprisonment, at least in Ngũgĩ's subsequent view of the Kenyan situation, has led to "a rebirth of a kind of national literature in the country" (*Moving* 94). For Soyinka, release from prison is release from death to life and a renewed affirmation of "his human identity" in community with others (278). In his diary, Soyinka assumes the role of prophet, visionary, and dreamer with "the implication ... that the dreamer is a dreamer for society" (Jones 225). Insistent on the universal nature of experience and suspicious of "literary ideology," Soyinka celebrates the African artist's "social vision" (*Myth* 61),[34] and *The Man Died* ends with both a "spiritual indictment and affirmation" (Fox 209). Soyinka, while affirmative, relies on a somewhat romantic view of the intellectual, and a spiritual conception of the nation, and, as Ngũgĩ noted, does not suggest clear alternatives to present problems (Lazarus, *Resistance* 205). Breytenbach proposes both a radical political restructuring and the quietistic consolations of Buddhism or Taoism, which seem to mesh easily with a refined existentialist despair. In the context of South Africa's subsequent renewed sense of nationhood, Breytenbach has said he feels "redundant" or at best ambivalent. He is suspicious of the debased language of patriotism: "Everybody who wants to be somebody in the country now lays claim to having been in the resistance movement; we are all of the ANC. Rumours of heroic feats abound" (Wood 28). In *Moving the Centre*, Ngũgĩ equates an affirmative future with escape from linguistic imprisonment. He unwillingly went into exile in England in 1982 and now in the United States, sadly discovering that "[e]xile can even be worse than prison" (106).

---

[34] See Appiah's critique of Soyinka's essentialism in his *In My Father's House* (78–81).

Chapter 6
The Global Intellectual: Conclusion

Part 1: Multiple Ngũgĩs

There are a number of different Ngũgĩs. Ngũgĩ's public image has been figured in radically varying ways as saint, ogre, demagogic ranter, myth, and postcolonial wizard. "Saint Ngugi" is the appellation used in Peter Nazareth's affectionate survey of his career ("Introduction" 1), and the "Ngugi ogre" or "Ngugi as political ogre" was a specter circulated (and actually hunted) by the state during the long years of the Moi regime in Kenya, as Carol Sicherman has shown.[1] We must see if this specter rises again, Lazarus-like, in what Ngũgĩ characterizes as the virtual rebirth of the former dictator after the 2013 elections in "A Dictator's Last Laugh." For some, Ngũgĩ remains the Marxist ranter of *Writers in Politics* hoarsely denouncing imperialism and neocolonialism, with the pentecostal fire of the secular preacher and a good deal of repetitious cliché, from the easy target of a "distinguished professor" chair at an American research university. In Kenya, where the relationship of the heroic, historic, and mythic may be somewhat opaque, we have the mythic Ngũgĩ, a figuration he has exploited to a degree in his autobiographical writing, regarding his life as witness to the embodiment of the major political and cultural developments of the past 50 years in his country and extending back to the nineteenth century.[2] Ngũgĩ's recognition of his position in a long genealogy of resistance was one consequence of his year-long detention without charge or trial when he was institutionalized by the nation, a deeply traumatic experience which he would come to regard as "a watershed in my life" (Wilkinson, "Ngugi" 211). It was a harshly "educational" experience for him, contingent as it was on his work in people's theater, and one that placed him in a national history of struggle, giving his words great moral authority, but it also has tended to become a defining feature of his intellectual reputation, as it has not been for a similarly distinguished African intellectual like Soyinka, for example.

---

[1] In particular, Sicherman focuses on the incidents in London in October 1984 when the long arm of the Moi regime instituted a campaign of alarmist misinformation within Kenya and in the United Kingdom, attempting to present Ngũgĩ as a political pariah and to silence him at the time of the rehearsals for a London production of Ngũgĩ and Mugo's *The Trial of Dedan Kimathi* which one Kenyan article claimed had been transformed into "a kind of communist musical set in Africa, with much clenching of raised fists and brandishing of automatic rifles" ("Ngugi wa Thiong'o as Mythologizer" 264).

[2] As Sicherman puts it, "Ngugi may be seen … as a mythologized figure in the line of Waiyaki, Kenyatta, and Kimathi" ("Ngugi wa Thiong'o as Mythologizer" 262).

We also have the "multiple Ngugis," including the "revolutionary romantic," that Nazareth uncovers in *Petals of Blood*, by which he designates that novel's polyphonic narrative voices in its implied author and authorial narrator.[3] Nazareth faults the novel's use of magic realism, though he does credit the unsentimental focus of "the village Ngugi" on rural history from below and also the novel's use of a griot-like character (120). He notes interestingly that Arnold Kettle, Ngũgĩ's professor at Leeds, "experienced some uneasiness" about the overly ideological nature of an early draft of *A Grain of Wheat*, maintaining that "Ngugi's real talent was as a writer of fables" (129 n15). If "fables" here may be linked to orature and by extension to Ngũgĩ's hybridized "litorature" (Ngũgĩ, "Orature" 3), this may well have been a prescient comment, anticipating the arrival of Ngũgĩ the "postcolonial wizard."[4] A final Ngũgĩ may be the emergent global intellectual, if we understand this figure to be the advocate, participant, and even embodiment of "globalectics," the subject of Ngũgĩ's most recent theoretical intervention.

Being a world-famous postcolonial artist-intellectual has its special challenges, as Ngũgĩ has learned over more than a half-century of intellectual labor and cultural activism. On the one hand, there is the very real danger of imprisonment, exile, and even assassination, but there is also, on the other hand, a perennial risk of misinterpretation or neglect. "A friend of mine," writes Walcott in a tribute to James, "said that writers have a longing to be jailed so they can say they are getting attention. Neglect is perhaps a greater insult than being put in prison" (45).[5] Living in a situation or a country in which the writer's imprisonment is "one of the highest compliments," however, is perilous (Moorsom quoted in Lazarus, "(Re)turn" 24).[6] For Ngũgĩ, moreover, "neglect" was never part of his fortunes before his imprisonment, though he has been marked as a former political detainee ever afterward, and he has been subject to other forms of violence, as noted in

---

[3] In this novel, Nazareth isolates the voices of a Christian Ngũgĩ, a political Ngũgĩ, a magic realist Ngũgĩ, an historical Ngũgĩ, and also a "revolutionary romantic" Ngũgĩ with elements of the "preacher" and "ideologue" ("Second Coming" 118–29, 127). Nazareth finds that "[t]he fragmented selves are not only in the tale but also in the teller" and he considers that the novel lacks a fully effective "revolutionary form" (122, 127).

[4] This phrase is used in the title of Gikandi's review of *Wizard of the Crow*.

[5] Achebe made a similar comment in a preamble to a lecture entitled "Art as Celebration." Referring to a comment made about the privileged position of intellectuals in Africa where speaking out could mean death, he facetiously apologized. Achebe himself would be victimized when he was maimed in a politically motivated car accident in Nigeria (a favored method of silencing writers due to the staggering number of road deaths in Nigeria and Kenya).

[6] Lazarus also cites a passage from *Detained* when Ngũgĩ is told by another inmate, It may sound a strange thing to say to you, but in a sense I am glad they brought you here. The other day … we were saying that it would be a good thing for Kenya if more intellectuals were imprisoned. First, it would wake most of them from their illusions. And some of them might outlive jail to tell the world. ("(Re)turn" 24)

Chapter 5, as well as a somewhat lazy "neglect." Hall has attacked a tendency in intellectual discourse toward the name checking of major intellectual figures like Gramsci and even Marx.[7] He notes the dangers of fetishizing "quotability" as Grant Farred puts it (Farred, "Introduction" 3–4),[8] a style of shorthand name and phrase reference that fails to engage with or to perform anything more than an "easy transfer of generalisations" (Hall, "Gramsci and Us").[9] As Hall writes in "Gramsci and Us," "We mustn't *use* Gramsci (as we have for so long abused Marx) like an Old Testament prophet who, at the correct moment, will offer us the consoling and appropriate quotation." Marx, in the post-Marxist period beginning in the 1970s, however, also has been "typecast," remarks Hobsbawm, more ominously and dismissively "as the inspirer of terror and gulag" (*How to Change the World* 398). Gramsci, too, he notes, has seen a similar but nearly opposite distortion in the movement from virtual anonymity after his death to his present fame and that of his equally famous critical phrases even among those who have never read his work (Hobsbawm 316).[10] Spivak also notes the commodification, homogenization, and distortion of Gramsci's terminology, including the "subaltern" and the "organic intellectual,"[11] and even extending to Gramsci's own transformation

---

[7] A note in the online pdf of this essay acknowledges, "This article was first published in *Marxism Today*, June 1987 and was based on a talk given at *Marxism Today*'s conference on Gramsci."

[8] Farred explains:
Distilled to its essence, Hall's is a call for the considered use of Gramsci's work. By extension, we can apply Hall's dictum to James scholarship and, indeed, to the use of Hall's own writing. Hall ... provides an injunction for intellectual and political responsibility aimed at ensuring a full, nuanced engagement with the work of intellectuals. ... "Abuse" is an intellectual approach that invariably leads to the emaciation of a thinker's work, quickly evacuating the writing of its ideological and political efficacy. More importantly, however, Hall challenges the way intellectuals use the work of major figures. ... [O]nce a figure such as a Gramsci or a James obtains a certain currency, and quotations flow glibly, their work lends itself easily to uncritical and indiscriminate appropriation. A quote from a prominent thinker should not, as it often does, function as a substitute for a substantive engagement with the issue at hand. (3–4)

[9] Elsewhere, Hall refers to a tendency toward "mimicry" or "ventriloquism" which in the absence of the formulation of new ideas "sometimes passes as a serious intellectual exercise" ("Cultural Studies" 286).

[10] Hobsbawm notes how the 1977 *Fontana Dictionary of Modern Thought* reduces its entry on Gramsci to the single word "hegemony" (339, 449 chap. 13, n. 3). He observes, however, how Gramsci has escaped the fate of Marxism, or "enclosure in academic ghettos," or even "becoming an 'ism'" (339).

[11] Spivak cautions that Gramsci's "notes to himself, by a very smart and sick man in jail" are accepted as "definitions," and their applications are sometimes wildly distorted: "The sentimental academic-populist version of the organic intellectual takes the counter-intuitive in Gramsci and turns it into something that is no more than commonsensical" (Bhattacharya, "Interview" 229, 230).

from Comintern-trained Marxist-Leninist to "liberal democrat" (Bhattacharya, "Interview" 221–2).[12] Similarly, Adorno lamented Nietzsche's reduction to "a few misunderstood slogans [that] have become the dubious common-property of the 'educated'" (133). Ngũgĩ is especially liable to this insubstantial, ready reference given his genius for coining evocative words and phrases such as "decolonizing the mind," "moving the center," "Afro-Saxon," "litorature," and "cyborature,"[13] as well as his tendency to reiterate and embellish his core ideas, particularly when retelling home truths from a position of exile.

Like Ngũgĩ, Adorno was an intellectual exiled in America from dictatorship. His notion of absolute intellectual detachment influenced Said's controversial elevation of exile as the necessary condition of the intellectual. Adorno was not a cosmopolitan intellectual enjoying the productive, temporary exile of the Caribbean and African exiles in Paris and London in the 1940s and 1950s—perhaps one root of the perennial nostalgia of the Négritude poets—who so influenced Ngũgĩ. In *Minima Moralia* (1951), the aphoristic philosophical meditations that take as their starting point the quandary of "subjective experience" (18), moreover, Adorno holds that

> [e]very intellectual in emigration is, without exception, mutilated, and does well to acknowledge it to himself, if he wishes to avoid being cruelly apprised of it behind the tightly-closed doors of his self-esteem. He lives in an environment that must remain incomprehensible to him, however flawless his knowledge of trade-union organizations or the automobile industry may be; he is always astray. Between the reproduction of his own existence under the monopoly of mass culture, and impartial, responsible work, yawns an irreconcilable breach. His language has been expropriated, and the historical dimension that nourished his knowledge, sapped. (33)

Adorno's torment, which he shared with Said, was partly the suffering of the lover of intellectually challenging music, like Schoenberg's, forced to endure popular music increasingly being piped into every cranny of the public sphere in America. Such an exilic mutilation of the sort to which Adorno points, however, is perhaps especially acute for a figure like Ngũgĩ, who was cut off from the source of his artistic inspiration in his homeland, and especially the creative mutation of his living mother tongue there, and to an extent relegated to the equally alienating abstract intellectual space of the "postcolonial" while pursuing his work as a university professor. Ngũgĩ moreover retains a haunting personal memory of the

---

[12] Spivak allows for the value of "intellectual activism that re-territorializes a powerful original" as in Ranajit Guha's Subaltern Studies collective's use of Gramsci's term "subaltern" (Bhattacharya, "Interview" 222). Young, in a perceptive, comprehensive account of Gramsci's postcoloniality, suggests that Spivak herself, not Gramsci, may be considered the subaltern's inventor, though he accepts that her intervention owes much to Gramsci's class-based analysis ("Il Gramsci meridionale" 31–2).

[13] Ngũgĩ coins "litorature" in "Orature in Education" (3) and "cyborature" in *Globalectics* (85).

anti–Mau Mau actions in colonial Kenya, part of what he refers to as the "African holocaust" (*Something Torn* 59), the violent resistance to which was partly inspired by antifascist struggle in Europe (Gilroy, *Darker* 77–8),[14] and the brutality of which is finally having an airing in the English courts.

Adorno's autobiographical text sustains at least a shifting focus on the question of the role of the intellectual after Auschwitz. Exiled by violence "under conditions enforcing contemplation" (18), Adorno confronts a new order of repression in America. In particular, this is the entrapment by the bureaucratization, institutionalization, and mechanization of the independent intellectual who, either from a need for money (the apparently oxymoronic "salaried philosophers" 74–5) or as a result of intellectual associations, is exposed to the dangers of complacency and conformism, amid the omnipresent oppression of mass popular culture and even the convention of separating work and leisure. Adorno writes that "one could no more imagine Nietzsche in an office, with a secretary minding the telephone in an anteroom, at his desk until five o'clock, than playing golf after the day's work was done" (130). In a climate in which intellectual labor is valued narrowly according to whether it is "necessary and reasonable," the productive spontaneity of free thought disappears (124). As a result, intellectuals mostly work with and write about the failings of other intellectuals, a masochistic narcissism that helps perpetuate a "prevalent anti-intellectualism" within the culture at large (28). The very success of modern, bureaucratic society makes intellectuals into a self-consuming machine, producing as a by-product a resigned sense of dissatisfied alienation: "Whatever the intellectual does, is wrong" (133).

In *The Pleasures of Exile* (1960, 1984),[15] Lamming addresses himself to a Caribbean audience about the predicament of the Caribbean writer in exile or upon emigration to the imperial center as well as this figure's unwillingness to return. Lamming begins his reflections on the condition of exile with a reference to the Haitian Ceremony of the Souls as a way to conjure the spirit of James's *The Black Jacobins* and to connect with a lost memory of African ancestors (*Pleasures* 9). It is a ceremony for the resurrection of the dead, "[t]hrough the perfected necrophily of the living," and in this ritual "we are allowed to tune in on the forgotten secrets of the Dead" (14). Lamming reconnects with this notion of a continuity between the living and the dead by witnessing mourners coming from a funeral when he first arrives in Africa (164). He feels transformed upon arrival when he first encounters the confidence of freedom in newly independent Ghana "as though the Haitian ceremony of the Souls had come real" (162). Lamming will later come face to face in supremely confident, death-phobic America with a land in which "[i]t didn't seem to anyone that death was a fact" (189).

---

[14] In a discussion of Primo Levi, Gilroy refers to Kimathi's moral imperative to embrace violence as being inspired by antifascist forces (*Darker* 77–8). In *The Black Atlantic*, Gilroy addresses the problematic associations between the holocaust and the experiences of diasporic Africans (213–8).

[15] This text, like *Minima Moralia*, influenced Said's reflections on exile. Lamming's importance for Ngũgĩ, especially in the late 1960s, cannot be overestimated.

For Lamming, however, exile is the condition of—not the intellectual—but the colonized and an integral part of colonialism's reciprocal nature (*Pleasures* 156, 229). As he says categorically, "[t]o be colonial is to be in a state of exile" (229). Exile is the quasi-existential separation of the colonized from meaningful rituals and also from language and its legacy of memories and associations. The Caribbean writer's exile is also "self-colonisation" (156), the embedding of the new mythic memory of the principle of England and Englishness and also the myth of the native other within the psyche. Lamming frames his reflections on the West Indies and his recounting of racist incidents in Britain with James's *The Black Jacobins*, but far more extensively with references to *The Tempest*, hinting at Euro-Caribbean links between the Martiniquean Empress Josephine, the heroic Toussaint-like James, and James as an alienated Ishmael. While claiming that the greatest mystery is why he and other Caribbean writers were able to resist the colonial "questioning [of] his very right to write"—a phrase with great significance for the young Ngũgĩ—and lacking "any previous native tradition to draw upon" (27, 38), Lamming gives little sustained attention to these writers' choice of exile, over and above the difficulty of making a career in the Caribbean given a widespread disinterest in reading and the complacency of the quasi-colonial society they have left behind. Home, however, still offers a needed nostalgic sustenance:

> I have lost my place, or my place has deserted me. This may be the dilemma of the West Indian writer abroad: that he hungers for nourishment from a soil which he (as an ordinary citizen) could not at present endure. The pleasure and paradox of my own exile is that I belong wherever I am. My role, it seems, has rather to do with time and change than with the geography of circumstances; and yet there is always an acre of ground in the New World which keeps growing echoes in my head. I can only hope that these echoes do not die before my work comes to an end. (50)

Lamming's exile is a natal alienation from the geography, culture, and language of Africa, a cultural landscape that can only be a place of disassociated memory. As Adorno says in a different context, however, to dismiss memory as "unpredictable, unreliable, irrational" and hence unworthy of serious consideration is to disregard "the historical dimension of consciousness" (122). In the case of an African political exile like Ngũgĩ, memory evokes a homeland, and in particular the remembered mother language may well assume the shape of the exile's home.

Moving from "Africa's holocaust" to "Africa's Renaissance" is a preoccupation of much of Ngũgĩ's recent critical and theoretical work (*Something Torn* 59), and a large part of this project is a concern with the Pan-African diaspora as in *Homecoming*, and with an enlargement of the postcolonial project. Ngũgĩ explicitly avoids engaging with those who would cite the spreading, continent-wide horror of "Africa's World War,"[16] with the recent nearly macabre addition of Hollywood

---

[16] See Gérard Prunier's exhaustive account of the ramifications of the Rwandan genocide in *Africa's World War: Congo, The Rwandan Genocide, and the Making of a Continental Catastrophe* (2009). Prunier cites Kenya's role in protecting the perpetrators for strategic political reasons (11–12, 199–200).

stars trying to negotiate peace with warlords or trying to save a Noah's Ark of representative Africa via international adoption in the glare of television cameras. There is also the looming threat from the purchase of vast stretches of agricultural lands by private interests seeking to profit from a projected global famine, the danger of a second economic colonialism governing the extraction of precious raw materials, and even the dependency generated by styles of domestic philanthropy such as Tony Elumelu's Africapitalism. In *Something Torn and New*, subtitled *An African Renaissance*, Ngũgĩ extends the notion of merely dreaming a more hopeful future that ends *Penpoints, Gunpoints and Dreams*. He refers there, as he had earlier in *Decolonising the Mind* (3), to the famous poem "Looking at Your Hands" from *The Hill of Fire Glows Red* (1951) by Martin Carter (1927–1997), the Guyanese poet, social activist, sometime diplomat, and political detainee, about dreaming to change the world in quasi-Marxist phrase (*Penpoints* 132).[17] Ngũgĩ in *Something Torn* extends his ongoing project of developing the history of anti-colonial resistance to include Ireland, and particularly what he reads as the English Renaissance's attempt to eliminate Irish linguistic and national identity, desiring merely to preserve the corpse of a dead culture to supply spiritual inspiration, when needed, for the development of an Anglo-Irish identity. This is the prospect of the postcolonial necrophilia touched upon earlier. He is concerned with the colonial framing of collective cultural identity, one of the central concerns of the postcolonial project.

Ngũgĩ's career-long concern with language has shifted more recently to a focus on memory or at least the relationship between the two. Memory—not language alone—is the storehouse of personal and collective cultural identity. In addition, he extends his consideration of African cultural identity to the African diaspora, as in *Homecoming* (focused on the Caribbean) with extensive references to Lamming and Kamau Brathwaite, though his primary concern is a reinvigorated attention to the legacy of slavery in America and the traces of a collective memory of Africa among African Americans in spirituals, blues, and jazz. As Gilroy argues in *Postcolonial Melancholia*, the collective memory of this history and its cultural resistance survive in descendants, and it is not the "intellectual property" of any particular group who are self-appointed "defenders of cultural and experiential copyright" (56). Ngũgĩ shares this collective memorial legacy, though he also seeks the decolonization of memory or more specifically the decolonization of African memory that was hijacked or supplanted by European memory (Ngũgĩ, "Europhone" 155–64). Slavery and colonialism are differently remembered historical traumas, he maintains, that have yet to receive proper global mourning. In *Something Torn*, Ngũgĩ advances a more methodical inquiry into Pan-African intellectual history of which he sees himself a part, with a lingering critique of Victorian attitudes to African history's nonexistence, Négritude, and bourgeois

---

[17] Carter's poetry's emphasis on poverty, nakedness, and emptiness, what he called "the university of hunger" ("University" 84–5), as well as flashes of revolutionary fervor, resembles Ngũgĩ's embrace of unadorned, grounded "poor theory" in *Globalectics* (2–5).

African intellectuals who participate in the burying of African languages. The book's title plays on the idea of rebirth and remembering with the notion of "re-membering," or putting together the anatomy of a dismembered idea and identity, that of the body of Africa itself.

Ngũgĩ's dream of an African renaissance may be opening at least in Kenya in a new willingness to confront colonial history, to hold perpetrators of atrocities to account, and to seek justice for survivors. This active re-membering of this historical trauma will be explored in a little more detail here due to its relevance for Ngũgĩ's work. In *A Secret History of Torture*, published in paperback by Portobello as *Cruel Britannia*, Ian Cobain considers the use of torture in colonial Kenya as part of a much wider employment of such techniques (78–90). The uncovering of documents about this period in Kenya, originally by Anderson and Elkins, has transformed national and international responses to the anticolonial conflict and has challenged African historiography (Branch xi–xvii). Examining secret Foreign Office files only recently opened in light of a case being brought forward at the High Court in London by Kenyan torture victims (88–90), Cobain details methods designed to break Mau Mau suspects psychologically, to maim or murder them, and to terrorize the wider population. These "Gestapo methods," as one perpetrator referred to them (80), were known to be illegal and much attention was given to keeping their use secret and to limiting the damage of employing them on the perpetrators themselves. President Obama's grandfather may well have been a victim of the indiscriminate use of torture and brutalizing violence during his six months of detention in this period. The exposure of a massacre at Hola camp caught the attention of the world, and particularly the English parliament, and led to the end of colonial rule in Kenya:

> The growing worldwide awareness that Britain's 'civilising mission' in East Africa had descended into barbarism led directly to British withdrawal from Kenya. Even Conservative MPs were admitting publicly that the affair had been hugely damaging to the country's reputation and began to accept that, while the British may have won the battle against the Mau Mau, they had lost the war to maintain control of the country. (87)

A sign of the still highly contentious nature of this history is an exchange about Cobain's book in the *Times Literary Supplement* (*TLS*).[18]

---

[18] In a review of Cobain's book, Calder Walton faults Cobain's failure to offer a historically specific use of "torture" and he disputes Cobain's claim that torture was part of English colonial policy. Walton maintains that his own research
> suggests that when torture did occur ... it occurred because of a failure to enforce recommendations, particularly from MI5, about how best to interrogate prisoners. MI5's policy for interrogations then was the same as it had been at Camp 020 [MI5's wartime interrogation center]: that prisoners could be subjected to mental pressure, but not physical violence, because to do so would be counter-productive. (Walton 8)

The issue of colonial torture practices in this period has recently become of more immediate concern as a suit brought by former Mau Mau detainees has made its way through the British courts. As of May 2013,

> The British government is negotiating payments to thousands of Kenyans detained and severely mistreated during the 1950s Mau Mau insurgency, in what would be the first compensation settlement resulting from official crimes committed under imperial rule. In a development that could lead to many other claims from around the world, government lawyers began the talks with Mau Mau veterans after being defeated in bids to prevent elderly survivors of the prison camps from seeking redress in British courts. The defeats followed discovery of a vast archive of colonial-era documents the Foreign Office (FCO) had kept hidden for decades. In the case of the Kenya conflict, the secret papers showed that senior colonial officials authorised appalling abuses of inmates held at prison camps, and that ministers and officials in London were aware of a brutal detention regime in which men and women were tortured and killed (Cobain and Hatcher 15).

Significantly, compensation for the possibly 10,000 victims may open claims from former prisoners in other British colonies that could easily reach tens of millions of pounds. In this respect, Kenya's Mau Mau becomes a precedent-setting example of anticolonial resistance, as Ngũgĩ has almost always maintained, despite the certain ambivalence in his early journalism examined in Chapter 2. Of the five claimants in the test case in British courts, two of whom were castrated, Wambugu Wa Nyingi testified that he was detained for nine years and felt "robbed of my youth": "There is a saying in Kikuyu that old age lives off the years of youth ... I have nothing to live off because my youth was taken from me" (quoted in Cobain and Hatcher 15).

In line with a new, more hopeful opening to history and to justice, truth, and reconciliation within Ngũgĩ's last three critical and theoretical works, despite colonialism's tragic legacy, there is also a reenergized return to the question of the role of the intellectual and a move toward decolonizing the postcolonial intellectual. While retaining the essence of his earlier conception of the intellectual as "a worker in ideas using words as the means of production" (*Penpoints* 90), a definition he repeats in "For Peace, Justice, and Culture: The Intellectual in the Twenty-First Century" (33), Ngũgĩ increasingly regards the intellectual as a type of interpreter whose work resembles that of the translator engaged in a conversation between texts, languages, creators, and readers, allowing open access to the body of intellectual capital. The traditional African oral intellectual or griot for Ngũgĩ is an articulate memory keeper and also a prophetic "scout and guide" for the people,

---

Cobain disputes Walton's contention that he claims that Britain had "a secret torture policy"; he argued somewhat more modestly "that there is evidence that the British authorities resort far more readily to torture than the British people recognize, and then act to conceal the evidence" (Cobain, "Letters" 6).

and while this tradition has not been severed (and hence in need of reinvention[19]), it was interrupted by the colonial experience. Colonialism styled the intellectual "interpreter as a foreign" or "double agent" whose loyalty was first and foremost to the international bourgeoisie rather than to the people (*Penpoints* 79, 95). These colonial and then postcolonial intellectuals enabled their own bondage, Ngũgĩ maintains, by using the colonizer's language and keeping their knowledge capital from the masses. *Penpoints*, which focuses on the relationship of the artist-intellectual and the state, devotes a chapter, "The Allegory of the Cave," to an examination of Plato's allegory and Ayi Kwei Armah's reinterpretation of it in a postcolonial context in *The Beautyful Ones Are Not Yet Born* (1968). While disputing Armah's assessment of Nkrumah, Ngũgĩ embraces Armah's implied hope for a generation of "Beautyful Ones" who will be born in the future. They will not participate in the intellectual and cultural exploitation, conducted in European languages, which for Ngũgĩ is "a kind of collective death-wish for the African-language intellectual tradition" (98).

In Ngũgĩ's reflections on colonial, neocolonial, and oral intellectuals, there are similarities with the influential position of Gramsci in his scattered remarks on intellectuals in his prison notebooks produced in the internal exile of jail. Referring mainly to Italy's experience, though elsewhere reflecting on Italy's own quasi-colonial internal, north-south dynamics and its imperial adventures, Gramsci distinguishes between a caste of traditional intellectuals, with distinct petty bourgeois origins and fantasies of being utterly autonomous while supporting the ruling class, and the "new intellectuals" whose expertise is more practical. He seeks both to widen the conception of the intellectual and to suggest ways of interrupting the reproduction of the intellectual class. Gramsci separates intellectuals who create knowledge in science, art, or technology from those who merely administer knowledge, the latter ever increasing in number and in their range of activities in modern society. Like Ngũgĩ, he holds that, while intellectual work is part of all human activity ("[t]here is an intellectual dimension to every human enterprise" [Ngũgĩ, "For Peace" 33]) and "[a]ll men are intellectuals," the majority lack this social designation (Gramsci, "Formation" 121).

Problems arise for Gramsci when contemplating the function and formation of "new intellectuals" who are a utopian creation, "an organic intellectual of democratic socialism" in Spivak's phrase (Bhattacharya, "Interview" 230). Firstly, these new intellectuals must be more pragmatic than the priestly caste of pampered, parasitic, and deluded traditional intellectuals (*Selections* 274): "The mode of existence of the new intellectual can no longer consist of eloquence, the external and momentary arousing of sentiments and passions, but must consist of being actively involved in practical life, as a builder, an organiser, 'permanently persuasive' because he is not purely an orator" ("Formation" 122). Secondly, Gramsci anticipates a struggle

---

[19] See Terence Ranger's "The Invention of Tradition in Colonial Africa" (211–62) and also Nicholas Dirks's discussion of the deployment of "culture" as a response to colonialism (1–25).

between traditional and new intellectuals as the latter attempt to "assimilate and conquer 'ideologically' the traditional intellectuals" (122), getting them to change their stripes and identify with the working class.[20] By this assimilation, traditional intellectuals would acknowledge that they are of "the same flesh and blood as the most humble, the most backward, and the least aware" (Gramsci quoted in Marks 16). Over and above the problem of "assimilation," the best method of forming new intellectuals is through democratizing access to education. Spivak maintains that Gramsci's focus on "instrumentalizing the 'new intellectuals'" is designed to produce "the subaltern intellectual" (Spivak, *An Aesthetic Education* 7). Ngũgĩ departs from Gramsci in maintaining "the primacy of the word" in the role of intellectuals ("For Peace" 33) and in his position on some of Gramsci's remarks on "'organic' intellectuals" ("Formation" 118).[21] While maintaining that classes create their own organic intellectuals, Gramsci adds an important qualification:

> [T]he mass of the peasants, although they carry out an essential function in the world of production, do not elaborate their own "organic" intellectuals, and do not "assimilate" any class of traditional intellectuals, although other social groups take many of their intellectuals from the peasant masses, and a great many of the traditional intellectuals are of peasant origin. ("Formation" 119)

While Ngũgĩ is just this type of intellectual of peasant origin, he has both re-assimilated himself and relentlessly called on others to do so, but he maintains a strong belief in the role of peasant-based oral intellectuals reaffirmed by this educational work at Kamĩrĩĩthũ. In this last respect, his work resembles Partha Chatterjee's call for a renewed attention via Gramsci to the peasantry (119–36), a type of Kenyan Subaltern Studies, conducted from the distance of exile.

As in some of his remarks about the collective authorship of the Kamĩrĩĩthũ plays such as the still-unpublished *Maitũ Njugĩra* (*Mother, Sing For Me*), Ngũgĩ accepts that he is both "interpreter" as well as "editor" of these texts (Bardolph and Durix 160), a contention that has implications for his view of the postcolonial intellectual. Even in his writing of Gĩkũyũ novels, such as *Caitaani Mũtharaba-inĩ* (*Devil on the Cross*), Ngũgĩ has said that he considers the actual composition or writing to have been a "collective" endeavor with the novelist again functioning as "a kind of editor" (Wilkinson, "Ngugi" 208), drawing on the historical and linguistic expertise of the peasantry: "the writer functions as an editor but using

---

[20] Gramsci "envisaged the intellectuals, proletariat and peasantry working together to bring about a fundamental political emancipation for the country as a whole" (Young, "Il Gramsci meridionale" 30–1). However, Gramsci may have considered traditional and organic intellectuals as being locked in a seemingly endless cycle of reproduction; as one of Gramsci's major interpreters, Said, put it, "the traditional intellectual was once an organic intellectual" (Said, "American Intellectuals" 144).

[21] See Hall's remarks on the problematic status of the organic intellectual, a figure who may be historically contextualized and whose value may be limited ("Cultural Studies" 288).

the imaginative sieve as an editorial machine"; "[i]n a sense all works of art are really acts of collaboration—and even the business of novel-writing" (Darah 191). In these remarks, Ngũgĩ goes some distance toward suggesting a distinctly African mode of creation as well as pointing to a distinctively collective role for the artist intellectual. By extension, it appears that he regards the African intellectual as a type of collective intellectual who is a memory keeper, and who also guides and voices collective aspirations and dreams, but who also functions as a conduit for the archive of technical, intellectual capital.[22] In this respect, Ngũgĩ's notion of the intellectual contains elements of the fluid, "relational" aesthetic of Glissant, and particularly its concern with decolonizing intellectual capital in a postcolonial world without attempting to erase its diverse legacies:

> There still exist centers of domination, but it is generally acknowledged that there are no exclusive, lofty realms of learning or metropolises of knowledge left standing. Henceforward, this knowledge, composed of abstract generality and linked to the spirit of conquest and discovery, has the presence of human cultures in their solid materiality superimposed upon it. And knowledge, or at least the epistemology we produce for ourselves from it, has been changed by this. Its transparency, in fact, its legitimacy is no longer based on a Right. Transparency no longer seems like the bottom of the mirror in which Western humanity reflected the world in its own image. (Glissant, *Poetics of Relation* 111)

Ngũgĩ's work points to a number of practical strategies for a decolonized epistemology and the creation of a more open-access archive of intellectual capital, as mentioned in Chapter 1. Over and above his long-standing recommendations regarding the transformation of English-only world literature departments and his advocacy of Africans writing in African languages, Ngũgĩ calls for the creation of an archive of texts and resources available via translation that would make accessible the legacy of knowledge of the Pan-African diaspora (*Something Torn* 127).[23] He also calls for a month, week, or day of global mourning to address the historical trauma of colonialism and slavery that would launch a celebration of African arts and culture, concluding with a projection into a more hopeful future. This is an expansion of Anderson's recommendation for a strictly Kenyan remembering, honoring, and mourning for figures like Dedan Kimathi and the 1,090 hanged at Kamĩtĩ prison (where Ngũgĩ was detained),[24] and reversing the attempt to bury the past (336–44). However, Ngũgĩ's primary recommendation has

---

[22] Raymond Suttner refers to collective intellectuals in his account of the liberation struggle in South Africa (119–21).

[23] At least one preliminary, English-language text of this sort may be Molefi Kete Asante and Abu S. Abarry's necessarily highly selective "book of sources" *African Intellectual Heritage*.

[24] In her account of anti–Mau Mau torture and sexual violence, Elkins gives extensive documentary evidence about Kamĩtĩ which was used for a variety of purposes in this period, including the incarceration of female Mau Mau suspects (221–32).

a distinctly geopolitical pragmatism. As he writes in a recent piece of journalistic commentary, a revitalized African Union is needed to redress the injustice of Africa's natural and human resources having been used "in the evolution of capitalism from its mercantile through its industrial to its current global financial dominance" as well as Africa's continuing role as "the west's playground" ("Unity" 19). Ngũgĩ has persistently called, from the early 1960s, for Pan-African and "third world" alliances that would supersede the boundaries of colonial states. In line with Césaire in *Discourse on Colonialism*, Ngũgĩ increasingly holds that "the *nation* is a bourgeois phenomenon" (74).

Part 2: Hybrid Nationalisms, the Postnation, and Globalization

Ngũgĩ's conception of the nature of the post-neocolonial nation incorporates hybrid nationalisms. As John Paden argues, a number of independent African nation states have been amenable to a variety of simultaneous national affiliations such as subnational ethnic nationalism, regionalism, Pan-Africanism, and "third world" solidarity (403–33). Such "multiple loyalties" suggest a reconceptualization of the idea of nationalism in Africa (433), basing the idea of the nation-state on various combinations of traditional or premodern models; regional, class-based, or transnational alliances; models based on the shared experience of anticolonial struggle; or neocolonial models. Ngũgĩ, too, sometimes seems to advocate competing nationalisms. For example, he wants a truly independent, harmonious Kenya to oppose domestic and multinational capitalist exploitation, but he also strives to foster a heightened sense of cultural identity in all Kenya's traditional ethnic nationalities. In addition, he wishes to erase the old colonial boundaries in favor of regional, Pan-African, and international "third world" and proletarian alliances. Similarly, he desires, in classic Marxist terms, reiterated by Cabral, the progressive dissolution of the nation with its colonial and neocolonial legacies, regarding the very idea of the state as repressive. However, as some of his earlier journalism indicates, Ngũgĩ may, like Cabral, see at least some of these seemingly competing nationalisms as progressive, developmental stages.

Ngũgĩ's early journalism calls for harmony among Kenya's ethnic nationalities, repeating the familiar colonial mantra of "tribalism" as the nation's greatest enemy.[25] Moreover, *Petals of Blood* is founded on the notion of such harmony, and in particular a union of traditionally competing pastoralists and cultivators in the interests of collective resistance. Ngũgĩ's last play at Kamĩrĩĩthũ, *Maitũ Njugĩra* (*Mother, Sing for Me*), a type of people's opera, incorporated different Kenyan languages. In the open space of the performance, a type of linguistic melting took place. The multiethnic audience had to interact to grasp the play's shifting linguistic and cultural registers, and at moments joined the performers on

---

[25] See Ngũgĩ's articles "Let's See More School Integration" of July 8, 1962; "How Much Rope?" of Sept. 16, 1962; "It's Time We Broke Up" of Oct. 20, 1963; and "How Do You Kill?" of July 5, 1964.

stage (Björkman 62, 87). The play reinterpreted the birth of the nation, particularly regarding the question of land purchase at independence (Delgado 130–46).

Ngũgĩ has long endorsed regional East African associations and international proletarian and "third world" unions, the latter as a bulwark against imperialism. In "Matigari and the Dreams of One East Africa" from *Moving the Centre*, Ngũgĩ recalls the racial and cultural diversity of the "Swahili village" near where he grew up, and the enjoyment of various foods during different Muslim, Christian, and African festivals. This cultural Swahili masala seems to model the potential for Ngũgĩ's unified East African homeland. In the essay, Ngũgĩ describes East Africa as a "kalaidoscope of colours, cultures, and contours of history," and he refers to the coastal cities of the region that the Angel Michael shows Adam before his ejection from the Garden in *Paradise Lost* (*Moving* 161). For Ngũgĩ, the places are "a kind of paradise regained through human efforts," a zone united by a shared history of resistance, a common geography, shared nationalities, and a shared pluralistic culture: "East Africa is really one country" (161, 162).

Ngũgĩ's support for an East African Federation as a first step toward progressive postnational development has been consistent throughout his career. His early journalism, explored in Chapter 2, argues that a nation built upon the contradictions of the colonial model will fail ("Let's Get Out" 39), and that the former colonial powers oppose union out of a desire for sustained exploitation. Writing as a Makerere undergraduate, Ngũgĩ sees student union activity at the region's university colleges and the creation of an East African University as potential paradigms for the proposed East African Federation. As he points out in August 1964, "most of the present African leaders served their political apprenticeship in their respective student organizations" ("Commentary" 6). His advocacy becomes increasingly strident as the individual countries in the proposed Federation gain and then consolidate independence before considering union, fearful of possible domination. For Ngũgĩ, however, creating a Federation of East Africa, that must be a political and not merely an economic association, has real urgency because of the example it would provide for Pan-African union. If this "test case" succeeds, a United States of Africa will not be far off, with the ultimate possibility of world union to follow ("Isn't It Time?" 31). Fired with the period's prevailing optimism for developing progressive alliances, the youthful Ngũgĩ even rhapsodizes in February 1963: "The African nations, being young, should now assume the role of a saviour to rescue a civilisation on the verge of decay. Their faith and optimism should act as the new beacons on top of Kilimanjaro to light not Africa alone but the Dark Continent of Europe as well" ("Don't Forget Our Destination" 12). Europe's salvation by Africa—something contemplated by Cabral in a different fashion—is still anticipated, of course, and, moreover, while East African union was nearly realized in 1963, the alliance split along ideological lines in a climate of mutual suspicion. Ngũgĩ still anticipates the creation of an East African Federation as "a prelude to the United States of Africa" (*Moving* 174, 176), a continental union that could tackle a myriad of shared problems such as the AIDS pandemic, genocidal civil wars, kleptocratic governments, and ecocide.

In the extensively revised and rewritten second edition of *Writers in Politics*, Ngũgĩ warns of the new transnational world order's threat to Africa's survival. He anticipates the combined might of a united America, Europe, and Japan, and their far-reaching "developmental" instruments, the international lending agencies such as the IMF and the World Bank, free trade blocs, the G7 Group of Industrialized Countries, and the UN Security Council (rev. ed., 126–31). These agencies, in coordination with neocolonial governments in client states, have had disastrous results, that only class-based or "third world" solidarity can remedy effectively.[26] To prevent Africa's total collapse and recolonization, Ngũgĩ reiterates his commitment to the idea of a Pan-African alliance formed in dialogue with the socialist forces of Asia and South America.

Distinctively African models for postnational alliance are proposed by Manthia Diawara and Appiah. Based, like the prospect of proletarian union, on a model of cooperative political economy, a radically different paradigm is imagined by Ngũgĩ's former colleague Diawara. For Diawara, the West African nation-state, from its inception, competed against and undermined the traditional regional marketplace and its control of economic and cultural interaction. Diawara conceptualizes the West African market as a "site of resistance" to the forces of globalization and a model for fluid postnational organization (123). He calls for "a regional identity in motion that is based on linguistic affinities, economic reality, and geographic proximity, as defined by the similarities in political and cultural dispositions grounded in history and patterns of consumption" (124). Similarly, Appiah welcomes the survival of "'premodern' affiliations, the cultural and political fretwork of relations through which our very identity is conferred" (171). While much less anxious than Appiah or Ngũgĩ to abandon the model of the nation-state in Africa, Appiah celebrates some states' willingness to withdraw from many aspects of people's social and economic lives, previously organized by the state, in favor of such traditional modes of affiliation. Facilitating, rather than directing, such social allegiances, the state allows greater popular participation, and, importantly for states like Kenya, checks the excesses of the state's rulers (167–71).

Ngũgĩ's own most far-reaching and unorthodox view of the post-neocolonial nation is outlined in *Penpoints*. Advancing his conception of the postcolonial intellectual as an activist who uses the resources of the traditional oral intellectual in order to effect a return to the source of cultural integrity, Ngũgĩ advocates a radically contemporary model for the postnation. Since the early 1980s, and in particular *Barrel of a Pen*, Ngũgĩ has insisted that a true national culture could be made readily accessible to a rural audience via modern technology such as film and video, but in *Penpoints* Ngũgĩ explores cyberspace as an accommodating vehicle

---

[26] Ahmad attacks the privileging of the nation as a site of resistance by "Third World Theory" in favor of global, class-based unions (*In Theory* 287–318). An international proletarian union to oppose the worst effects of globalization is explored extensively by Harvey (*Spaces* 39–45).

for contemporary performative orature: "Cyberspace, where we can already see the narrowing of the gap between signs, icons, and voices, is nearer to the world of the oral. In cyberspace resides the possible merger of the four aesthetic systems of the written, the oral, the theatrical, and the cinematic. Cyberspace orature may turn out to be the great oral aesthetic system of the future" (*Penpoints* 118). Ngũgĩ's argument in the series of lectures recognizes a dialectical relationship between the imprisoning neocolonial state, on the one hand, and the free space of art and cyberspace orature, on the other, that suggests cyberspace as a model of absolute freedom for the postnation itself. Cyberspace models Ngũgĩ's dream of Africa's future because of its circularity that "assumes a dynamic interplay of margins and centres" (115). Ngũgĩ's return to the future, his dream of a postmodern version of the postnation, differs from the models of Diawara and Appiah, who to varying degrees support traditional organizational alternatives or modifications to the existing nation-state in Africa.

While Ngũgĩ's construct is an ambitious and inevitably ambiguous political paradigm for the African postnation, partly designed to outwit the advance of the new transnational world order, it relies on a homogeneous, fetishistic notion of cyberspace itself and its absolute freedom within a globalized political economy, indicating a weakness in Ngũgĩ's view of the final stage in the progressive development of the postnation. As Saskia Sassen points out, cyberspace, far from being empty or ideologically neutral, is an intensely commodified and commercialized zone, and its open public space is increasingly threatened by further control, segmentation, and restriction, governed by the new structures of power (*Globalization* 177). As Fredric Jameson suggested nearly 30 years ago in a consideration of the postmodern "information revolution," in terms with which Ngũgĩ would no doubt agree, the commodification of knowledge and the new electronic information technology will do anything but allow free access, and this commodification will not be easily challenged even by new intellectuals: "the dystopian prospect of a global private monopoly of information," Jameson points out, will not be "reformed by however benign a technocratic elite" ("Foreword" xx). Moreover, the seemingly open, endless topography of cyberspace and the information technology sector is not without frontiers or boundaries, national or otherwise, but instead requires a vast human and material infrastructure often located in the new global cities, such as New York. Access to cyberspace, especially from the global margins, is controlled and restricted. In fact, Sassen argues, such technology may offer simply a new "spatialization of inequality" (182). If distribution of information technology in countries like Kenya is controlled by foreign capital, furthermore, "the goals of these investors may well rule and shape the design of that infrastructure. That is, of course, reminiscent of the development of railroads in colonial empires, which were clearly geared toward facilitating imperial trade rather than promoting the internal territorial integration of the colony" (192). Cyberspace, like the transportation system or the map, as David Harvey suggests, can become a totalizing device, as railways and maps did in Kenya's history (*Condition* 252).

Instead of being an imaginative space for the postnation, a zone of absolute freedom, as Ngũgĩ seems to envision it, cyberspace, like the border and the nation in colonial history, may best be considered a site of resistance. Similarly, globalization, with its much vaunted potential for loosening restrictions and even reconfiguring repressive national boundaries, may permit a yet more totalized imperialism, colonialism, and hegemony. If globalization is just something the developed "first world" does to the "third world," then the reconfiguring of nations may promise a yet more devastating exploitation. Though dreading "the ascendance of capitalist fundamentalism," Ngũgĩ dreams at the end of *Penpoints*, in classic Marxist terms, of the eventual "wither[ing] away" of the state, clearing a space for a "post-capitalist society [in which] ... culture and creativity will reign" (130, 131). Terry Eagleton, in a different context, however, warns of the danger of such "premature utopianism": "To wish class or nation away ... is to play straight into the hands of the oppressor" (24, 23). Inevitably, postnationalist struggle is articulated in the language of nationalism, and inextricably embedded in the very hegemonic discourse it seeks to abolish, "fighting on a terrain already mapped out by its antagonists" (24).

The narration of the birth of the postnation that Ngũgĩ hopes will be accomplished by cultural revival may be effected by the very forces of globalization that he deplores using his own methods. Ngũgĩ generally underplays the extent to which culture is already globalized (and he could not have anticipated the role of social media in the Arab Spring or the growing threat of cyber warfare). The globalization of popular culture, for example, through the very media Ngũgĩ embraces for liberation—film, video, and cyberspace—promotes not the films of Sembene or Ngũgĩ, but the celluloid product lines and invisible legitimizing ideology of Hollywood and the dot.com empires.[27] As Ngũgĩ's former colleague at the University of Nairobi, Taban Lo Liyong anticipated: "The poor of the world who buy silence with sweets and ice-cream / Will keep McDonald and the General in business / Regardless of ideology, change of regime, whims of the boss" (111). The border crossing of cyberspace is increasingly accomplished by the silent movements of global capital and the e-market. Already, as Sassen points out, "sovereignty has been decentered and territory partly denationalized," particularly for debtor governments virtually owned by investors (*Losing Control?* 28). Credit rating agencies naturally render life for the majority in such client states a Hobbesian existence of standardized poverty. Those who want people everywhere to learn how to stop worrying and love globalization promote the democracy and self-policing nature of capital and bond markets, and the protection offered all individuals, rather than citizens, by international human rights agreements that hold rogue states to account. These powerful geopolitical and transnational forces, however, already are effecting "the renationalizing of the nation as an idea" (Sassen, *Losing Control?* 62). The anticipated postnation could become merely

---

[27] Nkrumah noted this state of affairs in 1965 (246). See, too, Appiah (*In My Father's House* 58).

another version of the stateless nation denying former citizens the very means of survival. While the forces of globalization may unscramble Africa's national boundaries, they may also inaugurate a second scramble to carve up Africa.

Part 3: Globalectics

In the magisterial final chapter of *Globalectics: Theory and the Politics of Knowing* on orature, Ngũgĩ displays what a globalectic ethics or a world literary aesthetics might be, and he suggests a role for the global intellectual. He writes, by way of definition, that "Globalectics embraces wholeness, interconnectedness, equality of potentiality of parts, tension, and motion. It is a way of thinking and relating to the world, particularly in the era of globalism and globalization" (8). Clearly designed in part to take back the globe itself from globalization, Ngũgĩ's account of world literature, orature, and cyberspace orature resembles Spivak's advancement of comparative literature in *Death of a Discipline* which he cites briefly (57). Globalectics itself, linking the global and the aesthetic, resembles the role of the "planetary" in Spivak's formulation (*Death* 84, 96). It is also informed by Goethe's transnationalism, Marx's cosmopolitanism, as well as Glissant's poetics of relation, and it reintegrates a world disunited by economic, cultural, and political globalization. Ngũgĩ links globalectics to a democratization of old linguistic hierarchies, themselves extrapolated from Hegel's master-slave dialectic, and particularly he relates globalectics to the memo that launched a revolution at the University of Nairobi calling for the abolition of the English Department and its replacement with a Department of Literature. This plea was partly a blow against "intellectual self-enclosure" in national, cultural, generic, and linguistic silos (42), but as Ngũgĩ reflects on this historical moment nearly 50 years later, he sees its sweeping implications, including its influence on the birth of a discipline, postcolonial studies. The crucible of colonialism and its neo-colonial heir in that period of resistance to cultural oppression was enabling the emergence of a new type of intellectual: "it was the colonial order of knowledge, as in the Nairobi of the sixties that was now forming the postcolonial literary intellectual" (41).[28] The Nairobi curricular revolution, Ngũgĩ makes clear, along with the establishment of the journal *Transition*, "became synonymous with the birth of the postcolonial African intellectual" (53). Ngũgĩ's coauthors Henry Owuor-Anyumba and Taban Lo Liyong were both active in creative writing and orature, and well beyond a seemingly simple departmental name change, they sought a special reimagining of cultural centers and margins and an openness to the multidisciplinary, "interlinked nature of art forms in the traditional practice" (73), including the performative interaction of literature, orature, music, and drama. Ngũgĩ offers the illustration

---

[28] Ngũgĩ notes the significance of resistance in allowing this emergence: "a sense of universality was actually the foundation of the new [postcolonial] literature, and it was so precisely because it was a product of the struggle of the double consciousness inherent in the education of the colonial bondsman, now unified in resistance" (42).

of the Mau Mau fighters and other liberation movements in Africa who used transformed songs and hymns for educational, cultural, and strategic purposes. For Ngũgĩ the revolutionary movement in the postcolonial university, while focused on curricular reform and even institutional restructuring, drew on the insights of Goethe and Marx about the worlding of cultures, and suggests the formation of a new type of postcolonial artist intellectual, the global intellectual.

Ngũgĩ offers examples of "[r]eading globalectically," that are in actuality displays of power interrogating feudal, master-slave hierarchies, and he suggests an alternative future for the postcolonial. He also refers to future projects such as a study of "linguistic Darwinism" and he may also have in mind the subject of his recent *In the Name of the Mother: Reflections on Writers and Empire* (8). *Globalectics*' final chapter examines scenes in *Out of Africa*, *Tristes Tropiques*, and *Robinson Crusoe*, considering how they exclude the colonial or othered subject from history. Ngũgĩ performs a close reading of the type he endorsed earlier in the volume, though he is cautious of the dangers of an overreliance on formalism. His method thus marries Leavis with Kettle, though also adding Derrida and Marx. He also returns to *The Tempest*, though he doesn't refer again to Césaire's adaptation of Shakespeare's play as in previous discussions in *Globalectics*. Césaire has Caliban reject the name Prospero gave him as an "insult" and instead he insists that Prospero

> Call me X. That would be best. Like a man without a name. Or, to be more precise, a man whose name has been stolen. You talk about history ... well, that's history, and everyone knows it! Every time you summon me it reminds me of a basic fact, the fact that you've stolen everything from me, even my identity! Uhuru! (Césaire, *A Tempest* 20)

Caliban's speech in Césaire's work from 1969 in a few lines evokes the slave practice of linguistic debasement and control in America, the resistance to slave names in the example of Malcolm X and the descendants of the Nation of Islam's Wallace Fard Muhammad and Elijah Muhammad, and by implication the winds of independence in East Africa. Ngũgĩ's diasporic Pan-Africanism displays the breadth of postcolonial analysis, from an intertextual, creative perspective, but in *Globalectics* he wishes to situate the postcolonial in its historical moment, with all of its often-rehearsed problems, and to grow it into a broader, more inclusive, more worldly approach that shape shifts and synthesizes global cultural forms and flows. In this respect, the globalectic acts as a critique of the postcolonial despite its plurality and worldliness and its writers' intellectual grounding (49). The globalectic articulates "a web of connections of mutual dependence" (77). As with orature, it connects "nature, nurture, supernatural, and supernurtural," and, also, as in orature the teller of the tale is by implication a prophet (75, 79). This visionary, prophetic quality appears, as with the model of orature and "cyborature," to be part of the role of the global intellectual who can articulate a globalectics of mutual support and foster "the globalectic reading of texts and the world" (85).

In conclusion, *The Postcolonial Intellectual: Ngũgĩ wa Thiong'o in Context* has attempted to locate Ngũgĩ amid some of his major diasporic Pan-African influences and within the postcolonial intellectual tradition—as established by Said, Spivak, Bhabha, and Fanon—as well as within the tradition of perennial resistance to the apparently elitist, exclusionist, and essentialist notion of the intellectual. The appetite for intellectual murder, annihilation, or suicide— following from a deep-seated suspicion of the intellectual as a useless passion— continues to be robust. Despite this uneasiness and the recurrent announcements of the death of the intellectual, a preoccupation with the role of the intellectual (who speaks and for whom?) has been widespread in postcolonial studies, where it is frequently accompanied by autobiographical and autocritographic moments. Ngũgĩ is a particularly unusual, unlikely example while also being virtually the type of the postcolonial intellectual due to his own inherited subaltern status as part of the landless peasant class during the brutal anti–Mau Mau suppression in colonial Kenya that is only now being heard in British courts. His has been a particularly resolute refusal to elevate mental over manual or other labor,[29] though he has maintained a perception of intellectual work as primarily text based. Ironically, for a theorist most widely known for his advocacy of African languages, the study of world literature, and the role of culture in political struggle, Ngũgĩ's successful initiation as a member of the colonial intellectual elite was contingent on his facility in English.

Addressing his largely overlooked early work in Nairobi journalism with its ambivalent assumption of the perspective of the "abstract African" and focusing on his nonfictional critical, theoretical, and autobiographical texts, this book argues for Ngũgĩ's location as a postcolonial theorist. It traces the remarkable consistency but also the radical transformation of his intellectual stance, as he moved from evangelical Christianity, quasi-colonial amelioration or liberalism, and belief in salvation through education. Following from his encounter with James, Fanon, Marx, and also Arnold Kettle as well as the literature of the Caribbean in the periphery of the colonial homeland—the industrial northern city of Leeds—Ngũgĩ embarked on his own acquired class suicide in Cabral's terms. A strident advocacy of Marx followed in the 1970s and 1980s—Ngũgĩ's "orthodox Marxist phase" (Gikandi, *Ngugi* 11)—together with a certain hardening of attitudes and a much-heralded farewell to English and the Afro-Saxon novel. His reeducation continued via his experience in Gĩkũyũ popular theater at Kamĩrĩĩthũ, the resulting year-long political detention, and subsequent exile that continues to the present. Before these traumatic, transformative events, he was part of another, smaller collective at the University of Nairobi that authored a memo which launched a revolution. This opening salvo on the decolonization of literature teaching may also have

---

[29] See Rodney (*Walter Rodney Speaks* 113) and Jameson ("On Negt" 56–7) on this tendency among intellectuals. Lazarus suggests that postcolonial writers tend to enforce the distinction between writing labour and "the majoritarian (and mostly manual) forms of social labour" (*Postcolonial* 54).

indirectly inaugurated the so-called canon wars and accelerated the establishment of the discipline of postcolonial studies.

Ngũgĩ has become a major postcolonial critic and theorist, though he has often been regarded as a novelist whose critical/theoretical works are merely road maps for his own fiction and drama. He notably advocates for mental decolonization as extending well beyond "flag independence," the centrality of culture in political struggle and the human right to open access to intellectual capital, the dreaming of postnational futures, and the decolonization of the postcolonial intellectual. He has reconceptualized the African intellectual as one who can depart from a bourgeois, Western orientation, drawing on the prophetic voice of the traditional oral intellectual or griot, a collective intellectual who voices popular aspirations and whose works are at least partly the product of communal labor. The present project is inevitably preliminary and provisional as the domain of the intellectual and the discourse of intellectual representations are so vast and unwieldy, and because Ngũgĩ is a writer whose work is very much in progress, with five major new titles in the last eight years, at a time when the postcolonial imaginary progresses past its own "post" and rumors of its own demise, and as the task of the decolonization of the intellectual continues.

Works Cited

Abdullahi, Aminu. "Ngugi wa Thiong'o: James Ngugi." Interview with Ngũgĩ wa Thiong'o. *Ngũgĩ wa Thiong'o Speaks*. Ed. Reinhard Sander and Bernth Lindfors. 11–19.

Achebe, Chinua. *Hopes and Impediments, Selected Essays*. New York: Doubleday, 1989.

———. "An Image of Africa: Racism in Conrad's *Heart of Darkness*." *Hopes and Impediments*. Chinua Achebe. 1–20.

———. "The Novelist as Teacher." *Hopes and Impediments*. Chinua Achebe. 40–46.

Adesanmi, Pius. "Ngũgĩ and the Postcolonial." *Approaches to Teaching the Works of Ngũgĩ wa Thiong'o*. Ed. Oliver Lovesey. 53–9.

Adichie, Chimamanda Ngozi. *Americanah*. London: Fourth Estate, 2013.

Adorno, Theodor. *Minima Moralia: Reflections from Damaged Life*. Trans. E.F.N. Jephcott. London: Verso, 1974.

Ahmad, Aijaz. *In Theory: Classes, Nations, Literatures*. London: Verso, 2008.

———. "Jameson's Rhetoric of Otherness and the 'National Allegory.'" *Social Text* 17 (1987): 3–25. Rpt. in Ahmad's *In Theory: Classes, Nations, Literatures*. London: Verso, 1992. 95–122.

———. "The Politics of Literary Postcoloniality." *Race & Class* 36.3 (1995): 1–20.

Ali, Tariq. *Conversations with Edward Said*. London: Seagull, 2006.

———. "Remembering Edward Said." *Conversations with Edward Said*. Tariq Ali. 3–17.

Althusser, Louis. *Lenin and Philosophy and Other Essays*. Trans. Ben Brewster. London: NLB, 1971.

Amoko, Apollo Obonyo. *Postcolonialism in the Wake of the Nairobi Revolution: Ngugi wa Thiong'o and the Idea of African Literature*. New York: Palgrave Macmillan, 2010.

Amooti wa Irumba, Katebalirwe. "Ngugi wa Thiong'o's Literary Production: A Materialist Critique." D. Phil. Diss., University of Sussex, 1980.

Anderson, David. *Histories of the Hanged: The Dirty War in Kenya and the End of Empire*. New York: Norton, 2005.

Appiah, Kwame Anthony. "Africa: The Hidden History." Rev. of *Africa: A Biography of the Continent* by John Reader. *New York Review of Books*, 17 Dec. 1998.

———. *In My Father's House: Africa in the Philosophy of Culture*. Oxford: Oxford UP, 1992.

Araeen, Rasheed. "A New Beginning: Beyond Postcolonial Cultural Theory and Identity Politics." *Third Text* 50 (Spring 2000): 3–20.

Arendt, Hannah. *Men in Dark Times*. New York: Harcourt, Brace and World, 1968.

———. *On Violence*. New York: Harcourt, Brace and World, 1970.

Arnove, Anthony. "Pierre Bourdieu, the Sociology of Intellectuals, and the Language of African Literature." *Novel: A Forum on Fiction* 26.3 (Spring 1993): 278–96.

Aronowitz, Stanley. "On Intellectuals." *Intellectuals: Aesthetics, Politics, Academics*. Ed. Bruce Robbins. 3–56.

Asante, Molefi Kete, and Abu S. Abarry, eds. *African Intellectual Heritage: A Book of Sources*. Philadelphia: Temple UP, 1996.

Ashcroft, Bill. "Exile and Representation: Edward Said as Public Intellectual." *Edward Said: The Legacy of a Public Intellectual*. Eds. Ned Curthoys and Debjani Ganguly. 75–95.

———. "Introduction: A Convivial Critical Democracy—Post-Colonial Studies in the Twenty-First Century." *Literature for Our Times: Postcolonial Studies in the Twenty-First Century*. Ed. Bill Ashcroft, Ranjini Mendis, Julie McGonegal, and Arun Mukherjee. xv–xxxv.

Ashcroft, Bill, and Hussein Kadhim, eds. *Edward Said and the Post-Colonial*. Huntington, New York: Nova Science Publishers, 2001.

Ashcroft, Bill, Ranjini Mendis, Julie McGonegal, and Arun Mukherjee, eds. *Literature for Our Times: Postcolonial Studies in the Twenty-First Century*. Amsterdam: Rodopi, 2012.

Bardolph, Jacqueline. "Ngugi wa Thiong'o." Danassays.wordpress.com/encyclopedia-of-the- essay/ngugi-wa-thiong'o/

Bardolph, Jacqueline, and Jean-Pierre Durix. "An Interview with Ngugi wa Thiong'o." *Ngũgĩ wa Thiong'o Speaks*. Ed. Reinhard Sander and Bernth Lindfors. 157–65.

Baudrillard, Jean. "Intellectuals, Commitment and Political Power. Interview with Maria Shevtsova." *Baudrillard Live: Selected Interviews*. Ed. Mike Gane. London: Routledge, 1993. 72–80.

Beauvoir, Simone de. *Force of Circumstance*. Trans. Richard Howard. London: Penguin, 1968.

———. *The Mandarins*. Trans. Leonard M. Friedman. London: HarperCollins, 2005.

Bell, Bill. "Signs Taken for Wonders: An Anecdote Taken from History." *New Literary History* 43 (2012): 309–29.

Benda, Julien. *The Treason of Intellectuals*. Intro. Roger Kimball. Trans. Richard Aldington. New Brunswick, NJ: Transaction Publishers, 2009.

Benjamin, Walter. "Critique of Violence." *Selected Writings. Vol. 1: 1913–1926*. Ed. Marcus Bullock and Michael W. Jennings. Cambridge, MA: Belknap P of Harvard UP, 1996. 236–52.

Bhabha, Homi K. "Black and White and Read All Over." *Artforum* 34.2 (October 1995): 16–17, 114, 116.

———. "The Commitment to Theory." *The Location of Culture*. Homi K. Bhabha. 19–39.

———. "Draw the Curtain: Foreward." *Iranian Photography Now*. Ed. Rose Issa. Ostfildern, Germany: Hatje Cantz Verlag, 2008. 6.

———. "Foreword: Framing Fanon." *The Wretched of the Earth*. Frantz Fanon. Trans. Richard Philcox. New York: Grove P, 2004. vii–xli.

———. "Homi Bhabha." *Critical Intellectuals on Writing*. Ed. Gary A. Olson and Lynn Worsham. 36–41.

———. "Interrogating Identity: Frantz Fanon and the Postcolonial Prerogative." *The Location of Culture*. Homi K. Bhabha. 40–65.

———. "Introduction: Locations of Culture." *The Location of Culture*. Homi K. Bhabha. 1–18.

———. *The Location of Culture*. London: Routledge, 1994.

———. "The Postcolonial and the Postmodern: The Question of Agency." *The Location of Culture*. Homi K. Bhabha. 171–97.

———. "Postcolonial Authority and Postmodern Guilt." *Cultural Studies*. Ed. Lawrence Grossberg, Cary Nelson, and Paula A. Treichler. New York: Routledge, 1992. 56–68.

———. "Remembering Fanon: Self, Psyche and the Colonial Condition." *Black Skin, White Masks*. Frantz Fanon. Trans. Richard Philcox. London: Pluto P, 1986. xxi–xxxvii.

———. "Signs Taken for Wonders: Questions of Ambivalence and Authority under a Tree Outside Delhi, May 1817." *The Location of Culture*. Homi K. Bhabha. 102–22.

Bhattacharya, Baidik. "Interview with Gayatri Chakravorty Spivak." *The Postcolonial Gramsci*. Ed. Neelam Srivastava and Baidik Bhattacharya. 221–32.

Björkman, Ingrid. *"Mother, Sing for Me": People's Theatre in Kenya*. London: Zed Books, 1989.

Blake, William. "Auguries of Innocence." *Blake's Poetry and Designs*. Ed. Mary Lynn Johnson and John E. Grant. 2nd ed. New York: Norton, 2008. 403–5.

Bourdieu, Pierre. *On Television*. Trans. Priscilla Parkhurst Ferguson. New York: New P, 1998.

Branch, Daniel. *Defeating Mau Mau, Creating Kenya: Counterinsurgency, Civil War, and Decolonization*. Cambridge: Cambridge UP, 2009.

Brathwaite, Kamau. "*Limuru* and *Kinta Kunte*." *Ngũgĩ wa Thiong'o: Texts and Contexts*. Ed. Charles Cantalupo. 1–11.

Breytenbach, Breyten. *The True Confessions of an Albino Terrorist*. London: Faber, 1984.

Bronstein, Michaela. "Ngũgĩ's Use of Conrad: A Case for Literary Transhistory." *MLQ: Modern Language Quarterly* 75.3 (September 2014): 411–37.

Brutus, Dennis. *Letters to Martha and Other Poems from a South African Prison*. London: Heinemann, 1968.

Buhle, Paul. *C.L.R. James: The Artist as Revolutionary*. London: Verso, 1988.

Bunyan, John. *Grace Abounding to the Chief of Sinners*. London and New York: Oxford UP, 1966.

———. *The Pilgrim's Progress*. Oxford and London: Oxford UP, 1966.

Butler, Judith. "Interview." *Critical Intellectuals on Writing*. Ed. Gary A. Olson and Lynn Worsham. 42–52.

Cabral, Amílcar. "National Liberation and Culture." *Transition* 45 (1974): 12–17.
———. *Return to the Source: Selected Speeches of Amilcar Cabral*. Ed. Africa Information Service. New York: Monthly Review P, 1973.
———. *Revolution in Guinea: Selected Texts*. Ed. and Trans. Richard Handyside. New York: Monthly Review P, 1972.
———. *Unity and Struggle: Speeches and Writings*. Selected by the PAIGC. Trans. Michael Wolfers. New York: Monthly Review P, 1979.
Campbell, Horace. "Pan Africanism in the Twenty-First Century." *Pan Africanism: Politics, Economy and Social Change in the Twenty-First Century*. Ed. Tajudeen Abdul-Raheem. London: Pluto P, 1996. 212–28.
Cantalupo, Charles, ed. *Ngũgĩ wa Thiong'o: Texts and Contexts*. Trenton, NJ: Africa World P, 1995.
———, ed. *The World of Ngũgĩ wa Thiong'o*. Trenton, NJ: Africa World P, 1995.
Carter, Martin. "University of Hunger." *University of Hunger: Collected Poems and Selected Prose*. Ed. Gemma Robinson. Highgreen, Tarset, Northumberland: Bloodaxe Books, 2006. 84–5.
Césaire, Aimé. *Discourse on Colonialism*. Trans. Joan Pinkham. New York: Monthly Review P, 2000.
———. "An Interview with Aimé Césaire." [Conducted by René Depestre.] *Discourse on Colonialism*. Aimé Césaire. 81–94.
———. *A Tempest*. Trans. Richard Miller. New York: TCG Translations, 2002.
Chabal, Patrick. *Amilcar Cabral: Revolutionary Leadership and People's War*. Cambridge: Cambridge UP, 1983.
Chatterjee, Partha. "Gramsci in the Twenty-First Century." *The Postcolonial Gramsci*. Ed. Neelam Srivastava and Baidik Bhattacharya. 119–36.
Cheyette, Bryan. "A Glorious Achievement: Edward Said and the Last Jewish Intellectual." *Edward Said's Translocations: Essays in Secular Criticism*. Ed. Tobias Döring and Mark Stein. New York: Routledge, 2012. 74–94.
Chilcote, Ronald H. *Amílcar Cabral's Revolutionary Theory and Practice, A Critical Guide*. Boulder, CO: Lynne Rienner, 1991.
Clifford, James. "Taking Identity Politics Seriously: 'The Contradictory, Stony Ground ... .'" *Without Guarantees: In Honour of Stuart Hall*. Ed. Paul Gilroy, Lawrence Grossberg, and Angela McRobbie. 94–112.
Cobain, Ian. *Cruel Britannia: A Secret History of Torture*. London: Portobello, 2012.
———. "Letters to the Editor." *TLS* (22 Feb. 2013) No. 5734: 6.
Cobain, Ian and Jessica Hatcher. "Mau Mau Victims in Talks with UK over Compensation Payout." *Guardian Weekly*, 10 May 2013: 15.
Collini, Stefan. *Absent Minds: Intellectuals in Britain*. Oxford: Oxford UP, 2006.
Cone, James H. "'Let Suffering Speak': The Vocation of a Black Intellectual." *Cornel West: A Critical Reader*. Ed. George Yancy. 105–14.
Cudjoe, Selwyn R., and William E. Cain, eds. *C.L.R. James: His Intellectual Legacies*. Amherst: U of Massachusetts P, 1995.
———. "Introduction." *C.L.R. James: His Intellectual Legacies*. Ed. Selwyn R. Cudjoe and William E. Cain. 1–19.

Curthoys, Ned, and Debjani Ganguly, eds. *Edward Said: The Legacy of a Public Intellectual*. Victoria, Australia: Melbourne UP, 2007.

Dabashi, Hamid. *The Arab Spring: The End of Postcolonialism*. London: Zed Books, 2012.

Darah, G. G. "'To Choose a Language Is to Choose a Class': Interview with Ngugi wa Thiong'o." *Ngũgĩ wa Thiong'o Speaks*. Ed. Reinhard Sander and Bernth Lindfors. 181–97.

Davidson, Basil. "Remembering Cabral." *Review of African Political Economy* No. 58 (November 1993): 78–85.

Davies, Ioan. *Writers in Prison*. Toronto: Between the Lines, 1990.

De Andrade, Mário. "Biographical Notes." *Unity and Struggle: Speeches and Writings of Amilcar Cabral*. Amilcar Cabral. New York: Monthly Review P, 1979. xviii–xxxv.

Delgado, Celeste Fraser. "MotherTongues and Childless Women: The Construction of 'Kenyan' 'Womanhood.'" *The Politics of (M)Othering: Womanhood, Identity, and Resistance in African Literature*. Ed. Obioma Nnaemeka. London: Routledge, 1997. 130–46.

De Meneses, Filipe. *Salazar: A Political Biography*. New York: Enigma Books, 2009.

Depestre, René. "An Interview with Aimé Césaire." *Discourse on Colonialism*. Aimé Césaire. New York: Monthly Review P, 2000. 79–94.

Derrida, Jacques. *Monolingualism of the Other, Or, The Prosthesis of Origin*. Trans. Patrick Mensah. Stanford: Stanford UP, 1997.

De Villiers, John. "The Birth of a New East African Author." *Ngũgĩ wa Thiong'o Speaks*. Ed. Reinhard Sander and Bernth Lindfors. 7–9.

Dhondy, Farrukh. *C.L.R. James*. London: Weidenfeld & Nicolson, 2001.

Diawara, Manthia. "Toward a Regional Imaginary in Africa." *The Cultures of Globalization*. Ed. Fredric Jameson and Masao Miyoshi. Durham: Duke UP, 1998. 103–24.

Dickens, Charles. *Hard Times*. Ed. Fred Kaplan and Sylvère Monod. New York: Norton, 2001.

Dirlik, Arif. "The Postcolonial Aura: Third World Criticism in the Age of Global Capitalism." *Critical Inquiry* 20 (Winter 1994): 328–56.

Dirks, Nicholas B. "Introduction: Colonialism and Culture." *Colonialism and Culture*. Ed. Nicholas B. Dirks. Ann Arbor: U of Michigan P, 1992. 1–25.

Drew, Bettina. *Nelson Algren: A Life on the Wild Side*. Austin: U of Texas P, 1991.

Du Bois, W.E.B. *Darkwater: Voices from Within the Veil*. New York: Harcourt, Brace and Howe, 1920.

———. *The Souls of Black Folk*. Introduction by Donald B. Gibson. New York: Penguin, 1989.

Dumont, René. *False Start in Africa*. Trans. Phyllis Nauts Ott. 2nd ed. New York: Praeger, 1969.

Dumont, René, and Marie-France Mottin. *Stranglehold on Africa*. Trans. Vivienne Menkes. London: A. Deutsch, 1983.

Eagleton, Terry. "Nationalism: Irony and Commitment." *Nationalism, Colonialism, and Literature*. Ed. Terry Eagleton, Fredric Jameson, Edward W. Said. Minneapolis: U of Minnesota P, 1990. 23–39.

Egan, Susanna. "Breytenbach's *Mouroir*: The Novel as Autobiography." *Journal of Narrative Technique* 18.2 (1988): 89–104.

Elkins, Caroline. *Imperial Reckoning: The Untold Story of Britain's Gulag in Kenya*. New York: Henry Holt, 2005.

Eze, Emmanuel C. "The Colour of Reason: The Idea of 'Race' in Kant's Anthropology." *The African Philosophy Reader*. Ed. P.H. Coetzee and A.P.J. Roux. 2nd ed. London: Routledge, 2003. 430–59.

Fanon, Frantz. *Black Skin, White Masks*. Trans. Charles Lam Markmann. New York: Grove P, 1967.

———. *Les Damnés de la Terre* [1961]. Paris: François Maspero, 1974.

———. *Toward the African Revolution: Political Essays*. Trans. Haakon Chevalier. New York: Grove P, 1967.

———. *The Wretched of the Earth*. Preface by Jean-Paul Sartre. Trans. Constance Farrington. New York: Grove P, 1968.

———. *The Wretched of the Earth*. Commentary by Jean-Paul Sartre and Homi K. Bhabha. Trans. Richard Philcox. New York: Grove P, 2004.

Farred, Grant. "Introduction." *Rethinking C.L.R. James*. Ed. Grant Farred. 1–14.

———, ed. *Rethinking C.L.R. James*. Cambridge, MA: Blackwell, 1996.

Feal, Rosemary G. "From the Editor." Presidential Forum: The Role of Intellectuals in the Twenty-First Century. *Profession* (2006): 1–6.

Foot, Michael. "C.L.R. James." *C.L.R. James: His Intellectual Legacies*. Ed. Selwyn R. Cudjoe and William E. Cain. 98–105.

Foucault, Michel. "Intellectuals and Power: A Conversation between Michel Foucault and Gilles Deleuze." *Language, Counter-Memory, Practice: Selected Essays and Interviews*. Ed. Donald F. Bouchard. Trans. Donald F. Bouchard and Sherry Simon. Ithaca, NY: Cornell UP, 1977. 205–17.

———. "Technologies of the Self." *Technologies of the Self: A Seminar with Michel Foucault*. Ed. Luther H. Martin et al. Amherst, MA: U of Massachusetts P, 1988. 16–49. http://foucault.info/documents/foucault.technologiesOfSelf.en.html.

Fox, Robert Elliot. Rev. of *Poems of Black Africa* by Wole Soyinka. *African Literature Today* 11. *Myth and History*. Ed. Eldred Durosimi Jones. London: Heinemann, 1980. 209–12.

Friedberger, Heinz. "Kenyan Writer James Ngugi Interviewed in Nairobi." *Ngũgĩ wa Thiong'o Speaks*. Ed. Reinhard Sander and Bernth Lindfors. 39–42.

Froude, James Anthony. *The English in the West Indies, or The Bow of Ulysses*. 2nd ed. London: Longmans, Green, and Co., 1888.

Gakaara wa Wanjaũ. *Mau Mau Author in Detention*. Trans. Ngigĩ wa Njoroge. Nairobi: Heinemann Kenya, 1988.

Gates, Jr., Henry Louis. "Critical Fanonism." *Critical Inquiry* 17 (Spring 1991): 457–70.

Gérard, Albert S. *African Language Literatures: An Introduction to the Literary History of Sub-Saharan Africa*. Harlow, Essex: Longman, 1981.

Gĩchingiri Ndĩgĩrĩgĩ. *Ngũgĩ wa Thiong'o's Drama and the Kamĩrĩĩthũ Popular Theater Experiment*. Trenton, NJ: Africa World P, 2007.

———, ed. *Unmasking the African Dictator: Essays on Postcolonial African Literature*. Knoxville: U of Tennessee P, 2014.

Gikandi, Simon. "Between Roots and Routes: Cosmopolitanism and the Claims of Locality." *Rerouting the Postcolonial: New Directions for the New Millennium*. Ed. Janet Wilson, Cristina Şandru, and Sarah Lawson Welsh. London: Routledge, 2010. 22–35.

———. "Cultural Translation and the African Self: A (Post)colonial Case Study." *Interventions* 3.3 (2001): 355–75.

———. "Editor's Column: The End of Postcolonial Theory? A Roundtable." Ed. Patricia Yaeger. *PMLA* 635–6.

———. "Moments of Melancholy: Ngũgĩ and the Discourse of Emotions." *The World of Ngũgĩ wa Thiong'o*. Ed. Charles Cantalupo. 59–72.

———. "Ngũgĩ's Conversion: Writing and the Politics of Language." *Research in African Literatures* 23.1 (Spring 1992): 131–44.

———. *Ngugi wa Thiong'o*. Cambridge: Cambridge UP, 2000.

———. "Obama as Text: The Crisis of Double-Consciousness." *Comparative American Studies* 10.2–3 (August 2012): 211–25.

———. "The Postcolonial Wizard." Rev. of *Wizard of the Crow* by Ngũgĩ wa Thiong'o. *Transition* No. 98 (2008): 156–69.

Gilly, Adolfo. "Introduction." *A Dying Colonialism*. Frantz Fanon. Trans. Nell Salm. New York: Grove P, 1967. 1–21.

Gilroy, Paul. *The Black Atlantic: Modernity and Double Consciousness*. Cambridge, MA: Harvard UP, 1993.

———. *Darker Than Blue: On the Moral Economies of Black Atlantic Culture*. Cambridge, MA: Belknap P, 2010.

———. *Postcolonial Melancholia*. New York: Columbia UP, 2005.

Gilroy, Paul, Lawrence Grossberg, and Angela McRobbie, eds. *Without Guarantees: In Honour of Stuart Hall*. London: Verso, 2000.

Glaberman, Martin. "The Marxism of C.L.R. James." *C.L.R. James: His Intellectual Legacies*. Ed. Selwyn R. Cudjoe and William E. Cain. 304–13.

Glissant, Édouard. *Poetics of Relation*. Trans. Betsy Wing. Ann Arbor: U of Michigan P, 1997.

Graff, Gerald. "Arnold, Reason, and Common Culture." *Culture and Anarchy*. Ed. Samuel Lipman. New Haven: Yale UP, 1994. 186–201.

———. "Today, Tomorrow: The Intellectual in the Academy and in Society." Roundtable on Intellectuals. *PMLA* 112.5 (Oct. 1997): 1132–3.

Gramsci, Antonio. "The Formation of Intellectuals." *The Modern Prince and Other Writings*. Trans. Louis Marks. New York: International Publishers, 1992. 118–25.

———. *The Modern Prince and Other Writings*. Trans. Louis Marks. New York: International Publishers, 1992.

———. *Selections from Cultural Writings*. Ed. David Forgacs and Geoffrey Nowell-Smith. Trans. William Boelhower. Cambridge, MA: Harvard UP, 1991.

Granqvist, Raoul. "Ngugi wa Thiong'o: An Interview." *Ngũgĩ wa Thiong'o Speaks*. Ed. Reinhard Sander and Bernth Lindfors. 167–71.

Greaves, L.B. *Carey Francis of Kenya*. London: Rex Collings, 1969.

Grimshaw, Anna. *Popular Democracy and the Creative Imagination: The Writings of C.L.R. James 1950–1963*. New York: The C.L.R. James Institute. May 2001. www.clrjamesinstitute.org/popudem.html

———. "Preface." *The C.L.R. James Reader*. Ed. Anna Grimshaw. Oxford: Blackwell, 1992. vii–ix.

Grimshaw, Anna, and Keith Hart. "*American Civilization*: An Introduction." *American Civilization*. C.L.R. James. Cambridge, MA: Blackwell, 1993. 1–25.

Hall, Stuart. "The After-life of Frantz Fanon: Why Fanon? Why Now? Why *Black Skin, White Masks*?" *The Fact of Blackness: Frantz Fanon and Visual Representation*. Ed. Alan Read. 12–37.

———. "C.L.R. James: A Portrait." *C.L.R. James's Caribbean*. Ed. Paget Henry and Paul Buhle. 3–16.

———. "Cultural Studies and Its Theoretical Legacies." *Cultural Studies*. Ed. Lawrence Grossberg, Cary Nelson, and Paula Treichler. New York: Routledge, 1992. 277–94.

———. "Gramsci and Us." June 1987. http://www.hegemonics.co.uk/docs/Gramsci-and-us.pdf

Harasym, Sarah, ed. *The Postcolonial Critic: Interviews, Strategies, Dialogues*. New York: Routledge, 1990.

Harris, Lyle Ashton, et al. "Dialogue." *The Fact of Blackness: Frantz Fanon and Visual Representation*. Ed. Alan Read. 180–183.

Harvey, David. *The Condition of Postmodernity: An Enquiry into the Origins of Cultural Change*. Cambridge, MA: Blackwell, 1990.

———. *Spaces of Hope*. Berkeley: U of California P, 2000.

Hegel, Georg Wilhelm Friedrich. *The Philosophy of History*. Trans. J. Sibree. New York: Dover, 1956.

Hell, Richard [Richard Meyers]. *I Dreamed I Was a Very Clean Tramp, An Autobiography*. New York: HarperCollins, 2013.

Henry, Paget and Paul Buhle, eds. *C.L.R. James's Caribbean*. Durham: Duke UP, 1992.

———. "Preface." *C.L.R. James's Caribbean*. Ed. Paget Henry and Paul Buhle. vii–xvi.

Hindmarsh, Roland. "Cut the Cackle." Rev. of *A Short Guide to English Style* by Alan Warner. *Transition* No. 3 (Jan. 1962): 32–3.

Hobsbawm, Eric. *How to Change the World: Marx and Marxism 1840–2011*. London: Little, Brown, 2011.

Holden, Philip. *Autobiography and Decolonization: Modernity, Masculinity, and the Nation-State*. Madison, Wisconsin: U of Wisconsin P, 2008.

Holloway, Marvin. "Introduction." *A History of Pan-African Revolt*. C.L.R. James. 2nd ed. Washington, DC: Drum and Spear P, 1969. vii–viii.

Huddart, David. *Postcolonial Theory and Autobiography*. London: Routledge, 2008.

Hussein, Abdirahman A. *Edward Said: Criticism and Society*. London: Verso, 2002.

Idahosa, Paul. "James and Fanon and the Problem of the Intelligentsia in Popular Organizations." *C.L.R. James: His Intellectual Legacies*. Ed. Selwyn R. Cudjoe and William E. Cain. Amherst: U of Massachusetts P, 1995. 388–404.

Ikiddeh, Ime. "Foreword." *Homecoming: Essays on African and Caribbean Literature, Culture and Politics*. Ngũgĩ wa Thiong'o. London: Heinemann, 1972. xi–xiv.

Irele, Abiola. "In Defence of Negritude: A Propos of *Black Orpheus* by Jean Paul Sartre." *Transition* 3.13 (March–April 1964): 9–11.

———. "Négritude: Literature and Ideology." *The African Philosophy Reader*. Ed. P.H. Coetzee and A.P.J. Roux. 2nd ed. London: Routledge, 2003. 35–51.

Jacobs, J.U. "Breyten Breytenbach and the South African Prison Book." *Theoria* 68 (1986): 95–105.

———. "Confession, Interrogation and Self-Interrogation in the New South African Prison Writing." *Kunapipi* 13.1/2 (1991): 115–27.

Jaggi, Maya. "Ngugi wa Thiong'o: *Matigari* as Myth and History: An Interview." *Ngũgĩ wa Thiong'o Speaks*. Ed. Reinhard Sander and Bernth Lindfors. 261–73.

James, C.L.R. *American Civilization*. Ed. Anna Grimshaw and Keith Hart. Cambridge, MA: Blackwell, 1993.

———. "The Artist in the Caribbean." *The Future in the Present: Selected Writings*. C.L.R. James. London: Allison & Busby, 1977. 183–90.

———. *Beyond a Boundary*. London: Hutchinson & Co., 1963.

———. *The Black Jacobins: Toussaint L'Ouverture and the San Domingo Revolution*. New Edition. London: Allison & Busby, 1980.

———. "Foreword [1980]." *The Black Jacobins*. C.L.R. James. [v]–vii.

———. *A History of Pan-African Revolt*. 2nd ed. Washington: Drum and Spear P, 1969.

———. *Mariners, Renegades and Castaways: The Story of Herman Melville and the World We Live In: The Complete Text*. Intro. Donald E. Pease. Hanover and London: UP of New England, 2001.

———. "The Mighty Sparrow." *The Future in the Present: Selected Writings*. C.L.R. James. London: Allison & Busby, 1977. 191–201.

———. *Minty Alley*. Intro. Kenneth Ramchand. Jackson and London: UP of Mississippi and New Beacon Books, 1997.

———. *Nkrumah and the Ghana Revolution*. London: Allison & Busby, 1977.

———. "Preface to the First Edition [1938]." *The Black Jacobins*. C.L.R. James. ix–xi.

Jameson, Fredric. "Foreword." *The Postmodern Condition: A Report on Knowledge*. Jean-François Lyotard. Trans. Geoff Bennington and Brian Massumi. Minneapolis: U of Minnesota P, 1984. vii–xxi.

———. "On Negt and Kluge." *The Phantom Public Sphere*. Ed. Bruce Robbins. Minneapolis: U of Minnesota P, 1993. 42–74.

———. "Third-World Literature in the Era of Multinational Capitalism." *Social Text* 15 (Fall 1986): 65–88.
JanMohamed, Abdul R. "Worldliness-without-World, Homelessness-as-Home: Toward a Definition of the Specular Border Intellectual." *Edward Said: A Critical Reader*. Ed. Michael Sprinker. 96–120.
Jeyifo, Biodun. "Introduction: Wole Soyinka and the Tropes of Disalienation." *Art, Dialogue and Outrage: Essays on Literature and Culture*. Wole Soyinka. London: Methuen, 1993. ix–xxx.
Johnson, Clarence Shole. "Reading Cornel West as a Humanistic Scholar: Rhetoric and Practice." *Cornel West: A Critical Reader*. Ed. George Yancy. 312–34.
Johnson, Samuel. *The History of Rasselas, Prince of Abissinia*. Ed. D.J. Enright. London: Penguin, 1976.
Jones, Eldred Durosimi. *The Writing of Wole Soyinka*. 3rd ed. London: James Currey, 1988.
Kamenju, Grant. "Frantz Fanon." Rev. of *The Wretched of the Earth* by Frantz Fanon. *Transition* No. 26 (1966): 51–2.
Kanwar, Asha S., and Arnold Kettle. "An Interview with Arnold Kettle." *Social Scientist* 15.7 (July 1987): 54–61.
Kay, Hugh. *Salazar and Modern Portugal*. London: Eyre & Spottiswoode, 1970.
Kettle, Arnold. "The Artist and Politics." *Literature and Liberation: Selected Essays*. Arnold Kettle. Eds. Graham Martin and W.R. Owens. Manchester: Manchester UP, 1988. 35–48.
———. *Communism and the Intellectuals*. London: Lawrence & Wishart Ltd., [1965].
———. *An Introduction to the English Novel*. 2 vols. London: Hutchinson & Co., 1951, 1953.
———. *Literature and Liberation: Selected Essays*. Ed. Graham Martin and W.R. Owens. Manchester: Manchester UP, 1988.
Kettle, Martin. "What MI5's records on my father tell us about the uses of surveillance." *Guardian*. 28 July 2011. http://www.theguardian.com/commentisfree/2011/jul/28/mi5-security-service-records-my-father-surveillance
Killam, G.D., ed. *Critical Perspectives on Ngugi wa Thiong'o*. Washington, DC: Three Continents P, 1984.
Kristeva, Julia. *Hatred and Forgiveness*. Trans. Jeanine Herman. New York: Columbia UP, 2010.
———. "A New Type of Intellectual: The Dissident." Trans. Seán Hand. *The Kristeva Reader*. Ed. Toril Moi. New York: Columbia UP, 1986. 292–300.
———. "Thinking in Dark Times." Presidential Forum: The Role of Intellectuals in the Twenty-First Century. *Profession* (2006): 13–21.
———. *This Incredible Need to Believe*. Trans. Beverley Bie Brahic. New York: Columbia UP, 2009.
Kritzman, Lawrence D. "Simone de Beauvoir, the Paradoxical Intellectual." *PMLA* 124.1 (January 2009): 206–13.

Kumar, T. Vijay. "The Writer as Activist: An Interview with Ngugi wa Thiong'o." *The Writer as Activist: South Asian Perspectives on Ngũgĩ wa Thiong'o*. Ed. Bernth Lindfors and Bala Kothandaraman. 169–76.

Kyomuhendo, Goretti. *Waiting, A Novel of Uganda at War*. New York: The Feminist P, 2007.

LaCapra, Dominick. "Today, Tomorrow: The Intellectual in the Academy and in Society." Roundtable on Intellectuals. *PMLA* 112.5 (Oct. 1997): 1133–5.

Lai, Walton Look. "C.L.R. James and Trinidadian Nationalism." *C.L.R. James's Caribbean*. Eds. Paget Henry and Paul Buhle. 174–209.

Lamming, George. "C.L.R. James: West Indian: George Lamming Interviewed by Paul Buhle." *C.L.R. James's Caribbean*. Ed. Paget Henry and Paul Buhle. 28–36.

———. *The Pleasures of Exile*. London: Allison & Busby, 1984.

Landry, Donna, and Gerald MacLean. "Introduction: Reading Spivak." *The Spivak Reader: Selected Works of Gayatri Chakravorty Spivak*. Ed. Donna Landry and Gerald MacLean. 1–13.

———, eds. *The Spivak Reader: Selected Works of Gayatri Chakravorty Spivak*. New York: Routledge, 1996.

Lanzmann, Claude. *The Patagonian Hare: A Memoir*. Trans. Frank Wynne. New York: Farrar, Straus and Giroux, 2009.

Larsen, Neil. "Negativities of the Popular: C.L.R. James and the Limits of 'Cultural Studies.'" *Rethinking C.L.R. James*. Ed. Grant Farred. 85–102.

Lazarus, Neil. "Cricket and National Culture in the Writings of C.L.R. James." *C.L.R. James's Caribbean*. Ed. Paget Henry and Paul Buhle. 92–110.

———. "Mind the Gap: An Interview with Neil Lazarus [by Sorcha Gunne]." *Postcolonial Text* 7.3 (2012): 1–15.

———. *The Postcolonial Unconscious*. Cambridge: Cambridge UP, 2011.

———. "Representations of the Intellectual in *Representations of the Intellectual*." *Research in African Literatures* 36.3 (Fall 2005): 112–23.

———. *Resistance in Post-Colonial African Fiction*. New Haven: Yale UP, 1990.

———. "(Re)turn to the People: Ngũgĩ wa Thiong'o and the Crisis of Postcolonial African Intellectualism." *The World of Ngũgĩ wa Thiong'o*. Ed. Charles Cantalupo. 11–25.

Lenin, V.I. *Imperialism: The Highest Stage of Capitalism, A Popular Outline*. New York: International Publishers, 1970.

Lessing, Doris. "Introduction." *The Mandarins*. Simone de Beauvoir. 7–9.

———. *Walking in the Shade: Vol. Two of My Autobiography, 1949–1962*. London: HarperCollins, 1997.

Levi, Primo. *Survival in Auschwitz*. Trans. Stuart Woolf. New York: Collier, 1961.

Lindfors, Bernth. "Ngugi wa Thiong'o's Early Journalism." *WLWE: World Literature Written in English* 20.1 (1981): 23–41.

Lindfors, Bernth, and Bala Kothandaraman, eds. *The Writer as Activist: South Asian Perspectives on Ngũgĩ wa Thiong'o*. Trenton, NJ: Africa World P, 2001.

Lonsdale, John. "Kenya: Ethnicity, Tribe, and State." *openDemocracy*, 17 Jan. 2008, 1–3. http://www.opendemocracy.net/article/democracy_power/kenya_ethnicity_tribe_state

Lovesey, Oliver. "Chained Letters: African Prison Diaries and 'National Allegory.'" *Research in African Literatures* 26.4 (Winter 1995): 31–45.

———. "'Initiation for the Nation': Ngũgĩ wa Thiong'o's Writing for Children." *Voices of the Other: Children's Literature and the Postcolonial Context*. Ed. Roderick McGillis. New York: Garland, 2000. 193–210.

———. "The Last King of Africa: The Representation of Idi Amin in Ugandan Dictatorship Novels." *Unmasking the African Dictator: Essays on Postcolonial African Literature*. Ed. Gĩchingiri Ndĩgĩrĩgĩ. 85–109.

———. "Making Use of the Past in *Things Fall Apart*." *Genre: Forms of Discourse and Culture* 39.2 (Summer 2006): 273–99; rpt. in *Chinua Achebe's Things Fall Apart*. Ed. Harold Bloom. Bloom's Modern Critical Interpretations. New edition. New York: Infobase Publishing, 2010. 115–39.

———. *Ngũgĩ wa Thiong'o*. New York: Twayne, 2000.

———. "Ngũgĩ wa Thiong'o's Postnation: The Cultural Geographies of Colonial, Neocolonial, and Postnational Space." *Modern Fiction Studies* 48.1 (Spring 2002): 139–68. Rpt. in *Postcolonial Literary Studies: The First 30 Years*. Ed. Robert P. Marzec. Baltimore: Johns Hopkins UP, 2011. 199–224.

———. "Postcolonial Self-Fashioning in Sara Suleri's *Meatless Days*." *The Journal of Commonwealth Literature* 32.2 (1997): 35–50.

———, ed. *Approaches to Teaching the Works of Ngũgĩ wa Thiong'o*. New York: MLA Publications, 2012.

Macaulay, Thomas Babington. "Minute [on Indian Education. Feb. 2, 1835]." Bureau of Education. *Selections from Educational Records*. Part 1 (1781–1839). Ed. H. Sharp. Rpt. Delhi: National Archives of India, 1965. 107–17. http://www.mssu.edu/projectsouthasia/history/primarydocs/education/Macaulay001.htm

MacCabe, Colin. "Foreword." *In Other Worlds: Essays in Cultural Politics*. Gayatri Chakravorty Spivak. New York: Routledge, 1998. xii–xxvi.

Macey, David. *Frantz Fanon: A Biography*. 2nd ed. London: Verso, 2012.

Macpherson, Margaret. *They Built for the Future: A Chronicle of Makerere University College 1922–1962*. Reissue edition. Cambridge: Cambridge UP, 2009.

Maduakor, Obi. *Wole Soyinka: An Introduction to His Writing*. New York: Garland, 1986.

Makdisi, Saree. "Edward Said and the Style of the Public Intellectual." *Edward Said: The Legacy of a Public Intellectual*. Ed. Ned Curthoys and Debjani Ganguly. 21–35.

Maloba, W.O. "Ngũgĩ and Kenya's History." *Approaches to Teaching the Works of Ngũgĩ wa Thiong'o*. Ed. Oliver Lovesey. 60–75.

Mapanje, Jack. "Where Dissent Is Meat for Crocodiles." *The Chattering Wagtails of Mikuyu Prison*. Oxford: Heinemann, 1993. 80–81.

Marcuson, Alan, Mike González, and Dave Williams. "James Ngugi Interviewed by Fellow Students at Leeds University." *Ngũgĩ wa Thiong'o Speaks*. Ed. Reinhard Sander and Bernth Lindfors. 25–33.

Margaretta wa Gacheru. "Ngugi wa Thiong'o Still Bitter over His Detention." *Ngũgĩ wa Thiong'o Speaks*. Ed. Reinhard Sander and Bernth Lindfors. 91–7.

Marks, Louis. "Introduction." *The Modern Prince and Other Writings*. Antonio Gramsci. New York: International Publishers, 1992. 11–18.

Marrouchi, Mustapha. "Counternarratives, Recoveries, Refusals." *Edward Said and the Work of the Critic: Speaking Truth to Power*. Ed. Paul A. Bové. Durham: Duke UP, 2000. 187–228.

Martini, Jürgen, Anna Rutherford, Kirsten Holst Petersen, Vibeke Stenderup, and Bent Thomsen. "Ngugi wa Thiong'o: Interview." *Ngũgĩ wa Thiong'o Speaks*. Ed. Reinhard Sander and Bernth Lindfors. 115–27.

McCarthy, Conor. *The Cambridge Introduction to Edward Said*. Cambridge: Cambridge UP, 2010.

McClintock, Anne. "The Angel of Progress: Pitfalls of the Term 'Post-Colonialism.'" *Social Text* 31–32 (1992): 84–98.

McCulloch, Jock. *In the Twilight of Revolution: The Political Theory of Amilcar Cabral*. London: Routledge, 1983.

Memmi, Albert. "The Impossible Life of Frantz Fanon." *The Massachusetts Review* 14.1 (Winter 1973): 9–39.

Michael, John. *Anxious Intellects: Academic Professionals, Public Intellectuals, and Enlightenment Values*. Durham: Duke UP, 2000.

Mignolo, Walter D. "Today, Tomorrow: The Intellectual in the Academy and in Society." Roundtable on Intellectuals. *PMLA* 112.5 (Oct. 1997): 1140–41.

Miller, J. Hillis. "Today, Tomorrow: The Intellectual in the Academy and in Society." Roundtable on Intellectuals. *PMLA* 112.5 (Oct. 1997): 1137–8.

Mkandawire, Thandika. "African Intellectuals and Nationalism." *African Intellectuals*. Ed. Thandika Mkandawire. 10–55.

———, ed. *African Intellectuals: Rethinking Politics, Language, Gender and Development*. Dakar: CODESRIA Books, 2005.

Moi, Toril. *Simone de Beauvoir: The Making of an Intellectual Woman*. 2nd ed. Oxford: Oxford UP, 2008.

Moore-Gilbert, Bart. *Postcolonial Life-Writing: Culture, Politics and Self-Representation*. London: Routledge, 2009.

———. *Postcolonial Theory: Contexts, Practices, Politics*. London: Verso, 1997.

Moser, Gerald M. "The Poet Amílcar Cabral." *Research in African Literatures* 9.2 (Autumn 1978): 176–97.

Msimang, Nonqaba. "Ngugi: In His Own Words." *Ngũgĩ wa Thiong'o Speaks*. Ed. Reinhard Sander and Bernth Lindfors. 325–31.

Mwangi, Evan Maina. *Africa Writes Back to Self: Metafiction, Gender, Sexuality*. Albany, NY: State U of New York P, 2009.

———. "Contextualizing Untranslated Moments in Ngũgĩ's Prose and Drama." *Approaches to Teaching the Works of Ngũgĩ wa Thiong'o*. Ed. Oliver Lovesey. 93–113.

———. "'Spare Kenyans This Intellectual Hypocrisy.' *Daily Nation* 8 Feb. 2000." Online posting. 9 Feb. 2000. List for African Literature and Cinema. http://www.h-afrlitcine@h-net.msu.edu

Nagenda, John and Robert Serumaga. "A Discussion between James Ngugi ... John Nagenda and Robert Serumaga . . . ." *Ngũgĩ wa Thiong'o Speaks*. Ed. Reinhard Sander and Bernth Lindfors. 21–4.

Nandy, Dipak. "Arnold Kettle and English Marxist Literary Criticism." *Literature and Liberation: Selected Essays*. Arnold Kettle. Ed. Graham Martin and W. R. Owens. Manchester: Manchester UP, 1988. 1–17.

Natsoulas, Theodore. "The Politicization of the Ban on Female Circumcision and the Rise of the Independent School Movement in Kenya: The KCA, the Missions and Government, 1929–1932." *Journal of Asian and African Studies* 33.2 (May 1998): 137–58.

Nazareth, Peter. "Introduction: Saint Ngũgĩ." *Critical Essays on Ngũgĩ wa Thiong'o*. Ed. Peter Nazareth. 1–16.

———. "Is *A Grain of Wheat* a Socialist Novel?" *Critical Perspectives on Ngugi wa Thiong'o*. Ed. G.D. Killam. 243–64.

———. "The Second Coming: Multiple Ngugis in *Petals of Blood*." *Marxism and African Literature*. Ed. Georg M. Gugelberger. Trenton, NJ: Africa World P, 1986. 118–29.

———. "Teaching *A Grain of Wheat* as a Dialogue with Conrad." *Approaches to Teaching the Works of Ngũgĩ wa Thiong'o*. Ed. Oliver Lovesey. 165–70.

———, ed. *Critical Essays on Ngũgĩ wa Thiong'o*. New York: Twayne, 2000.

Neuman, Shirley. "Autobiography: From Different Poetics to a Poetics of Difference." *Essays on Life Writing: From Genre to Critical Practice*. Ed. Marlene Kadar. Toronto: U of Toronto P, 1992. 213–30.

Ngũgĩ wa Thiong'o. "African Culture: The Mistake That Kenyatta Made." *Sunday Post* 6 Aug. 1961: 10.

———. "An African Says 'The African Personality Is a Delusion': Do Tigers Have 'Tigritude'?" *Sunday Post* 7 May 1961: 12.

———. "African Writers Need a New Outlook." *Sunday Nation* 2 Dec. 1962: 29.

———. "Art Experiment Which Deserves to Succeed." *Sunday Nation* 29 Dec. 1963: 31.

———. *Barrel of a Pen: Resistance to Repression in Neo-Colonial Kenya*. London: New Beacon Books, 1983.

———. "Big Day for God's Children." *Sunday Nation* 30 Dec. 1962: 25.

———. "Can the Educated African Meet This Challenge?" *Sunday Post* 27 May 1962: 31.

———. "A Change Has Come Over the Land—A Sense of Destiny Moves in Most People." *Sunday Nation* 2 June 1963: 5.

———. "Commentary." *Daily Nation* 8 Aug. 1964: 6.

———. "Commentary." *Daily Nation* 14 Aug. 1964: 6.

———. "Commentary." *Daily Nation* 18 Aug. 1964: 6.

———. "Commentary." *Daily Nation* 19 Aug. 1964: 6.

———. "Co-operative Spirit Is Not Enough." *Sunday Nation* 3 Feb. 1963: 4.

———. *Decolonising the Mind: The Politics of Language in African Literature*. London: James Currey, 1981.

———. *Detained: A Writer's Prison Diary*. London: Heinemann, 1981.
———. *Devil on the Cross*. Trans. Ngũgĩ wa Thiong'o. London: Heinemann, 1982.
———. "A Dictator's Last Laugh." *New York Times* 15 March 2013: A25.
———. "Don't Forget Our Destination." *Sunday Nation* 10 Feb. 1963: 12, 35.
———. *Dreams in a Time of War, A Childhood Memoir*. New York: Pantheon, 2010.
———. "Europhone or African Memory: The Challenge of the Pan-Africanist Intellectual in the Era of Globalization." *African Intellectuals: Rethinking Politics, Language, Gender and Development*. Ed. Thandika Mkandawire. 155–64.
———. "Even Brothers Can Cut Throats." *Sunday Nation* 17 Feb. 1963: 4.
———. "For Peace, Justice, and Culture: The Intellectual in the Twenty-First Century." Presidential Forum: The Role of Intellectuals in the Twenty-First Century. *Profession* (2006): 33–9.
———. "The Future and the African Farmer." *Sunday Nation* 3 June 1962: 33.
———. *Globalectics: Theory and the Politics of Knowing*. The Wellek Library Lectures in Critical Theory 2010. New York: Columbia UP, 2012.
———. *A Grain of Wheat*. Rev. ed. London: Heinemann, 1986.
———. "Here's the Kenya I Want." *Sunday Nation* 12 Aug. 1962: 28.
———. "He's Africa's Poet-Statesman." *Daily Nation* 10 July 1964: 6.
———. *Homecoming: Essays on African and Caribbean Literature, Culture and Politics*. London: Heinemann, 1972.
———. "How Do You Kill These Tribal Feelings?" *Sunday Nation* 5 July 1964: 6.
———. "How Much Rope Should Opponents Be Given?" *Sunday Nation* 16 Sept. 1962: 9.
———. "I Hope This Theatre Group Won't Die, Too." *Sunday Nation* 19 July 1964: 6–7.
———. *In The House of the Interpreter, A Memoir*. New York: Pantheon, 2012.
———. *In the Name of the Mother: Reflections on Writers & Empire*. Nairobi: East African Educational Publishers; Woodbridge, Suffolk: James Currey, 2013.
———. "In the Old Days It Was for the Old Men to Drink—Now Even Children Tread on the Toes of Their Fathers." *Sunday Nation* 12 May 1963: 9.
———. "Introduction." *Africa's Cultural Revolution*. Okot p'Bitek. Nairobi: Macmillan, 1973. ix– xiii.
———. "I Say Kenya's Missionaries Failed Badly." *Sunday Nation* 6 Jan. 1963: 5.
———. "Isn't It Time the Public Were Asked about Federation?" *Sunday Nation* 1 Sept. 1963: 31.
———. "It's Time We Broke Up This Tribal Outlook." *Sunday Nation* 20 Oct. 1963: 33.
———. "Lack of Communication May Be Barrier to an Africa United States." *Sunday Nation* 22 Sept. 1963: 14.
———. "Let's Get Out of the Dark and Take a Look at the Sun." *Sunday Nation* 17 June 1962: 39.

———. "Let's See More School Integration." *Sunday Nation* 8 July 1962: 25.
———. "Let Us Be Careful about What We Take from the Past." *Sunday Nation* 5 Aug. 1962: 31.
———. "The Letter That Made My Heart Sink Inside Me." *Sunday Nation* 15 Sept. 1963: 15.
———. *Matigari*. Trans. Wangũi wa Goro. Oxford: Heinemann, 1987.
———. "Mboya Is Right—Education Is an Investment." *Sunday Nation* 21 Apr. 1963: 10, 33.
———. "More Is Needed from Educated Africans." *Sunday Nation* 7 June 1964: 9.
———. *Moving the Centre: The Struggle for Cultural Freedoms*. London: James Currey, 1993.
———. "A Multi-Centred Globe: Translation as the Language of Languages." *Literature for Our Times: Postcolonial Studies in the Twenty-First Century*. Ed. Bill Ashcroft, Ranjini Mendis, Julie McGonegal, and Arun Mukherjee. 117–23.
———. "Must We Drag Africanness into Everything?" *Sunday Nation* 2 Sept. 1962: 30.
———. "The Negro Is a Myth." *Daily Nation* 9 Apr. 1964: 6.
———. "A New Mood Prevails." *Sunday Nation* 24 Nov. 1963: 14.
———. "The New Voices: Some Emerging African Writers." *Sunday Post* 4 June 1961: 11.
———. "Now Let's See More Flexibility from University Colleges." *Sunday Nation* 7 July 1963: 31.
———. "Now the Emphasis Must Be on Co-ops." *Sunday Nation* 16 Aug. 1964: 6.
———. "The Oasis That Is Makerere." *Sunday Nation* 24 Mar. 1963: 30.
———. "Orature in Education." *Approaches to Teaching the Works of Ngũgĩ wa Thiong'o*. Ed. Oliver Lovesey. 1–4.
———. *Penpoints, Gunpoints, and Dreams: Towards a Critical Theory of the Arts and the State in Africa*. Clarendon Lectures in English Literature 1996. Oxford: Clarendon P, 1998.
———. "Pensions—We Still Can't Rest Satisfied." *Sunday Nation* 14 June 1964: 3.
———. *Petals of Blood*. London: Heinemann, 1977.
———. "Preface." *Secret Lives and Other Stories*. Ngũgĩ wa Thiong'o. [xi–xiii].
———. "Respect Will Come When We Are Self-Sufficient." *Sunday Nation* 17 Mar. 1963: 29.
———. *The River Between*. London: Heinemann, 1965.
———. "Role of the Press." *Sunday Nation* 23 Dec. 1962: 6.
———. *Secret Lives and Other Stories*. London: Heinemann, 1975.
———. "Social Problems of the New Villages: A Challenge to African Leaders." *Sunday Post* 20 Aug. 1961: 12.
———. *Something Torn and New: An African Renaissance*. New York: Basic Books, 2009.
———. "Swahili Must Have Its Rightful Place." *Sunday Nation* 23 Sept. 1962: 12.
———. "Teachers, Too, Want Cash!" *Sunday Nation* 21 June 1964: 6.

———. "The Three Levels of Independence." *Sunday Nation* 27 Oct. 1963: 39.

———. "Unity Is Still an African Dream." *Guardian Weekly* 188.25 (31 May 2013): 19.

———. "Wanted—A Proper Place for Art." *Sunday Nation* 23 Dec. 1962: 11.

———. "We Must Halt Spread of 'Freedom Army'." *Sunday Nation* 28 Oct. 1962: 31.

———. *Weep Not, Child*. London: Heinemann, 1964.

———. "What Do We Really Mean by Neutralism?" *Sunday Nation* 19 Aug. 1962: 30.

———. "What is Happening about Federation?" *Sunday Nation* 26 Aug. 1962: 30.

———. "Why Don't These Two Leaders Learn from History?" *Sunday Nation* 30 Sept. 1962: 31.

———. "Why Not Let Us Be the Judges?" *Sunday Nation* 29 July 1962: 4.

———. "Why Shakespeare in Africa?" *Daily Nation* 22 Apr. 1964: 6.

———. *Wizard of the Crow*. Trans. Ngũgĩ wa Thiong'o. New York: Pantheon Books, 2006.

———. *Writers in Politics*. London: Heinemann, 1981.

———. *Writers in Politics: A Re-engagement with Issues of Literature and Society*. Revised edition. Oxford: James Currey, 1997.

Ngũgĩ wa Thiong'o, Henry Owuor-Anyumba, Taban Lo Liyong. "On the Abolition of the English Department." *Homecoming: Essays on African and Caribbean Literature, Culture and Politics*. Ngũgĩ wa Thiong'o. 145–50.

Ngũgĩ wa Thiong'o and Manthia Diawara, dir. *Sembene: The Making of African Cinema*. Prod. Tisch School of the Arts, New York University, and Manthia/Ngũgĩ Production in association with Channel 4 Television U.K., 1994.

Nicholls, Brendon. *Ngugi wa Thiong'o, Gender, and the Ethics of Postcolonial Reading*. Farnham, Surrey: Ashgate, 2010.

Nkosi, Lewis. "The Birth of the African University." *Words and Worlds: African Writing, Theatre, and Society*. Ed. Susan Arndt and Katrin Berndt. Trenton, NJ: Africa World P, 2007. 31–44.

Nkrumah, Kwame. *Africa Must Unite*. London: Mercury Books, 1963.

———. *Neo-Colonialism: The Last Stage of Imperialism*. London: Heinemann, 1965.

Nnolim, Charles E. "Background Setting: Key to the Structure of Ngugi's *The River Between*." *Critical Perspectives on Ngugi wa Thiong'o*. Ed. G.D. Killam. 136–45.

Norridge, Zoe. "Why Ngugi wa Thiong'o should have won the Nobel prize for literature." *Guardian* Books Blog. 8 Oct. 2010. http://www.guardian.co.uk/books/ booksblog/ 2010/oct

Obama, Barack. *Dreams from My Father: A Story of Race and Inheritance*. New York: Broadway Paperbacks, 2004.

Olson, Gary A. and Lynn Worsham, eds. *Critical Intellectuals on Writing*. New York: SUNY Press, 2003.

Omari, Emman. "Ngugi wa Thiong'o Speaks! 'I Am Not above the Contradictions Which Bedevil Our Society'." *Ngũgĩ wa Thiong'o Speaks*. Ed. Reinhard Sander and Bernth Lindfors. 129–35.

Owusu, Kwesi. "A Political Choice." Interview with Ngũgĩ wa Thiong'o. *Ngũgĩ wa Thiong'o Speaks*. Ed. Reinhard Sander and Bernth Lindfors. 233–8.

Paden, John N. "African Concepts of Nationhood." *The African Experience*. Vol. 1. Ed. John N. Paden and Edward W. Soja. Evanston: Northwestern UP, 1970. 403–33.

Parker, Bettye J. "BBC Interviews Ngugi wa Thiong'o." *Ngũgĩ wa Thiong'o Speaks*. Ed. Reinhard Sander and Bernth Lindfors. 57–66.

Parry, Benita. "Overlapping Territories and Intertwined Histories: Edward Said's Postcolonial Cosmopolitanism." *Edward Said: A Critical Reader*. Ed. Michael Sprinker. 19–47.

———. "Signs of Our Times: A Discussion of Homi Bhabha's *The Location of Culture*." *Learning Places: The Afterlives of Area Studies*. Ed. Masao Miyoshi and Harry D. Harootunian. Durham, NC: Duke UP, 2002. 119–48.

Pease, Donald E. "C.L.R. James's *Mariners, Renegades and Castaways* and the World We Live In." *Mariners, Renegades and Castaways*. C.L.R. James. vii–xxxiii.

Peck, Richard. "Hermits and Saviors, Osagyefos and Healers: Artists and Intellectuals in the Works of Ngugi and Armah." *Research in African Literatures* 20.1 (Spring 1989): 26–49.

Perloff, Marjorie. "The Intellectual, the Artist, and the Reader." Roundtable on Intellectuals. *PMLA* 112.5 (Oct. 1997): 1129–30.

Philcox, Richard. "On Retranslating Fanon, Retrieving a Lost Voice." *The Wretched of the Earth*. Frantz Fanon. Trans. Richard Philcox. New York: Grove P, 2004. 241–51.

Posnock, Ross. "How It Feels to Be a Problem: Du Bois, Fanon, and the 'Impossible Life' of the Black Intellectual." *Critical Inquiry* 23 (Winter 1997): 323–49.

Povey, John. Rev. of *Writers in Politics*. *World Literature Today* 55.4 (Autumn 1981): 717.

Poyner, Jane. *J.M. Coetzee and the Paradox of Postcolonial Authorship*. Farnham, Surrey: Ashgate, 2009.

———. "J.M. Coetzee in Conversation with Jane Poyner." *J.M. Coetzee and the Idea of the Public Intellectual*. Ed. Jane Poyner. 21–24.

Poyner, Jane, ed. *J.M. Coetzee and the Idea of the Public Intellectual*. Athens: Ohio UP, 2006.

Prunier, Gérard. *Africa's World War: Congo, the Rwandan Genocide, and the Making of a Continental Catastrophe*. Oxford: Oxford UP, 2009.

Pugliese, Cristiana. *Author, Publisher and Gĩkũyũ Nationalist: The Life and Writings of Gakaara wa Wanjaũ*. Bayreuth: Bayreuth African Studies, 1994.

———. "The Organic Vernacular Intellectual in Kenya: Gakaara wa Wanjau." *Research in African Literatures* 25.4 (Winter 1994): 177–87.

Quayson, Ato. "Introduction: Postcolonial Literature in a Changing Historical Frame." *The Cambridge History of Postcolonial Literature*. 2 vols. Ed. Ato Quayson. Cambridge: Cambridge UP, 2012. Vol. 1:1–29.

Rabaka, Reiland. *Africana Critical Theory: Reconstructing the Black Radical Tradition, from W.E.B. Du Bois and C.L.R. James to Frantz Fanon and Amilcar Cabral*. Lanham: Lexington Books, 2009.

Radhakrishnan, R. "The Intellectual." *A Said Dictionary*. R. Radhakrishnan. Malden, MA: Wiley-Blackwell, 2012. 48–53.

———. "Postcoloniality." *A Said Dictionary*. R. Radhakrishnan. 86–91.

———. "Theory, Democracy, and the Public Intellectual." *PMLA* 125.3 (May 2010): 785–94.

———. "Toward an Effective Intellectual: Foucault or Gramsci?" *Intellectuals: Aesthetics, Politics, Academics*. Ed. Bruce Robbins. 57–99.

Ramchand, Kenneth. "Introduction." *Minty Alley*. C.L.R. James. Jackson and London: UP of Mississippi and New Beacon Books, 1997. 5–15.

Ranger, Terence. "The Invention of Tradition in Colonial Africa." *The Invention of Tradition*. Ed. Eric Hobsbawm and Terence Ranger. Cambridge: Canto, 1992. 211–62.

Read, Alan, ed. *The Fact of Blackness: Frantz Fanon and Visual Representation*. London: Institute of Contemporary Arts, 1996.

Rich, Adrienne. "Legislators of the World." *Guardian*. 18 Nov. 2006. http://www.guardian.co.uk/books/2006/nov/18/featuresreviews.guardianreview15

Robbins, Bruce. "Introduction: The Grounding of Intellectuals." *Intellectuals: Aesthetics, Politics, Academics*. Ed. Bruce Robbins. ix–xxvii.

———. *Secular Vocations: Intellectuals, Professionalism, Culture*. London: Verso, 1993.

———, ed. *Intellectuals: Aesthetics, Politics, Academics*. Minneapolis: U of Minnesota P, 1990.

Rodney, Walter. *How Europe Underdeveloped Africa*. London: Bogle-L'Ouverture, 1972.

———. *Walter Rodney Speaks: The Making of an African Intellectual*. Ed. Robert A. Hill. Trenton, NJ: Africa World P, 1990.

Ross, Andrew. "Civilization in One Country? The American James." *Rethinking C.L.R. James*. Ed. Grant Farred. 75–84.

———. "Defenders of the Faith and the New Class." *Intellectuals: Aesthetics, Politics, Academics*. Ed. Bruce Robbins. 101–32.

Said, Edward W. "American Intellectuals and Middle East Politics." Interview with Bruce Robbins. *Intellectuals: Aesthetics, Politics, Academics*. Ed. Bruce Robbins. 135–51.

———. *Beginnings: Intention and Method*. New York: Columbia UP, 1975, 1985.

———. *Culture and Imperialism*. New York: Vintage, 1994.

———. "Intellectuals in the Post-Colonial World." *Salmagundi* No. 70/71 (Spring–Summer 1986): 44–64.

———. "The Intellectual in the Post-Colonial World: Response and Discussion." Conor Cruise O'Brien, Edward Said, and John Lukacs. *Salmagundi* No. 70/71 (Spring–Summer 1986): 65–81.

———. *Joseph Conrad and the Fiction of Autobiography*. Cambridge, MA: Harvard UP, 1966.

———. "My Right to Return." *Power, Politics, and Culture: Interviews with Edward W. Said*. Ed. Gauri Viswanathan. New York: Pantheon, 2001. 443–58.

———. *Out of Place, A Memoir*. New York: Vintage, 1999.

———. *Representations of the Intellectual, The 1993 Reith Lectures*. New York: Vintage, 1996.

———. "A Standing Civil War: On T.E. Lawrence." *Reflections on Exile and Other Essays*. Edward W. Said. Cambridge, MA: Harvard UP, 2000. 31–40.

———. *The World, the Text, and the Critic*. Cambridge, MA: Harvard UP, 1983.

Said, Edward, Jennifer Wicke, and Michael Sprinker. "Interview with Edward Said." *Edward Said: A Critical Reader*. Ed. Michael Sprinker. 221–64.

Sander, Reinhard, and Bernth Lindfors. "Chronology." *Ngũgĩ wa Thiong'o Speaks*. Ed. Reinhard Sander and Bernth Lindfors. [xvii]–xxvi.

———. "Introduction." *Ngũgĩ wa Thiong'o Speaks*. Ed. Reinhard Sander and Bernth Lindfors. xi–xiii.

Sander, Reinhard, and Bernth Lindfors, eds. *Ngũgĩ wa Thiong'o Speaks: Interviews with the Kenyan Writer*. Trenton, NJ: Africa World P, 2006.

Sander, Reinhard, and Ian Munro. "'Tolstoy in Africa': An Interview with Ngugi wa Thiong'o." *Ngũgĩ wa Thiong'o Speaks*. Ed. Reinhard Sander and Bernth Lindfors. 43–56.

Sandgren, David P. *Mau Mau's Children: The Making of Kenya's Postcolonial Elite*. Madison, Wisconsin: U of Wisconsin P, 2012.

Sartre, Jean-Paul. *Anti-Semite and Jew: An Exploration of the Etiology of Hate*. Trans. George J. Becker. New York: Schocken, 1976.

———. "Black Orpheus." Trans. John MacCombie. *The Massachusetts Review* 6.1 (Autumn 1964–Winter 1965): 13–52.

———. "A Friend of the People." *Between Existentialism and Marxism*. Jean-Paul Sartre. Trans. John Matthews. London: Verso, 1983. 286–98.

———. "A Plea for Intellectuals." *Between Existentialism and Marxism*. Jean-Paul Sartre. Trans. John Matthews. London: Verso, 1983. 228–85.

———. *What Is Literature?* Trans. Bernard Frechtman. New York: Philosophical Library, 1949.

———. *The Words*. Trans. Bernard Frechtman. New York: Vintage, 1981.

Sassen, Saskia. *Globalization and Its Discontents*. New York: New Press, 1998.

———. *Losing Control? Sovereignty in an Age of Globalization*. New York: Columbia UP, 1996.

Saunders, Doug. "It's Not a 'Universal Rape Culture'—It's India." *Globe and Mail* 5 Jan. 2013: F9.

Savory, Elaine. "Postcolonialism and Caribbean Literature." *The Cambridge History of Postcolonial Literature*. Ed. Ato Quayson. Cambridge: Cambridge UP, 2012. Vol. 1: 215–49.

Scalmer, Sean. "Edward Said and the Sociology of Intellectuals." *Edward Said: The Legacy of a Public Intellectual*. Ed. Ned Curthoys and Debjani Ganguly. 36–56.
Schipper, Mineke. *Beyond the Boundaries: Text and Context in African Literature*. London: Allison Busby, 1989.
Schwarz, Bill. "Becoming Postcolonial." *Without Guarantees: In Honour of Stuart Hall*. Ed. Paul Gilroy, Lawrence Grossberg, and Angela McRobbie. 268–81.
Schwerdt, Dianne. "An Interview with Ngugi." *Ngũgĩ wa Thiong'o Speaks*. Ed. Reinhard Sander and Bernth Lindfors. 279–88.
Sharma, Govind N. "Ngũgĩ's *Detained* as a Modern *Consolatio*." *Research in African Literatures* 19 (1988): 520–28.
Shelley, Percy Bysshe. "A Defence of Poetry." *English Romantic Writers*. Ed. David Perkins. New York: Harcourt, Brace and World, Inc., 1967. 1072–87.
Sheridan, Alan. *André Gide, A Life in the Present*. Cambridge, MA: Harvard UP, 1999.
Shohat, Ella. "Notes on the 'Post-Colonial.'" *Social Text* 31–32 (1992): 99–113.
Sicherman, Carol. *Becoming an African University: Makerere 1922–2000*. Trenton, NJ: Africa World P, 2005.
———. "The Leeds-Makerere Connection and Ngugi's Intellectual Development." *Ufahamu* 23.1 (1995): 3–20.
———. "Ngugi's British Education." *Ngũgĩ wa Thiong'o: Texts and Contexts*. Ed. Charles Cantalupo. 35–46.
———. "Ngugi's Colonial Education: 'The Subversion . . . of the African *Mind*.'" *Critical Essays on Ngũgĩ wa Thiong'o*. Ed. Peter Nazareth. 17–47.
———. *Ngugi wa Thiong'o: The Making of a Rebel*. London: Hans Zell, 1990.
———. "Ngugi wa Thiong'o as Mythologizer and Mythologized." *From Commonwealth to Post-Colonial*. Ed. Anna Rutherford. Sydney: Dangaroo P, 1992. 259–75.
Slaymaker, William. "Mirrors and Centers: A Rortyan Reading of Ngũgĩ's Liberation Aesthetics." *Research in African Literatures* 26.4 (Winter 1995): 94–103.
Smith, Paul. *Discerning the Subject*. Minneapolis: U of Minnesota P, 1988.
Smith, Sidonie. "The Other Woman and the Racial Politics of Gender: Isak Dinesen and Beryl Markham in Kenya." *De/Colonizing the Subject: The Politics of Gender in Women's Autobiography*. Ed. Sidonie Smith and Julia Watson. 410–35.
Smith, Sidonie, and Julia Watson. *Reading Autobiography: A Guide for Interpreting Life Narratives*. Minneapolis: U of Minnesota P, 2001.
Smith, Sidonie, and Julia Watson, eds. *De/Colonizing the Subject: The Politics of Gender in Women's Autobiography*. Minneapolis: U of Minnesota P, 1992.
Sontag, Susan. *Regarding the Pain of Others*. New York: Farrar, Straus and Giroux, 2003.
Soyinka, Wole. *The Man Died: Prison Notes of Wole Soyinka*. New York: Noonday, 1972.

———. *Myth, Literature and the African World* [1976]. Cambridge: Cambridge UP, 1990.

———. "Neo-Tarzanism: The Poetics of a Pseudo-Tradition." *Transition* 48 (1975): 38–44.

———. *Of Africa*. New Haven: Yale UP, 2012.

———. "The Writer in a Modern African State." *The Writer in Modern Africa: African-Scandinavian Writers' Conference, Stockholm 1967*. Ed. Per Wästberg. 14–21.

Spivak, Gayatri Chakravorty. *An Aesthetic Education in the Era of Globalization*. Cambridge, MA: Harvard UP, 2012.

———. "Bonding in Difference: Interview with Alfred Arteaga." *The Spivak Reader: Selected Works of Gayatri Chakravorty Spivak*. Ed. Donna Landry and Gerald MacLean. 15–28.

———. "Can the Subaltern Speak?" *Marxism and the Interpretation of Culture*. Ed. Cary Nelson and Lawrence Grossberg. Urbana: U of Illinois P, 1988. 271–313.

———. *Death of a Discipline*. New York: Columbia UP, 2003.

———. "Edward Said Remembered on September 11, 2004: A Conversation with Gayatri Chakravorty Spivak [by Ben Conisbee Baer]." *Edward Said: A Legacy of Emancipation and Representation*. Ed. Adel Iskandar and Hakem Rustom. Berkeley: U of California P, 2010. 53–9.

———. "Explanation and Culture: Marginalia." *In Other Worlds: Essays in Cultural Politics*. Gayatri Chakravorty Spivak. 139–60.

———. "French Feminism in an International Frame." *In Other Worlds: Essays in Cultural Politics*. Gayatri Chakravorty Spivak. 184–211.

———. "How to Read a 'Culturally Different' Book." *An Aesthetic Education in the Era of Globalization*. Gayatri Chakravorty Spivak. 73–96.

———. *In Other Worlds: Essays in Cultural Politics*. New York: Routledge, 1998.

———. "More on Power/Knowledge." *The Spivak Reader: Selected Works of Gayatri Chakravorty Spivak*. Ed. Donna Landry and Gerald MacLean. 141–74.

———. "Ngũgĩ wa Thiong'o: In Praise of a Friend." *Approaches to Teaching the Works of Ngũgĩ wa Thiong'o*. Ed. Oliver Lovesey. 5–7.

———. "The Politics of Interpretations." *In Other Worlds: Essays in Cultural Politics*. Gayatri Chakravorty Spivak. 161–83.

———. *The Post-Colonial Critic: Interviews, Strategies, Dialogues*. Ed. Sarah Harasym. New York: Routledge, 1990.

———. "Preface." *An Aesthetic Education in the Era of Globalization*. Gayatri Chakravorty Spivak. ix–xvi.

———. "Subaltern Studies: Deconstructing Historiography." *In Other Worlds: Essays in Cultural Politics*. Gayatri Chakravorty Spivak. 270–304.

———. "Subaltern Talk: Interview with the Editors." *The Spivak Reader: Selected Works of Gayatri Chakravorty Spivak*. Ed. Donna Landry and Gerald MacLean. 287–308.

———. "Three Women's Texts and a Critique of Imperialism." *Critical Inquiry* 12.1 (Autumn 1985): 243–61.

———. "Translator's Foreword." *In Other Worlds: Essays in Cultural Politics*. Gayatri Chakravorty Spivak. 245–56.

———. "Translator's Preface." *Of Grammatology*. Jacques Derrida. Trans. Gayatri Chakravorty Spivak. Baltimore: Johns Hopkins UP, 1976. ix–lxxxxvii.

Sprinker, Michael, ed. *Edward Said: A Critical Reader*. Oxford: Blackwell, 1992.

Srivastava, Neelam. "The Travels of the Organic Intellectual: The Black Colonized Intellectual in George Padmore and Frantz Fanon." *The Postcolonial Gramsci*. Ed. Neelam Srivastava and Baidik Bhattacharya. 55–79.

Srivastava, Neelam, and Baidik Bhattacharya, eds. *The Postcolonial Gramsci*. New York: Routledge, 2012.

Surin, Kenneth. "'The Future Anterior': C.L.R. James and Going *Beyond A Boundary*." *Rethinking C.L.R. James*. Ed. Grant Farred. 187–204.

Suttner, Raymond. "The Character and Formation of Intellectuals within the ANC-led South African Liberation Movement." *African Intellectuals*. Ed. Thandika Mkandawire. 117–54.

Taban Lo Liyong. "Ministers to the Toothless." *Ariel: A Review of International English Literature* 29.2 (April 1998): 111.

Tobar, Hector. "Ngugi wa Thiong'o Soars 'In the House of the Interpreter'." *Los Angeles Times* 16 Nov. 2012. http://articles.latimes.com/2012/nov/16/entertainment/la-ca-jc-ngugi-wathiongo-20121118

Tolstoy, Leo. *Childhood, Boyhood and Youth*. Trans. C. J. Hogarth. New York: Knopf, 1991.

Trivedi, Harish, with Wangui wa Goro. "Ngugi wa Thiong'o in Conversation." *Ngũgĩ wa Thiong'o Speaks*. Ed. Reinhard Sander and Bernth Lindfors. 399–413.

Veeser, H. Aram. *Edward Said: The Charisma of Criticism*. New York: Routledge, 2010.

———. "Introduction: The Case for Confessional Criticism." *Confessions of the Critics*. Ed. H. Aram Veeser. ix–xxvii.

———, ed. *Confessions of the Critics*. New York: Routledge, 1996.

Viswanathan, Gauri. *Masks of Conquest: Literary Study and British Rule in India*. London: Faber and Faber, 1990.

Wainaina, Binyavanga. "Kenyans Chose a Leader We Felt Could Bring Peace." *Guardian Weekly* 188.14 (15–21 March 2013): 19.

Walcott, Derek. "A Tribute to C.L.R. James." *C.L.R. James: His Intellectual Legacies*. Ed. Selwyn R. Cudjoe and William E. Cain. 34–48.

Walder, Dennis. *Postcolonial Nostalgias: Writing, Representation, and Memory*. New York: Routledge, 2011.

Wali, Obiajunwa. "The Dead End of African Literature?" *Transition* 4.10 (September 1963): 13–15.

Walton, Calder. "Old Tin Eye." Rev. of *Cruel Britannia: A Secret History of Torture* by Ian Cobain. *TLS* (15 Feb. 2013): 7–8.

Warner, Alan. *Shakespeare in the Tropics*. London: Oxford UP, 1954.

———. *A Short Guide to English Style*. London: Oxford UP, 1961.

Wästberg, Per. "Opening Remarks." *The Writer in Modern Africa: African-Scandinavian Writers' Conference, Stockholm 1967*. Ed. Per Wästberg. 9–13.

Wästberg, Per, ed. *The Writer in Modern Arica: African-Scandinavian Writers' Conference, Stockholm 1967*. New York: Africana Publishing Corporation, 1969.

Watson, Julia, and Sidonie Smith. "Introduction: De/Colonization and the Politics of Discourse in Women's Autobiographical Practices." *De/Colonizing the Subject: The Politics of Gender in Women's Autobiography*. Ed. Sidonie Smith and Julia Watson. xiii–xxxi.

The Weekly Review. "An Interview with Ngugi." *Ngũgĩ wa Thiong'o Speaks*. Ed. Reinhard Sander and Bernth Lindfors. 85–9.

West, Cornel. "Afterword." *Cornel West: A Critical Reader*. Ed. George Yancy. 346–62.

———. "The Dilemma of the Black Intellectuals." *The Journal of Blacks in Higher Education* No. 2 (Winter 1993–1994): 59–67.

Wilkinson, Jane. "African Diaries." *Autobiographical and Biographical Writing in the Commonwealth*. Ed. Doireann MacDermott. Sabadell, Spain: Editorial AUSA, 1984. 247–53.

———. "Ngugi wa Thiong'o." An Interview with Ngũgĩ wa Thiong'o. *Ngũgĩ wa Thiong'o Speaks*. Ed. Reinhard Sander and Bernth Lindfors. 199–214.

Williams, Patrick. "'Like wounded birds'? Ngugi and the Intellectuals." *The Yearbook of English Studies* 27 (1997): 201–18.

———. "Nothing in the Post?—Said and the Problem of Post-Colonial Intellectuals." *Edward Said and the Post-Colonial*. Ed. Bill Ashcroft and Hussein Kadhim. 31–55.

Wolin, Richard. *The Wind from the East: French Intellectuals, the Cultural Revolution, and the Legacy of the 1960s*. Princeton: Princeton UP, 2010.

Wong, Jan. *Red China Blues: My Long March From Mao to Now*. Toronto: Doubleday, 1997.

Wood, James. "An Afrikaner Trapped in No Man's Land." Interview of Breyten Breytenbach. *Guardian Weekly* (9 Jan. 1994): 28.

Worcester, Kent. *C.L.R. James: A Political Biography*. Albany: State U of New York P, 1996.

Wynter, Sylvia. "Beyond the Categories of the Master Conception: The Counterdoctrine of the Jamesian Poiesis." *C.L.R. James' Caribbean*. Ed. Paget Henry and Paul Buhle. 63–91.

Yaeger, Patricia, ed. "Editor's Column: The End of Postcolonial Theory? A Roundtable with Sunil Agnani, Fernando Coronil, Gaurav Desai, Mamadou Diouf, Simon Gikandi, Susie Tharu, and Jennifer Wenzel." *PMLA* 122.3 (2007): 633–51.

Yancy, George. "Cornel West: The Vanguard of Existential and Democratic Hope." *Cornel West: A Critical Reader*. Ed. George Yancy. 1–16.

———, ed. *Cornel West: A Critical Reader*. Malden, MA: Blackwell, 2001.

Young, Robert J. C. *Colonial Desire: Hybridity in Theory, Culture and Race.* London: Routledge, 1995.

———. "Edward Said: Opponent of Postcolonial Theory." *Edward Said's Translocations: Essays in Secular Criticism.* Ed. Tobian Döring and Mark Stein. New York: Routledge, 2012. 23– 43.

———. "Il Gramsci meridionale." *The Postcolonial Gramsci.* Ed. Neelam Srivastava and Baidik Bhattacharya. 17–33.

———. "Postcolonial Remains." *New Literary History* 43.1 (2012): 19–42.

———. *Postcolonialism: An Historical Introduction.* Oxford: Blackwell, 2001.

———. *White Mythologies: Writing History and the West.* London: Routledge, 1990.

Žižek, Slovoj. "Interview with Katie Engelhart." *Salon.* 29 Dec. 2012. http://www.salon.com/2012/12/29/slavoj_zizek_i_am_not_the_worlds_hippest_philosopher/

———. *Violence.* London: Profile Books, 2009.

Index

Abyssinia, League for the Protection of 89
Abrahams, Peter 66, 161
  Tell Freedom 161
Achebe, Chinua 2–3, 3n7, 9, 10, 12, 20n39, 23, 33, 45–6, 61, 72, 100, 115, 142, 159, 174n5
  attempted assassination of 174n5
  on *Heart of Darkness* (Conrad) 23
  works
    "Art as Celebration" 174n5
    "The Novelist as Teacher" 3, 115
    Things Fall Apart 3n7, 72, 159
Adesanmi, Pius 10
Adichie, Chimamanda Ngozi 111n54
  Americanah 111n54
Adorno, Theodor 17, 20, 41, 94, 144, 176–7, 178
  on the experience of exile 177, 178
  on the intellectual in America 177
  Minima Moralia 176, 177, 177n15
African-Scandinavian Writers' Conference (Stockholm) 82n17
African Writers of English Expression, Conference of (Makerere) 45, 133
Ahmad, Aijaz 33, 34, 164n30, 187n26
  critique of Bhabha 33–4
Algeria 7, 8, 12, 19, 35, 36, 99, 101, 106, 108, 109, 110, 116
All Africa People's Conference (Accra) 106
Althusser, Louis 108, 122–3
  Lenin and Philosophy 122–3
Amoko, Apollo Obonyo 10, 48–9, 49n12, 135n21
  on 'African universities' and universities in Africa 48–9
  on Ngũgĩ as postcolonial intellectual 10, 48–9
Amooti wa Irumba 127, 155, 156, 157
Anderson, David 4, 87, 180, 184
Angola 119

Antilles, the 34, 109, 111, 112
anti-Semitism 12–13, 111; *see also* Jean-Paul Sartre, *Anti-Semite and Jew*
Appiah, Kwame Anthony 48, 48n11, 76n2, 130, 133, 172n34, 187, 188, 189n27
  In My Father's House 48, 48n11, 130–31, 133, 172n34, 189n27
Arendt, Hannah 1n1, 76, 76n2, 107, 108, 109, 109n50, 144
  Men in Dark Times 1n1
  On Violence 76n2, 107, 108, 108n49, 109, 109n50
Armah, Ayi Kwei 37, 182
  The Beautyful Ones Are Not Yet Born 37, 131, 182
Arnold, Matthew 18, 47, 51, 57, 59, 64, 64n22, 83, 83n20
  cultural anarchy 47
  and the English public school 47, 57–8, 161
  Rugby 47
  and Thomas Arnold 47
Arnove, Anthony 10, 38n65, 133
  on Ngũgĩ as postcolonial intellectual 10
Ashcroft, Bill 12n27, 13n30, 17
Austen, Jane 59
auto/biography 6, 8, 14, 15, 22, 34, 49, 79, 80, 139–40, 162, 165, 165n31, 167, 192
  and auto-critical moments 15–16, 40, 132, 134, 139, 144, 192
  and Cabral 111
  and Fanon 111
  and Gikandi 144, 144n12
  and James 80, 80n14, 81, 83–4
  national 40, 142–3
  and Ngũgĩ 40, 85, 115, 117, 132, 134, 138, 139, 140–42, 143, 144, 145, 149–50, 155–63, 173
  fiction of 149–51, 156–7, 162–3

interviews and 153–4, 155
memoirs of 155–63
postcolonial 15, 139–40, 143–4
and postcolonial identity politics 143–4
and the prison diary 40, 139, 143, 163–72
and the relational 40, 141, 141n8, 142, 184
and Soyinka 143
and Spivak 22n42, 25–6
and Tolstoy 148

Baldwin, James 73
Barthes, Roland 32n61, 47, 96
    Mythologies 47
Baudrillard, Jean 6, 7, 7n16
Beauvoir, Simone de 7, 8, 9, 99, 108
    and the intellectual 7, 8–9, 108–109
    and relationship with Nelson Algren 8
    and relationship with Sartre 8–9
    works
        Force of Circumstance 99, 108–109
        The Mandarins [*Les Mandarins*] 7, 7n15, 8–9
Benda, Julien 13n29, 18, 19
    La Trahison des Clercs 18
Benjamin, Walter 4, 108
Berlin Conference (1885) 118
Bethune, Norman 98–9n43
Bhabha, Homi 3, 5, 10n19, 13, 16, 30–35, 36, 79n12, 101, 192
    and the committed intellectual 30–31, 33
    critical appraisal of 31–3, 31n60
    on Fanon 32, 34–5, 101, 108
    on the location and sanction of utterance/articulation 31, 32, 33, 36
    and the positionality of the postcolonial intellectual 30–31, 33–4
    and the postcolonial intellectual, privileged hybridity of 32, 33, 35
    and the uses of history 32, 32n61
    works
        "Black and White and Read All Over" 33
        "The Commitment to Theory" 31, 34
        "Draw the Curtain" 31
        "Foreword" to *Black Skin, White Masks* (Frantz Fanon) 34, 108
        "Foreword" to *The Wretched of the Earth* (Frantz Fanon) 108, 108n48
        "Interrogating Identity: Frantz Fanon and the Postcolonial Perspective" 34
        The Location of Culture 13, 32
        "The Postcolonial" 31
        "Postcolonial Authority and Postmodern Guilt" 32n61
        "Remembering Fanon" 34
        "Signs Taken for Wonders" 32, 33
Bible 55, 77, 80, 89n30, 100, 101, 128, 166, 172
    and biblical allusions/references in Ngũgĩ's works 36, 138, 151, 162, 172, 173
    and biblical stories as tools of revolution/liberation 4, 36, 166
    I Corinthians 56
    Gospels 36, 136
    King James Version of 162
'Biggles' stories 162
Black Atlantic 5, 12, 12n28, 13, 23, 132n17, 177n14
Blake, William 130
    "Auguries of Innocence" 130, 130n13
Blyden, Edward Wilmot 12
Booth, General William 64
Boupacha, Djamila 8
Bourdieu, Pierre 2, 10
bourgeoisie
    black 72n31
    colonial / neocolonial 123, 124
    international / capitalist 121, 182
    liberal 123
    native 30, 72n31, 130
    petty 40, 49, 82, 82n19, 93, 117, 120, 121, 122, 123, 124, 125, 127, 129, 130, 151n18, 185
    revolutionary 120
    Westernized / nationalist 99, 102, 107
Brathwaite, Kamau 43n1, 179
    "*Limuru* and *Kinta Kunte*" 43n1
Brecht, Bertolt 77, 154
Breytenbach, Breyten 4, 163, 164, 165–7, 168, 170, 172

imprisonment of 163, 166–7, 168, 169–70, 170–71
works
   Mouroir: Mirrornotes of a Novel 172
   The True Confessions of an Albino Terrorist 40, 164n29, 165, 167, 170
Britain 3, 4, 7, 15, 19, 20, 23n45, 25, 31, 41, 43, 45, 49, 55, 74, 75n1, 76n3, 78, 79, 80, 80n13, 82, 83, 84, 85, 87, 92, 93, 96, 96n42, 97, 118, 119, 132n17, 145, 147n14, 172, 178
Bronstein, Michaela 79n9
Brontë, Charlotte 23
   Jane Eyre 23
Brutus, Dennis 72n31, 164, 167
   Letters to Martha 164, 164n29, 167
Buddhism 167, 169, 170, 172
Buhle, Paul 80, 81, 81n15, 88
Bunyan, John 165
   Grace Abounding to the Chief of Sinners 165
   The Pilgrim's Progress 160, 165
Butler, Judith 1–2
   Giving an Account of Oneself 2n4
   Precarious Life 2n4

Cabral, Amílcar 1, 17, 40, 81, 107, 116–26, 128, 129, 130, 131, 132, 154, 185, 192
   assassination of 119, 121, 123, 123–4n8, 126
   life of, in comparison with Ngũgĩ's 117
   and class 118, 120, 120n6, 121–3
   and "class suicide" 17, 107, 116, 122–3, 125, 130
   and culture 116, 124–5
   on education 120, 121
   and the intellectual
      revolutionary 81, 116, 120–22
      artist 123
      colonized 124
      postcolonial 124
   and liberation, struggle for 116, 119–21
   on Marxist-Leninism, limitations of 40, 118, 119
   and the peasantry 40, 116, 119, 120, 121, 122, 124–5
   and the poetry of 116n3, 125
   on the post-independence nation 124
   on "re-Africanization of minds" 124
   and "the return to the source" 40, 73, 116, 124, 125, 132, 187
   on tribalism 117
   on violence 119
   works
      "Determined to Resist" ["Practical Problems and Tactics"] 117
      "Identity and Dignity in the Context of the National Liberation Struggle" 124
      "National Liberation and Culture" 118
      Return to the Source 40, 118, 119, 121, 123, 124–5, 126
      Revolution in Guinea 117, 118, 119, 120, 121, 122, 123
      Unity and Struggle: Speeches and Writings 117, 119, 121, 124, 125
      "The Weapon of Theory" 118
Caetano, Marcelo, 125, 126
   and neo-Salazarism 125
Camus, Albert 7, 9
Cape Verde 116, 118, 119, 123–4n8, 125
Caribbean 39, 48, 71n29, 73n34, 74, 75, 77, 78, 79, 79n12, 80, 81, 82, 83, 84, 88, 89, 90, 94, 98, 111, 116, 121, 142, 146, 176, 177, 178, 179, 192
Carter, Martin 142, 179, 179n17
   The Hill of Fire Glows Red 179
   "Looking at Your Hands" 179
   "Poems of Affinity" 142n9
   University of Hunger 142n9, 179n17
Castro, Fidel 85, 89
Césaire, Aimé 7, 34, 71, 71–2n29, 73, 73n33, 74, 82, 84n23–24, 88, 99, 116, 136, 185, 191
   on Marxism and Communism, limitations of 74, 84n23–n24
   works
      Discourse on Colonialism [*Discours sur le Colonialism*] 73, 74, 84n23, 185
      Notebook of a Return to My Native Land [*Cahier d'un retour au pays natal*] 71, 73n33, 136
      A Tempest 191

Chabal, Patrick 119, 123–4n8
Chakava, Henry 148
Chilcote, Ronald 120n6
China 98–9n43, 103, 126, 135n20
Chomsky, Noam 6, 109
class suicide 17, 40, 98, 107, 116, 122–3, 125, 130, 192
Cobain, Ian 4, 87, 180, 180n18, 181
Coetzee, J.M. 5n12
Collini, Stefan 1, 1n1, 13n29, 17–18n35
Communism 84, 47n10, 63, 129, 135
   and Communists/Communist Party 8, 8n17, 58, 74, 76, 76n3, 84n23–n24
Conrad, Joseph 16, 21, 45, 47, 47n9, 60, 76, 76n4, 79, 79n9, 103, 145, 151, 154
   novels of, as subject of Ngũgĩ's undergraduate and graduate work 45, 47, 47n9
   works
      Heart of Darkness 23
      Nostromo 60, 79, 79n9–n10, 103
      Under Western Eyes 47n9, 76, 76n4, 79, 79n9, 103
cricket 47, 80, 81, 83, 94, 96–7, 96n42

Damas, Léon Gontran 71
Davidson, Basil 124, 123–4n8
   "Remembering Cabral" 124, 123–4n8
Deleuze, Gilles 27, 28, 29
   "Intellectuals and Power" 27, 28
Derrida, Jacques 22, 23, 24, 27, 139n2, 191; *see also* Gayatri Chakravorty Spivak
   Of Grammatology [*De la Grammatologie*] 23, 24
Dickens, Charles 47, 50n15, 58, 59, 78, 157
   Great Expectations 157
   Hard Times 50n15, 58, 59
   Oliver Twist 157
Douglass, Frederick 84n22, 97
Du Bois, W.E.B. 12, 83, 84, 111, 111n53, 121, 128, 140, 161
   Darkwater 138
   The Souls of Black Folk 13, 111
Dumont, René 88n29

East Africa 45, 46, 50, 58, 60, 61, 62, 65, 100, 136, 154, 180, 186, 191
East African Standard 51

education
   colonial and neocolonial 3, 6, 15, 23, 28, 39, 48, 57–60, 83–4, 85, 92, 107, 109, 117, 121, 132n17, 145–6, 150, 151
   and colonial schools 15–16, 46–8, 100, 117, 134, 145, 160n24
   and the colonial university 3, 39, 48–9, 107, 117, 121
   and in the postcolony 93, 117, 135–6
educational institutions
   Alliance High School (Kenya) 43, 44, 45, 46, 47, 48, 50, 51, 54, 57, 67, 75, 83, 135, 145, 151, 160–3
   and *Alliance High Magazine* 52
   Beijing University 135n20
   Cambridge University 44n4, 76, 147
   Columbia University 17
   Cornell University 25
   Gĩkũyũ Independent School 46, 145
   Harvard University 16, 148
   Leeds University (U.K.) 40, 46n8, 47n9, 48, 49, 57, 75, 76, 77, 78, 100, 101, 127, 129, 146, 174
   Makerere University College (Uganda) 43, 43n2, 44n3, 45, 45n5–n6, 46, 46n8, 47, 48, 49, 50, 50n16, 52, 57, 58, 59, 60, 67, 72, 74, 75, 77n5, 78, 99, 133, 134, 145, 163, 186
   and *The Makererean* 45
   New York University 134, 147
   Oxford University 76, 147
   Princeton University 15
   Smith College 147
   University of Calcutta 25
   University of California, Irvine 147
   and the International Center for Writing and Translation 147
   University of Nairobi 3, 100, 135, 146, 189, 190, 192
   Yale University 147
Eliot, George 46
Elkins, Caroline 4, 87, 160, 180, 184n24
Elumelu, Tony 179
   Africapitalism 179
Engels, Friedrich 89, 92, 123, 127, 154
   Anti-Duhring 127
   Socialism: Scientific and Utopian 127
England *See* Britain

Fanon, Frantz 5, 7, 11n23, 12, 13, 30, 32, 34–5, 36, 40, 48, 68n25, 71–2n29, 73, 73n34, 75, 76, 78, 81, 84, 84n25, 87, 88, 95n39, 98–113, 98n43, 108n48, 116, 117, 126, 127, 128, 136, 137, 140, 154, 192
   on Communism and Marxism, limitations of 84
   on the intellectual 98–9, 102–103
   on psychic liberation 74, 104, 109
   and psychopathology of colonialism 100–101, 103, 111–13, 137
   on violence 106–109
   works
      Black Skin, White Masks [*Peau Noire, Masques Blancs*] 11n23, 34, 71–2n29, 95n39, 100, 100n44, 102, 103, 108, 111–13, 128, 137
      A Dying Colonialism [*L'An Cinq de la Révolution Algérienne*] 109, 110
         "Algeria Unveiled" 109
         "This Is the Voice of Algeria" 110
      Toward the African Revolution 105, 106, 107, 109, 110
      The Wretched of the Earth [*Les Damnés de la Terre*] 17–18n35, 32, 34, 68n25, 73, 77, 100–104, 105–106, 107, 108, 108n48, 109, 110, 112
         "On National Culture" 101
         "The Pitfalls of National Consciousness" 102
         "On Violence" 106–109
Farrington, Constance 102, 103
fascism 9, 40, 79, 84n22, 115, 119, 127
   and anti-fascism 8, 177, 177n14
female circumcision *see* female genital mutilation
female genital mutilation 53–4, 109–110, 110n51
feminism, French 26
Foucault, Michel 2n4, 4, 6, 13, 18, 19, 27, 27n56, 28, 29, 30, 108, 128, 141, 143
   "Intellectuals and Power" 27, 28
   "Technologies of the Self" 141, 143

France 7, 7n15, 8, 34, 35, 74, 82, 90, 91, 92, 95n39, 106, 111, 112, 119
Francis, Edward Carey 44–5, 44n14, 161, 162
   on Mau-Mau 44–5, 161
Frankfurt School 96n42
Freire, Paolo 129
Freud, Sigmund 111, 140n3
Froude, James Anthony 89
   The English in the West Indies 89, 89–90n33

Gakaara wa Wanjau 134, 160n25, 161n26
Garvey, Marcus 50, 74, 86, 88
   and the 'Back to Africa' campaign 86
Gates, Henry Louis Jr. 35, 148n17
Ghana 3n7, 50, 84, 85, 92, 123, 177
Gichamu theatre group 129
Gĩchingiri Ndĩgĩrĩgĩ 146n13, 153n19
Gide, André 8n17
Gikandi, Simon 10n20, 33, 38n65, 110n51, 111n53, 128, 133, 139, 141, 144, 144n12, 148n16, 153, 174n4, 192
Gĩkũyũ Independent Schools Association 110
Gilroy, Paul 12, 12n28, 13, 132n17, 177, 177n14, 179
Glissant, Édouard 142, 142n10, 184, 190
   Poetics of Relation [*Poétique de la Relation*] 142, 142n10, 184
globalization 4, 11–12n26, 37, 41, 62, 79, 124, 128, 136, 142, 185, 187, 187n26, 189–90
Goethe, Johann Wolfgang von 190, 191
Gordon, Lewis 153n20
Goretti Kyomuhendo 156
   Waiting 156
Gorky, Maxim 77
   Mother 77
Gosse, Edward 15
   Father and Son 15
Graff, Gerald 2, 64n22
Gramsci, Antonio 2n4, 17, 18, 19, 36, 41, 43, 84n25, 119, 121, 130, 132n17, 155, 175, 175n7–n11, 176n12, 182–3, 183n20
Grimshaw, Anna 80n14, 81, 83n20, 97
griot 38, 41, 132, 136, 142, 174, 181, 193
Guevara, Che 82n18, 118, 128

Guinea-Bissau 115, 116, 118–19, 120, 120n6, 121, 122, 123, 123–4n8, 125

Haggard, H. Rider 162
Haiti 75, 89, 91, 177; *see also* San Domingo
Hall, Stuart 34, 82, 89, 91, 96n41, 97, 101, 175, 175n8–n9, 183n21
Harlem Renaissance 71, 74
Hart, Keith 80n14, 83n20
Harvey, David 38n65, 187n26, 188
Hazlitt, William 96, 96n42
Hearne, John 77n7
Hegel, Georg 64, 75, 76n2, 99, 100, 105, 111, 128, 142, 190
　　and the master-slave dialectic 99, 100, 105, 128, 190
　　The Philosophy of History 76n2
Hell, Richard 2n5
Henderson, Ian 65
Hindmarsh, Roland 50, 60n19
Hobsbawm, Eric 126, 126n9, 128, 175, 175n10
Hola Camp 51, 180
Holden, Philip 140, 141n7, 143
Homer 142
Huddart, David 15n32, 22n42, 139n2, 141, 143
Hughes, Thomas 47, 161
　　Tom Brown's Schooldays 47, 161
Huxley, Elspeth 46

ICC: International Criminal Court 4, 65, 66, 126
Idahosa, Paul 94, 99
Ikiddeh, Ime 78, 79
India 11n24, 19, 23, 25, 26, 28, 29, 30, 43, 48
intellectual, the
　　abolitionist 84n22, 97
　　academic 1, 11n25, 13, 19, 30, 33, 175n11
　　African 36–8, 48, 70, 92–3, 102, 105, 112, 129, 180, 181–2
　　alienated 16, 58, 69, 92–3, 95, 97–8, 101–102, 103, 107, 121, 132, 132n17, 134, 178
　　and anti-intellectualism 1–2, 2n5, 15, 70n28, 177
　　artist 32, 38, 65, 66, 67, 68, 80, 101, 102, 103, 104, 105, 123, 129–31, 132, 136, 152, 156, 174, 182, 184, 191
　　black 20, 33, 34, 72n31, 80, 84n25, 42n28, 111n53, 132n17, 153n20
　　border 20
　　bourgeois 30, 33, 72n31, 82, 82n19, 102, 106, 117, 121–3, 124, 152, 179–80
　　celebrity 13–14, 18, 20, 22, 25, 148, 153, 153n20
　　collective 19, 27, 36, 40, 41, 98, 141, 183–4, 184n22, 193
　　colonized / colonial 7, 32, 33, 39, 48, 84n25, 102, 103, 104, 107, 108, 121, 124, 133, 134, 151, 182, 193
　　committed 30–31, 32, 33, 98n43, 153
　　contemporary debate over the role of 1–2, 3–5
　　cosmopolitan 5n13, 9, 32, 144, 176
　　dark times for 1, 1n1–n2
　　death of 1, 10, 192
　　decolonization of 38, 39, 41, 43, 124, 181–2, 193
　　diasporic 9, 12, 20, 22n42, 105, 112–13, 140
　　dissident 5, 14, 16, 18, 99, 101
　　embedded 22, 82, 82n18
　　and exile, the experience of 20, 21, 33, 35, 80n13, 92–3, 98–9, 105, 173, 176–8
　　First World / Western 27, 28, 29, 30, 92, 97, 110, 132, 135, 151
　　global 35, 37, 40, 41, 173–93
　　guerrilla 82, 82n18
　　immigrant / migrant 30, 33
　　native 27–8, 37, 43, 91, 103
　　neocolonial 33, 102, 130, 132, 182
　　new 5, 33, 37, 41, 132n17, 182–3, 188, 190, 192
　　oral 20n39, 41, 132, 141, 152, 181–2, 183, 187, 193
　　organic 31, 84, 84n25, 132n17, 134, 152, 175, 175n11, 182, 183, 183n20–n21
　　paradoxical 8–9, 17, 33
　　and the postcolonial project 2, 33
　　in post-war Europe and Britain 7–9

prophetic 27, 136, 181, 191–2, 193
public 1–2, 2n4, 4, 5, 5n12, 7–9, 11,
    11n25, 13n30, 17–21, 33, 153n20
revolutionary / radical 6, 9, 10, 16, 22,
    28, 29, 30, 30n59, 40, 68, 79n12,
    80, 81, 82, 99, 118, 120, 132
'Saidian' 20n39
specular 20n39
specific 18–19, 27, 30
subaltern 29, 38, 175, 183
and subject positions of 22
syncretic 20n39
Third World 6, 9, 11–12n26, 20, 22, 30
traditional *see* universal
true 19, 22
universal ('classic' or 'traditional')
    1, 5–6, 18, 19, 27, 30, 33, 108,
    132n17, 182–3, 183n20
vacillating 68, 97, 113, 149, 151,
    151n18, 152
Ireland 137, 179
Irele, Abiola 70, 70n28, 71–2n29

Jacobs, J.U. 164n29, 165
James, C.L.R. 23, 39–40, 47, 50, 66,
    66n23, 68, 71, 71n29, 73n33, 74,
    75–92, 75n1, 79n11–n12, 80n13–
    n14, 81n15, 82n19, 83n20, 84n22,
    96n42, 103, 116, 128, 136–7, 161,
    175n8, 177, 178, 192
and Africa 82–3
and the African intellectual 92–3
on art and artists 94
and autobiography 80, 80n14, 94–5,
    96–7
and the Caribbean 80–83
and colonial education of 83–4
Communism and Trotskyism, break
    with 84–5
and diasporic pan-African history in
    the struggle against colonialism 74,
    75, 76–7, 79, 81, 83–4, 85–6, 87,
    89–91
Ellis Island imprisonment of 23, 94–5
intellectual biography of 80–98
and the intellectual, abolition of 97–8
on journalism and national
    consciousness 50–1
on Marxism, limitations of 40, 84–5

on Mau Mau 87, 87n28
and 'The Mighty Sparrow' 94n38
on *Moby Dick* and Herman Melville
    23, 23n44, 68, 94–6, 95n40, 96n41
and the myth of Africa 75n1, 103
on Négritude 71, 73n33
on Nkrumah and the Ghana Revolution
    92–3
on *Pierre* (Melville) 96
on Shelley, Percy Bysshe 68
and the Promethean hero 68, 68n26
works
    American Civilization 68, 79n12,
        80n14, 83n20, 84n22, 97–8
    "The Artist in the Caribbean"
        71n29, 94
    Beyond a Boundary 47, 66n23, 83,
        96–7
    The Black Jacobins 71, 71n29, 75,
        85, 89–91, 89n31–n32, 91n34,
        92, 94, 112, 177, 178
        on Toussaint L'Ouverture 85,
            89–91, 178
    A History of Negro Revolt 75
    A History of Pan-African Revolt
        75, 85, 86, 87n28
    *Mariners, Renegades and
        Castaways: The Story of
        Herman Melville and the World
        We Live In* 23n44, 68, 68n26,
        80n14, 94–6
    Minty Alley 83n21
    *Nkrumah and the Ghana
        Revolution* 50, 75n1, 84, 85,
        89n32, 92–3, 116, 136–7
Jameson, Fredric 164n30, 165, 188,
    192n29
Johnson, Samuel 130
    Rasselas 130, 130n14
John the Baptist 136, 138
Jung, Carl 111

Kamenju, Grant 99
Kamĩtĩ Maximum Security Prison 146,
    165, 170, 184, 184n24
Kant, Immanuel 63, 108
Kanwar, Asha S. 76n3
Kaunda, Kenneth 88, 143, 163
    Zambia Shall Be Free 143

Kenya Land and Freedom Army 55, 129
Kenyatta, Jomo 50, 52, 53, 64, 67, 69, 71,
    83, 126, 134, 139, 141, 142, 158,
    163, 164, 168, 173n2
  Facing Mount Kenya 52, 53, 134, 139,
    141
Kenyatta, Uhuru 4, 65, 126
Kettle, Arnold 40, 46n8, 76, 76n3, 77,
    79n10, 129, 174, 191, 192
  "The Artist and Politics" 76n3
  Communism and the Intellectuals 129
  An Introduction to the English Novel
    76n3, 79n10
Kettle, Martin 76n3
Kībaki, Mwai 65, 145, 146, 148
Kimathi, Dedan 87, 116, 129, 135, 170,
    173n2, 177n14, 184; see also
    Ngũgĩ wa Thiong'o, fiction, *The
    Trial of Dedan Kimathi*
Koestler, Arthur 7, 9
Kristeva, Julia 1n2, 5, 5n13–n14, 26
  About Chinese Women 26
  Hatred and Forgiveness 5n13
  The Incredible Need to Believe 5
  on the public intellectual 5
  "Thinking in Dark Times" 1n2

Lacan, Jacques 102, 111
Lamming, George 20, 41, 71n29, 79,
    79n11, 81, 82, 83, 86, 94, 154, 177,
    178, 179
  and exile, the experience of 177–8
  on James's *The Black Jacobins* 89n30
  works
    "C.L.R. James" 79n11, 82, 83
    In the Castle of My Skin 79
    The Pleasures of Exile 71n29, 82,
      84, 89n30, 177–8
Lancaster House Conference 62
languages, African 37–8, 39, 41, 45–6,
    46n8, 49, 60, 105, 115, 116n1,
    120, 121, 127, 128, 129, 131, 132,
    133–7, 142, 143, 144, 146, 148,
    155, 161, 168, 179–80, 182, 184,
    185, 192
  Afrikaans 168
  colonial 10, 39, 43, 49, 133, 143, 182
  as cultural archive 40, 116, 132,
    179–80

Gĩkũyũ 9, 38n65, 61, 67, 79, 104,
    116n1, 129, 132, 134–5, 143, 145,
    146, 147, 148, 152, 154, 159, 163,
    168, 170, 183, 192
  indigenous 14, 39, 60, 129
  and memory 132, 133, 136–7, 168,
    179–80
  Sheng 9, 133
  Swahili 38n65, 60, 76, 76n2, 127, 132,
    136, 186
Lanzmann, Claude 7
Lao Tze 128
Lawrence, D.H. 71, 78, 154
Lawrence, T.E. 35, 35n62
Lazarus, Neil 9, 10, 10n19–n20, 19, 19n37,
    81, 94, 96n42, 126n9, 156, 172,
    174n6, 192n29
  on Ngũgĩ as postcolonial intellectual
    9–10
Leavis, F.R. 46, 48, 58, 60, 76, 76n3, 191
Lenin, V.I. 77, 88, 89, 98, 118, 123, 125,
    127, 154
  The Heritage We Renounce 125
  *Imperialism, The Highest Stage of
    Capitalism* 77, 127
  on neocolonial imperialism 127n11
Lessing, Doris 7–8, 8n17, 76n3
  Walking in the Shade 8, 8n17, 76n3
Levi, Primo 167, 177n14
  Survival in Auschwitz 167, 177n14
Lévi-Strauss, Claude 108
Lindfors, Bernth 49n13, 52, 147, 154, 155n21
literature, comparative 147, 190
literature, world 10n19, 14, 142, 153,
    184, 190, 192
London 7, 8, 32, 34, 39, 43, 45, 58, 80, 83,
    83n1, 84, 94, 146, 173, 173n1, 176,
    180, 181
Lonsdale, John 117
L'Ouverture, Toussaint 85, 89–91, 91n34
Lovesey, Oliver 4n10, 26n54, 72n30, 78,
    112n55, 131n15, 147n15, 153n19,
    159n23, 163n27, 171n33
Lu Xun 103

Macaulay, Thomas 27, 28, 37, 43, 47, 48,
    58, 84n22, 91
  "Minute [On Indian Education]" 27–8,
    37, 58

Index

McCarren Immigration Bill 95
McCulloch, Jock 118, 118n4, 119n5, 120, 121, 122n7, 124, 125, 126n10
Macey, David 99, 101, 101n46, 106, 108n48, 111
McLuhan, Marshall 4
  The Gutenberg Galaxy 4n11
  Understanding Media 4n11
Makdisi, Saree 18n36
Malcolm X 191
Maloba, W.O. 35n63
Mandela, Nelson 141, 143, 163
Manthia Diawara 147, 187
Mao Tse-tung 45, 99, 98–9n43, 118, 131
  and Maoism 5n14, 135, 135n19
Mapanje, Jack 164, 164n29
  The Chattering Wagtails of Mikuyu Prison 164n29
Marcuson, Alan 44n4, 76, 78, 145, 149, 152
Martinique 34, 35, 71, 98n43, 99, 109, 111, 112, 113, 178
Marx, Karl 27, 46n8, 48, 73, 73n33, 74, 77, 81, 89, 108n49, 118, 122, 123, 126, 126n9, 127, 128, 154, 175, 190, 191, 192
  Capital 122, 127
  Class Struggles in France 128
  Communist Manifesto 77
  The Eighteenth Brumaire of Louis Bonaparte 27, 128
  The German Ideology 127
  Introduction to Political Economy 127
Marxism 11, 22, 27, 31, 40, 76n3, 77, 78, 80, 82n19, 84–5, 99, 100, 118, 126, 126n9, 127, 128, 173, 175, 175n7, 175n10, 179, 185, 189, 192
  and post-Marxism 11, 126
Marxist-Leninism 119, 126, 176
Maspero, François 101
Mathenge, Stanley 87, 152
Maugham, Somerset 46
Mau Mau 3, 4, 35n63, 39, 44–5, 46, 54–7, 62–3, 87, 87n28, 100, 100–101n45, 106, 107, 112, 115, 116, 145, 152, 156, 158, 158n22, 161, 162, 165, 166, 170, 180–81, 191; *see also* Edward Carey Francis; C.L.R. James

aesthetics 4, 165
  campaigns against 3, 4, 39, 65, 110, 112, 151, 160–61, 163, 166n25, 177, 180–81, 184n24, 192
  detainees 3, 4, 51, 87, 112, 161, 166, 177, 180, 181, 184n24, 192
  and the Emergency 53, 62, 87
  and policy of terror in colonial Kenya 3, 4, 51, 87, 110, 145, 160–61, 160n25, 180–81, 180n18, 184n24
  revisionist histories of 4
Mboya, Tom 58, 59, 106, 161
Melville, Herman 23n44, 68, 68n26, 94–6, 95n40; *see also* C.L.R. James
  Moby Dick 23, 68n26, 94–6, 96n41
  Pierre 96
Memmi, Albert 98, 99
Michelet, Jules 92, 92n35
Mill, John Stuart 15, 19, 63
  Autobiography 15
modernism / modernity 4, 12, 37, 66, 68, 71, 74, 79n12, 81, 91, 115, 119, 129, 141, 143, 149, 150, 159
Moi, Daniel arap 4, 66, 125, 126, 146, 147, 173, 173n1
Moi, Toril 8
Moore-Gilbert, Bart 15n32, 31n60, 33, 73, 139n1, 140, 140n5, 141n8, 143
Mottin, Marie-France 88n29
Mphahlele, Ezekiel 54
  Pot of Tears 54
Mũtirii 134, 147, 148
Mwangi, Evan 133n18
Mwangi, Wallace 145, 159

Naipaul, V.S. 20, 94
Nairobi 4, 9, 39, 43, 45, 48, 49, 52, 54, 110, 146, 147, 148, 154, 159, 192
narodism 125
native informant 21, 25, 37, 39, 50, 132, 141, 158
Nazareth, Peter 60n18, 78, 79n9, 173, 174, 174n3
Négritude 11n23, 39, 67, 70–74, 86, 99, 101, 103, 104, 105, 111, 112, 116, 121, 125, 137, 142n10, 176, 179
Neto, Agostinho 121
New Historicism 14, 30, 32
New York 2n5, 4, 15, 20, 148n17, 188

Ngũgĩ wa Thiong'o
and the aesthetics of decolonization 40, 115
on African writing in English 116, 116n1, 128, 133–4, 143, 184
and Afro-Caribbean literature 48, 74, 75, 77–80, 192
and the Afro-Saxon 128, 133, 176, 192
on authorship, the nature of 183–4
biography of 145–8
and the birth of postcolonial studies 3, 79, 135, 190, 190n28, 193
Cabral's influence on 40, 116–18, 119, 121, 123, 124, 125–7, 128–9, 130, 131, 132, 185, 186, 192
and the call for an African Renaissance/renewal 9, 37, 38, 41, 46, 69, 88, 128, 136–8, 178–9, 180, 184, 185–6
and canon reform and educational decolonization 3, 23, 23n43, 40, 59–60, 135–7, 184, 190–91, 192
censorship of 147, 149, 153; see also imprisonment of
Césaire's influence on 71–2, 73–4, 84n23, 136, 185, 191
and Christianity and the colonial Church 36, 44, 50, 47–8, 47n10, 52, 63, 138, 141, 149, 151, 162, 165–6, 192
class position of 3, 35, 183, 192
colonial education of 43–9, 78, 145, 157–8, 159–62
  at Alliance High School 43–5, 46, 47, 48, 49, 145, 160–63
  at Gĩkũyũ Independent School 46, 145
  at Leeds University 40, 46n8, 47n9, 48, 49, 75–8, 77n5, 100, 101, 127, 129, 146, 174
  at Makerere University College 45–6, 47, 48, 49, 50, 76n5, 145–6
on culture and African languages 37, 38, 40, 41, 46, 60, 115, 116, 117, 121, 128–9, 131–2, 133–5, 146, 148, 155, 168, 180, 184, 192
Fanon's influence on 36, 40, 48, 63, 63n25, 73, 75, 76, 77, 78, 99–113, 117, 127, 128, 136, 137, 140, 154, 192
fiction
  The Black Hermit 45, 69, 104, 146
  "The Black Messiah" 47, 146
  Caitaani Mũtharaba-inĩ; see *Devil on the Cross*
  Devil on the Cross 10, 104, 110, 134, 141, 145, 146, 152, 153, 163, 168, 172, 183
  A Grain of Wheat 47n9, 56, 76n4, 79, 79n9, 103, 145, 146, 151, 152, 162, 163, 174
  "I Try Witchcraft" 52, 149
  I Will Marry When I Want 104
  Maitũ Njugĩra; see *Mother, Sing For Me*
  Matigari 9, 10, 21n41, 61, 87, 104, 110, 145, 146, 147, 152, 153, 162, 171, 172, 186
  Matigari Ma Njirũũngi; see *Matigari*
  "A Meeting in the Dark" 150
  Mother, Sing For Me 104, 183, 185–6
  "Mugumo" 150, 162
  Mũrogi wa Kagogo; see *Wizard of the Crow*
  "My Childhood" 52, 149
  Ngaahika Ndeenda; see *I Will Marry When I Want*
  'Njamba Nene' children's fiction 112
  Njamba Nene and the Cruel Chief 157
  oral intellectuals in 152
  Petals of Blood 58, 60, 61, 104, 131, 135, 145, 146, 150, 151, 152, 153, 174, 185
  The River Between 47, 51, 53, 57, 103, 109, 141, 145, 146, 150, 151, 152
  Secret Lives 145, 149
  The Trial of Dedan Kimathi (co-authored with Micere Mugo) 87, 173n1
  troubled intellectuals in 9, 40, 47, 149–52
  Weep Not, Child 46, 55, 57, 103, 110, 145, 146, 150, 151, 156, 157, 162

Wizard of the Crow 3–4, 9, 110, 111, 126, 133, 145, 147, 148, 148n16, 152–3, 174n4
films 147, 147n14–n15, 189
   Africa in Sweden 147
   Blood-Grapes and Black Diamonds 147
   Sembene: The Making of African Cinema (co-director, Manthia Diawara) 147
and the global postcolonial 137–8, 190–93
and hybrid nationalisms 185–90
imprisonment of 134–5, 146, 154, 163, 167–8, 169, 170, 171, 173, 184, 192
and the intellectual
   African 35, 36–8, 129–30, 131–2, 181–2, 190–91
   border 20
   collective 37, 131, 182–4, 184n22, 193
   exiled 20, 35, 173, 178
   global 190–91
   as interpreter 181–2
   native 43
   politically committed 35, 36, 129–30, 131, 154–5, 181–3, 187
   in the postcolony / neocolony 131–2, 154–5
   prose style of 36
James's influence on 39–40, 74, 75–99
journalism of 39, 45, 46, 47n10, 49–71, 86, 110, 139, 146, 181, 185, 186
   advertisements accompanying 49
   on alcoholism 53
   on the arts and Indigenous drama 54, 60–61, 66–7
   bibliography for 49n13
   on Christianity and the colonial Church 47, 47n10–n11
   on cultural tradition 53, 54, 63–4
   for *Daily Nation* 46, 49, 55, 57, 65, 71, 73
   and editorial intrusion 50, 52; *see also* censorship of
   on education 57–60
      of African leaders 46
      agricultural equality, gender and class in 53
      and Makerere 50, 50n16, 57, 58; *see also* education; education institutions, Makerere University College
   on the Emergency, social and cultural problems created by 53
   on employment
   on land redistribution in Kenya 53
   on languages, African 60–61
   on liberation, economic, national, political, and psychological 51, 64–5
   on Mau Mau 55–7, 65
   on Négritude 70–4; *see also* Négritude
   the 'New Villages' 53
   on old age security 53
   on Pan-Africanism 57, 60–61, 62, 64–5, 186; *see also* Ngũgĩ wa Thiong'o, and the call for an African Renaissance/renewal; Pan-Africanism
   on post-independence Kenya 52
   on publication, African language 61–2
   on psychological colonization 51
   for *Sunday Nation* 47, 49, 50, 50n16, 51, 52, 54, 55, 57, 58, 59, 60, 61, 62, 63, 64, 65, 68, 69, 70
   for *Sunday Post* 49, 61, 69, 71
   on teachers, native Kenyan and expatriate 53
   on tribalism 57, 68, 117, 185, 185n25; *see also* Ngũgĩ wa Thiong'o, on tribalism as creation of colonialism
and the Kamĩrĩĩthũ Community Educational and Cultural Centre 54, 104, 129, 134–5, 146, 146n13, 154, 170, 173, 183–4, 185, 192
Lamming's influence on 20, 77, 79, 94, 154, 177n15, 179
and Marxism/Leninism 126–8, 130
on memory 132, 133, 136, 167–8, 179–80
and mental decolonization 35, 68, 69, 74, 104, 124, 134, 136, 193

on modern media and technology 110, 131, 187–9
and name change 43n1, 146, 158
Nobel Prize in Literature, nominee for 3, 3n8
non-fiction; *see also* journalism
   Barrel of a Pen 102, 102n47, 110, 117, 129, 131, 164n29, 170, 187
   "Church, Culture and Politics" 47
   Decolonising the Mind 10, 46n8, 78, 79, 100, 102n47, 115, 132, 133, 134, 139, 145, 146, 165, 168, 179
   Detained: A Writer's Prison Diary 40, 80, 143, 157, 163–72, 174n6
   "A Dictator's Last Laugh" 66, 125, 173
   Dreams in a Time of War 40, 132, 156–60, 161
   "Europhone" 37, 38, 63n20, 179
   "For Peace, Justice and Culture: The Intellectual in the Twenty-First Century" 5, 36, 37, 138, 181, 182, 183
   Globalectics 2, 3, 10, 10n19, 12, 23n43, 41, 45, 46n8, 51, 73, 75, 76, 76n3, 84n23, 99, 100, 102, 102n47, 103, 107, 111, 115, 116, 128, 130, 131, 133, 136, 138, 142, 144, 148, 174, 176n13, 179n17, 190–91
   Homecoming 2, 3, 47, 48, 75, 77, 77n6, 78, 99, 102, 102n47, 110, 115, 117, 129, 133, 135, 136, 138, 146, 178, 179
      "Towards a National Culture" 133
   In the House of the Interpreter 40, 44, 44n3, 50, 50n15, 51, 52, 54, 62, 135, 138, 145, 149, 151, 160–63
   In the Name of the Mother 2n6, 191
   'Introduction' to Okot p'Bitek's *Africa's Cultural Revolution* 129
   "Kenya" 117
   Moving the Centre 36, 72, 77, 79, 80, 80n13, 89, 94, 100, 102, 102n47, 111, 115, 117, 131, 134, 147, 162, 164n29, 172, 176, 186
      "Biggles, Mau Mau and I" 162
      "The Ideology of Racism" 111
      "Matigari and the Dreams of One East Africa" 186
      "A Multi-Centered Globe" 132
   "On the Abolition of the English Department" (co-authored with Taban Lo Liyong and Henry Owuor-Anyumba) 3, 58, 135–6, 190, 192
   Penpoints, Gunpoints, and Dreams 4, 36, 37, 38, 40, 91, 102n47, 110, 115, 128, 131, 132, 136, 137, 138, 144, 147, 179, 181, 182, 187, 188, 189
      "The Allegory of the Cave" 182
   Something Torn and New: An African Renaissance 4, 38, 40, 50, 84n23, 89, 102n47, 103, 115, 116, 128, 132, 136, 148, 177, 178, 179, 184
   "A Study of the Theme of Alienation in the Fiction of the West Indies, with Particular Reference to the Novels of George Lamming" 77
   This Time Tomorrow 146
   "Unity Is Still an African Dream" 164n28, 185
   Writers in Politics 30, 78, 102n47, 115, 117–18, 126, 130, 131, 132, 133, 146, 165, 173, 187
on orature 23, 35, 104, 117, 133, 136, 157, 174, 187–8, 190, 191
and cyberspace 41, 110, 136, 187–9, 190
and cyberture / cyborature 136, 176, 176n13, 191
and litorature 174, 176, 176n13
and the peasantry 117, 135, 183–4
as postcolonial theorist 2–3, 192–3
and the postnation 185, 187–8, 189
representations of 173–4, 174n3

and Shelley, Percy Bysshe 68
   on tribalism as creation of colonialism
      39, 117, 185
Nietzsche, Friedrich 176, 177
Nigeria 72, 163, 166, 174n5
Nkosi, Lewis 48, 49
Nkrumah, Kwame 83, 86, 92–3, 106, 116,
      123, 143, 161, 163, 182, 189n27
   Africa Must Unite 93, 93n37
   *Ghana: The Autobiography of Kwame
      Nkrumah* 143
Nyere, Julius 60, 86, 88

OAU: Organization of African Unity 119
Obama, Barack Hussein 3, 3n9, 111n53,
      148n17, 180
Oginga Odinga 65, 143
   Not Yet Uhuru, An Autobiography 143
   and Raila Odinga 65
Okot p'Bitek 129
   Africa's Cultural Revolution 129
On the Road (Jack Kerouac) 101
Orwell, George 21, 127
Owuor-Anyumba, Henry 3, 136, 190

Padmore, George 83, 84, 84n25, 85, 88,
      161
Pan-Africanism 7, 9, 12, 37, 38, 39, 41,
      57, 71, 74, 75, 76, 78–9, 80, 83–4,
      85–6, 88, 93–4, 99, 100, 103, 106,
      116, 119, 121, 130, 132, 132n17,
      136–7, 142, 178, 179, 184–5,
      186–7, 191, 192
Paradise Lost (John Milton) 186
Paris 5, 5n14, 7, 27, 39, 71, 74, 82, 116,
      125, 167, 176
Pascal 98
Penpoint 45, 146
Philcox, Richard 73n34, 98n43, 101,
      108n48
Plato 4, 37, 113, 128, 131, 142, 143, 144,
      154
   and allegory of the cave 131–2, 144,
      182
   Republic 131
popular culture 4, 40, 43, 94, 95, 96n42,
      112, 132, 177, 189
Portugal 7, 40, 115, 118, 119–20, 121 124,
      123–4n8, 125, 126

postcolonialism
   debate over 10–12, 20, 20n38, 30
   paradox of 5n12
   and postcolonial necrophilia 40, 115,
      137, 179
   project of 40, 179
postmodernism 11, 11–12n26, 19, 32,
      32n61, 35, 141, 188
poststructuralism / poststructuralist 5n14,
      11, 14n31, 31, 32, 36
Povey, John 126–7
Presbyterian Church of East Africa,
      General Assembly of the (March
      1970) 47

Quayson, Ato 10n20, 12

racial profiling 148, 148n17
Radhakrishnan, R. 2n4, 14n31, 16, 20n40
Ravenscroft, Arthur 76
Renaissance, English 137, 179
Rich, Adrienne 1n2, 67n24, 69
   "Legislators of the World" 1n2, 67n24
Robben Island 163
Robinson Crusoe (Daniel Defoe) 191
Rodney, Walter 78n8, 80, 81, 82, 82n18,
      128, 192n29
   How Europe Underdeveloped Africa
      82, 128
   *Walter Rodney Speaks: The Making of
      an African Intellectual* 78n8, 82,
      82n18, 128, 192n29
Rousseau, Jean-Jacques 24, 63

Said, Edward W. 1, 1n2–n3, 2, 3, 5, 5n12,
      9, 9n18, 13–22, 25, 32, 33, 35, 36,
      73n33, 79, 80, 81, 85n26, 86n27,
      92, 130, 140, 141, 143, 156, 176,
      177n15, 183n20, 192
   autobiographical self-construction of
      13–15, 22, 140–41
   and auto-critical moments 15–16
   as a dissident intellectual 13–14,
      15–17, 18n35–n36
   on Conrad 16
   on the intellectual 13–22, 21n41, 35
   intellectual biography of 13–15
   on James 80–81, 85n26
   and Palestine 15, 16n33, 17, 20, 22

on Swift as intellectual 1n3, 17, 20, 130
works
   Beginnings: Intention and Method 16
   Culture and Imperialism 21, 73n33, 80, 81, 85n26
   "The Intellectual in the Post-Colonial World" 21
   Joseph Conrad and the Fiction of Autobiography 16, 16n33
   Mimesis 36
   "My Right to Return" 17
   Orientalism 14n31, 16, 36
   Out of Place 14, 15–16, 141, 156
   Representations of the Intellectual: The 1993 Reith Lectures 1n2–n3, 9, 17–21, 22
   "Third World Intellectuals / Metropolitan Culture" 22
   The World, the Text, and the Critic 16, 17, 18
Salazar, António de Oliveira 125–6
Salih, Tayeb 34
   Season of Migration to the North 34
San Domingo 85, 89, 90; *see also* Haiti
Sartre, Jean-Paul 1, 5, 6, 8, 9, 11, 11n23, 12, 13, 30, 70n28, 101, 101n46, 105, 108, 108n49, 111, 128
   Anti-Semite and Jew 6
   "Black Orpheus" 11, 11n23, 72n29, 101, 105, 111
   as Dubreuilh in Beavoir's *The Mandarins* 8–9
   "A Friend of the People" 5, 6
   on the intellectual, classical / universal 5–6, 12–13
   on Négritude 105, 111
   "A Plea for Intellectuals" 5, 6
   'Preface' to Fanon's *The Wretched of the Earth* 101, 101n46, 108
   "What Is Literature" 5
   The Words 6
Sembene Ousmane 104, 131, 147, 189; *see also* Ngũgĩ wa Thiong'o, films
   God's Bits of Wood 104
Senghor, Léopold Sédar 7, 9, 70, 70n28, 71, 74, 105
Shakespeare, William 53, 55, 59, 60, 64, 66, 68, 154, 162, 191; *see also* tragedy, Shakespearean
   Caliban 64, 66n23, 191
   The Tempest 64, 66, 178, 191
   Romeo and Juliet 150
Shelley, Percy Bysshe 68, 69, 130n14
   Defence of Poetry 68, 69, 130n14
   Prometheus Unbound 68
Sicherman, Carol 38n65, 45, 45n5–n6, 46, 46n8, 52, 52n17, 76n4, 77n5, 77n7, 164n29, 173, 173n1–n2
Smith, Sidonie 139, 140, 143
Sorel, Georges 109
   Réflexions sur la violence 109
South Africa 49, 56, 86, 106, 119, 163, 168, 171, 172, 184n22
Soviet Union (the Soviets) 7, 8n17, 9, 58, 76n3, 84, 85, 88, 92, 118, 119, 126, 145
Soviet Writer's Union 58, 146
Soyinka, Wole 9, 20n39, 40, 72, 72n31, 73, 73n32, 74, 129, 142, 143, 166, 167, 168, 172, 172n34
   and imprisonment 163, 166, 167, 168, 169, 170
   and release from prison 171–2
   works
      Aké: The Years of Childhood 156
      The Man Died 40, 164, 165, 166, 170, 172
      Myth, Literature and the African World 72, 172
      Of Africa 73
      Season of Anomy 172
      A Shuttle in the Crypt 172
      "The Writer in a Modern African State" 72, 73
spirituality, African 115, 116n2, 133, 136, 138
Spivak, Gayatri Chakravorty 1n2, 3, 5, 11, 12, 13, 22–30, 32, 35, 139n2, 175, 175n11, 176n12, 182, 183, 190, 192
   autobiographical construction of 22n42, 22–6
   and auto-critical moments 24
   as celebrity intellectual 25
   colonial education of 23, 23n45
   and deconstruction 24, 24n48, 25, 25n51, 30
   intellectual biography of 22–5

on *Jane Eyre* (Charlotte Brontë) 23, 26
on the location and sanction of utterance 28–30
on Ngũgĩ 30
and the planetary 190
and postcolonial studies 24n47
subject positions of 24–7, 25n49–n52, 35, 36
as translator of Jacques Derrida's *De la Grammatologie* [*Of Grammatology*] 23–4
works
    An Aesthetic Education in the Age of Globalization 25, 37n64, 183
    "Can the Subaltern Speak?" 11, 11n22, 25, 26–9, 26n55, 35–6
    Death of a Discipline 37n64, 190
    "Edward Said" 1n2
    "Explanation and Culture: Marginalia" 25n52
    "French Feminism" 26
    "How to Read a Culturally Different Book" 23
    In Other Worlds 24n47
    "Politics of Interpretation" 30
    The Post-Colonial Critic: Interviews, Strategies, Dialogues 22, 24, 25, 26, 26n53, 30, 35
    "Subaltern Studies" 29, 30n59
    "Subaltern Talk" 23, 26, 26n55, 30
    "Three Women's Texts and a Critique of Imperialism" 23
    'Translator's Foreword' to Mahasweta Devi's "Draupadi" 25n51, 28
    'Translator's Preface' to Derrida's *De la Grammatologie* [*Of Grammatology*] 24, 24n46
Stalin 3n17, 91
Stalinism 8n17, 76n3, 79, 84, 84n24, 92
subaltern 2, 3, 6, 26, 33, 36, 38, 43, 76n2, 143, 144, 156, 158, 175, 176n12, 183, 192
Subaltern Studies 22, 26, 29, 176n12, 183
Suleri, Sara 15, 26
    Meatless Days 15, 26n54
Surin, Kenneth 83n20, 96n42

Swift, Jonathan 1n3, 17, 20, 130; *see also* Edward Said
    "Voyage to the Country of Houyhnhnms" 17

Taban Lo Liyong 3, 135–6, 189, 190
Tanzania 86, 88, 120, 147
Taoism 138, 167, 172
Taylor, Charles 4
Thandika Mkandawire 131
Tolstoy, Leo 52, 148–9, 150, 154, 162
    Childhood, Youth and Boyhood 52, 148–9, 162
torture, in colonial Kenya 180–81, 180n18, 184n24
tragedy
    Aristotelean 89
    Shakespearean 89
Transition 45, 54, 190
Tressell, Robert 77
    Ragged Trousered Philanthropists 77
Trevor-Roper, Hugh 75, 76n2
Trinidad 81, 83, 84n24, 96
Trotsky, Leon 80, 84, 89, 92, 96
Truth and Reconciliation Commission 56

Uganda 44, 45, 145, 146, 156, 163
Umoja 147

Veeser, H. Aram 13–14, 14n31, 139n2
Viswanathan, Gauri 23, 28

Wali, Obiajunwa 46, 46n7, 133
Walcott, Derek 80n13, 81, 174
Warner, Alan 43n2, 49, 49n14, 50, 59, 60, 60n19, 68
    and Alliance-inculcated English prose style 49–50, 49n15
    A Short Guide to English Style 49–50, 49n14, 60, 60n19
    Shakespeare in the Tropics 59, 68–9
Washington, T. Booker 162
    Up from Slavery 162
Watson, Julia 139, 140, 141, 143
West Indies 35, 47, 71, 71n29, 77, 77n6, 78, 79, 80, 82, 83, 84, 85, 88, 89–90n33, 96, 97, 178
West, Cornel 2, 132n17, 148n17, 153, 153n20

Wilkinson, Jane 154, 164, 173, 183
Williams, Patrick 9, 9n18, 126n9, 147n14
Williams, Raymond 46n8, 77
Wolin, Richard 5n14, 7, 27, 108, 135n19

Yeats, W.B. 115, 137

Young, Robert C. 12, 14n31, 20, 32, 33, 43, 106, 123, 176n12, 183n20

Žižek, Slavoj 11, 11n24, 107, 108
   Violence 108
Zuka 146